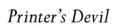

Printer's Devil

*The publisher gratefully acknowledges
the generous contribution to this book provided
by the Simpson Humanities Endowment Fund of
the University of California Press Foundation.*

Printer's Devil

MARK TWAIN AND THE AMERICAN PUBLISHING REVOLUTION

Bruce Michelson

UNIVERSITY OF CALIFORNIA PRESS

BERKELEY LOS ANGELES LONDON

University of California Press, one of the most distinguished university presses in the United States, enriches lives around the world by advancing scholarship in the humanities, social sciences, and natural sciences. Its activities are supported by the UC Press Foundation and by philanthropic contributions from individuals and institutions. For more information, visit www.ucpress.edu.

University of California Press
Berkeley and Los Angeles, California

University of California Press, Ltd.
London, England

Library of Congress Cataloging-in-Publication Data

Michelson, Bruce, 1948–
    Printer's devil : Mark Twain and the American
publishing revolution / Bruce Michelson.
        p.   cm.
    Includes bibliographical references and index.
    ISBN-13 978-0-520-24759-8 (acid-free paper)
    ISBN-10 0-520-24759-0 (acid-free paper)
        1. Twain, Mark, 1835–1910—Knowledge—Printing.
2. Printing in literature.   3. Printing—United States—
History—19th century.   4. Publishers and publishing—
United States—History—19th century.   5. Authors and
publishers—United States—History—19th century.
I. Title.

PS1342.P67M53   2006
818'.409—dc22   2005034481

Manufactured in the United States of America

15   14   13   12   11   10   09   08   07   06
10   9   8   7   6   5   4   3   2   1

This book is printed on New Leaf EcoBook 50, a 100% recycled fiber of which 50% is de-inked post-consumer waste, processed chlorine-free. EcoBook 50 is acid-free and meets the minimum requirements of ANSI/ASTM D5634–01 (*Permanence of Paper*).

For Barbara Elizabeth Yates

CONTENTS

ILLUSTRATIONS

PREFACE

This book grew out of many conversations about the information revolution that engulfs us and the relevance of Mark Twain to our thinking about it. The literary text is encountered now as an electronic wraith as well as a physical object, and authors living and dead are sailing through cyberspace like Captain Stormfield on his comet. The printed word is challenged and reified by elegant technologies of sight and sound; cultural experience, globalizing and incorporated, grows gaudier and noisier every week. For so many reasons, then, the time is ripe for another book about a writer who told his last stories with primitive implements—ink and pencil and typewriter—at the opening of the last century!

Mark Twain is often remembered as an American pioneer. We know him as a voice for a new populace, as an early, bold explorer of impossible modern questions—about social and political identity and the innermost actualities of the self. Grounded in facts from his life, each reconstruction connects him to our world. Each provides a measure of continuity and depth to an endless dialogue about who and where we are, historically and morally, and how we came to be here.

But we also need a heightened sense of how Mark Twain responded to technological upheavals that resemble and foreshadow our own predicaments. What palpable consequences, and darker implications, did Sam Clemens foresee or experience firsthand as he joined in a revolution that changed every major process for representing and disseminating human experience? He was a printer, investor, inventor, publisher, amateur illustrator, and media celebrity as well as a literary artist. His identities were many, and his life was rich and complex; and every venture into it benefits from prodigious work by others to sort out this history and discover its meaning.

At the Mark Twain Papers and Project at Berkeley, Robert Hirst, Victor Fischer, and Lin Salamo have invested decades in organizing and promulgating one of the world's most extensive archives on one author. For a generation of scholars, these guardians have been gracious with their expertise. Very carefully, Vic read through much of what I had drafted, fixing inferences and catching important factual errors. With a sharp eye and a level of Twain-savvy shared by very few other people on this planet, Bob took on the entire book with breathtaking energy and generosity, making many additional repairs and offering contexts and nuances that I could never have achieved on my own. Lin Salamo and Neda Salem provided guidance and encouragement as I wandered into unpublished material. As a Mark Twain scholar whose store of knowledge is astounding, Barbara Schmidt graciously combed through a draft of the manuscript, rescuing it from other omissions and errors. Susan K. Harris, Peter Messent, Tom Quirk, Gregg Camfield, and Don Florence, who represent the imaginative vitality and eloquence that flourish in the study of American literature, coaxed several chapters into better shape. Closer to home, my friends Dale Bauer, Nina Baym, Audrey Hodgins, Gordon Hutner, Trish Loughran, John Timberman Newcomb, and Robert Dale Parker all worked hard to improve my drafts.

In the later years of the twentieth century, when Roland Barthes was upsetting people with his talk of "the death of the author," he didn't know the half of it, the scope of what was about to come down. Barthes himself was gone before the compounding of authorial "death" by download and upload, by renegade blogs and fan-sites, by e-text, hypertext, Webcast, and podcast, epistemological violence that can be accomplished now with mouse and keyboard or merely on a handset. The interpretive dilemma that held his attention was the comparatively limited problem of the alienated printed page. Magnified and cut loose now, these enigmas shadow every encounter with "literature," "authors," and "texts" as artifacts of rag and cellulose or as flashes of media lightning. These issues transform the understanding of the cultural past and of Mark Twain as an icon within it.

We are lucky, therefore, to have scholars who understand the cultural and cognitive predicaments of the twenty-first century, even as they affirm, with creativity and enthusiasm for historical truth, that the Mark Twain legacy is alive and that it matters. Louis Budd, Vic Doyno, Michael Kiskis,

Leland Krauth, Ann Ryan, Gary Scharnhorst, Laura Skandera Trombley, John Bird, and Jeffrey Steinbrink are leaders in this cohort, and their friendship and advice have steadied me as this project took shape. At the University of Virginia, Steve Railton's Web sites on Mark Twain have grown into an essential source for facts and images; Kent Rasmussen's *Mark Twain, A to Z* has been a blessing for confirming details about Sam Clemens and his world. For particulars about Sam's experiences as an apprentice printer in Hannibal and nearby towns, I learned much at the State Historical Society of Missouri, in Marion County archives at the Hannibal Public Library, and from Henry Sweets at the Mark Twain Boyhood Home and Museum. As director of Rare Books and Special Collections at the University of Illinois Library, Barbara Jones guided me to stronger connections between Mark Twain's career and the important work of the American Printing History Association and the Society for the History of Authorship, Reading, and Publishing. Also with Rare Books and Special Collections at the University of Illinois Library, Alvan Bregman was a companion in the search for illustrations to accompany this text. Crucial details were contributed by Jo Kibbee, head of Reference at the University of Illinois Library; Marguerite Lavin at the Museum of the City of New York; Margaret Moore and Jeffrey Nichols at the Mark Twain Memorial in Hartford; and Dave Thomson, the antiquarian book expert Kevin MacDonnell, and several archivists at the Library of Congress and the Smithsonian Institution, talented people who prefer to stay anonymous. Over the past three years, I have had the pleasure of working with Heather Bouwman, Andrew Moss, and Tessa Oberg, three gifted, conscientious research assistants who brought dimensions to this tale that I never anticipated.

As an iconic career and a body of written work, "Mark Twain" exemplifies American vitality but also the turbulence of modern life. I came through this encounter with him only because my closest companions, Theresa, Hope, and Sarah Michelson, create together a sacred realm of wit, poise, decency, energy, and joy—essential to the chase and to the adventure of being alive.

ONE

Samuel Clemens and the Printed Word

SAM

The first surviving image of him is tiny, compared to most of the copies—retouched and reprinted, digitized and uploaded. Only about two inches wide and three high, arched at the top, this daguerreotype comes down to us still in its original pocket-sized wooden case, enameled and hinged, with a padded lining and a tiny clasp. A handwritten inscription in ink on the lining gives a date: December 1850. But behind the picture is a paper backing with the name "G. H. Jones" written in pencil (a byline, probably) and a different date, "Nov. 29th." Sam Clemens was born on November 30, 1835, so the odds are good that this was a birthday present.[1] The cap on the boy's head suggests a charred popover on a bush of hair; in his eyes and posture there is truculence. Elbows flared, he grips at waist level what looks to be a *SAM* belt buckle, flaunting it like a talisman. The image presents him backwards, and this device he holds is a composing stick, an adjustable clamp used for setting and holding movable type since the time of Gutenberg. When the picture was taken, Sam Clemens was an apprentice printer with about two years' experience in the shop of Joseph C. Ament, on a scant team of men and boys who turned out the *Missouri Courier,* a four-page local weekly newspaper with a pathetically ambitious name. The composing and printing were accomplished in one room, upstairs from a drugstore on Main Street in the village of Hannibal (only thirty years old at that time, with a population of approximately three thousand white citizens and several hundred black slaves).[2] In that room, the craft was practiced with apparatus and rituals essentially unchanged from what they had been two centuries before.

The equipment in the *Courier* office probably included one or two hand-operated bed-and-platen presses; cubbyholed upper and lower wooden cases, slant mounted, holding the lead alloy fonts and the larger wood-carved headers; a couple of imposing-stones roughly four feet long and two feet wide; cast-iron chases,[3] wooden side-sticks, and quoins for holding the set type in position; and a leakproof iron inking table. To print out copies of the weekly edition, Joe Ament's crew applied ink by hand to the form (the typeset page or pages to be produced in one impression), moistened and positioned each sheet by hand, removed each from the press by hand, hung each of them up to dry, and later folded them and stacked them—everything here was done by hand. In a printer's manual from 1853, the Philadelphia typographer Thomas F. Adams describes one key ritual of the printer's craft, the actual production of the sheets on a conventional handpress. From this headlong two-sentence paragraph, several antique terms need glossing: a *rounce* is a handle for running the press-carriage (holding the form of set type) in and out of the press; a *tympan* is a light-duty frame, covered with cloth, where the paper sheet is laid; a *frisket* is a frame of iron that is lowered onto the sheet to keep it in place and prevent smearing of the ink.

> [T]he puller places his body almost straight before the near side of the tympan; but nimbly twists the upper part of his body a little backwards towards the heap, the better to see that he takes but one sheet off, which he loosens from the rest of the heap by drawing the back of the nail of his right thumb quickly over the bottom part of the heap, (but in the reiteration, care should be observed to draw the thumb on the margin, or between the gutters, that the sheet may not smear or set off,) and, receiving the near end of the sheet with his left hand fingers and thumb, catches it by the further edge with his right hand, about four inches from the upper corner of the sheet, and brings it swiftly to the tympan, and having the sheet thus in both his hands, lays the further side and two extreme corners of the sheet down even upon the further side and extreme further corners of the tympan sheet; the sheet being now properly laid on, he supports it in the centre by the fingers of the left hand, while his right hand, being disengaged, is removed to the back of the ear of the frisket, to bring it down upon the tympan, laying, at the same moment, the tympan on the form. He then, with his left hand, grasps the rounce, and with a moderate strength quickly turns it in; after pulling, he

gives a quick and strong pressure upon the rounce, to turn it back, and run the carriage out again: as soon as he has given this pressure, he disengages his left hand from the rounce, and claps the fingers of it towards the bottom of the tympan, to assist the right hand in lifting it up, and also to be ready to catch the bottom of the sheet when the frisket rises, which he conveys quick and gently to the catch; and while it is going up, he slips the thumb of his left hand under the near lower corner of the sheet, which, with the assistance of his two fore-fingers, he raises, and by so doing allows the right hand also to grasp it at the top, in the same manner, which lifts the sheet carefully and expeditiously off the points, and nimbly twisting about his body towards the paper bank, carries the sheet over the heap of white paper to the bank, and lays it down upon a waste sheet or wrapper, put there for that purpose; but while it is coming over the white paper heap, though he has the sheet between both his fore-fingers and thumbs, yet he holds it so loosely, that it may move between them as on two centres, as his body twists about from the side of the tympan towards the side of the paper bank.[4]

The result is one printed side of one sheet of paper. Repeat the entire process always exactly right, about one thousand times (for the back of each sheet must be processed this way as well), and a crew of men and boys could produce one five-hundred-copy four-page daily or weekly newspaper for a small town. In the American heartland at the end of the 1840s, the printing office of a "county paper" was a site of complex hard labor and technological entropy, a preindustrial environment whose components Benjamin Franklin, Peter Zenger, or any first-generation colonial printer would have recognized as kin to gear and procedures in their own establishments so long before.

While Sam was learning his first trade in Hannibal, however, nearly every phase in the production and distribution of printed words and images was undergoing radical reinvention in the American metropolis. About ninety miles south of Joe Ament's shop, St. Louis newspapers were spinning off daily editions in tens of thousands of copies, using massive type-revolving presses driven by steam engines; one of these papers, the *Missouri Republican*, had been operating such a powered press as early as the spring of 1836.[5] By May of 1853, when Sam resolved to quit working for essentially nothing at his brother Orion's hand-pulled, half-starved *Hannibal Daily Journal* and seek a job instead where this potent technology was flourishing, the St. Louis production plants around Leclede's Landing were also deploying automatic sheet feeders and high-speed cutting and folding machines.

And beginning in December 1847, the newsrooms there could also exploit a telegraph network to Chicago, New Orleans, and the East Coast.[6]

With St. Louis as a prime target, the American railroad system was fiercely on its way. By 1850, major cities of New England and the Middle Atlantic were webbed by a system that at the beginning of 1830 had not existed at all, and whose mileage of operational track had quadrupled in the past ten years. A franchise had been established to drive a line quickly into the West, from Cincinnati through Vincennes, Indiana, and out to the docklands of Illinoistown, now known as East St. Louis, just across the Mississippi River.[7] A few blocks east of the St. Louis printers' row, the second-busiest port in the United States was processing hundreds of freight-laden steamboats every month, moving nearly every variety of manufactured product—including books, magazines, newspapers, lithographs—on the longest navigable river system in the world. By 1854, the city had acquired its own type foundry, which one municipal history has described as big and modern enough to supply a complete outfit for a newspaper on one day's notice. The local industries in that year also included "six lithographic, printing, and engraving establishments, four steel and copper plate engraving and three wood engraving" businesses, and "six book binderies and eight book and job offices."[8] In 1853, on Locust Street near the harbor, the first stereotype plant west of the Mississippi had opened for business; another began operations soon after, on the now-obliterated Republican Alley, named for the city's most influential journal.[9]

By the time Sam held his breath for his first daguerreotype, the "Great Revolution in Publishing," as it was being called in the popular press, was already old news and a mainstay for economic growth in dozens of larger American cities.[10] Up in Hannibal, however, the arrival of any steamboat— they stopped there about three times per week—was still a town-stopping event.[11] There were no telegraph lines within easy reach; no local printer worked with the aid of any power source other than human muscle, or equipment faster or more sophisticated than a Washington double medium handpress. And a railroad line to Hannibal from anywhere else was a subject for civic deliberation and collective hope only.[12]

Even so, though high-volume print technology and modern communications were absent from Marion County, fruits of this revolution were ominously abundant, literally stacking up at the landings and the post office: cheap books by the bundle from New York, Boston, Philadelphia, and

Cincinnati; lavishly illustrated mass-market national monthlies, printed only a few days before in sprawling factories hundreds of miles to the east; and genuine city newspapers, often with a dozen pages or more, eight or ten columns across, flaunting their "telegraph intelligence," still fresh in the hour of publication. Facing competition like this, a newspaper in an American small town had a life expectancy of only months before it fell prey to its own antiquated production methods—a horse-drawn, dirt-road distribution system, too few subscribers, stale news, scant revenue, exhausting physical effort—and the owner, editor, and publisher (very often the same individual) sold the remaining assets to other dreamers.[13] The eager-looking boy in this daguerreotype was learning printing as a traditional craft. Each day at his job, however, he bore witness to an upheaval that was giving reproduced words and pictures a dominion that had been unimaginable as recently as the year of his birth.

In January 1851, about a month after the likeness was taken, Sam and his younger brother Henry ended their apprenticeship with Joe Ament and migrated over to Orion's shop, where the eldest Clemens brother was struggling to merge the ruins of two other local weeklies, the *Western Union* and the *Hannibal Journal,* into one viable business.[14] No one knows exactly where the picture was made, but we can guess that the upside-down composing stick in the boy's hands and the three metal or hardwood large-font type letters arranged in it were borrowed from either Orion's inventory or Ament's. Neither of these shops was more than a three-minute walk from anywhere in the heart of the village or from the house where the Clemens family lived and that in happier times they had owned—but that now, after the sudden untimely death of John Marshall Clemens, Sam's respected but insolvent father, they had sold off and were leasing back. To ease the financial burden on the family, Sam himself had been boarding with Ament. "G. H. Jones," the penciled name behind the picture, remains a mystery. Perhaps he worked at Ballard's Daguerrean Rooms, which was advertising regularly in Ament's paper at that time and was located on Hill Street at the corner of Bird, above the Great Western General Store, three blocks from the *Courier.* But even the shop isn't certain: as a new technology, daguerreotypes were a national craze, and in 1850 there were several sources in the small village, including one establishment on a boat, anchored in Bear Creek near the steamboat landing.

Depending on the material, letters of movable type are either cast or

FIG. I The "printer's devil" and the stick of type. Mark Twain Papers, Bancroft Library, University of California, Berkeley.

carved in reverse. Daguerreotypes, which are produced with no negative, are also by nature reversed, for a daguerreotype is essentially a stabilized mirror image. Coated with a silver emulsion, a copper plate is exposed to light for about thirty seconds, after which the likeness caught on the plate is fixed with mercury vapors, covered with a sheet of glass, and bordered with metal tape to prevent oxidation from destroying the picture. To provide clients with the corrected likeness they would probably want, a competent daguerreotypist could arrange a good mirror in front of the subject and take the picture from the reflection.[15] With this boy's likeness, however, the rectifying step was eliminated, and the reason is the type. Although capital *A*'s and *M*'s in conventional fonts look much the same in reverse as when viewed straight on, there is no way to turn an *S,* with its solid body or shank, so that it matches the letter on the printed page.[16] Therefore, because the composing-stick *SAM* could not be maneuvered to read properly, the letters had to go in backwards, like a word set for type, and the image had to be made without the usual reversing, allowing the typeface to appear in the desired sequence and the right way around—which means that the human face becomes the face in a mirror. From the primordial years of photography in the American outback, a "special effect": a trivial conspiracy among Sam Clemens, Mr. G. H. Jones or whoever operated the light trap, the English language, and the pathologies of two media, one of them stubbornly medieval and the other in its rambunctious infancy. At the beginning of the story, the truth is flipped around, in a sense, for the sake of a good illusion. So what? In the history of Sam Clemens and Mark Twain, is this a paradox with an edge to it? Maybe not—but in the encounter between this rising, ramifying information age and Mark Twain as a writer and American icon, richer and wilder anomalies would follow, and the modest headwaters of that history may rise here.

Mark Twain's involvement with the American publishing revolution, which began in earnest when he was a child, absorbed him professionally and imaginatively as a teenager and continued to obsess him as a reporter, storyteller, traveling entertainer, author of books, entrepreneur, and international celebrity. Sprawling and intense, the story ranks as a great adventure from the American industrial age, a tale of a boy from a technological nowhere, rising to the wave tops in a relentless typhoon of innovation—and later in his life nearly drowning in that storm. Mark Twain's biography has become a national literary treasure in its own right; for students of American cultural history, that narrative can be the most compelling and significant story associated with his name. Nonetheless, when attention turns to his obsessive involvement with the logistics of printing and publishing, what usually unfolds is a cautionary fable about squandered genius and lost time. Only a couple of commentaries, brief and recent, have proposed that Mark Twain's enthusiasm for big, fast machines and the possibilities of automatic production, in the publishing industries or out beyond them, might actually make some of his texts more interesting, more relevant to our own cultural experience, rather than drive those texts to ruin as they did his personal finances.[17] Typically, when accounts of Mark Twain's life and work turn to his adult adventures in technology and the publishing business—automated typesetting, the American Publishing Company, his own Charles L. Webster & Company (a.k.a. WebsterCo), Harpers, Kaolatype, steam pulleys, bed sheet clamps, cash registers, and all the rest[18]—the mood turns somber: if only he had poured his energy exclusively into writing, putting out of his mind that exquisitely complicated equipment, those squabbles over rights and patents, those grandiose and quick-profit publishing schemes or corner-the-market aspirations, leaving all such bother to partners and underlings. If only a delegation of perspicacious friends had locked him up for a couple of decades in that gazebo writing-lair built for him by his in-laws Susan and Theodore Crane on their breezy hilltop east of Elmira, or in his own writing-and-billiards hideout atop the extravagant Nook Farm house in Hartford. If only Mark Twain had consented to be our American Proust, relentlessly immersed in his art, and hadn't sought also to be the Andrew Carnegie of a media revolution, and sometimes its P. T. Barnum. The bookshelves are well stocked with narratives of Mark Twain's publishing business infatuations and disasters, his self-destructive episodes of expertise and prognostication with regard to the production and marketing of printed images and words. There is no question that these enthusiasms could wreak havoc with his morale and pull him away, for long intervals, from concentration on his own writing.

But Mark Twain's infatuation with the hardware and possibilities of print media deepens and complicates many important imaginative texts that he *did* manage to write. Because Sam Clemens was trained as a printer before he was professionally trained to do anything else, and because the logistics and potentialities of printing and publishing were a focus of his attention throughout his career, causing him to involve himself in nearly every phase of designing, producing, and selling books, newspapers, and national magazines, this passionate attention resonates in the structure of his narratives, the essence of the wit, the voices of the prose—and in themes that have established Mark Twain as a consummately American and "modern" author.

Printer's Devil inquires into that presence. Mark Twain thought deeply about the cultural and psychological impact of the industrializing media that began to overwhelm the United States as he was growing up. His writing is energized and informed by his response to a cataclysmic expansion and transformation of publishing, a turmoil of innovation. He wrote about the impact upon culture and public life and upon the nature of the American self.

"THE LARGEST AMOUNT OF BRAIN LABOUR EVER UNDERTAKEN"

From the whole project, only one great specimen survives, a prototype from the middle years of a convoluted catastrophe.[19] Nine feet long and about six feet high at the top of the raceway where the proprietary brass type cascaded into the forms, this version is about 7,550 pounds of steel, with roughly eighteen thousand moving parts,[20] most of which (contrary to some disparaging contemporary reports) functioned reliably in a sixty-day test run at the *Chicago Herald* in the autumn of 1894. About twenty years after the Paige Company's demise, an extensive British survey of recent typographical progress included a long description, contributed by Charles E. Davis (endorsed here as a "distinguished mechanical engineer"), covering the history and capabilities of "the Paige composing, line-justifying, and distributing machine" as a technical achievement without equal in the history of printing. Summarizing the test at the *Herald*:

> [T]he Paige compositor, with all delays counted against it, delivered more corrected live matter to the imposing stone, ready for the formes, per operator employed, than any one of the thirty-two Linotype machines which were in operation in the same composing department, although the latter had had several years' use on newspaper work. This record may fairly claim never to have been equalled by any composing machine on its maiden trial: moreover, the composition which the compositor turned out was, in artistic merit, equal to the finest book work ever set by hand.
>
> The Paige compositor has been pronounced by competent engineers to be the foremost example of cam mechanism ever produced in the United States, if not in the whole world, and to have performed by positive mechanical devices the largest amount of brain labour ever undertaken.[21]

Davis may not have been entirely impartial about all this, having created many of the blueprints for the machine himself and having supervised the construction of every model.[22] But certifiably marvelous or not, this "foremost example of cam mechanism ever produced in the United States, if not in the whole world" (381), was a commercial dead end by 1894, and its frightening complexity was only one of the reasons. While the Paige was devouring most of Sam Clemens's personal wealth and much of his wife Olivia's inheritance from her late father, the prosperous coal merchant Jervis Langdon,[23] the Anglo-American printing industries were leaving behind any imperative to mechanize the skilled manual work of conventional typesetting. The Paige's most dangerous competition had abandoned that process altogether, like wooden-peg house framing or whale-oil lamps.

This one surviving iteration, which sulked for about fifty years in the brick basement of the most outlandish mansion in what was once the enclave for Hartford's elite, has recently been hauled to a spacious new museum on the property. To move the machine a few dozen yards cost about $30,000. The high price seems appropriate to the whole history of the Paige—and also to this dream house, which several bad investments in publishing and information technology, culminating with this disaster, ultimately forced the Clemens family to close down and sell. In more than a dozen years of the compositor's development, Clemens had poured in at least $150,000—an enormous personal outlay for that time, yet less than a tenth of the total cost for the project.[24] When staff at the Mark Twain Memorial polish up their prize, its finely finished surfaces regain their seductive glow. Certainly Clemens was seduced, and he remained in its thrall for most of those fifteen years—but not because he was naive about this machine or the reality of its quick-evolving competition. One of his weaknesses was that he knew *too much* about such matters, that he was blinded by his own personal experience with printing, his insider's appreciation for typesetting done right, and the great promise that this device alone was someday going to fulfill. Four centuries of hand-accomplished printing, centuries of drudgery and fallibility, would here be ended. He experimented with drafting encomiums himself, in the voice of a veteran printer:

> To begin, then, the operator makes a dart at the keys with both hands; a word instantly appears in the raceway before him; it came from the channels under the glass, but too quickly for anyone to see how it was done. The machine takes the measure of that word, automatically, & then passes it

FIG. 2 The surviving prototype of the Paige compositor, in its new setting at the Mark Twain House. Courtesy of the Mark Twain House & Museum, Hartford, Connecticut.

along to the front tooth of the long comb; it measures the next word & the next, and passes them to the comb-teeth; & so on & so on, stringing the words along the raceway about three inches apart until the operator touches the justifying bar; by this time the machine has exactly determined what kind of spaces are required in that line, & as the procession moves past the space-sash, the proper spaces emerge & take their places between the words, the completed line is then gently transferred to the galley by automatic mechanisms, & the thing regarded for four centuries & a half as an impossibility is accomplished. And no spacing by hand could be so regular, no justifying by hand could be so perfect.[25]

Compared to first-generation commercial models of Ottmar Mergenthaler's Linotypes and Tolbert Lanston's Monotypes in the 1880s and early 1890s, the Paige compositor was a leap beyond in sophistication. Casting type in slugs from a reservoir of molten lead, tin, and antimony, the first

Linotypes on the market could not justify the lines they produced; they were hot and unpleasant to work with; and also unlike the Paige, Mergenthaler's contraptions of wire rods and light-gauge tubing looked flimsy and vulnerable. They were certainly not the kind of brawny gear that had shaped the masculine aesthetic of a nineteenth-century print shop. Moreover, the Paige was designed (and incessantly redesigned) to accomplish more by itself than any other typesetting machine on the market. Not only would it collect, set, and justify its brass type perfectly for transfer to the press; its most remarkable capability—its madness, as it turned out—was its configuration to distribute the "dead matter" as well. In other words, when a form of set type was repositioned in the compositor after use on a press, the Paige would supposedly "read" and sort all of the component material—type letters, punctuation, em spacers, everything—back into correct position for immediate use on another job. No other typesetting machine in development anywhere could do such work,[26] which had vexed print shop apprentices, "printer's devils" like the young Sam in the daguerreotype, since the dawn of the industry and which had consumed so much of his professional time in Hannibal, Keokuk, Quincy, St. Louis, New York, Philadelphia, and other towns where as a "wandering comp" he had supported himself in the trade. Like the casting of slugs on demand, the Linotype's handling of "dead matter" was an outlandish shortcut—the used slugs were merely discarded into a melting-kettle for recasting. The Linotype was *not* intended to replicate the functions of a human typesetter—Mergenthaler's machine altered the typesetting process in its fundamentals rather than attempting to copy every traditional move. Right from the start, the Paige was meant to be the complete mechanical tradesman that Mark Twain dreamed of and that those British print historians effusively remembered. It was to be the ultimate employee, obedient, reliable, tireless, deathless; no days off, no pay, no membership in fractious unions. To Sam Clemens around 1890, as a veteran author and businessman fed up with bureaucracy, professional incompetence, wildcat strikes, and other money-gobbling expenses in getting his own books through the publishing process and out to the public, a machine like this could signify much. It was wealth and power, perpetual publication, even a kind of transcendence from the frailty and forgetfulness endemic to the culture and the flesh. From another note, apparently to himself, trying out some publicity rhetoric around 1889:

We are now ready to prove by practical test, on any day, or every day, that either of our apprentices can earn as much in a day or a week at 4 cents per 1000 ems, solid matter, corrected, as the average book-compositor can earn at 40. Proof to be corrected for nice spacing, justification, & typographical errors.

Also, that either of our apprentices can turn out as much corrected book-matter per hour or day or week, as can one man on a MacMillan, Burr, or Thorne machine in four hours or four days or four weeks.[27]

Power this robot with one of Tesla's new electric motors—James Paige also experimented, for a while, with a competing device, running on direct current rather than alternating, and Clemens bought into that ill-fated project as well[28]—and some dimension of Mark Twain himself might possibly continue forever—a printer liberated from toil, an author redeemed from the blundering and recalcitrance of human hirelings, an artist indemnified against oblivion and the world's caprices by an engineered embodiment of his own dreams, revolutionizing an industry on which, only in his lifetime, the cultures of the West had come to depend. In other holograph pages from around 1885 there are outbursts of anxious self-reassurance about a happy ending, just out of sight, a release from even the fallibility and mortality of other machines:

It is safe even in the awkwardest hands; it is hardly possible to get it out of order.

All its parts are made of steel; it is good for an indefinite number of years without repairs.

Anybody who can read, can *set* type with it.

And it does its own distributing, automatically, & without anybody's interference or assistance. . . .

Two persons are required; a man or a girl to *set* type by operating the keys; and a girl to justify. . . .

The machine applies a test, automatically, to every type that enters it from the distributor—with this result:

It throws out all broken type;

Also all weak type;

Also all turned letters;

Also all type that are turned end-for-end;

Also all "wrong font" type.

A type *cannot break* in the machine.
It does not *wear* the type, or injure it in any way.[29]

As early as 1885, however, the competition was treacherous. By the end of the next year, Linotypes on the market were accomplishing the basics of typesetting well enough, and improved models from the Baltimore plant—the Blower Linotype (1889), which used forced air to move the cast matrices into position, and the Simplex (1890), exploiting gravity for these manipulations—also found buyers. Some of Mergenthaler's first production models were deployed at Whitelaw Reid's *New York Tribune* in 1886, when the Paige was still only blueprints;[30] and the wealthy and ruthless Reid, whom Clemens despised, became a major investor in the Paige's most powerful competition, eventually driving Mergenthaler himself out of the company he had created.[31]

Clemens was keeping an eye on these developments, just as he had paid attention to nearly every important innovation in printing and publishing since his days at the *Hannibal Journal.* But like many other people who knew the industry well,[32] he fixed his gaze on the wrong competition, on a handful of systems configured to work with movable type of the traditional variety. He refused to recognize the significance of technology that broke away as radically as the Linotype.[33] And looking in the wrong direction, he found plenty to worry about. In the mid-1880s, after fifty years of British, French, and American experiment with automated typesetting, there were contrivances on the market that also worked with the kind of type that Sam had known since his youth. None of these machines was anywhere near as sophisticated or complete as the Paige was going to be, but some of them did function essentially as advertised; and as affordable options for American printers they too were gnawing into the potential market. A Rogers Typograph, for example, operated only at about half the speed of a Blower Linotype, but a Rogers also cost about $500 less—in those years not a trivial price advantage—and it performed reliably enough to win a national competition sponsored by the American Newspaper Association in 1891.[34] A couple of years later, Wilbur Scudder introduced the Monoline, a line-casting machine that was similarly slow, compared to both the hypothetical and the actual velocity of the Paige, but also cheaper and attractive to smaller publishers: $1,000 to buy, $250 per year to rent,[35] compared to the $6,000 or even $12,000 that the Paige would eventually need to sell for (according to Sam's jittery private calculations)[36] if the company was to turn a profit or merely survive.

Most of the competing equipment weighed hundreds of pounds less than the Paige; mechanically simpler, it could be shipped and maintained at remote locations with less trouble and expense—and worst of all, by the beginning of the 1890s it was in production. By the close of 1892, when after seven years of development the Paige was still not ready for a serious commercial trial, even the *Helena Daily Journal* (Montana), the *Idaho Statesman* (Boise), the *Astoria* on the Oregon coast, and South Dakota's *Pioneer Times* had Linotypes or other automated typesetting machinery in their workrooms.[37] Moreover, because Linotypes and Monotypes cast matrices as needed, they effectively ended a dependency upon type foundries to supply replacement inventories of fonts, a dependency that had troubled printers since the advent of metal type in the Renaissance.[38] From that perspective, the Paige was again a long safari in a wrong direction, requiring a permanent chattel relationship between the machine's operators and whatever foundry could produce the special brass type with the intricate scoring required for the distribution process. The financial panic of 1893 was a concluding stroke of dismal luck.

With these other contraptions, however, there was no intimation of personal immortality. They assisted only; they did not presume to construct in steel a human being. Only the Paige could signify the kind of redemption Mark Twain wanted, a postponed bonanza that would turn the impatient, aging writer into a media tycoon, a peer at last with plutocrats of the steel, oil, and publishing industries, men whose hospitality and friendship Clemens had come to relish. If the Paige succeeded as he had dreamed it would, it would make Mark Twain a commanding figure in the greatest information technology upheaval since the advent of movable type and handpresses in Mainz in the fifteenth century. And when the final failure of the Paige, along with the ignominious end of the Kaolatype illustration process and red-ink publishing projects of his Charles L. Webster & Company, led to bankruptcy, he was sixty years old.

The financial fall of Mark Twain was a mess of misfires and disasters, including a "Memory Builder" game for the daily newspapers, the direct-current electric motor, a lavishly illustrated subscription book that would supposedly sell for a thousand dollars a copy,[39] and the *Library of American Literature,* more comprehensive (and more expensive) than any anthology before it in the history of American publishing. The Paige was only Mark Twain's Vicksburg siege in a fiscal terrain so baffling that charting it in detail would require a Corps of Engineers. The root of the defeat, however, was the way that technological and business possibilities related to printing and publishing ramified in his imagination.

The Kaolatype Company, which Clemens founded, and into which he eventually poured more than $50,000 of his own money, centered on a new process for printing illustrations. The patents had been controlled by Dan Slote, former companion on the 1867 *Quaker City* trip that led to *The Innocents Abroad.* Using a matrix of fine clay as a step in transferring images to printable plates—as a shortcut and a cost savings—Kaolatype was only one new and dubious trick in a range of fresh strategies to replace conventional wood and steel engraving in the late 1870s.[40] Enthralled by what Slote had shown him, Clemens purchased a four-fifths share of the patented process in February 1880, keeping Slote as treasurer of the company. As Sam described its future in a euphoric letter to Orion, Kaolatype (with Clemens's money and personal influence backing it) would "utterly annihilate & sweep out of existence one of the minor industries of civilization, & take its place—an industry which has existed for 300 years—& doubtless many attempts have been made to knock the bottom out of its costliness before. Perchance I am mistaken in this calculation, but I am not able to see how I can be."[41] By autumn of that year, Clemens was imagining himself smarter than all the competition:

> I wrote to you last March that I believed I had invented an idea that would increase the value of Kaolatype a hundred fold. It was to apply it to the *moulding* of bookbinders' brass stamps, in place of *engraving* them. Ever since then I have been trying to find somebody who could invent a flux that would enable a body to mould hard brass with sharp-cut lines & perfect surfaces.
>
> But every brass-expert laughed at the idea & said the thing was absolutely impossible. But at last I struck a young German who believed he could do it. I have had him under wages for 3 months, now, night & day, & at last he has worked the miracle. . . . His flux, & his method of using it, are marvelously original & ingenious, & are patentable by themselves. He & Slote came up yesterday, bringing six specimens of moulded brass stamps, & I contracted to pay him $5,000 when he is able to put his patents into my hands and assign me a one-third ownership in them for America and Europe, & pay him $150 a month to go on & perfect his methods, & also the attendant expenses. I never saw people so wild over anything.[42]

Early in his health-wrecking business relationship with his obsessive uncle, Charles Webster was drafted into overseeing this project when Clemens and

Slote quarreled over money and management, and through much of 1881 Clemens's letters to Webster clang with prognostications about brass. Eventually Sam succeeded in pressuring James Osgood into trying the process for the embossed binding of *The Prince and the Pauper*—but its viability for the original purpose, reproducing illustrations quickly and inexpensively for high-volume printing on a powered press, remained a matter of uncertainty. By the spring of 1881, Clemens's suspicions had been aroused as he received conflicting advice from outside experts, scrutinized details of the technology, and wondered what it could really do.[43] Artists hired by Osgood to illustrate in *Life on the Mississippi* rebelled against its use; the Kaolatype production shop burned down under suspicious circumstances shortly before Clemens was to inspect it firsthand; and Dan Slote, who died in 1882, went to his grave maligned by Clemens as a thief. And while he fulminated about a succession of real and imagined infringements on the patent, the technological upheaval in book and magazine illustration refused to let up. Whether or not it actually worked as advertised, Kaolatype vanished in a sea of viable alternatives.

One more Gilded Age dream that came to nothing—and Sam's high hopes and volatility in pursuing them may suggest a deficit of good sense. But in the turbulent world of American publishing, other heretical ideas had already made Mark Twain into a genuine international star. Sam Clemens did not invent subscription bookselling, and as a young writer in Nevada and California he had not actively sought a pact with it. This rambunctious new industry found *him,* and in subsequent years it was crucial in keeping Mark Twain connected to a huge audience and making money for him at levels never reached before by American writers. As one of seven subscription-trade houses in Hartford (in 1869 there were five more in Chicago, four in Philadelphia, three in Cincinnati, and at least nine more scattered in other major cities),[44] the American Publishing Company was popular entertainment and fast profit, with no serious aspirations to become a dignified imprint. Elisha Bliss and his son Frank favored hefty, gilt-embossed volumes, stuffed with pictures and written in styles appropriate to the tastes and reading skills of ordinary villagers and farmers. Right after the Civil War, thanks to a new railroad network hurried into the hinterlands to link up the Union states and territories, subscription publishers could contract out a massive first printing, with duplicate electroplates, to firms at scattered locations; bind the book at one plant or several; and do a synchronized, stunning national release through a system of affiliates. When *Roughing It* was released in the United States in 1872, for example, it was shipped out from regional warehouses in Chicago, Toledo, Cincinnati, Philadelphia, Boston, and San Francisco, as well as Hartford, where most of the production was done.[45] The APC and the other major subscription houses could saturate the continental United States with editions and print runs that would have astounded a Boston Brahmin before the Civil War—fifty thousand, seventy thousand copies or more, gaudily adorned, jammed with pictures, and vended nationwide in a matter of months.[46]

After the success of *The Innocents Abroad,* which had sold more than eighty thousand copies through Elisha Bliss's door-to-door sales force in a year and a half, Mark Twain wrote most of his books until about 1895 with this format and market in mind, sometimes insisting that his publishers secure advance sales in the tens of thousands before he completed the manuscript.[47] When his work also proved popular in England and other far-off places, and when pirate editions elsewhere cut into his profits, he made himself a storm center of international copyright disputes and negotiations, mastering intricate maneuvers for protecting his rights and royalties in the Commonwealth.[48] As a world-famous writer he was willing at times to market a different identity abroad than at home, to bowdlerize his books for overseas sensibilities, or to downplay, in advertising campaigns, the satiric heat of his own volumes even in the United States.[49] By the mid-1890s, when some of the illustration technologies that ended Kaolatype simplified the printing of photographs in newspapers and magazines,[50] Mark Twain began posturing for the cameras as frequently and effectively as any other American author of his day.

Mark Twain adored the toys and the potent inventions of this new age in communications. He bragged about being the first American author to have a manuscript typed up before he revised it and the first citizen in Hartford to have a telephone in a private residence. But while he was infatuated with this revolution, he was also wary of its consequences for American cultural life and for personal identity. He configured his artistic aspirations and writing strategies to exploit new technologies and possibilities of an age of print, inflecting some of his narratives to ponder the impact of publishing on a massive scale and the disruptive presence of printed texts from afar in a naive cultural context. Though he could be catastrophically wrong in guessing the technological and economic future of this print revolution, his errors were rooted in his own extraordinary experience of its past and present, and one book can only begin to explore the influence upon his literary work. To do so, a tight focus must be maintained to avoid floating away into enigma variations on "Mark Twain and Modernity." I want to stay with the following objectives.

The first is to review briefly how the life of Sam Clemens, and the career and public identity of Mark Twain, took shape under the pressure of this revolution. The technological skills that Clemens learned in his youth, the radical innovations that he encountered firsthand and that as an author and celebrity he exploited with enthusiasm and skill, bringing down financial disaster and personal anguish when he tried to become a major force in the industry—these are landmarks in the life and a recurring presence in the literary texts. What happens if we think about "Mark Twain" as a cultural phenomenon in which the latest technologies of publishing and the art of the writer are conjoined? As American literature and culture have achieved respectability as academic subjects, the incentive has been strong to imagine our major authors as somehow escaping contamination by the publishing systems of their own moment unless the artist consciously chose to make the world of smokestacks, presses, and business deals a significant subject. In popularized stories of our own cultural history, the impression is conveyed that the corporate and technological embroilment, or outright seduction, of good American authors is a disaster of only recent vintage. From our survey courses and from the general histories and the introductions in big-selling literary anthologies, many thousands of intelligent Americans come away every year assuming that a manuscript accumulating on the writing tables of Fitzgerald, Cather, Hemingway, Ellison, or anyone else from about 1865 to the advent of the desktop computer was essentially the same kind of project as a sheaf of pages quilled out for local handpress printers by Rawson, Equiano, Irving, or Cooper. The innovations that reconstructed American publishing after 1840, changes that only increased in scope and fury through the end of the nineteenth century, altered nearly everything that a "book" was and could be—not only its physical construction, demographic reach, and economic value but also its potential as a cultural artifact and even its epistemology. Every decade of Clemens's life from 1850 through 1900 brought radical disruptions in that reality, and in every one of those decades he re-created himself as an author to respond to that new world.

The second objective is to observe how these technological transformations manifest themselves in Mark Twain's texts—not only in their embellishment but also in how they are written and structured as prose—and how this print revolution is engaged as a *subject* in these texts. Enthusiastic about innovations cascading into the industry, Mark Twain was also sensitive to their impact upon culture, upon personal and collective conduct, the contingencies of seeing and telling, the aesthetic tastes and political sentiments of a vast public, the reach and authenticity of fame, and the thematic stability and cultural longevity of printed discourse and literary art. The compounding strangeness of reporting and reading in such a context turns up early in his work—even before there was a Mark Twain. And when he achieved international celebrity, he wrote about that too, the intoxication of launching printed discourses and images across thousands of miles at unknowable audiences, the intensifying rivalries between image and word and also between the mediated and the direct experience. As a boy in Hannibal and as a reporter in the West, Clemens played exuberantly with the paradoxical authority of the printed page; as an aging eminence in American culture, he understood the new world of print as a darker dilemma, connected to mysteries of knowing and being.

Third, there is the abiding, metamorphic presence of the Mark Twain legacy, and its special importance now, in the midst of another media revolution, an exponential intensification and complication of the crisis that broke out in Mark Twain's childhood. When Clemens died in 1910, "Mark Twain" had already become a global entity, uncannily versatile, rising from the printed page to slip away on projected light and electromagnetic frequencies whose exploitation had begun only in the final years of his life. No other "great author" from the American nineteenth century enjoys such all-weather vogue as a mass culture icon in the twenty-first—in part, perhaps, because our own century continues to construct "author" and "celebrity" in configurations that Sam Clemens played a role in pioneering. He poured his energies into establishing the rules of games we still play. He invented a new kind of immortality, a protean omnipresence suited to a new age with little faith in the divine, yet much veneration for supposedly human media contrivances. As we search for not-so-distant mirrors of our own "accelerated grimace," for precedents or guidance in re-creating "literature" and the American author as subjects that are somehow still consequential to our cultural life, the evolving phenomenon of Mark Twain is an excellent place to begin.

The patronage of a county newspaper is too frequently the most pitiful, beggarly thing in the world.

Fulton Telegraph, February 2, 1849

WILL PEOPLE WHO OWE US
PLEASE CALL AND PAY UP?
WE NEED THE MONEY AND HAVE NO TIME TO COLLECT IT.

Hannibal Daily Journal, August 24, 1853

Not a single literary work of genuine originality published in book form before 1850 had any commercial value to speak of until much later, and most of our classics were financial failures—Poe's and Hawthorne's tales, Emerson's essays and poems, Melville's *Mardi,* Thoreau's *Week.*

WILLIAM CHARVAT,
Literary Publishing in America

Sam Clemens had his first collisions with this new information age in Joe Ament's shop, setting type and printing the sheets according to the old ways while depending on stories that by the end of 1847 were reaching St. Louis on telegraph lines and churning up to Hannibal by steamboat days later.[51] When Sam and his brother Henry left the *Missouri Courier* in 1851 to help Orion (ten years older, and freshly returned from years of work as a printer in the newspaper-publishing business of St. Louis) in turning out a four-pager variously called the *Western Union,*[52] the *Hannibal Journal and Western Union,* the *Hannibal Weekly Journal,* and the *Hannibal Daily Journal,* the three Clemens brothers probably had nothing more modern to work with than two serviceable handpresses and no direct or reliable access to the electronically transmitted "intelligence" that filled the St. Louis papers, feeding and intensifying a public appetite for news speeding in from afar. As late as May 1853, as Sam was getting ready to flee his brother's enterprise and head for St. Louis, Orion's paper was still publishing pleas for a basic telegraph hookup to Hannibal.[53]

As for the actual presses on which Sam mastered the craft, published his own first experiments as a writer, and experienced (literally hands on) the paradoxical transient permanence of printed words, we can close in tighter. About two years before Orion bought the *Journal* and merged its equipment and subscription base into his struggling *Western Union,* Robert Buchanan, one of the *Journal*'s previous owners (the masthead's list of publishers and partners shifted frequently in the late 1840s), was advertising his shop's availability for job-printing work, listing "two excellent presses" and embellishing the ad with a small off-the-shelf illustration, called by printers a "dingbat," showing what might be a version of a Washington hand-press, which by that time was established as a machine of choice for small American printing operations.[54] A better clue turns up in the *Journal* a year before. In February 1848, citing health problems and seeking buyers for his paper and shop, Buchanan published a list of the assets:

> This Establishment has been in successful operation for the last six years and upwards, and enjoys, at this time, the most profitable run of Job Work and Advertising of any other paper in the State, out of St. Louis, with a flattering promise of a large increase of subscription, job work, and Advertising.
>
> The materials of the office consist of a first rate new Double Medium "Washington" Press; an elegant second hand "Imperial" Press; (both Iron;) and Plain, Fancy, and Ornamental Type, from Nonpareil up to the largest size Wooden Type, suitable for all descriptions of printing, from a *visiting card to the largest sized poster,* with all other fixtures required about a city Printing Office.
>
> All the Ornamental, and most of the large Job Type, is entirely new, having been recently purchased at the "Cincinnati Type Foundry." A Practical Printer, wishing to go into business, could not do better than to embrace this opportunity. Application should be made early, post-paid, to J. S. BUCHANAN.
>
> *Hannibal, February 3, 1848*

Shortly afterward, instead of selling the paper and the inventory outright, Buchanan transferred his share of the business to his son and a partner named Joseph G. Easton, and the *Journal*'s "Prospectus," published regularly afterward in the summer of 1848, boasts of the freshness of its gear and the improving speed with which news from afar was now coming in—by steamboat from St. Louis, where the papers were getting it by wire:

> Not more than a year since, the office was thoroughly refurnished with a first rate new Press, and full supply of new type, and since that time, the "Journal" has issued upon a neatly printed double medium sheet; and we are not afraid to say, will compare, under all the circumstances, with any paper in the State. . . .
>
> Whatever transpires in St. Louis on one day, we receive the next by 3 o'clock, P.M.—from all the prominent cities of the East, on the wings of lightning and

steam, we receive the most important news in three days—it has even come to our hands in thirty hours from Philadelphia. We know the transactions of New Orleans in seven days from the time they transpire; and that time will soon be reduced by Telegraph, more than half, between these points.[55]

With regard to commerce and the circulation of news in the later 1840s, the "wings of steam" were figuring in Hannibal's commercial and cultural life, but "wings of lightning" were a prerogative of larger places. About these presses: "double medium" signifies the maximum size of the sheet that this configuration[56] of the Washington press could accommodate. By the middle of the nineteenth century, paper dimensions had been standardized by large-scale manufacturers, and the smallest sheet suitable for conventional printing press use, "medium," was nineteen by twenty-four inches. "Medium-and-half" was twenty-four by thirty; "double medium," a preferred size for a folded four-page newspaper, measured twenty-four by thirty-eight.[57] With a Washington double-medium handpress, therefore, a printer could produce one impression of two newspaper pages with a single pull.[58] A print run of four hundred four-page newspapers would require eight hundred impressions, one for each side of each sheet—with an interval for the first-side impressions to dry. If an experienced crew working at full speed in optimal conditions could be expected to produce about 160 to 200 impressions in one hour,[59] then a complete run, allowing time for changing forms and drying and folding the sheets, would require at least half a working day. A heavier London-made machine standing on ornate cast-iron legs with animal-paw feet, the Imperial handpress had a platen that was operated with a leaf spring, making it exceptionally powerful for impressions.[60] But the Imperial was configured to take a much smaller sheet: on extant models in the United States and Australia, the chase is only about fifteen inches by twenty, making it unsuitable for turning out a newspaper with the sheet dimensions of either the *Western Union* or the *Journal*.[61] A standard outfit, then, for a small-town printer. For comparison: by 1848, with multicylinder, type-revolving presses, also manufactured by the Hoe Company or one of its several competitors, a newspaper in a large American city could count on producing six thousand to ten thousand double-sided impressions in a single hour. If Orion Clemens was so cash-strapped in his Hannibal printing days that he could never pay his brothers for their work, it seems doubtful that he could have financed major improvements on the equipment he acquired with the *Journal*.

Patent Washington Printing Press.

The celebrity which our Patent Washington and Smith Hand Presses have obtained during the last forty years, renders any remarks upon their superiority unnecessary. They are elegant in appearance, simple, quick and powerful in operation, and combine every facility for the production of superior printing. Each press is tried at the manufactory, and warranted for one year.

Sizes and Prices.

	Platen.	Bed.	Weight boxed.	Price.
Foolscap	14½ × 19½ inches	18 × 24 inches	710 lbs	$250.00
Medium	19 × 25 "	22½ × 29½ "	1,310 "	300.00
Super Royal	22½ × 28 "	26 × 32½ "	1,475 "	330.00
No. 1	21 × 30 "	24½ × 34½ "	1,510 "	345.00
" 2	22 × 32½ "	25½ × 37 "	1,540 "	360.00
" 3	23 × 35 "	26½ × 39½ "	1,870 "	375.00
" 4	24 × 37 "	27½ × 41½ "	1,980 "	390.00
" 5	25 × 39 "	28½ × 43½ "	2,150 "	415.00
" 6	26 × 41½ "	29½ × 46 "	2,270 "	435.00
Mammoth	34½ × 43½ "	38½ × 48 "	"	575.00

Above price includes two pairs of Points, 1 Screw Wrench, 1 Brayer, 1 Slice and 1 extra Frisket.

Boxing and Carting or Carting and Putting-up, $7.50. If the frame is made to be taken to pieces, $15 extra.

Terms of Payment—Cash at manufactory in New-York.

Until inventory lists turn up from the 1853 sale of the *Journal*'s remains to another rival paper, the *Hannibal Tri-Weekly Messenger* (the number of newspapers that sprouted and perished quickly in American small towns before the Civil War is astounding), the best assumption is that much of Sam's education in the printer's craft, and most of his time as the stand-in boss of this county paper's work crew (when Orion was out of town, which happened frequently, Sam was left in charge of all phases of production), centered on this Washington double-medium press—and that when he escaped to St. Louis in his eighteenth year, and subsequently rambled around for months as a journeyman printer in publishing centers on the East Coast, he crossed a technological great divide, encountering and participating in production processes whose complexity and scale were truly in another dimension.

Among the letters that survive from these first adventures in high-speed automated printing, one stands out, sent by Sam from Washington, D.C., for publication in the *Muscatine Journal,* and dated February 17 and 18, 1854. Orion had moved upriver to publish this paper after his failure in Hannibal. Eighteen years old now, the younger brother muses on the sight of Ben Franklin's handpress, conserved in the Museum of the Patent Office, and on the radical transformation of printing in Sam's own lifetime: "The bed is of wood and is not unlike a very shallow box. The platen is only half the size of the bed, thus requiring two pulls of the lever to each full-size sheet. What vast progress has been made in the art of printing! The press is capable of printing about 125 sheets per hour; and after seeing it, I have watched Hoe's great machine throwing off its 20,000 sheets in the same space of time, with an interest I never before felt."[62]

Before the Washington encounter with Franklin's press, Sam had worked for several weeks at a printing establishment on Cliff Street in lower Manhattan, very near the mighty Harper establishment, while an "Exhibition of the Industry of All Nations" was in full swing in an American "Crystal Palace" on Reservoir Square, at Sixth Avenue between Fortieth and Forty-Second Streets, where the New York Public Library stands now. Strongly promoted by the publishing magnate George Palmer Putnam, this world's fair was housed in a domed, cruciform pavilion of glass, five acres under one roof. It was New York's architectural and industrial answer to the other Crystal Palace across the sea, which had housed Prince Albert's 1851 "Great Exhibition" in Hyde Park. In the grand concourses of the Manhattan show, along with a colossal statue of George Washington on horseback and smaller

𝕰ight 𝕮ylinder 𝕿ype-𝕽evolving 𝕻rinting 𝕸achine.

FIG. 4 One of Hoe's "great machines," commercially available in the early 1850s: sixteen thousand printed sides per hour, from the Hoe Company catalog. By 1856, ten-cylinder models were being advertised as reaching twenty thousand sides per hour. Rare Books and Special Collections Library, University of Illinois at Urbana-Champaign.

effigies of Ethan Allen and Daniel Webster (on their own two feet), there was another equestrian work, a real crowd pleaser in bronze by a sculptor named Kiss, purporting to show the Queen of the Amazons attacked by a lion. Amid such company, which also included three fountains, a baptismal font, and a solid iron palmetto tree, Putnam had arranged for two state-of-the-art, steam-driven automatic presses—each operated by only one human being—to print the exposition's weekly journal, the *Illustrated Record,* every day before the eyes of the visiting multitudes.[63] But Putnam did not choose "Hoe's great machine" for this center-stage demonstration of printing prowess, opting instead for a current model of the steam-driven Adams bed-and-platen press, which was revolutionizing book production (more about the importance of the Adams equipment later in this chapter), and a "steam cylinder printing machine" from the New York firm of A. B. Taylor and Sons, especially for printing illustrations.[64] Preferring a spectacle of sheer Yankee productivity rather than finesse, an issue of the *Scientific American* grumbled that these exhibits in the east nave of the palace were not appropriately up to date:

Two printing presses have been introduced into the Palace, and are kept at work on the Illustrated Catalogue. We have been informed that Messrs. Hoe are not going to have one of their large lightning presses on exhibition. The reason given is, they could not get the requisite quantity of room to erect and work it. We regret this, because we are sure that this press would command the admiration of all. It would especially arrest and rivet the attention of all our foreign brethren. Applegarth's great press was at the London Exhibition; why should not Hoe's be at the American? A working model of Wilkinson's new press is to be on exhibition, but that is not enough, in justice to *our country*, we want to see the biggest and fastest press in America at the Exhibition.[65]

Sam must therefore have had his first encounters with Hoe's behemoth somewhere else on his East Coast ramble, possibly at more than one location in Washington or Philadelphia, or nearby in New York City, where the Hoe Company had its headquarters on Gold Street, about two blocks from where Sam was working (Hoe's three New York factories at that time were several blocks farther uptown, on Broome, Sheriff, and Columbia).[66] But on the young Missourian the Exhibition certainly made an impression of its own; he wrote about it to his sister Pamela Moffett in St. Louis, probably in early September 1853—the earliest surviving manuscript of a personal letter from Samuel Clemens:

> From the gallery (second floor) you have a glorious sight—the flags of the different countries represented, the lofty dome, glittering jewelry, gaudy tapestry, &c., with the busy crowd passing to and fro—tis a perfect fairy palace— beautiful beyond description.
>
> The Machinery department is on the main floor, but I cannot enumerate any of it on account of the lateness of the hour (past 1 o'clock). It would take more than a week to examine everything on exhibition; and as I was only in a little over two hours to-night, I only glanced at about one-third of the articles; and having a poor memory, I have enumerated scarcely any of even the principal objects. The visitors to the Palace average 6,000 daily—double the population of Hannibal. The price of admission being 50 cents, they take in about $3,000.[67]

Even if he had wandered the palace only on that evening, Sam would have rolled through one "gallery" and "court" after another featuring innovations in typography, inks, bookbinding, papermaking, every modern aspect of the printing industry. The U.S. exhibits included at least three different displays of new electrotype and stereotype technology; seven printing presses other than the featured Adams and Taylor equipment; and new machines for cutting and folding newspapers, turning out lithographs, manufacturing paper, and "paging the sheets of blank books." From Saxony there was a new process for casting type; the British sent a "slide-lever improved lithographic press-registering machine for chromo or color printing" and many specimens of the latest in book production; and French participants sent a new design for an iron lithographic press and eighteen other exhibits under the general category of "Paper and Stationery; Types, Printing, and Bookbinding." There were thousands of innovations here to catch the imagination of an ambitious young man, far more fresh and professionally relevant technology than Sam had ever encountered elsewhere in a single place.[68]

In the spring of the year before, while Sam was still in Missouri, slipping jokes, poems, and pseudonymous comic letters and even giddy woodcuts into the news-starved columns of the *Hannibal Journal,* he was in the midst of a contradictory education—in the volatility and mortality of words and the hard rituals of handpresses and movable type—not unlike what Franklin had learned two centuries before, or what William Dean Howells, only two years younger than Sam, was facing as an apprentice in similar shops in rural Ohio. When the "author" must also edit his copy, set the type, check proofs, position forms, operate the press, sort dead matter back into the cases, and clean up for the next day's work, "writing" can be understood as a process with more attendant complexities and responsibilities than are knowable from merely generating manuscript for others to decode and publish.

About the literary dimensions of an education in a traditional print shop, that much is a commonplace; but other anomalies were here to be faced as well, also related to the strangeness of setting your own words in type for their mayfly life on a page of a county paper. Loaded into a composing stick, written words acquire heft; a conscientiously corrected form, ready for the press, is a weighty object with tedious work invested in its making, a construction with physicality that the same discourse scrawled on a piece of paper cannot come near. And a stack of printed, folded journals, each containing its replica of one's own discourse, might intimate that something consequential, or even permanent, had been achieved in that effort. Even in a place as small as Hannibal, however, tomorrow's flurry of newspapers from your own workroom, from other shops in town, or from enormous establishments far away smothers the verbal spark and banality of yesterday, and every hand-set, copyedited, and hand-printed page of local discourse is fated to fall fast into oblivion. From the colonial period through the early years of the nineteenth century, there were conscientious American private citizens who made a practice of sewing and binding local newspapers into books for preservation[69] because in those earlier times the printed word could seem so dear. The Columbia *Morning Intelligencer,* a Tennessee contemporary of Orion's *Daily Journal,* lamented the decline of the practice: "It is much to be regretted that it is not more generally customary to preserve and bind for future use the newspaper of the day. . . . In a few years, the newspaper now so lightly esteemed, would become the most interesting and accurate daguerreotype of the past, and every year would add to its value."[70] By the time Sam entered the trade, however, the sheer volume of American periodical discourse was reducing such conservation into an eccentric hobby for shut-ins or a chore for professional archivists. If his Hannibal experience as a teenaged writer-editor-printer conditioned Sam Clemens to involve himself, throughout his later life as an author, in all the processes through which imaginative effort becomes a published artifact in a national and international market, that early experience may have also have taught him lessons in the treacherous epistemology, and the dubious cultural value, of the printed word.

With the peculiar dynamics and interconnections of byline, public identity, and private self, Sam Clemens had youthful adventures as well. When he began to set and print his own writings in the *Journal* he did so anonymously, with cryptic or comic pseudonyms or no name on the piece at all. He slipped in one-sentence gags, poems, and counterfeit letters from the public. He even produced and printed clumsy woodcuts, satirizing (and also envying) the large and fancy illustrations that had lately become features in national weeklies and monthlies.[71] His bogus bylines— "Rambler," "Grumbler," "A Son of Hannibal," "Saverton," and "Josh"— might indicate conflict in the *Journal*'s office—Orion trying to rein in his frisky younger brother, and Sam in insurrection—or perhaps a deception they conspired in together, a workroom pretense that there were more contributors to this newspaper, more readers of it, and more to provoke those readers than was actually the case. On his own, Sam would continue these quirky experiments in self-effacing self-exhibition after he left Orion's employ, publishing here and there as Thomas Jefferson Snodgrass, Soleleather,[72] Sargent Fathom, and W. Epaminondas Adrastus Blab. Later, from the Nevada Territory, his first sketch to win national attention was an anonymous hoax news report about a petrified man discovered in the desert near Virginia City, where Sam was reporting and fabricating "intelligence" for the *Territorial Enterprise.* To reach a wide audience and keep it entertained, Sam Clemens wrote as nobody many times before he ever wrote as Mark Twain.

In that Hannibal shop, however, what was the relationship between this flamboyant self-erasure and the physical work of setting and printing these sheets of news? The skills and labor of the apprentice can alienate: every handwritten word, whether by your own or some other hand, becomes a work order for the multistage production of a different kind of artifact. Each word becomes a professional challenge of mechanical assembly: pull the right type from the cases; set each letter in the chase, tight, justified, watching the spelling (always backwards), and doing this carefully, lest the whole assemblage crash into "pi"—a professional humiliation, and grounds for dismissal in shops where efficiency is required. Later you will operate the press with main strength, in another compound process to be repeated carefully for every impression. If imaginative and humorous writing requires an increment of caprice, there is very little of that in the toil of carrying the results through these rituals of publication. And when your own words occupy only small space on an ephemeral sheet of local gossip and advertisements, or at most a column or two in a daily journal that will be kindling and wrappings tomorrow—what then? Which alternative is the riskier: signing your true name to your own words and launching them into brief circuits of ridicule and guaranteed oblivion? Or preempting such a quick journey into the dark by obliterating yourself *before* the diurnal or weekly futility of small-town publishing can do that service for you?

A different path of speculation leads to essentially the same omega point: in the middle of the American nineteenth century, daily and weekly newspapers, even these four-pagers, were an incantation of names, an exposition of identities that in a strict sense were fraudulent. Such-and-such a person, probably unknown to most readers as anything more than this name, reportedly did this or that notorious thing, and in its particulars the report that followed was possibly wrong; another name on the page was said to have died yesterday, or to have been arrested, or elected to something, or to have jumped or been pushed through some other ordinary portal that counts as a significant passage in American village life. To glance over stale sheets of published local news is to bear witness to fruitless clamoring for the instant of recognition—tomorrow morning's lesson in the vanity of today's byline—or for some species of transcendence, some kind of escape from utterance and identity as these ephemeral configurations of ink. And when one of the names associated here with setting the type and printing the sheets is the same as the one taking credit for the story? This is disturbance of the hierarchies, the "printer's devils" usurping what little dignity and authority there is in backcountry editorial Pandemonium. No glory accrues to a journal for having its apprentices write the copy, as well as set it in type and run it through the press: journalism requires genuine or affected demarcations between the authors of the words and the folk who blacken their hands with the chases and the machines. Because Franklin understood that, in his own printer days he concocted a succession of contributors—Poor Richard, Silence Dogood, Polly Baker—to take responsibility for wit and heresy coming from himself. According to the rituals of movable type, discourse is supposed to run gauntlets of review: you edit me, I copyedit you, and from these exchanges of labor printed texts emerge that are implicitly certified as worth reading. Paltry authorial "me" inflates into editorial "us." One modern paradox, of course, is that the editorial inflation of celebrity "me's," synthetic personalities pumped up and floated sky-high with published words and pictures, is a high-profit business of globalized media. Round and round it goes. Even in a place like Hannibal, however, on the periphery of this Great Revolution, allowing the lowly printers to write the words—or rather, allowing word to circulate that the printers are *also* writing the words—is putting the small mammals in charge of the zoo, compromising whatever dignity might be aspired to by a struggling county paper.

After Orion purchased the *Hannibal Journal* in the fall of 1850, merged it with his *Western Union,* and persuaded his two brothers to leave Joe Ament's *Courier* and join this new enterprise, Orion's print shop continued for another eighteen months, surviving an office fire in January 1852 and removals to other work spaces, perhaps including a temporary setup in the parlor of the Clemens family house.[73] In March 1853, still without a telegraph news service, or reporters, or most of the other amenities of a modern metropolitan newspaper, and straining to hold his audience against other local journals and the St. Louis and national competition, Orion resolved to produce the village's first *Daily Journal* in addition to the *Weekly.*[74] It is not surprising that Sam took leave from this exhausting experiment only a few weeks after it got underway. About six months later, Orion himself had reached the end, and by the middle of September he had sold off the remains of the *Journal* and moved away to try again in Musca-tine.[75] The surviving numbers of the *Daily Journal* tell much about the rough times of small-scale regional publishers as national media powered up and spread out. For the opening six weeks of its operation, Orion published almost nothing on his front and back pages except advertisements for much grander periodicals. With automated production plants, these new period-icals, packed with words and pictures, could charge less for a year's sub-scription than either the *Daily Journal* or the *Weekly* because of a plunge in the cost of serviceable paper (another story of rapid technological change), advantages in other production costs, and a sharp cut in federal postal rates for printed matter.[76]

For two or three dollars per year, a Marion County family could immerse itself in pictures and competent prose. The *Southern Literary Messenger, Blackwood's, Arthur's Home Magazine, Harper's New Monthly Magazine, Godey's Lady's Book, De Bow's Review,* the *Dollar Newspaper, Peterson's Magazine*—in effusive advertisements they are all here, promising a much better reading experience, in content and production values, than these des-perate village imprints that carried their notices. Published in Philadelphia, *Scott's Weekly Paper* credited its success to the fact "that it presents more read-ing matter, of a better quality, in a more elegant style, and at a cheaper rate than any other publication; and that its literary and news contents have met the wants of the great mass of the American people, by combining interest, instruction, and amusement to a degree hitherto unparalleled." All this for two dollars a year. An annual subscription to *Scott's Weekly* had run as high as nine dollars only three years before. As the strongest-selling of the American "women's magazines," *Godey's Magazine and Lady's Book* was claiming a monthly circulation of sixty-eight thousand copies as early as the spring of 1850.[77] And founded by America's largest publishing house in June 1850, *Harper's New Monthly Magazine,* published on Franklin Square in Manhattan, was already boasting "a regular monthly issue of more than 100,000 COPIES, and . . . still steadily and rapidly increasing." For only thirty-six cents per year, Hannibal subscribers were promised "the most attractive and most useful Magazine for popular reading in the world; and the extent to which their efforts have been successful is indicated by the fact, that it has attained a greater circulation than any similar periodical ever issued." The *Knickerbocker Magazine,* the *Home Journal* (another national weekly), and the *Musical World and Times* (also a weekly) were advertised as a set, available at a package price:

These three publications will post a family up in regard to everything worth knowing:—Art, Science, Literature; music, painting, sculpture; inventions, discoveries; wit, humor, fancy, sentiment; the newest fashions and other attractions for ladies; choice new music for the Sabbath, the church, and the firesides; reviews and criticisms of Musical Works, Performers and Performances; in short, the very pick and cream of Novelty, Incident, History, Biography, Art, Literature and Science; including whatever can be given in periodicals to promote Healthy Amusement and Solid Instruction in the family, and help make it Better, Wiser, and Happier, may now be obtained for FIVE DOLLARS.

Celebrating the cut in postal rates (thanks to the expanding, competitive rail and steamboat networks and a long fight in Congress), *Blackwood's* was also offering a package deal, five substantial journals for one rock-bottom price: "The postage on Blackwood and the Four Reviews is now but 72 cents a year. Prior to 1843, it was $6.80; the subscription price of Blackwood at the same time was five dollars a year. It is now but three dollars, and when taken with any of the four Reviews, but two dollars a year!!" Against all this, Orion's *Daily Journal* was trying to charge two dollars, in advance, for a three-month subscription—essentially three months of additional repetitious advertisements for these superior alternatives.

The rise of high-volume national periodicals in the 1840s had been paralleled by the exponential expansion of American book publishing. With the standard handpress and clumsy technology for creating printable copies of forms, it is no surprise that as late as Sam's childhood the total annual output of new book titles by publishers in the United States could be stacked on one library table. Addressing the New York Book Publishers Association at a banquet in the Crystal Palace on September 27, 1855, George Palmer Putnam, a presiding elder in the industry now (though he had lost a fortune producing the *Illustrated Record* at the Exhibition),[78] spoke proudly about the growth of the industry between Sam's infancy and his adventures as a young "jour printer" on the East Coast. Between 1830 and 1842, Putnam noted, 623 original books had been published in America, an average of fifty per year. In 1853 alone, the total was 420, an increase of more than 800 percent in the annual output. But what had really skyrocketed were the print runs: "for 20 years ago," he said, "who *imagined* editions of 100,000 or 75,000, or 30,000, or even now the common number of 10,000?"[79]

Other changes in Boston, New York, and Philadelphia book publishing from the year of Sam's birth through the end of his Hannibal apprentice-ship will underscore how rapidly the American industry had expanded. In 1835, a typical print run for a new book was five hundred to one thousand copies, commonly subsidized by the author and produced by a local pub-lishing house that also operated as printer, wholesaler, and retailer.[80] The national circulation of books was a haphazard negotiation of auctions and bulk sales.[81] To ship a box or bale of printed material from New York only as far as Buffalo in 1835 required about nine days of transport by boat, and news about books, authors, or anything else still traveled only as paper doc-uments at comparable speeds, either floating the watercourses or moving overland by horse or mule at an average speed well under ten miles per hour. The first railroad line in the United States, a thirty-mile connection within eastern Massachusetts, had gone into service only five years before Sam was born; Morse's first operational long-distance telegraph line, a forty-mile run between Baltimore and Washington, D.C., was not accomplished until Sam was five years old. From the middle 1830s until his majority, the radi-cal inventions, upgrades, and successful implementations that transformed American printing and publishing came on in such profusion that a full survey would require several chapters.

Even so, these transformations have remained a sideline interest in the teaching and narrating of American literary history. About the unprece-dented best-sellers that hit America hard at midcentury, including Susan Warner's *The Wide, Wide World* and Stowe's *Uncle Tom's Cabin,* much is said about "popularity" and compelling or timely content and surprisingly lit-tle about technological developments that made possible these gigantic print runs and nationwide sales and the dramatic increase of print as a pres-ence in American cultural and political life.[82] In 1826, Cooper's *The Last of the Mohicans* achieved best-seller status with a total sale of about 5,700 copies; in 1842 his novel *Wing-and-Wing* was also a notable success, at fewer than thirteen thousand produced for the year.[83] About a dozen years after, *Uncle Tom's Cabin* overwhelmed the American reading public with combined print runs that were forty times greater, and neither critical acclaim nor moral timeliness can account for that scale of popular success.[84]

What else lay behind it? One year before the serialization of *Uncle Tom's Cabin* began in the *National Era,* the Boston quarterly *Littell's Living Age* surveyed the industrial power that was amassing in American publishing. Recognizing the importance of Longman's, Putnam's, Lea and Blanchard, and the "four or five large bookselling and publishing firms . . . in full operation" in Cincinnati, the account culminated with a tour of the mighty Harpers plants along Cliff Street in lower Manhattan:

> Within their own establishment, all the details and machinery of publishing are carried on, with the exception of paper-making and type-founding. Their extensive range of buildings, equal to six or seven five story houses, they divide into the several departments of composing rooms, stereotype foundery, press rooms, warehouses, bindery, &c. Nineteen double medium power presses, besides Napier presses, are constantly throwing off printed sheets, to the extent of some 70 reams per diem; while in the bindery 50 barrels of flour are required for making paste every year, as well as 1,200 dozen sheepskins. . . . Over 40,000 lbs. of metal are used per annum for casting stereotype plates, of which their vaults contain about $300,000 worth; they also have about 70,000 lbs. of various founts of type in their composing rooms. . . . Their annual sales have been estimated in round numbers at 2,000,000 volumes, including pamphlets.[85]

In December 1853, these Harpers plants were all destroyed in a huge fire that burned two other nearby publishing houses as well. The Harpers Company rebuilt on a grander scale;[86] and in 1857, when the company launched *Harper's Weekly,* national sales above 120,000 copies for that journal were quickly achieved and sustained.[87] The production and transshipment of the printed word had modernized so rapidly, and in so many ways, that after more than three hundred years of comparative stasis a new era for the cultures of the West had begun. The right published text could now be a momentous national event and a financial bonanza. To exploit these new possibilities, a new kind of American author would emerge, an author who understood the industry to the core, who was enthralled by its dynamics, and who would dedicate his or her career to being a leader within it.

FIVE INNOVATIONS

Between 1830 and 1855, there were at least seventy decisive inventions and patents related directly to American printing and publishing. While many of these changes pertained to the automation and powering of presses, nearly every apparatus and process for producing and transporting the printed word was also significantly enhanced. Even Sam's composing stick, the traditional implement of the apprentice, underwent several overhauls before he grew into a full-time writer, with five American patents recorded to improve it between 1855 and 1860.[88] More important than any cavalcade of patents, obviously, was the widespread commercial adoption of new and faster production equipment, and trade journals like the *Inland Printer* (founded in 1883 as a national journal dedicated to this technology) prospered for decades on illustrated advertisements for the latest gear.[89] Mechanized sheet feeders and page cutters; machines for sewing signatures, for embossing and gluing covers, for applying the ink—each of these developments had an impact, and sorting them out and assessing their relative importance is an ongoing project in American technological history. Between 1840 and the end of the Civil War, however, when Mark Twain emerged as a writer for this newly accessible national public, five developments loom large in expanding and reinventing the American publishing industry. Each of them attracted Clemens's attention early and held it long; each permanently altered the economic and cultural power of the printed page.

Stereotype and electrotype   For accomplishing large-scale print runs on multiple presses, the optimal process in the United States between about 1820 and 1840 was the stereotype. Before 1820, printing in England and North America nearly always meant printing from movable type set in a form and locked in the iron matrix called a chase; and for multiple presses to be engaged in producing the same document (Thomas Paine's widely circulated *Common Sense* is a classic example), the text had to be reset for each machine from scratch. The process was not only time consuming and expensive but also temporary, for very few shops could afford to keep their movable type locked indefinitely in heavy forms, which were also susceptible to collapse if transported out of the shop. A subsequent printing therefore usually required another round of labor at the composing stones and copyediting tables.

Developed first in England around 1820, the first viable stereotype processes allowed printers to acquire serviceable casts of their forms of set and justified type, but with some compromise in register (print quality) and durability. To create a stereotype before 1840, the form was covered with plaster to create a mold, which was then filled in with molten lead or some other soft metal. When this casting was cooled and put through a polishing process, the result was a printable duplicate of the original form. Though there were improvements to stereotyping over the period between the advent of this process and the mid-1840s, stereotypes wore out quickly; they were bulky and liable to breakage, and they commonly produced impressions of inferior register compared with competent printing from the original form. One other major drawback of stereotypes was their unsuitability for duplicating engraved illustrations. With woodcuts and intaglio steel engraving (dominant processes for printing illustrations before 1860), detail and subtlety were lost in a transfer to a stereotype—which is a reason why in books from American publishers before 1850, including Putnam's, Harper, and Ticknor and Fields, high-quality images were often printed on a different press from the letter text and tipped in, and pictures of any sort were scarce, compared to the content of national publications only a few years after.

As a dramatic improvement upon the first generation of stereotypes, the electrotype was also pioneered in London,[90] but the American engraver Joseph A. Adams is credited with making the process commercially viable around 1845. Compared to conventional stereotyping, electrotyping was a technical and economic breakthrough not only for publishers of books and large-circulation journals but also eventually for shrewd authors. To produce an electrotype by the Adams method, a mold of wax was taken from the form and coated in black lead. This mold was immersed in a radical apparatus, a lead-acid battery that resembled a large, low wooden chest. Within the battery, an electric current applied thin, even layers of copper to the lead surface. The resulting electrotype was a lightweight, sharp, robust facsimile of the form. When backed with tin and polished, it could produce thousands of high-quality impressions without showing significant wear. Moreover, the electrotype facilitated a profusion of book and periodical illustration, for relief wood engravings and steel engravings could now be reworked into "electros" with high resolution and at low cost.[91] When *Godey's Lady's Book,* climbing toward a national monthly circulation of 150,000 by the end of the 1850s,[92] promised its subscribers "splendid engravings on steel," and "four times as many steel engravings . . . as any other magazine,"[93] and when *The Innocents Abroad,* in 1869, was announced to America as a new Mark Twain book with "over two hundred illustrations!"[94] electrotypes were making possible that flood of images.[95]

For publishers and authors, the electrotype process offered additional advantages: electrotypes were tougher than stereotypes and could be shipped safely, facilitating simultaneous publication in dispersed locations; and because they were thin and durable they could be stored much more conveniently,[96] retrieved for later editions, leased or sold to other publishers, transferred to the author if he or she could negotiate a reprinting with another house, or owned by the author from the outset in contractual arrangements for the first edition. No matter who owned them, the publishing industry had never before achieved such easy, durable conservation of the typesetter's handiwork. Because of "electros," or "plates," tens of thousands of nearly identical, lavishly illustrated APC copies of *The Innocents Abroad, A Tramp Abroad,* and *Adventures of Huckleberry Finn* could be ready to go, all across the country, on publication day;[97] subsequent print runs, years later, required no resetting of the text. Some of the British editions of Mark Twain's work were published by the distinguished London house of Chatto and Windus from the same electros used by his American publishers. And in Mark Twain's incessant and spirited interactions with his publishers—the APC, Chatto and Windus, Osgood, Harpers, and his own Webster Company—the whereabouts and control of the "plates" are frequently, and with good reason, a focus of his concern.

Something more should be said about the cultural impact of the process from which the electrotype derived, this use of induced electric current to apply an exquisitely thin, smooth façade of one metal or alloy upon some other. Beyond the production of high-quality replicas of set type and engravings, electroplating processes played havoc with the Western decorative arts and rituals of status display by multiplying and deepening the confusion on the streets about authenticity and intrinsic value. In the American and European metropolis after about 1857, it was suddenly harder to distinguish the real thing from the imitation, a precious object from a plausible low-priced knock-off. Households of moderate means could now serve tea from a silver service, and if that silver were only a slick coating upon a casting of tin, guests in the parlor would have trouble telling the difference. Daughters of ordinary families could be sent to soirées with affordable golden finery on the wrist, the office clerk could sport a gaudy watch in the waistcoat pocket—and middle-class life acquired a luster that only twenty years before had been exclusive to the rich.

For artists and craftsmen who lived by catering to those elites, a new and easy technology for deception was no happy development. In the Paris journals of the 1840s and 1850s, August Luchet, a versatile artist, dramatist, and critic, and also one of the livelier curmudgeons of his time, raged that these new shortcuts to flash were bringing French culture to ruin. "The fraudulent has taken us captive and governs us all," he said, referring to all the paste jewelry and plated inventories in the Boulevard *magasin;* "fraudulence is everything and everywhere; it feeds us, it dresses us, it adorns us, it houses us; it provides our pleasures and our education, our literature and our arts!"[98] With less hyperbole but greater effect on the tastes of English and American educated classes, John Ruskin and William Morris also bemoaned the industrialized dominion of the superficial and the bogus. Ruskin's recompense was that the main museum dedicated to his life, and to his crusade for authenticity and good taste, eventually rose in Sheffield, the same city that in his lifetime became synonymous with the production of silver plate, and where Ruskin had tried so hard to lift the British worker out of ignorance and confusion with free public lectures and gallery collections paid for out of his own pocket.

It was electroplating technology, in other words, that actually gilded the "Gilded Age" that Mark Twain and Charles Dudley Warner named and satirized but also exploited in their collaborative novel by that name. In several dimensions, an age of electrochemical imposture had arrived—and though it did not bring what Luchet had feared, the obliteration of discernible difference between the genuine and the bogus, it did make discrimination more of a challenge, and aesthetics in the West acquired interesting new problems to wrestle with. In the *literary* arts, a fresh legion of avowed or serendipitous American "Realists," relishing the writer's antique game of revealing truth behind deceptive façades, could now wander all day in cultural settings with ingenious counterfeiting on every side. This Gilded Age in which Clemens reached his prime was a funhouse of shiny surfaces—including the realms of creativity and fame where he sustained his own career. In an unsent letter, drafted in 1887, he mused that "[r]eputation is a hall-mark: it can remove doubt from pure silver, and it can also make the plated article pass for pure."[99] "Illusion and reality" is a very old literary theme, but in Mark Twain's prime the illusions were better made, and more treacherous, because electroplating made possible the deception and the dazzle, and also the enhanced power of print to address these lies.

The rapid development and deployment of powered type-revolving and automated bed-and-platen presses   Distinctions are important here: through much of the nineteenth century after about 1835, the type-revolving or rotary press played a major role in the cultural conquest of America by national circulation newspapers and magazines, and daily or weekly print runs of tens of thousands of copies had become routine in major cities as early as 1845.[100] A different kind of automation, however, was required for book work, where the quality of the printing was expected to be higher. For book production, the crucial development in Mark Twain's lifetime was the Adams press, which first reached the American market in 1836. The Adams was a powered[101] bed-and-platen press, which means that its impressions were achieved by forcing two flat surfaces together rather than by moving the sheet under or over a revolving cylinder. This bed-and-platen system remained preeminent for book publishers into the 1870s, when the electrotype achieved dominion throughout American publishing, overcoming a concern that rotary press systems could damage stereotypes produced by older technologies.[102] In the bed-and-platen arrangement, the accuracy of a well-operated handpress was conserved; with the Adams, the inking, sheet positioning, and sheet removal were automated and synchronized with other steps in the printing process. One crucial component of the Adams, a major reason for its success in the marketplace, was its proprietary mechanized *fly,* an apparatus for delivering sheets from the press without stopping or slowing the operation. With a corresponding mechanism for positioning blank sheets, the Adams could perform an intricate production ballet—with no human intervention—a wonder that the 1848 patent renewal describes as follows:

> The nippers will then immediately be made to draw said sheet from the tympan.—Said sheet as it slides from said tympan, and as the frisket is carried along under it, drops down upon the frisket as herein before described.— Thus the sheet will be introduced between the platen and the forme of types, and when the motion of the frisket carriage is arrested, the sheet will have been brought into a proper position to receive an impression. —A little before this happens the bed . . . will begin to rise, and immediately after said sheet has become stationary, will be forced up by the continued action of said alternator, and other parts of the mechanism, until the forme of types is carried into contact with the said sheet and against the platen with sufficient force to produce an impression.[103]

With the widespread adoption of the Adams press, much of the expensive physical labor of book printing was eliminated, and publicity illustrations of the Adams and its various imitators often included the figure of a young woman tending the machine, apparently alone, a reassurance to prospective buyers that less muscle (and lower pay) could now suffice on the production floor. As the Hoe Company was swelling into national dominance in press design and manufacture, it bought out Isaac Adams's patents and operations in 1857 (after a decade of patent infringement);[104] and by 1870 Hoe was offering the Adams in more than fifty configurations.[105] After the Civil War, however, competition came on strongly, most notably in the

FIG. 5 An Adams press from 1867, the year of Mark Twain's voyage on the
Quaker City. From *A Short History of the Printing Press, And of the Improvements
in Printing Machinery from the Time of Gutenberg up to the Present Day* (New
York: Printed and published for Robert Hoe, 1907), 13.

form of the Napier (another bed-and-platen press), and rotary "perfecting"
presses, including new models of the Bullock, capable of printing both sides
of a sheet in one motion, and at a level of quality suitable for book production. When Mark Twain turned to writing books, these were the favored
machines in large-scale American book publishing. And when he became
a book publisher himself, the speed and quality of the available equipment
loomed often in this thinking. In a notebook entry from 1884–85, Clemens
smolders about the production of the Webster Company's first great success,
the *Personal Memoirs of U.S. Grant,* and contrives a brusque message to
Charles Webster:

> I ordered 6 sets of plates—and think I remember your taking the respon-
> sibility on yourself of disobeying it. . . .
> How many presses?
> 37 Bullocks?
> Then they can do the 300,000 in a single day of 24 hours.
> 1 Bullock can do it in 40 days.
> 2 Adams in 40.
> Your printers have been using 1 press, & that not all the time.
> These 300,000 should all have been ready Sept 1, using a single bullock
> press.
> Lot of presses?—You only needed 1.[106]

Though the sheets-per-hour production rate of an Adams or a Bullock never approached the velocities of the multicylinder Hoes in the largest newspaper plants, a reliable pace of five hundred to a thousand sheets per hour, for book-quality production, left modern handpresses in the dust.

The mechanized manufacture of low-cost paper This innovation proved as important to the expansion of American publishing as the developments in the technologies for printing words. In Sam's youth, the major component of this transformation was the adoption in North America of the Fourdrinier and Gilpin processes, which had begun to revolutionize production in England in the first two decades of the nineteenth century. Manufacturing paper in continuous lengths—to accomplish this, some of the early Fourdrinier models were almost a thousand feet long—the mechanization ended the cottage-industry practice of producing paper in individual sheets, each fabricated and dried on a separate frame.[107] The raw material utilized in the Fourdrinier process was a radical improvement, an emulsion called "stuff," produced in a high-pressure boiler with induced alkali. Unlike the recipes it replaced, "stuff" did not require protracted fermentation, and its principal component could be cotton fiber rather than the perennially scarce commodity of washed and sorted rags.[108] As the most efficient cotton producer in the world, the United States was eminently ready for this kind of innovation. As Fourdrinier equipment came to dominate the North American paper market, other modifications and shortcuts arrived in a stream; and though the quality of much of the paper on the market declined, so did the price. By 1850, especially at publishing houses in proximity to paper manufacturers, the raw material costs, even for very large print runs, were no longer a serious financial concern. As for paper manufactured entirely from wood pulp, 1843 is a date assigned to the advent of that technology; however, newsprint and serviceable cellulose paper for book production would not become significant in American publishing for another thirty years.[109] It was the mechanization of papermaking, rather than radical alteration of its basic materials, that fed the powered presses and slashed the cost of publication in the decades before 1880.

The rapid expansion of railroad and telegraph networks The importance of both railroad and telegraph systems to every dimension of American history has been so thoroughly documented that there is no reason to delve into it here, beyond observing that with regard to refurbishing and contextualizing the history of American literature some catching up still needs to be done. Before 1830 neither system existed at all. In the early 1840s, by connecting to the Great Lakes and river traffic, the rails had cut the required time for freight shipment from major East Coast cities to the Mississippi River from weeks or even months to seven days or less; by 1852 six rail lines had penetrated the Appalachians; and two years later, an important branch of the network reached Chicago, thereby connecting systems on the East Coast with fleets on the Illinois and upper Mississippi rivers.[110] Lading fees and long shipping delays for cargo, and consequently for postal service, no longer obstructed the growth of national-market periodicals; a heartland was open as a publishing marketplace. The drop in federal postal rates for printed matter, as celebrated in the *Blackwood's* advertisements in Orion's paper, had been a matter of contention in Congress as awareness spread that a new and threatening era in communications had dawned. The Jackson administration had resisted the cutting of mail rates for newspapers and publications, fearing that the industrializing American cities of the Northeast would soon call the cultural and political tune for much of the republic. The Jacksonians were not wrong about this; *Adventures of Huckleberry Finn* addresses the cultural shock wave they saw coming.

Often using the same right-of-way as the rails, and stretching westward in tandem with that system or even ahead of it, the Western Union Company's telegraph network was transcontinental by the end of 1856, moving news, publicity, business arrangements, and printable discourse across the nation within hours. Soon these systems were selling or transporting not only printed matter but also the publisher's agents and sometimes the authors themselves as drummers for their own writing. When Mark Twain took his one-man stage-show "The American Vandal Abroad" on a crisscross through the upper Midwest in 1869, playing meeting halls and opera houses, building a constituency for his first real book, rails and wires made that campaign possible. And when the APC and other big subscription houses succumbed at the end of the nineteenth century, they were killed off by the same rail and telegraph systems that had fostered the door-to-door selling: the transport and communications network was so complete by 1900 that the canvassers could no longer stay ahead of the retailers.[111] The Hoe Company's enormous powered presses moved by rail, as did the juggernaut "webs," or rolls, of newsprint that they consumed. Rails and telegraph lines created the American publishing industry as a national presence, and they also created Mark Twain.

Technical advances and cost-reductions in printing illustrations These advances have been mentioned with regard to the electrotype process and the failure of Kaolatype. From Sam's adolescence onward through the establishment of Mark Twain as a figure known across the world, this information age was pictorial as well as verbal. As a massive dissemination of printed images in periodicals and books transformed the American experience of reading,[112] the new imperative for visual experience transformed Mark Twain's thinking about the books that he intended to write, the subjects he wrote *about,* his rhetorical style, and the tastes and values of the audience he was writing to. By the time he contracted with Elisha Bliss and the American Publishing Company for a travel book about the 1867 *Quaker City* excursion, the APC was already America's most successful producer of volumes packed to the boards with pictures and sold directly to the public.[113] As a selling point in the subscription-book trade, the quantity and diversity of visual experience mattered more than quality or taste in design or execution, or originality, or ethical conduct with regard to the use of images belonging to others. In building *The Innocents Abroad,* with 234 ILLUSTRATIONS touted on its title page, the APC staff followed strategies they had used with Albert Deane Richardson's *Beyond the Mississippi* (1867), which sold over one hundred thousand copies, and other tomes they had produced before Mark Twain signed on. Buying pictures from several artists of varying stature and skill, the APC also republished pictures from their own previous editions, along with copies of work by other artists, doing all this with an unsteady concern for provenance and copyright.[114] When *The Innocents Abroad* established Mark Twain as an author of picture-laden books, he began to play a central role in designing books that followed, hiring his illustrators, vetting their pictures, doing images himself—and collaborating, now and then, in the piracy of other people's work.

In April 1867, as Mark Twain's first slim collection of comic sketches was at press, he wrote to the *Alta California* that the gilt picture embossed on the cover might prove as commercially and artistically important as the prose inside. Another self-deprecating joke, to be sure—but also another hint that this aspiring author cared much about images and appearances, especially in work published under his new name:

Webb . . . has fixed up a volume of my sketches, and he and the American News Company will publish it on Thursday, the 25th of the present month. He has gotten it up in elegant style, and has done everything to suit his own taste, which is excellent. I have made no suggestions. . . . Its price is $1.50 a copy. It will have a truly gorgeous gold frog on the back of it, and that frog alone will be worth the money. I don't know but what it would be well to publish the frog and leave the book out.[115]

Mark Twain's involvement in the illustration and design of his own books between 1871 and the end of the 1890s is being skillfully chronicled by others, and his professional and financial involvement with new technologies for reproducing pictures will be a theme in this book. These technological and cultural upheavals related to the reproduction and distribution of visual experience are important not just to understanding Mark Twain's work but also to recognizing the larger predicament of imaginative literature in the American Gilded Age. The imperative and challenge of the published image shadows nearly everything that Mark Twain and the publishers of his books attempted in their quest for a national audience. Colorful lithographs (chromos) on the walls refreshed the imaginative environment of the private home; steel engravings, heliotypes, and published photographs altered the nature of American celebrity and public deportment; a profusion of illustrations in books and magazines transformed the American reading experience and the imaginative process of writing.

As lithography caught on in the United States, and especially with the advent and popularity of chromolithography, much of the American public achieved, by the middle of the nineteenth century, unprecedented access to seductive visual experience, including easy access to "fine art." Opening for business in the early 1820s, the first commercial lithographic presses in the United States produced black-and-white images with more and better detail than standard woodblock engraving. About thirty years later, the chromolithograph enhanced that appeal by adding a minimum of three colors to the print and often many more, sometimes achieving subtle gradations by the use of twenty to forty separate stones to produce a single image. Taking an early lead in the mass production of "chromos," Cincinnati for two decades was the center of the trade,[116] but strong competition arose in Chicago, Buffalo, Philadelphia, Boston (where Prang and Mayer, ancestor of the prolific Louis Prang and Company, opened for business in

1856),[117] and New York, where the now-legendary Currier and Ives would enter the industry in 1857.

By 1870, the American home or office could be cheaply adorned with panoramas of the Hudson River; the ivied tomb of George Washington; vistas of the Rocky Mountains or the Bernese Oberland; battle scenes and tableau moments from popular plays and epic poems; or portraits of statesmen, generals, or Parnassian authors. As chromos took hold as a national fad, the array of color pictures for sale on Main Street grew to fabulous dimensions; and when steam-powered production came to chromolithography around the end of the Civil War, it multiplied an established system of large-scale manufacture. Images in color had never before played such a role in ordinary life. This was spectacle and visual companionship for the millions, and as early as the end of the 1850s, as refinements in the technology were enhancing the complexity of color and register (reproduction of fine detail), even the *London Art Journal* conceded that the mass-produced chromo could now offer the world a plausible replica of "the artist's own best style."[118]

In North America, however, industrialized duplication of gallery-level art in the mid- and later nineteenth century was a sideline, as a constellation of large companies produced nearly every variety of polychrome image that could be sold openly without breaking the law. By 1890 there were seven hundred establishments producing chromos in the United States,[119] and as early as 1870, the single firm of Currier and Ives had to be long-winded merely to list the categories of pictures they offered: "Juvenile, Domestic, Love Scenes, Kittens and Puppies, Ladies Heads, Catholic Religious, Patriotic, Landscapes, Vessels, Comic, School Rewards and Drawing Studies, Flowers and Fruits, Motto Cards, Horses, Family Registers, Memory Pieces and Miscellaneous in great variety. . . ."[120] Six years later, "Prang's Chromo," as the company called itself in one of its "Popular Art" circulars, was offering faithful copies of western landscapes by Albert Bierstadt and Thomas Moran; paintings by Correggio and Landseer; Civil War sketches by Winslow Homer; dozens of botanicals, motto cards, friendship cards, and moralizing schoolroom decorations; and dozens and dozens of portraits: Gilbert Stuart paintings of George and Martha Washington, and fine-art and photographic likenesses of Beethoven, Byron, Booker T. Washington, William Cullen Bryant, Ulysses S. Grant and a host of Union generals living and dead, Longfellow, Sumner, Stowe, Andrew Johnson, Daniel Webster, and of course Abraham Lincoln.[121] To a scattering nation, you could now be known everywhere by your face—and known only or primarily *for* that face if you were lucky or savvy enough to achieve a visually arresting personal style.

Lithographs and chromos, steel engravings and woodcuts: a dozen years after the Civil War, these popular methods for illustrating on paper would be joined by what Mark Twain, writing from Paris, touted to his publishers as "the new photo processes," cutting-edge technologies for transferring drawn or painted images onto electroplates for printing in magazines and books. As early as 1860, however, to gaze at faces of American "notables" a citizen was no longer required to queue up at the galleries or purchase a costly volume with the occasional tipped-in steel engraving or a frontispiece portrait beneath an onionskin shroud. When the Civil War began, subscribers to *Harper's Weekly* could leaf through many vivid representations of current events and heroes of the hour. By the time the Confederacy collapsed, printed images were an abundant cultural fodder that ordinary Americans knew and craved. In the two decades after the war, the "photo processes" came on in a rush: heliotype, stipple, mezzotint, halftone, photoengraving, rotogravure, photo-electrotypes, zinc-etching, photo-zincographs. As Mark Twain achieved stardom in American public and literary life, the technological sophistication of printed pictures grew complex and protean, with competing nomenclatures, ephemeral tricks, and fundamental changes. Around the time that Mark Twain finished *Huckleberry Finn,* several strategies could produce electrotype-ready illustrations with techniques involving a coating of gelatin reactive to light, generating a relief surface on a flat matrix of copper, zinc, or stone. Though printed photographs in newspapers and magazines would not become common until about 1890, almost every year between 1875 and 1900 brought an improvement in the production of pictures, exploited by major publishers of books and well-financed national journals.

Fast production, cheap materials, lavish illustration, a blitz of selling—when Mark Twain was in his prime as a writer, the machinery of American publishing could get a new book into final shape by hustling forward on several tracks at once. In July of 1889, when Fred J. Hall (who had replaced the ailing, exhausted Charles Webster as chief of operations at Sam Clemens's company) wrote to "Mr. Clemens" about production plans for *A Connecticut Yankee,* his prose matched the breathless pace at which they both wanted to proceed:

Mr. Beard is to begin work at once, in fact is at work now, and the first thing to make is the cover for the book, so we can have the die cut. In illustrating the book he is to take it up *chapter by chapter.* I have made arrangements with the Electrotyper so that all drawings delivered to him in the morning he will give us plates of the same day, that all drawings delivered to him in the afternoon, he will give us plates of the next morning. Now as fast as these drawings are completed and plates made they can be put into the printers hands.

Of course the printer will begin to set up in galley-proofs and as fast as the cuts are completed they will be put in their proper places and he can go ahead and make up the pages and cast plates, and when he has plates enough cast to make a form up, it can be put on the press and the work of printing it commenced. In this way the drawings, setting up in galley-proof, the composition, electrotyping and printing can all be going on at the same time. Then as soon as we have enough of the book set up to be absolutely sure that our calculation as to the pages is correct, we can have a dummy made and Russell (the binder) can be making covers, so that while the book is being printed the most elaborate part of the binding can be going on. As fast as the signatures are printed that can be turned over to the binder and he can be folding them, in this way the entire pro[c]ess of book making can be going on, at the same time, from the binding down to the illustrating.[122]

Five developments, then, among hundreds that transformed the publishing of words and pictures in America during Mark Twain's lifetime. For theorizing the cultural impact of all this change in the media of the West, there is no shortage of available guidance. First published in 1936, Walter Benjamin's celebrated commentary on the general subject, "The Work of Art in the Age of Mechanical Reproduction,"[123] is a standard point of embarkation: in an age of industrialized copying and disseminating, "that which withers," says Benjamin, "is the aura of the work of art" (221), by which he means its uniqueness, its centrality to a "secular cult of beauty" dating from the Renaissance (224). He posits that around 1900 lithography, photography, and other methods of duplication had achieved "a standard that not only permitted [them] to reproduce all transmitted works of art and thus to cause the most profound change in their impact upon the public" but also gave the duplicate "a place of its own among the artistic processes" (219–20). In a profusion of replicas, the excitement and meaning of the direct encounter are diminished, along with the feeling of imme-diacy and innocence; and the artist, excluded or liberated from the old rit-uals of authenticity, is eventually absorbed into politics.

These are useful, canonical perceptions, but as time passes their limita-tions become clearer. What does an age of manufactured images signify for a different species of artist, sharing in that experience and seeking to under-stand it, yet also exploiting it: an artist like Mark Twain, whose medium and livelihood were mechanically reproduced verbal discourse—literary art cre-ated to be experienced as a downpour of reproduction, as an adventure in the inauthentic, and usually accompanied by duplicated pictures, often by unknown hands? What can the experience be for us, in our own moment, as we reopen these books, reading the words and gazing at the printed images? Writing from the media context of Paris in the Thirties, Benjamin (like most of his contemporaries) also could not foresee the global tri-umph, at the end of his own century, of varieties of art with no aura of the sort he described, no implicit artist to connect with imaginatively, and no "original," no text or physical artifact to discover and venerate beneath the reprints, remixes, morphs, and on-screen wholesale reinventions perpe-trated with ordinary software and a few touches on a keyboard. Mark Twain was the first American author to embrace and shudder at a new chaos of high-volume, high-resolution duplication, and over the course of his career in writing and publishing, his speculations about the consequences, for culture and literary art, sometimes ventured farther into the darkness than Benjamin's.

Systematic aesthetic and cultural theorizing has had a hard time with Mark Twain. For that reason, a wilder work on the modern pressure of the verbal and the visual, something like Guy Debord's *La société du spectacle* (1967),[124] seems a livelier springboard for speculations about the strangeness of Mark Twain's artistic predicament in his own time, a heyday of printed images, and also about the strangeness of our own situation as we try to negotiate his picture-laden books in our own moment, amid a daily assault of media beyond anything that he or Benjamin imagined. As mid-1960s Paris contended with the cultural imperialism of Hollywood, with Panavision projectors in the Boulevard cinemas and the Gaullist ORTF erupting in three-gun color from the television sets at home, Debord raged against a future addicted to the artificial and the vicarious. His France, his world, was degenerating into a lonely collectivity of submission to on-slaughts of manufactured images, of gazing fixedly at counterfeits and impersonations—and consuming, and thinking, as dictated by "*le spectacle.*" For Debord, the real menace was not mass distraction and wasted mental energies but rather what he called a "permanent opium war" (44) against individual sobriety, against the basic capacity to tell the actual from the nonsense or sort out one's own personal identity from lurid accumulations of prescribed adulation and desire. *La société du spectacle* is a series of quick tirades, unexpected opportunistic incursions into Marx, strange *aperçus* about Gallic anarchism and also about an unstoppable (and opaque) cultural conspiracy that Debord refers to as "pseudo-cyclical time." Like his forebear Luchet, amid the ramifying fraudulence of the Second Empire, Debord as a public intellectual did not favor modulated pronouncements. The spectacle triumphant, he declares, "grasped in its totality is both the result and the project of the existing mode of production. It is not a supplement to the real world, an additional decoration. It is the heart of the unrealism of the real society. In all its specific forms, as information or propaganda, as advertisement or direct entertainment consumption, the spectacle is the present model of socially dominant life" (6).

If this Situationist polemic hasn't kept all of its freshness, there are provocations here worth mulling over with regard to the international success of Mark Twain as both author and "image" and also to the complications (for the artist and the private self) of jostling for top position in a volatile marketplace of international fame. In 1902, the Houston Ice and Brewery Company of Houston, Texas, selling "Reputation Beer," used brightly colored metal signs featuring lithographed portraits of six American men of "Reputation," with only brief monikers below the pictures. "Barnum" is here, and "Buffalo Bill," and "Grant," and "Jefferson," referring to the actor Joe Jefferson—and here also is "Mark Twain." Other than the faces and these terse labels, there are no cues as to who these people are or what these "Reputations" are founded on. There are no testimonials for the beer either.[125] For these Houston brewers, what was required to sell the product was fame itself, pure and simple—or more precisely, the fame of a few human faces that most adult Americans around 1900 knew from other published images. "Known to Everyone—Liked by All" was a slogan on a Wolf Brothers cigar box, also from the turn of the century, featuring Mark Twain's portrait and his name in block red letters, a signature, and again no endorsement for the product and neither an image nor a mention of cigars. When your words reach millions and your likeness, liberally positioned among those printed words, grows larger and more vivid from one best-seller to the next, and when the full growth of this new kind of celebrity means that a likeness can fly free of the printed words and the deeds, becoming an icon in its own right in popular culture, then "identity" grows problematic in at least two dimensions: for the culture seeking to imagine and understand you and for whoever it is that you think you really are. Debord on the ontological and psychological catastrophe of modern celebrity, as a collateral contrivance of *le spectacle:*

> Being a star means specializing in the *seemingly lived;* the star is the object of identification with the shallow seeming life that has to compensate for the fragmented productive specializations which are actually lived. Celebrities exist to act out various styles of living and viewing society unfettered, free to express themselves *globally.* They embody the inaccessible result of social *labor* by dramatizing its by-products magically projected above it as its goal: *power* and *vacations,* decision and consumption, which are the beginning and end of an undiscussed process. In one case state power personalizes itself as a pseudo-star; in another a star of consumption gets elected as a pseudo-power over the lived. But just as the activities of the star are not really global, they are not really varied. (60)

This is also *enragé,* and in applying any fraction of this to Mark Twain one might recall that the primordial "photo op" did not become technologically possible until the last twenty years of his life and that in his final decade the motion picture was still only a curiosity. From his adolescence onward, however, Sam Clemens wrote and lived with an industry that had suddenly achieved a power to saturate nations with printed discourse and mediated visual experience. Along with everything else that transpired in the production and marketing of printed pages from 1840 onward, this combination plunged Mark Twain into a world's fair of imaginative and artistic challenge.

TWO

The Mischief of the Press

The technology of the modern printed text: the boy's fascination with all this—as an evolving, anomalous force, as well as a promise of imaginative freedom and money—can be traced back to within a year or two of the *SAM* daguerreotype. In 1851 and 1852, Sam had experimented now and then with writing reports and humorous sketches about life in his hometown; but beginning in the autumn of 1852, and especially in the following spring, he began to focus on cultural and cognitive absurdities of the trade he was learning and the national industry in which he participated. In a splash of comic material scattered through the May issues of the *Daily Journal*—anonymous jokes and short poems that are convincingly credited to him now,[1] along with counterfeit letters, supposedly from outraged members of the reading public—the satire turns reflexive. It pokes at the doubtful authority of reportage and editorial comment in small-circulation papers; at the pumped-up indignation of people eager for any space in the pages he helped produce; at the chronic scarcity of fresh, interesting news when the telegraph was still excruciatingly far away; and at the recourse to mindless filler, even in single-sheet imprints like the *Journal.* But this Maytime exuberance also targets basic peculiarities about modern printed discourse, especially when small-scale publishers were shriveling in the heat of "steam and lightning" journalism. Sam was already playing with the inherent foolishness of believing at face value the output from *any* press, hand-pulled or otherwise, and the "aura" of credibility attributed by a reading public to transcribed verbiage simply because it was competently set in movable type.[2] This commonplace gullibility was just then growing worse as national journals took hold and hundreds of thousands of Americans acquired subscriptions to stacks of printed discourse produced by people they would never encounter and in cities they had never been near. In the first two weeks of May 1853, "Rambler" and "Grumbler" put on their scrimmage in the *Journal;* both of them were concocted and ghostwritten by the same kid brother jack-of-all-printing-trades operating with too little supervision in Orion's shop. "Rambler" sends in a poem; "Grumbler" writes to complain about it—and insulting letters back and forth appear through May 13:

> In your paper of yesterday I find that I have attracted the notice of a _____ fool. I had fondly hoped that I would not again be troubled with that class of individuals. But alas for me! I was doomed to be disappointed. Here, now, comes poor pitiful "Snooks," charging upon me. I am wholly unable to comprehend his "pitiful" article. It has been subjected to the criticism of several, and none have been able to make "sense" of anything he has said. He calls me a "Cox-Comb." I will not say that he belongs to that long eared race of animals that have more head and ears than brains. It is the custom from whence I hailed for a man to act just as I have, without having every "puny puppy" that runs the streets, whining at his heels. His piece is couched in exceedingly bad taste.
>
> RAMBLER[3]

Sam's fun may have been shut down by Orion, who had been out of town while most of this was going on. The cooked-up animosity might have been meant to attract a few more paying customers for the *Journal,* like street idlers drawn to a Bricksville dogfight. But a typical dogfight has clearer motives: because the notes among Rambler, Grumbler, and Snooks have no content other than indignation, one theme becomes clear: that time and passion invested in producing rhetoric for one issue of a village newspaper, or in reading such nonsense and getting emotionally involved in it, is energy down the drain. The contrived cause of the argument, a short poem that Sam published as "Rambler" on May 6, was three ponderous stanzas with the delightful title "TO MISS KATIE OF H———L," poking fun not only at Hannibal as a place to be "of" (perhaps epitomized for Sam by the antiquated manual-labor "H———L" of Orion's paper, from which Sam would depart for better equipment and higher pay a few weeks later) but also at hair-trigger sanctimony, the potential for public outrage at printed indecency even when it isn't there. Other possible implications lurk on the edges: that no one else actually reads what anyone writes or prints; that in forms of set type, inert contrivances of metal and wood, dark magic can be concealed, including a power to cause trouble even with blank spaces. Though there is no point in bearing down on jokes in a struggling small-town paper, Sam's earliest experiments suggest an exuberant young mind discovering strange dimensions in his trade.

About ten years later, when Sam began to publish as Mark Twain and took up "reporting" for a bigger and more important newspaper, the Virginia City *Territorial Enterprise,* his first national stir (thanks to the wire services) was another anonymous story, a hoax about a discovery of a petrified man in the mountains of the Nevada gold country: "[T]he attitude was pensive, the right thumb resting against the side of the nose; the left thumb partially supported the chin, the fore-finger pressing the inner corner of the left eye and drawing it partly open; the right eye was closed, and the fingers of the right hand spread apart."[4] Mark Twain's marvel thumbed its nose at a spate of dubious and sensational discoveries around this time, also promulgated by a young and ever-hungry telegraph news system. Seven years later, George Hull's notorious "Cardiff Giant" made money for several shrewd men (eventually including P. T. Barnum, who exhibited a replica, a fake of the fake), all of them knowing that much of the American public felt a stronger pull to media-pumped sensation than to verifiable fact. But Twain's dreamed-up stone corpse also winked at the riskiness of believing, and disseminating, news dispatches of any sort clattering in from nowhere, with no bylines affixed, on a national tangle of wires that only compounded the alienation from a verifiable source: the rapid evolution of "news" from testimony by known human reporters into patterns of electrical pulses with no provenance.[5] As a reporter in San Francisco in 1865, not long after "Petrified Man," Mark Twain took aim again at the endemic peculiarities of published discourse, and the satire sometimes reached a higher level of intensity. During this period, the best sketches implicate "Mark Twain" himself. As he becomes a conspicuous presence in the text— no longer an implicit "I" reporting and merely responding but a consequential Somebody involved in the action and flaunting at times a feeble and ludicrous authority derived, by circular reasoning, from the fact of being published—he also becomes an identity *of* the medium, embodying and giving voice to its strangeness, even its madness. Mark Twain in San Francisco is another full-blown enigma of the printed page.

In the summer of 1865, a six-week series for the San Francisco *Califor-*

nian, "Answers to Correspondents," was a hilarious set of omniscient replies to fictitious inquiries on a galaxy of subjects, the running gags being the absurdity of the idea that one ordinary human could know it all—or knows anything at all—because he or she writes for a newspaper and that newspapers and magazines, on the basis of their handsome, solemn fonts and layouts, or the lists of worthies on the masthead, are to be regarded as repositories of wisdom and truth. For the *Enterprise* and the San Francisco *Golden Era* in 1863 and 1864, Mark Twain had tried his hand at burlesque columns of advice and connoisseurship far beyond his reach, satirizing, among other things, the ego inflation made possible by access to a printing press, the rising pretensions of Wild West newspapers, and the credulousness of readers. He had written commentaries on curing a cold, fancy architecture, and the latest women's fashions adapted (and butchered) from Paris originals. A long bombastic print feud with his friend Clement T. Rice, referred to as "The Unreliable," played with the dubious authority of Washoe journalism and of the entire profession to which they belonged.

Nothing before "Answers to Correspondents," however, which ran for five weeks in June and July of 1865, compares as a satire on knowingness, on the evolving bizarre relationship between print media and the American public and between the modern journalist and his own words. Mark Twain offers "answers" on American history, geometry, poetic taste, morals and philanthropy, mothering, acting, and the politest way to present flowers to a diva after a performance:

> ARTHUR AUGUSTUS.—No, you are wrong; that is the proper way to throw a brickbat or a tomahawk, but it doesn't answer so well for a boquet—you will hurt somebody if you keep it up. Turn your nosegay upside down, take it by the stems, and toss it with an upward sweep—did you ever pitch quoits?— that is the idea. The practice of recklessly heaving immense solid boquets, of the general size and weight of prize cabbages, from the dizzy altitude of the galleries, is dangerous and very reprehensible. Now, night before last, at the Academy of Music, just after Signorina Sconcia had finished that exquisite melody, "The Last Rose of Summer," one of these floral pile-drivers came cleaving down through the atmosphere of applause, and if she hadn't deployed suddenly to the right, it would have driven her into the floor like a shingle-nail. Of course that boquet was well-meant, but how would you have liked to have been the target? A sincere compliment is always grateful to a lady, so long as you don't try to knock her down with it.[6]

With the advent of nationwide print media stardom, strategies developed quickly for acquiring it and holding onto it, and one of these tricks has remained a favorite to this day: to bemoan—at shrewdly timed intervals and to as large a public as possible—the sensational vicissitudes of being a star. After the Nevada and San Francisco years, *The Innocents Abroad,* and *Roughing It* had given Mark Twain sufficient dimensions as a presence in American popular culture, he began to experiment along these lines, enhancing his reputation by satirizing his own celebrity as a maestro of published discourse. The best of these circular and paradoxical caprices, "An Encounter with an Interviewer," was first published in 1874, gaining a wider audience in reprints over the next decade. Louis Budd has described how it became an international favorite among Mark Twain sketches in Clemens's lifetime, reprinted widely and translated into French, German, Polish, Romanian, Russian, and other languages before 1900,[7] when Henri Bergson wrote about it in *Laughter* as a prime specimen of modern comic technique. This sketch is also one of the first interesting texts by any American about the ramifying strangeness of fame after the Civil War, as mechanized and incorporated media were taking hold. Approaching forty when he wrote it, Mark Twain was still relatively new as an American sensation—but so was the phenomenon of the interview. In a study of the form, Michael Schudson has found that no interviews of public figures turn up in wide-circulation journals in the United States before the 1850s and that when Horace Greeley interviewed Brigham Young in Salt Lake City in 1859, intending national publication of their conversation together, the concept was still exotic enough to require an explanatory preface by Greeley when the piece was printed.[8] Other histories of the interview note that the term does not even appear in the *Oxford English Dictionary* before 1869—around the time that the *Chicago Tribune,* the *Nation,* and the *Galaxy* were all decrying the practice as a rampant new offense against responsible journalism.[9] Why such consternation from these media powers, and so early in the game? Schudson speculates that the interview was a transgression of important imaginary boundaries between the spoken and written word, the teller and the listener, the author and the reader:

> [T]he relation of the interviewer to the interviewee is amoral. The interviewee, for the interviewer, is a means to an end and no more. Where newspaper reporting differs from private detective work is that the object of sur-

veillance is a public person or a person in his or her public light, and the client of the surveillance is not an individual but a readership, an entity with a plausible moral and political claim on us. Interviewers accommodate readers to a certain set of expectations of privacy and publicity, of journalist as account-giver and accountant, of professionals as proxies, of irony as a mode of assertion. In this they also flatter the public, give it an overinflated sense of its importance, encourage in leaders not only sensitivity to public opinion but sycophantic submission to popular prejudice.[10]

Mark Twain's "An Encounter with an Interviewer" begins this way:

The nervous, dapper, "peart" young man took the chair I offered him, and said he was connected with the *Daily Thunderstorm,* and added,—
"Hoping it's no harm, I've come to interview you."
"Come to what?"
"*Interview* you."
"Ah! I see. Yes,—yes. Um! Yes,—yes."
I was not feeling bright that morning. Indeed, my powers seemed a bit under a cloud. However, I went to the bookcase, and when I had been looking six or seven minutes, I found I was obliged to refer to the young man. I said,—
"How do you spell it?"
"Spell what?"
"Interview."
"O my goodness! What do you want to spell it for?"
"I don't want to spell it; I want to see what it means."
"Well, this is astonishing, I must say. *I* can tell you what it means, if you—if you—"
"O, all right! That will answer, and much obliged to you, too."
"I n, *in,* t e r, *ter,* inter—"
"Then you spell it with an I?"
"Why, certainly!"
"O, that is what took me so long."
"Why, my *dear* sir, what did *you* propose to spell it with?"
"Well, I—I—I hardly know. I had the Unabridged, and I was ciphering around in the back end, hoping I might tree her among the pictures. But it's a very old edition."[11]

To this supposedly befuddled Mark Twain, the patient visitor explains, "[I]t is the custom, now, to interview any man who has become notorious."

"Indeed! I had not heard of it before. It must be very interesting. What do you do it with?"

"Ah, well,—well,—well,—this is disheartening. It *ought* to be done with a club in some cases; but customarily it consists in the interviewer asking questions and the interviewed answering them. It is all the rage now." (584)

When Mark Twain (as this importuned "I") browses his bookcases for seven minutes in search of a definition for *interview,* he becomes the fool of the piece, or perhaps he merely plays the fool for his visitor—but in those seven minutes of silence, which according to the rituals of interview are supposed to be taken up with somebody asking questions and someone else answering or evading them, boundaries between common sense and stupidity seem to evaporate. For no matter what definition Mark Twain might find on his shelves, what can the word *interview* actually signify, as a variety of verbal text that supposedly conveys meaning, or facts, or some species of truth? When "professional" interviewers ask their supposedly necessary questions, adopting a voice and a sensibility that are only dubiously their own, and when the "interviewee," in this case a "notorious" comic writer, responds to such questions—perhaps with candor, or perhaps from some evasive or unsteady masquerade of candor, as a way of clarifying or complicating (or both at once) the masquerades inherent in humor, or for that matter in any kind of authorship—then what manner of discourse can come out of such a mess? Is *every* interview by nature a travesty of a conversation? And farther out: What kind of textual transaction can unfold, *in print,* as a transcript of one writer purportedly interrogating another writer—especially this kind of "another," a writer who makes his living in part by challenging the cultural constructions of seriousness and truth on the printed page? "Encounter with an Interviewer" is a short, wild ride through multiple levels of lunacy inherent in the conducting, writing, doctoring, and eventual public consumption of printed conversation with media-savvy celebrities.

Though the scripted drama of the interview, of premeditated question and supposedly thoughtful answer, enacts a sincere exchange, or even something like intimacy, any such pretensions in the published text are suspicious or outright false. Though the social informality and intellectual freedom of American-style conversation are represented, they are also betrayed, for in this ritual from a new age of print one of the enacted voices will do little more than ask, and the other is required to divulge. As an

author writing about being an author being queried and written *about,*
Mark Twain usurps the ritual and performs it backwards—first by keeping
his mysterious silence and then by asking the questions himself and dealing out absurd answers to the off-the-shelf interrogations coming at him
from this reporter.

Ultimately, however, "An Encounter with an Interviewer" becomes an
encounter with the incongruities of a cultural practice much bigger than
this asking and answering of canned questions or the playing of roles to fill
space in newspapers. The fundamental delusion under attack here is the
delusion that we are indeed whoever or whatever it is that we say we are, or
even *think* we are, especially when the identity in question is constructed
in print for a public composed of thousands or millions of strangers. Into
the swing of this pseudoconversation at last, the *Daily Thunderstorm* reporter, like some primordial version of a Diane Sawyer, tries to get personal:

Q. Had you, or have you, any brothers or sisters?
A. Eh! I—I—I think so,—yes—but I don't remember.

Q. Well, that is the most extraordinary statement I ever heard!
A. Why, what makes you think that?

Q. How could I think otherwise? Why, look here! who is this a picture of on
the wall? Isn't that a brother of yours?
A. Oh! yes, yes, yes! Now you remind me of it, that was a brother of mine.
That's William,—*Bill* we called him. Poor old Bill!

Q. Why? Is he dead, then?
A. Ah, well, I suppose so. We never could tell. There was a great mystery
about it. . . .

Q. Well, I never heard anything like this. *Somebody* was dead. *Somebody* was
buried. Now, where was the mystery?
A. Ah, that's just it! That's it exactly. You see we were twins,—defunct and I,—
we got mixed in the bath-tub when we were only two weeks old, and one
of us was drowned. But we didn't know which. Some think it was Bill,
some think it was me.

Q. Well, that *is* remarkable. What do *you* think?
A. Goodness knows! I would give whole worlds to know. This solemn, this
awful mystery has cast a gloom over my whole life. But I will tell you a
secret now, which I never have revealed to any creature before. One of us
had a peculiar mark, a large mole on the back of his left hand,—that was
me. That child was the one that was drowned. (585–86)

Thread this labyrinth of pata-logic, and you end up in one of those loops of reasoning that turn up often in Mark Twain's wit. So the person who consents to the interview is really not Mark Twain at all but his dead brother, who at some time back in their mutual infancy (when individual identity might be more an abstraction or a parental hope than a real thing) became by accident a changeling, thanks to a moment of family stupidity. So whoever it is that is being interviewed, here and now, is reporting that he himself is still trying to figure out what it means to be here, answering these questions as both a print celebrity and another sort of person, dead for almost forty years. If the answers flying back at the interviewer make no sense, then perhaps the American cult of individuality might also be, in some sense, senseless—since all of us, and especially the "notorious" among us, carry given names and burdens of identity that are never truly our own, speaking and answering in borrowed voices, becoming both ourselves and other than ourselves when we speak with feigned candor to strangers or write words for the printed page.

Plenty of existential confusion to fill the room, but are other relationships suggested here, relationships between this ridiculous conversation and recent upheavals in printing and publishing? Two men eventually settle down in chairs, evidently with accumulations of books along the wall, books that may have taught their proprietor nothing, remedied no idiocy. After this host pokes about (perhaps in earnest, perhaps as a put-on or a stalling tactic) to find out what *interview* means, he shape-shifts from the intended victim into the predator, this man of print who supposedly doesn't know how to spell. Picture the "peart" reporter from the absurdly named newspaper—some journal in the outback or in such a cutthroat market of big-city dailies that it needs the outlandish name and sensational content to survive. The paper is a daily thunderstorm of words, articles, scareheads, and interviews with nobody that go nowhere and neither comprehend nor flaunt their own absurdity as Mark Twain's travesty of an interview does. The sketch is an usurpation in a larger sense: real interviewers are out there in force, pandering to this national "rage," and one recourse for fending them off is to interview yourself as a preemptive burlesque, thereby inhibiting the burlesque that these others would make of you, adducing or fabricating your own words and publishing them for their own aggrandizement and profit, not your own. And in *their* newspaper, not your own: absorbing the first of his many losses in media enterprises, Clemens had sold his one-third interest in the *Buffalo Express* in 1871. Ultimately Mark Twain *does* interview himself here. These voices are all his, the self as "dialogic" in a very real way—yet also as a travesty of the dialogic principle.

But such complications only enrich the broad delights of "An Encounter," the pleasures emanating from an intuitive and collective understanding that flourishes in a culture awash in prose and in pictures of authors and entertainers. In a published interview with a famous writer, an invasion of privacy is both enacted and parodied, for the privacy of the performing public author is either compromised already or rendered irrelevant by the author's own decision to transform his "I" into a focus for media attention. Or just possibly (and paradoxically) that privacy is rendered more private, more secure, *because* of that public identity, whether it be genuine in some sense or counterfeit in all dimensions. For when the comic writer dramatizes and caricatures his own actions and perceptions for an enormous and scattered audience, plays to the crowds and poses for the illustrators, distances open between what he writes and says and who he believes himself to be, and the media upon which he thrives can have little understanding or respect for that separation. The personal angst that results can become another resource that he and the media can exploit together in endless spirals of production. This is only a pedantic way of describing the dynamics of enterprises like *People* magazine, *Vanity Fair,* and the *E!* Network and other cable-television channels dedicated to self-sustaining exposure— including, of course, exposés of the celebrity's performative outrage and suffering at so much exposure.

Playfully, "An Encounter with an Interviewer" takes us close to the origins of globalized public identity. Though the *Daily Thunderstorm*'s interviewer flees in confusion, his cohorts and posterity will multiply and conquer. More than a century after Mark Twain's imaginary first reckoning with this new journalistic gambit, the interviewers have won, and notoriety of any sort can trigger encounters commencing as this one does, with a call to share wisdom and confidences that you yourself are assumed to be either unable or unwilling to promulgate on your own. As a writer for publication, you say more or less what you want, crafting identity, voice, a body of perceptions and opinions for the permanent yet ephemeral artifice of print. Precisely, and perhaps skillfully, you write what you intend—or at least what your editors and publishers will allow to pass. And after some sufficient quantity of print has been circulated, the constructed identity grows fat enough, in the estimation of other writers, to warrant expeditions by others to gather words from you that are supposedly *not* edited, not mediated:

spontaneous utterance to complement, or subvert, the measured identity that you have constructed within the medium.

Is such a practice inherently malicious? In our own time, any number of ball players, movie actresses, and politicians have been maimed by the free swing of their own spoken discourse, the offhand wisecrack tossed in the general direction of a reporter, with insufficient awareness that when words spoken turn into words *printed* they undergo a metaphysical change, losing their context, echoing and re-echoing until the damage is done and PR agents arrive with retractions and explanations—and eventually the crowd drifts away, looking for some other public mortification.

Even so, there is no point in dismissing a thriving journalistic practice like interviewing as inherently malignant. At the heart of the interview there can be a curiosity extending beyond mere voyeurism, a wish to apprehend and present an actual human being off guard. An interview with a writer intrinsically recognizes the peculiarity of writing—*by* the writer, or from or *about* the writer. The contrivances of the travel book, the comic sketch, or the novel bring the reporters to the door, searching for something genuine behind all that. But laid out in paragraphs, and advancing the illusion that each word there is spontaneous and faithfully recorded and that two interacting voices, set down in black alphabets on paper, suffer no loss of content and quality in that translation—the interview itself is illusion as well, a pretense of candid revelation and honest listening, another masquerade, this time involving not one writer but two.

Roots of this sketch may run deep in Sam Clemens's formative years. Though much has been said about Mark Twain's abiding interest in twins, doubles, and alternative identities (an interest that obviously flares up in "An Encounter with an Interviewer"), that interest may have been sparked or fueled during Sam's first stint of work at the *Missouri Courier*. Over the course of a few days in November 1849, Sam was required to interact physically, as well as imaginatively, with a sensational story floating upriver from the St. Louis dailies. This was a story with brothers, mistaken identities, revolution on the Continent, a great deal of money, and a murder, a story blurred and muddied by a succession of reporters, editors, and typesetters. On October 29, 1849, some kind of disturbance broke out at one of the leading hotels of St. Louis. The *Republican* led with the story on Tuesday, and Ament's *Missouri Courier* borrowed from the *Republican* for page 2 of the weekly edition for Thursday, November 1:

Horrid Murder

Five men were shot at the City Hotel in St. Louis on Monday night, by two men, strangers, who gave their names as Gonzales de Montezquie and Rignard de Montezquie. The names of the persons shot were: Albert Jones, killed, T. K. Barnum, nephew of the proprietor of the Hotel, badly wounded, Capt. D. H. Hubbell, of Liberty, Mo., H. M. Henderson, and Macomber, steward of the hotel, wounded. The men affect insanity, and say they were commanded to kill by God. They were perfect strangers, and had no possible motive to commit such a deed.

One week later, on November 8, the *Courier* republished the corrections and expansions that the *Republican* had offered its own readers on October 31. The names of the alleged killers (or killer, for one stubborn mystery was which of them had pulled the trigger) were now partially repaired into "Gonzalve de Montesquiose" and "Raymond de Montesquiose," gentlemen traveling "in fine style, being provided with large wardrobes, and in every necessary for comfort and amusement. Their trunks were searched yesterday evening, and found to contain nothing but gentlemen's paraphernalia and $1,455 in gold in two separate bags." Ament and his apprentices also transcribed the perverse cheerleading in the St. Louis paper:

> We have seldom seen greater excitement manifested in this community, than was displayed during the whole of yesterday, produced by the tragedy of the previous night at the City Hotel, an imperfect account of which we gave in our last issue. The particulars, as we have been able to gather them, as well as such rumors as bear upon the case or tend to explain in the least degree the mysterious cause of this terrible deed, will be found in what follows: . . .
>
> They claim to be of a family of some distinction in France, the eldest of the two bearing the title of Count. The younger states that their father was killed in the outbreak of last February, and in consequence of their connection with the events of that period, and opposition to the Republican government, they were compelled to flee the country.

The shooter turned out to be Gonsalve, and the twice-butchered family name eventually proved to be Montesquieu. In following weeks, the story continued to suggest plotlines for a page-turner. After both brothers were jailed for the murder, they had to be spirited down an adjoining alley for safer keeping at the residence of the bishop of St. Louis to evade a mob that was working itself up for a lynching. Eventually transferred to army custody at the Jefferson Barracks on the Mississippi several miles south of downtown, the brothers were later tried for the shooting and acquitted on a plea of insanity.[12] Luigi and Angelo, the rich, noble "extraordinary twins" idling through America in *Pudd'nhead Wilson,* may have origins here, along with the murder mystery and the mistaken-identity motif that help to move this novel forward. There might also be a connection to Mark Twain's recurring and sometimes hotheaded interest in the insanity plea, an interest turning up now and then in his work for twenty years after. What young Sam also saw, however, as the small shop in which he worked reset and printed this succession of mangled, overheated reports, was modern journalism in action, an explosively growing industry in which the truthful representation of personal identity and the accuracy of salient facts would matter much less than sensational telling at the highest possible speed.

Oddly enough, the *Courier's* most extensive coverage of the City Hotel shootings occurred in the same issue as a lengthy report of two grisly killings in Clemens's home county, a crime that has earned more attention from Mark Twain's biographers as an early and durable focus of his imagination. This was the murder of two white children, a girl "about 13 years of age, well grown," and a boy "about 10," daughter and son of one Michael Bright, by a black slave in the woods near Philadelphia, Missouri, a Marion County village about twenty-five miles northwest of Hannibal. The *Courier* reported it on page 2—in its own prose, this time—as "[o]ne of the most horrible murders and fiendish acts" imaginable. "In cruelty and atrocity, it was indeed worthy only of the arch fiend himself. The heart sickens and the blood curdles in our veins at the bare recital." That ugliness did not restrain the *Courier* from dishing out the gore, reporting that the girl's ears had been cut off, along with part of her nose, and that she had been raped. As for the suspect, the paper reported that "on his person" he had "marks . . . indicating his participation in the most fiendish part of the act," meaning not the murder but the sexual violation.

Considerably mollified and racially rearranged, this atrocity echoes in the menace of Injun Joe in *The Adventures of Tom Sawyer,* the racial outcast in the woods who threatens mutilation and murder. Putting out the *Courier's* November 1 issue may indeed have jolted Sam's imagination, and it may have helped awaken him to another truth—that this expanding and evolving empire, the American press, had a voracious hunger for mayhem to publish, that its customers craved mayhem to read, and that the bigger the medium grew the stronger those appetites would become. Writing at almost the same time, Henry Thoreau in Concord observed heretically that the daily newspapers, fatted now by telegraph and brought home by rail, provided a sluice-flow of news that nobody really needed, narratives that only cluttered and stupefied the mind. "If we read of one man robbed," he says, "or murdered, or killed by accident, or one house burned, or one vessel wrecked, or one steamboat blown up, or one cow run over on the Western Railroad, or one mad dog killed, or one lot of grasshoppers in the winter, we never need read of another. One is enough. If you are acquainted with the principle, what do you care for a myriad instances and applications?"[13] Out in Hannibal, some of the young men caught up in the industry may have had similar sentiments; but their professional complicity required them to express that resentment only around the edges, usually as fillers for page spaces shorter than a column inch. In the *Hannibal Daily Journal* of May 13, 1853, there is a squib, possibly by Sam, about the tandem beneficence of the rail and steamboat systems, bringing news of catastrophe and bringing catastrophe for news: "The telegraph wires between the East and St. Louis surely do not work well. The St. Louis papers of yesterday contain no accounts of further loss of life by railroad or steamboat. According to lately established custom, something of the kind should happen every day."

The next day's *Journal* developed the same theme into a quick hoax:

TERRIBLE ACCIDENT!
500 MEN KILLED AND MISSING!!!

We had set the above head up, expecting (of course) to use it, but as the accident hasn't happened yet, we'll say

(To Be Continued)

Though the joke alludes to the headlong, perilous mechanization of American life, it also suggests the complicity of the *Journal* itself, and all of its competition, in the voyeuristic promulgation of horrors. If disasters of this sort have become inevitable, then media dependency upon such disasters is also inevitable—and so thoroughly that generic headlines might as well be set up now and kept at the ready. In fact, one such "Terrible Accident!" that had not happened quite yet was the boiler explosion of the steamboat *Pennsylvania* on June 13, 1858. Working as a cub pilot at that time, Sam would find a job for his younger brother Henry on that boat before a fistfight with a pilot named Brown caused Sam to be dropped from the crew. Staying with the *Pennsylvania,* Henry would be scalded fatally in the wreck. Were the Clemens brothers callous and sophomoric, five years before all this, when they published such jokes about mayhem on the river? Yes indeed—if the jokes were exclusively or primarily about that. But there is another target here, the medium itself, which, like the Walrus in *Through the Looking-Glass,* weeps copiously for the victim oysters even as it devours them. One exclamation point after "Terrible Accident," and after "Missing" three more. Even if such a headline were precisely true in the moment of its publication, who or what is to be imagined as doing the exclaiming? The anguished cohort at the *Daily Journal?* Barbarous boys, elated by disasters when they happen to somebody else? Why worry over such small items in a desperate little paper that Sam worked on as a teenager, with little firsthand moral experience in a larger world? Only because they suggest that as one of the daily makers of the *Journal* Sam understood his own complicity in a national enterprise of telling, an enterprise that was already growing intractable and strange and would become more so as technologies of mass communication took control of American culture.

Nevertheless, this dynamic relationship among newspapers, news services, and bloodletting was also divided significantly on the basis of modernization and operational scale. With staff, capital, and fast connections to local police departments and reports from farther off, American newspapers in big cities could report violence, and sometimes even incite it, without undue fear of suffering it directly. In smaller towns, however, the one-man printer-publisher was an easier target for retribution should the paper indulge in unpopular reports and editorials. November 1837 saw the broad-daylight, mob-action murder of the abolitionist newspaperman Elijah Lovejoy not far downriver in Alton, Illinois. Lovejoy had moved his operations there after several narrow escapes from angry readers in St. Louis and the repeated wrecking of his equipment. The Alton killing was a jamboree of mainstreet lawlessness in which the printing office was burned and Lovejoy's offending handpress was broken up and heaved into the Mississippi.

This was only one of several notorious incidents in Sam Clemens's boyhood, when storefront publishers around the country were assaulted or murdered or had their offices torched for whatever offending words were printed there. In 1844, a deputation sent by Joseph Smith and his brother Hyrum destroyed the gear of the Nauvoo, Illinois, *Expositor* for aligning itself too stridently against the neighboring community of Latter-day Saints. With Sam and Henry working with him now as typesetters and general helpers, Orion Clemens ran the following item on August 14, 1851, in one of the final issues of the *Western Union,* a story about a small journal in the Wild West, where gold fever and hostilities between white and Mexican populations were rampant: "A horrible murder has been perpetrated at Sonora. Some persons who took offense at an article in the Sonora Herald, went to the room of one of the editors, dragged him out of bed and shot him through the head. They also killed two other persons connected with the office, and wounded three others who went to their assistance."

When Mark Twain was reporting for the *Territorial Enterprise* about a dozen years later, he had a close call with such recriminations, coming close to fighting a duel over a tasteless line in an article about a local charity and quitting the town soon after, hastily and in disgrace.[14] First published in the *Buffalo Express* on September 4, 1869, Mark Twain's sketch called "Journalism in Tennessee" is a dreamed-up reminiscence about one day of overheated prose and cartoonish violence in the bush leagues of the American media. The sketch plays with a reality that Clemens had left behind only about five years before and that better capitalized and mechanized projects (the kind that Mark Twain was affiliating with now) were driving into extinction. The one-room, two-man office of the *Morning Glory and Johnson County War-Whoop* is a shooting gallery where the combative paper's aggrieved constituency fire revolvers through the front door and the window and drop hand grenades down the stovepipe. The absurd name of the paper is an exaggeration, yet not a very great one. In the middle of the nineteenth century, Tennessee could lay claim to a local journal called the *Clarksville Tobacco Leaf,* which competed with the *Clarksville Rough and Ready,* the *Memphis Avalanche* (mentioned in the sketch), the *Pulaski Chanticleer,* the *Springfield Spy,* the *Carthage Casket,* the *Nashville Daily Orthopolitan,* the *Shelbyville Patrician,* and the *Nashville Central Primate.*[15] Also, the hot prose in the *War-Whoop* echoes, with amusing distortions, the free-swinging editorials that were common in regional partisan papers in this state, which had been the arena for the rise of Stonewall Jackson, for John Sevier and the "State of Franklin," for violent turmoil over abolitionism and states rights, and for bloody battles of the Civil War. The following is an 1868 growl from the Shelbyville *Republican* on the perennial problems of county papers—too little money, too few subscribers, no respect: "There are many families who claim they are 'too poor to take a paper'; but did any one ever hear of a family too poor to keep one or more good-for-nothing, snarling, yelping dogs, whose keeping every year, cost more than enough to pay for several good family newspapers, that it would be a source of intelligence, comfort, and profit to the household?"[16] In Mark Twain's sketch there is no nostalgia for lost intimacy among writer, publisher, and public, for that relationship is portrayed here as lethal. When the narrator announces his decision to depart from that Johnson County office, he implies, with a mingled playfulness, that American journalists elsewhere can now expect the perquisite of professional aloofness and personal safety: "But to speak the plain truth, that sort of energy of expression has its inconveniences, and a man is liable to interruption. You see that, yourself. Vigorous writing is calculated to elevate the public, no doubt, but then I do not like to attract so much attention as it calls forth. I can't write with comfort when I am interrupted so much as I have been to-day. I like the berth well enough, but I don't like to be left here to wait on the customers."[17]

First published in the *Galaxy* about a year later, "How I Edited an Agricultural Paper, Once" can be read as a companion piece to "Journalism in Tennessee," for both of them caricature the back-country archipelago of small-circulation papers where Clemens had apprenticed as a printer and writer for handpress publication. When looked at together, more emerges thematically than a lighthearted adieu to the old ways. In the "Agricultural Paper" sketch, the Mark Twain who works briefly as a replacement editor is a journalist of the new breed, a self-important professional who assumes that he can write about anything—and much of the comedy that ensues involves the nonsense he publishes and the local reaction to it when he is required to turn out authoritative-sounding items about growing crops and caring for animals. This little newspaper actually has a subject and the competence to address it, and its readers also have a measure of expertise. When he is tossed out of the job by the real editor, who returns suddenly to handle the emergency, Mark Twain launches into a tirade about this paper's provincial audience and limited aspirations, a tirade that kicks back at himself as an up-to-date variety of editor, the species that knows "journalism" and nothing else, and at the *ignis fatuus* rise and expansion of metropolitan and national periodicals:

> I tell you I have been in the editorial business going on fourteen years, and it is the first time I ever heard of a man's having to know anything in order to edit a newspaper. . . . Who write the dramatic critiques for the second-rate

papers? Why, a parcel of promoted shoemakers and apprentice apothecaries, who know just as much about good acting as I do about good farming and no more. Who review the books? People who never wrote one. Who do up the heavy leaders on finance? Parties who have had the largest opportunities for knowing nothing about it. . . . Who write the temperance appeals and clamor about the flowing bowl? Folks who will never draw another sober breath until they do it in the grave. . . . *You* try to tell *me* anything about the newspaper business! Sir, I have been through it from Alpha to Omaha, and I tell you that the less a man knows the bigger noise he makes and the higher salary he commands. . . . I said I could make your paper of interest to all classes, and I have. I said I could run your circulation up to twenty thousand copies, and if I had had two more weeks I'd have done it. And I'd have given you the best class of readers that ever an agricultural paper had—not a farmer in it, nor a solitary individual who could tell a watermelon from a peach-vine to save his life.[18]

As manual, community-based publishing fades from the American scene, so does a measure of courage and competence. More than a century after they were written, these sketches can seem prophetic: the latest information age will bring with it a globalized sententious promulgation of misinformation and vacuity. If the *War-Whoop* is (or was) an insignificant and half-crazy backwoods paper, at least there is a tinge of heroism in its effort; and if these agricultural papers are doomed, then the dissemination of truth will not benefit from their passing. Between the end of the Civil War and 1875, when Mark Twain had given up on direct involvement in running newspapers and became instead a stockholding member of the board of directors of the American Publishing Company, he wrote several other sketches about the rhetoric and peculiar rituals of the American print media. There were hoax articles, parodies of fashion and sports reporting, of advice columns and civic-booster propaganda, of court proceedings and travel accounts; there were travesties of filler-pieces from the wire services, travesties of fundamental processes of reporting or narrating anything. In 1870, he published a burlesque woodcut "Map of Paris," a travesty of the armchair war correspondent's professional aspiration to report first, fastest, and least accurately. As satire, most of these efforts seem innocuous when compared to his earlier and riskier insurgencies against the new print media as an inducement to voyeurism and a disruption of the reader's ability to think straight. The notorious "Bloody Massacre" hoax, which appeared in the *Territorial Enterprise* in October 1863 in the midst of the real carnage of the Civil War, was a made-up news report about the slaughter of a family somewhere in Ormsby County, Nevada. The luridness and implausibility of details were evidently intended to tip off vigilant readers—but when the hoax was revealed it caused outrage, and Mark Twain for several years after was required to explain his way around it.

As a different kind of satire, more carefully aimed at the new mass medium to which Mark Twain himself sought access, the four short chapters of "Lucretia Smith's Soldier" appeared in December 1864 in the *Californian*. Spreading his work out to other journals beyond the *Territorial Enterprise*, including several recent appearances in the San Francisco *Golden Era* and the *New York Sunday Mercury*, Mark Twain was knocking on the portals of bigger-circulation regional publications—and with "Lucretia Smith's Soldier" he aligned himself with those journals and against the national weeklies and monthlies in which he had yet to appear. Battling each other for subscription bases in towns where all fresh news had been local only a few years before, *Harper's Weekly, A Journal of Civilization* (founded in 1857, and already boasting a regular circulation well above one hundred thousand copies, jumping to twice that number on special occasions) and its national-market competitors were constructing an American culture in which sentiment could be orchestrated, or at least coercively reported as a matter of coast-to-coast urgency. Loaded with engraved images of the latest action—some of these illustrations were two-page spectaculars, two feet across and a foot high—*Harper's Weekly* was taking on the cultural and political role that *Life Magazine* would play for Americans during the Second World War and that *Time, Newsweek,* Fox News, and CNN have played in the Gulf Wars and continue to play when blood spills in formerly far-off places. America was extensively telegraph-wired by the time the Civil War began, and battles fought in the valleys of the Rappahannock, the Tennessee, and the Mississippi were quickly rattling the newsrooms in the Sierras and beyond. When the weeklies arrived a few days after, they carried a punctual, stunning harvest of fact, pseudofact, and emotional calibration for Americans generally sympathetic to the Union cause.

It is a commonplace that war plays havoc with truth and that enthusiastic and patriotic reportage literally in the heat of battle requires extensive sorting out by cooler heads later on. The styles and subjects of the printed images are easier to negotiate, in a quest for the actual, than the prodigious weekly offerings of nonpareil print, four long columns across, that make up the typical *Harper's* page of verbal text. The portrait of the general might be trusted, the dramatic battle moment perhaps not. The handsome cutaway diagram of a Union Monitor-class ironclad might have a basis in reality; the cutaway of the Confederate submarine *Hunley,* which sank deep without being captured, is conjectural, with no acknowledgment of that fact. But Mark Twain's attention and resentment were focused on the printed words—not only what they said but *how* they were printed.

Published in December 1864, "Lucretia Smith's Soldier" is a story of a self-centered New England girl, a generic young man, and their mutual sentimental education by *Harper's Weekly.* Mark Twain attached a preface to the sketch to make certain this time that the tone and target of his satire would be clear:

[NOTE FROM THE AUTHOR. *Mr. Editor:* I am an ardent admirer of those nice, sickly war stories in *Harper's Weekly,* and for the last three months I have been at work upon one of that character, which I now forward to you for publication. It can be relied upon as true in every particular, inasmuch as the facts it contains were compiled from the official records in the War Department at Washington. The credit of this part of the labor is due to the Hon. T. G. Phelps, who has so long and ably represented this State in Congress. It is but just, also, that I should make honorable mention of the obliging publishing firms Roman & Co. and Bancroft & Co., of this city, who loaned me *Jomini's Art of War,* the *Message of the President and Accompanying Documents,* and sundry maps and military works, so necessary for reference in building a novel like this. To the accommodating Directors of the Overland Telegraph Company I take pleasure in returning my thanks for tendering me the use of their wires at the customary rates. The inspiration which enabled me in this production to soar so happily in the realms of sentiment and soft emotion, was obtained from the excellent beer manufactured at the New York Brewery, in Sutter street, between Montgomery and Kearny. . . .][19]

Invoking the telegraph news service and a local beer incongruously called "New York" (suggesting the cosmopolitan East, where the Harpers factories throbbed, where national attitudes were mandated, and where perhaps the beer was better) and a healthy pile of back issues, Mark Twain preambles a tale of catastrophes observed from an ambiguous remove. The Civil War is geographically far away, yet also fulsomely here on the tabletop; a young woman responds to mass violence and mass media assault privately, yet also as one of the masses. Lucretia Borgia Smith, a Massachusetts girl ruthless and hypocritical enough to be a trivial copy of her namesake, browbeats a generic young clerk named Reginald de Whittaker into enlisting in the

Union Army because every well-accoutered young woman requires a worshipful man in harm's way, a Special Someone in a blue uniform for her to emote about back home, someone to "breathe her name as he breasted the crimson tide of war!" (131). After a scolding by Lucretia, poor Reginald, who has said nothing about having already enlisted, departs for the army without another word. When she learns that Whittaker is soldiering without being *her* soldier, Lucretia fumes at being "unrepresented" in the ultimate drama. "Drat it!" she says to herself—and seeing a wire report that a soldier named Whittaker has been wounded and lies in a Washington hospital, Lucretia gleefully catches a train to Washington to posture as an Angel of Mercy in the ward, tending to the wounded boy whose face she cannot see. After three weeks of this altruism, however, the head bandages of the patient come off. "O confound my cats," says Lucretia, "if I haven't gone and fooled away three mortal weeks here, snuffling and slobbering over the wrong soldier!" Mark Twain's closing: "Such is life, and the trail of the serpent is over us all. Let us draw the curtain over this melancholy history— for melancholy it must still remain, during a season at least, for the real Reginald de Whittaker has not turned up yet."

In the 1864 numbers of *Harper's Weekly,* the stack that Mark Twain says he was looking at and "admiring" as he worked up his own tale, there are several stories carrying signs of kinship to the love life and travails of Lucretia Smith. "Becky Vane's Valentine," which appeared on February 20, tells of an Angel of Mercy in the Union field hospitals, tireless and saintly in her ministrations. The prose was fulsome enough to catch the eye of a wry budding realist:

> The stars of the chill February night hung like golden shields over the red glow that announced the near approach of sunrise when Becky Vane, wrapped in a gray shawl that made her look like a little nun, came out of her tiny cabin to begin the day's labors in those long, blank-looking hospital wards. For poor Charley Bryan had floated down the turbid currents of the river Death with the turn of the night, and Becky knew that she must make his shroud by noon! Do not shrink, reader; these are but the veritable records of hospital life! She had seen death in many shapes during this last winter, and ceased to fear his ghastly accessories—this noble girl! (122)

Becky Vane's anonymous creator may have been none other than Horatio Alger Jr., who was supplying *Harper's Weekly* with numerous one-hanky tales of love and woe, honing skills that would make him a print sensation and a wealthy man after the war.[20] Apparently Clemens knew nothing about Alger as yet, and there was nothing as yet to set Alger apart from a crowd of such contributors. Sentimental fiction for the popular press was a thriving activity. A couple of weeks later, a thickly sliced awakening-conscience story, suggestive of the inner life (such as it is) of Lucretia Smith, turns up in "The Heart of Miriam Clyde." A lovely, haughty young woman, Miriam has rejected the love declarations of Hammond Vinton (in stories of this kind, which appeared nearly every week in 1864, the noble young lovers often have gorgeous romantic names, and the "poor Charleys" are the interchangeable wounded), and he has gone off to war with a heavy heart. Summer gives way to winter; Miriam grows appropriately pale and anxious. News comes that Hammond has been wounded in battle, and Miriam realizes that in a sense she has missed the boat that the saintly Becky could sail on:

> She could not go to him. She had no right; and there was no way in which she could get special tidings. Would he live or die? How slowly the days went by! How she questioned if every morning sun shone upon his living face! How she longed to know of every sunset whether its red rays fell athwart his grave! If he could only live! She thought she could bear that he should never forgive the past—that he should be nothing to her any more—if only she could know that he was in the same world; hear his voice sometimes, sometimes look into his eyes.[21]

Six more weeks go by, and on a night in June we see Miriam "alone in her northern room":

> She did not hear her door open. She started when she felt a touch upon her shoulder, and turned round to see Hammond Vinton standing there, his face pale as death, his figure attenuated, one sleeve empty at his side, and only the old smile curving his mustached lip to tell her it was not his wraith.
> She was too weak to bear such a surprise. The color fled from face and lips, and she sank helpless and white as a wreath of snow at the feet of the returned soldier. (135)

Troths are pledged, and love triumphs. "The Heart of Miriam Clyde" could be a source or a specific target for Mark Twain's parody, but so could at least half a dozen other stories in the weeks that followed. The bad writing is a sitting duck for satire, yet there is something else here too, possibly more troubling to a reporter who has tried a few small-scale transgressions of his own with regard to reportage and hoaxes, nonsense and truth. These intensely sentimental stories of women sacrificing themselves in the wards or women waiting heroically back home almost never have a byline, and they are never labeled as fiction. Printed in the same font with everything else on the *Harper's Weekly* page, they snuggle in with the news items, assumedly to be accorded the same level of attention and credibility as "Hospital and Camp Incidents," a regular feature about real life near the battlefields. In Hannibal, Virginia City, and California, Mark Twain had published nonsense as news, but he usually had made the difference self-evident to attentive readers—or so he believed when he wrote those items. If you read carefully, you could discern that your leg was being pulled. These *Harper's Weekly* tales of love and war, however, were written and typeset into a different universe. In the layout of the *Weekly's* influential pages, fact and fallacy were blended, apparently not by mistake but by design, and possibly with recognition that in a time of high emotions hokum of this sort could sway the hearts of thousands of readers.

In some ways, therefore, "Lucretia Smith's Soldier" is more unsettling than the "Bloody Massacre" hoax in the *Territorial Enterprise* in the previous year, a tasteless account of a man in the outback slaughtering his family, a fake news item that readers took seriously and that consequently got Mark Twain into local trouble. The story of Lucretia Smith is a story about the pernicious power of stories, minds warped and lives ruined by what people are reading in the new national media. The overheated discourse of these journals, at that moment the preeminent source for news of the crisis and guidance in how to imagine it and feel it, can make modern Americans become what they see and read. It can teach self-centered people the postures of love and altruism; it can turn New England towns and Washington military hospitals into sentimental theater. A young man has gone off to war and lies maimed in a hospital, not for the Cause, but out of servile infatuation for a young woman obsessed with her own social status and derivative performance as a heroine in a *Harper's Weekly* story. Mark Twain's sketch insinuates that in 1864 there was nothing hypothetical about either of these people. As her name suggests, Lucretia might be a species of predator to be found in any age. But the motive and cue for her contrived passions, for pushing "poor," unromantically named Whittaker into combat, and for sweeping in to serve nobly thereafter in the Washington wards is the mass-market press, portrayed in the preface as inflicting its own kind of violence on America, a psychological and cultural mayhem with physical injury as only one sort of collateral damage. The opening intimation is that this story is *true* in a sense, not a complete hoax like the "Bloody Massacre," implying that there are actual people out there living and dying according to codes of conduct and psychological behavior acquired from the national weeklies. Lucretia's *un*reality, therefore, has a twist to it, for Mark Twain has invented her to represent a type that invents herself from the stuff of the "real" world she lives in, this new world of print, thereby becoming no more real, even in the context of fiction, than the made-up sentimental heroines she admires.

If fictions on the printed page and fictions in the heads of credulous readers can no longer be told apart, then is media sentimentality the fundamental satiric target of this story? One culprit is sentimentality that refuses to keep its proper cultural place, in three-volume novels, stage melodramas, keepsake albums, engraved tableaux, and bathetic poems, and not commingle with news reportage; another is a corporate print industry with fresh technologies to spew the pernicious emulsion nationwide. Yet there might be another culprit, lurking lower, evidenced strongly in the rhetorical style in which this story is told. In the narrative voice of "Lucretia Smith's Soldier" there is little hint of moral outrage; instead there is a pervasive emotional numbness about the industrialized narration of "the red tide of war," an indifference as to whether that telling is true, treacherous, or satiric. Actual violence, stereotypes with made-up names: the story itself even seems complicit, giving us what "we" will want or expect—a tale of spurned adoration and of sacrifice—while impugning all motives, not only of Lucretia and Whittaker, but also of ourselves as readers, of Mark Twain himself as the storyteller, and perhaps of anyone who pays attention to printed discourse about this national disaster—in which printed discourse is part of the disaster itself.

In 1864, from what geographical or political vantage point could such a moral perspective, such performative indifference, be a moral option for an American writer? Mark Twain and his audience—this outer orbit of readers who are in every sense closer to the *Californian* than they are to *Harper's Weekly*, but who presumably know both well—are three thousand miles from the field hospitals and the tangle of lethal trenches around Atlanta and Petersburg. California in 1864 is a kind of limbo, part of an embattled Union, yet comfortably removed from most of the trouble and danger.

With no California regiments under fire in Virginia and Georgia, this safer American public was breasting a red tide of narratives rolling in from a storm of violence thousands of miles away, news and maps and images and fiction in a bewildering blend—and authentic "New York" San Francisco beer to help local readers sort it out.

"Lucretia Smith's Soldier" is a small regional rebellion against the empire of New York and Eastern-city print, against far-off writers and publishers who launch this material into the West wholesale, yet who know the West not at all. In these parts the war is *foreign,* yet *Harper's Weekly* and its competition are writing it as a war in which everyone is directly involved. As a kind of reverse regionalism, Mark Twain's subversive Civil War story does not meet the Eastern menace head on so much as scurry about in the shadows of its colossal presence, and there is an element of self-conservation in the two key decisions about situating the narrative—the action itself, as well as the site of the publishing. Lucretia and Whittaker, after all, are not a local girl and boy of the West. They are presented as New Englanders, so that Mark Twain's circle of Californian readers can imagine these two as creatures as consolingly *un*like themselves; and a satire in a regional paper can take its swipes at a huge, distant media production system with assurance that it will pay little heed. The scale of the quarrel, such as it is, is off—and that discrepancy in scale affords Mark Twain a measure of artistic safety. The Lucretia Smiths of America are not going to read "Lucretia Smith's Soldier," at least not until long after this war is over, the real hospitals are emptied out, and the high emotions (real or print-tutored) have cooled down. When Mark Twain made his move into the new "big time" in the years after the Civil War, writing for publications that did operate on the scale that the Harper Company and its *Monthly* and *Weekly* had achieved, fifteen years would pass before he published another narrative with such an edge to it—about the dangerous psychological and cultural powers of the American mass media, within which he would build his career.

THREE

'But Now Everybody Goes Everywhere'

Detailed plans and prophetic ecstasies, complicated failures and mountainous archives—hard-core Mark Twain enthusiasts can wander endlessly in a sprawling paradise of esoteric fact and heady speculation. But to bring him home to us now, to imagine his relevance to contemporary concerns about the fate of the printed word, the imperative is to reopen the major texts. From early in his career, shorter pieces suggest that Twain was already thinking about social and psychological consequences of an influx of print from a publishing industry equipped to overwhelm an American public on both coasts and deep in the hinterland. In longer works, however, we can see Mark Twain enthralled with the construction and pictorial embellishment of his own narratives, yet also pondering the cultural consequences of this print revolution he was trying to exploit. Several of his biggest-selling books were nonfiction—more or less; and in this group the travel books have held up well as popular entertainments and as centers of intellectual interest, especially when they are read for glimpses of an American character discovering himself, finding a voice, amid challenging circumstances.

The travel book that Mark Twain had most control over was *A Tramp Abroad,* published by the APC in 1880. Before he started to write it, and with no authorization from either Frank or Elisha Bliss, Mark Twain, living in Paris, hired the principal illustrator himself and began supplying him with images to adapt and copy. Planning to produce other pictures on his own, he lobbied the APC to try new technologies for transferring and printing images for a book that existed only in his mind. Later on, while the manuscript of *A Tramp Abroad* was still in production in Hartford, Mark Twain meddled vigorously in its national marketing campaign. Also important: for the first and only time, with regard to the four travel books published while Clemens was alive, the actual excursions described in *A Tramp Abroad* were almost entirely of his own choosing. With money, freedom, and an international reputation, Mark Twain and Joe Twichell could go wherever they wanted. No obligations to an organized tour with hundreds of others, as had been true for *The Innocents Abroad;* no ambition to strike gold or eke out a living and avoid the numerous options for being killed in the Wild West, as with *Roughing It;* no need to learn the perilous routes and arts of a riverboat pilot *(Life on the Mississippi)* or work his way out of debt by trekking to wherever packed lecture halls were booked for him *(Following the Equator).* This "tramp" in the summer and fall of 1878, and the volume that appeared in America and Great Britain about two years after, were Mark Twain's like no other nonfiction work with his name on the cover.

An anomaly that informs this narrative, however, is that many of the places that Mark Twain visited and wrote about could *not* be imaginatively his own, as other places and excursions had been "his" in previous memoirs of personal adventure. Though the Grand Tour of Europe had been an Anglo-American upper-class practice for more than a century, the 1867 *Quaker City* pleasure trip was an unprecedented event for American travelers in the numbers it brought along, and the Middle Eastern segment of the itinerary included ventures into rough territory. During the gold rush, the intermountain West in 1863 was a frontier with plenty of imaginative breathing room. In 1874, when Sam was considering a memoir of his cub-pilot adventures, Joe Twichell hailed it as "a virgin subject to hurl into a magazine!"[1]—and Howells, in the *Atlantic,* serialized "Old Times on the Mississippi" through seven issues as something fresh and new. But in western Europe in 1878, Mark Twain found himself in landscapes that had been conquered by a new and eccentric breed of writer-adventurers, by side-wheel steam packets and ingenious railway engineering, by touring agencies for the middle classes, and by an inundation of published images and prose. To finish *A Tramp Abroad,* Mark Twain struggled. Though many of the illustrations in the book represent what he saw, they also ridicule and subvert modern rituals of looking, the commodification of seeing. The verbal text is the voice and record of a tourist in a crowd, laughing and chafing at the too-close, too-numerous companionship of other publications that impinged on everything Mark Twain was supposed to look at and every way to respond.

What did he think he was doing when he decided to write a European travel book for mass-market subscription sale, a book for readers scattered across the American landscape and for an additional market in the British Isles? Who did he think those readers were, and what did he imagine they wanted? Some of the evidence is grim. In August of 1889, while planning the campaign to sell *A Connecticut Yankee in King Arthur's Court* by subscription, Fred J. Hall wrote to Clemens about the mood of their American "General Agents" and veteran canvassers who had represented WebsterCo in the past. Hall saw these contractors as fed up with old-style exploitation by the publishers—including the practice of requiring these agents to guarantee a minimum number of sales. He recommended some stick-and-carrot experimentation to keep them on the job. This was a fast, confidential message, and the punctuation and spelling peculiarities are Hall's:

There is one thing certain, and that is that the guarantee business is "played out." We wish to say this now so that you will understand that it will be impossible to get guarantees from the best subscription men to take any definite number of the book,—they simply won't do it. They would not do it on the "SHERIDAN" except in a way that really did not bind them at all and we could not enforce. The large guarantees secured on the Pope and McClellan books which General Agents could not fulfill and never have, has created a general revulsion against guarantees. However, we will *try* and see if we cannot secure small guarantees at least, from all of our best General Agents.

We will have a clause in the contract, if possible, to arrange it, whereby we will be enabled to cancel a contract at once if a General Agent is not doing his duty; by holding this over him we may be able to keep him spurred up to his work. What do you think of this idea? It is an old one but has not been used for some time. We usually spend from $1500 to $2500 in advertising whenever we get out a first class book like your own, we might cut down our advertising say $500 and take that $500 and divide it into prizes to be given to agents who sell the greatest number of books in one year after its publication, for instance, the agent who sold the greatest number should receive $200.00 the second should receive $100.00 the third $75.00 the fourth $60.00 the fifth $50.00 and the sixth $40.00, this would make $525.00 in prizes. We know that this would be a great inducement to some of our best agents to stick to the book and work very hard, and think it would pay. It would be understood, that canvassers who work for General Agents, should bring in a sworn affadavit as to the number of orders taken by them, they should also bring an affadavit as to the orders taken by them sworn to by the General Agent for whom they worked. We know that there are one or two of our best agents that would not stick to the book for one year unless there is an inducement of this kind.[2]

General Agents and lowly canvassers, high-pressure sales campaigns with gimmicks and side-deals, unenforceable agreements among publishers, sellers, and customers, and plenty of acrimony to go around: in most histories of American book publishing, the forty liveliest years of the subscription trade are recalled without fondness,[3] and when sales tapered off and major firms like WebsterCo and the APC either folded or drifted away from the business before 1910, the sour reputation that the practice left behind had truth at the core. Drilling its agents in the hard sell and scattering them onto city streets and mud tracks to outlying farms, the subscription-book trade of the later nineteenth century harassed the public with tomes that could exemplify bad taste in several dimensions at once—verbal and intellectual content, quality of illustration, general egregiousness of design. The targeted customers were a new *demos,* ordinary people in far-flung locations, people facing long winters with dull company and scant experience in choosing worthwhile books to enrich life or merely pass the time. A generation before Mark Twain first connected with this business, veteran drummers were describing bluntly the clientele and the requisite sleight-of-hand for moving the product: "In canvassing men not familiar with books, and they comprise the majority, it is best to keep your book in your hand, turn over and show the most interesting portions, directing attention to such parts as you think most likely to interest them, otherwise, ten chances to one, they will turn to uninteresting things, waste time, get but an imperfect idea of the work, and not subscribe."[4]

From other veterans of these sales forces, the testimony bolsters an impression achieved by a browse through a stack of these peddled books: that the subscription trade's two fundamental contributions to American culture were exploitation of naive tastes and simple aspirations to learn or be amused and imaginative abuse of the people who did the direct selling.[5] But if the American subscription-book trade often pandered and played rough (at times even with its own authors), it can also be understood as a kind of insurgency. Venal or not, the trade resisted a class-based cultural complacency and decorum in a publishing system previously led by companies headquartered in the Eastern cities—companies that had shown little interest in a marketing system to reach Americans in outlying states and territories, where sizable audiences were springing up.

Sidestepping the haphazard structures of the conventional wholesale and retail market for books[6] and evading also the influence of metropolitan reviewers, the subscription business offered direct transactions, convenient for the consumer as well as discreet. By 1870, the subscription houses had stunned American publishing with an array of enormous print runs, best-sellers sold predominantly door-to-door.[7] To be sure, some of the postwar subscription books from the various Bliss imprints (the company operated in Hartford under several names) and also from the Hubbard Brothers, the J. B. Ford Company, John C. Winston, Park Publishing, and the Charles Webster Company could shimmer with piety and feigned erudition, especially compared to the "dime novels" pouring from the New York house of Beadle and Adams and from competitors in that trade who by the close of the 1870s had oversaturated the market and drained the profit from cheap sensational fiction.[8] These companies sold instant-heirloom family Bibles and "Family Companions" to Scripture; hagiographies of political, military, and religious leaders, including the current president and the pope;[9] and effusive memoirs of Holy Land tours, often by roving pastors and missionaries from various Protestant faiths.[10] In 1874, the most venerated prose author in America, Harriet Beecher Stowe, placed with the Ford house a collection of short sketches called *Women in Sacred History;* her influential coauthored book on modern housekeeping, *The American Woman's Home,* was also sold door-to-door, as was Horace Greeley's magisterial two-volume Civil War history, *The American Conflict,* which came with steel portrait engravings and a six-square-foot hand-colored map of "The Seat of War." In the early 1880s, Park Publishing, another Hartford subscription house, mounted a campaign to market *The Life and Times of Frederick Douglass, Written by Himself* directly to African Americans—a milestone in recognizing a new constituency.

A few years after *A Tramp Abroad,* in the midst of the Paige compositor nightmare, the cumbersome and costly *Library of American Literature* project, and everything else that Mark Twain's WebsterCo was taking on, Twain had been planning to produce a subscription-sale book that would top them all for ambition and elegance. What he had in mind was the ultimate art volume, a comprehensive illustrated catalog of the William Thompson Walters collection, a magnificent Baltimore trove of Old Masters. In May of that year, he wrote to Hall with regret that capital for the project had not materialized:

Dear Mr. Hall:

The proposed book was to be infinitely grander & finer than any ever issued in any country in the world. There were to be 600 copies for

Europe & 600 for America, all marked and numbered—& the plates then broken up. Price, $1,000 apiece. All the canvassing to be done by a single individual; his commission $100 a copy; his total profit something over $100,000; ours $700,000, or $800,000 after paying back the original cost, of $200,000 or $250,000. I said that there was reputation in it for us—& cash.[11]

If WebsterCo had produced the book, it might have been a breakthrough into supreme respectability, an achievement to eclipse even the *Library of American Literature*. It also might have brought on the company's bankruptcy a few years sooner. As the nineteenth century ended, American subscription houses were scattering to chase the interests and money of a volatile, diminishing consumer base. In the 1890s, the Globe Bible Publishing Company, a large Philadelphia firm, branched out with volumes about Arctic exploration, Civil War generals, "Photographs of the World," an illustrated catalog of the 1893 Columbian Exposition in Chicago, current events books about the Boer War and the Spanish-American War, an overview of the preceding one hundred years, and even a life of the consummate American hustler P. T. Barnum, "Written by Himself," with a useful appendix called "The Art of Money Getting, or Golden Rules for Making Money."

Whether or not they aspired to gentility, American subscription-book publishers often violated the decorum favored by the larger conventional houses of the time, especially the decorum of textual embellishment and cover design. Between 1865 and 1880, and despite the adoption of electrotype technology for illustration in national weeklies and monthlies, new volumes by Lippincott, Appleton, Ticknor and Fields, Harpers, Putnam, and other mainstream houses continued to avoid disrupting the down-the-page procession of the verbal text with outbreaks of images, especially when the intended market was adult American readers. Visual enhancements of essay collections, memoirs, Bibles, histories, and novels from reputable trade publishers were normally exercises in moderation compared to those of subscription editions. When the blue cloth cover, tastefully embossed in gold or silver, took dominion everywhere as a style for binding,[12] that fashion emanated from the established houses, most notably Ticknor and Fields, as an experiment to distinguish their own volumes from any lower species and to promote a high-class uniformity and aesthetic serenity when their specimens were gathered on the shelves. When a dozen APC subscription volumes from the 1870s are set together in the same way, the effect is suggestive of a street fair. If the "blue and gold mistake" of midcentury genteel bookbinding became such a cliché as to attract the wit of Emily Dickinson and blunt cautionary advice from Charles Webster against following this trend with the cover design of *Huckleberry Finn,*[13] such uniformity, like the sparsely figured contents of these volumes, defended the primacy of the printed word.

From the early decades of the nineteenth century, however, the cover design of English and American travel books was another story, and the ostentation here cannot be blamed entirely on the vulgarity of subscription companies. Even respected trade houses in London and Edinburgh seemed to regard accounts of exotic adventure as license for flashy embossed center vignettes and exuberant patterns on the bindings. On the actual pages of the retailed travel book, however, the standard practice with regard to deploying printed images was again to favor quality and measure, or at least a dearth of images, rather than dazzle and profusion. Travel book or no, an illustration in a conventional trade book in the 1860s and 1870s was commonly a plate tipped in for emphasis or momentary indulgence at measured intervals. Following a solid tradition in Anglo-American bookmaking (enforced in earlier decades of handpress and powered-press production by the complications and expense of mixing pictures with text in forms and stereotypes), the visual and the verbal experiences were usually not shuffled together.

Exploiting the versatility of the electroplate, the ostentatious, picture-giddy subscription book represented liberation from technological and aesthetic inhibition—much as the cultural context of the book, the milieu in which it was acquired and read, was liberated from inhibitions of urban literary life, from middle-class and aristocratic conventions of propriety and taste. When signatures of friends and acquaintances were glimpsed on the sign-up pages at the back of the canvasser's circular as it was popped open to complete the sale, then so much the better, as all of these buyers would be joining a little league of their own. Subscription-trade books could provide an alternative adventure in entertainment and aesthetic choice, and if some of the big-selling titles won scant respect from American cultural arbiters in newspapers and magazines, then scorn or inattention from those communities counted for little. Now and then, of course, a subscription book did crash the borders, winning respect from educated, "serious" readers and establishing itself as a literary work of genuine value. As companies in the subscription trade maneuvered erratically to enhance their respectability, even abstaining (occasionally) from binges of pictures as a primary value, these houses produced books that achieved canonical status or influenced American literary and cultural history. *The Innocents Abroad* and *A Tramp Abroad* from the APC are two of these; and from the Charles Webster Company, *Personal Memoirs of U.S. Grant,* the *Library of American Literature, A Connecticut Yankee in King Arthur's Court,* and *Adventures of Huckleberry Finn.*

In its most vigorous years in the quarter-century after Appomattox, the subscription-book industry accounted for as much as three-quarters of annual book sales in the United States,[14] and by operating at such a scale the system also complicated the reception and cultural status of the mechanically reproduced image. Even with lithographs and chromos flourishing as cheap commodities in those years, the image-laden book had an aesthetic role of its own to play, a more important role than merely expanding the range of mediated visual experience in ordinary American homes. Not only did these bulky books bring more images into private life; they forced those images into aesthetically challenging contexts, violating conventional zones of separation or repose between one visual encounter and the next and between the visual encounter and the verbal. Hanging on a wall, at a spot selected by its owner, or keeping its place on one page in an album of pictures produced by the same technology, a purchased chromo or a lithograph was commonly an experience apart or an object in a consistent company. A printed image in an APC tome jammed with them, however, is lost in an avalanche of pictures and words, and if Walter Benjamin was only enunciating the obvious when he asserted that mechanical reproduction "withers" what he called "the aura of the work of art" by obscuring or abolishing the imagined sanctity of the original,[15] he was perhaps more astute in observing that the *printed* picture could also foster a kind of freedom, aesthetic as well as commercial, whereby the duplicate allows the "art" to escape "from its parasitical dependence on ritual" and that in an era overwhelmed by the duplicated image "the work of art reproduced becomes the work of art designed for reproduction" (224). Chromo reproductions of works by Old Masters played such a role in later decades of the nineteenth century. Working artists, even distinguished ones as far back as Sir Joshua Reynolds, learned to produce "original art" with an eye trained on the potential market for engraved *copies* of the image they were creating.[16] Within the verbal-textual anarchy of a Mark Twain travel book, the profusion of printed pictures "designed for reproduction" can foster a different kind of escape, and from more than ritualized dependences—unless this hazy term *ritual* encompasses also those idiosyncratic personal rituals of knowing, or believing we know, exactly what kind of visual artifact we are looking at, and how carefully to look at it, and why.

The APC strategy for book illustration involved not only plenitudes of pictures but also a muddling of representational styles, levels of competence, and discriminations between "original" and "copy," including distinctions that Benjamin's essay seems to construe as absolute between "art" and anything else. When Elisha and Frank Bliss produced a subscription book, "original" illustrations were commissioned from artists under contract to make them for this particular verbal text and were subsequently engraved— sometimes by the artist himself but often by other hirelings of the company—and then published in a miscellaneous context, with images borrowed from other books published by the same house, or purchased or pirated from books by other companies, or obscurely acquired and silently modified in the editorial process. With no system of credits or permissions for these pictures, there was commonly no way for a curious reader to figure out who had done what, or whether the ultimate source was a photograph, a painting, a verbal description, hearsay, or fantasy. Now and then, a signature of an artist or craftsman did survive on the electroplate for the edition; more frequently, however, these illustrations were created unsigned, and potentially incriminating names on co-opted original works were expunged along the way. The result can be a funhouse of dubious visual encounters: fresh or recycled engravings of lithographs copied in turn from other lithographs or woodcuts or photographs (sometimes of the correct object or landscape, sometimes not); pictures based (perhaps) on no actual visual experience, whether direct or derivative; engraved copies (sometimes faithful, sometimes not) of work by artists with whom the publisher had no legal or financial arrangement at all. In the Mark Twain books published by the APC, and especially in *A Tramp Abroad,* there could be additional oddities, including counterfeit pages of holograph manuscript by people either living or dreamed up (one such pseudodocument, an illustration showing an illegible scrawl supposedly by Horace Greeley, provides a cue for an extended joke in *Roughing It*) and engravings or photographic-process reproductions of supposedly spontaneous handwritten notes and doodles from Mark Twain himself, purportedly "on the spot" and in the actual heat of artistic inspiration, in the course of his "tramp" through Germany and the highlands of Switzerland and France.

In *The Innocents Abroad, Roughing It,* and *A Tramp Abroad,* this restless and miscellaneous inventory of things to look at, including images three or more levels of remove from anything that could pass as original, might be understood as matching the verbal narrative's unpredictable shifts in subject and mood, as well as its occasional forays into adaptation and piracy. But the interaction here among printed words and adapted images has additional dimensions. In each case, Mark Twain comprehended from the start that he was writing an *illustrated* book, and in constructing these two volumes about the Old World he knew that his own verbal narrative, even as a screed of words as yet without pictures, would be about the freedom and the culturally conditioned rituals of *seeing,* the imaginative coercion of pilgrimage to Great Sights, the conflict between spontaneity and prescribed etiquette in the moment of bearing witness—especially in a context where printed pictures and verbal narratives by others were closing in. He was writing about the modern American traveler's daily imaginative challenge to discern and cherish one's own genuine and immediate perceptions (whether verbal or visual) against the seductive, omnipresent recourse, the mass-marketed aesthetic and psychological copy of the copy. Moreover, to read these profusely illustrated APC editions is to encounter American graphic art itself in metamorphosis, the engraved image transformed by the grace (or curse) of the electrotype and other intervening technologies into a commonplace and a subject for commonplace gazing.

By mechanical power, nearly every established artistic style was being propelled into the public domain. Especially in these European travel books, the range of visual and verbal experience suggests a disheveled campaign to flaunt a Yankee right of casual, honest observation and freedom of representation. In these books the faraway physical and cultural locale, made too familiar by those other publications, is recovered as an opportunity for indulgence in any narrative mode that suggests itself, as well as any mode or quality of visual art, from postcards and crude cartoons all the way to elegant, panoramic landscape paintings fit for a Royal Academy show in London or a Paris annual *Salon. A Tramp Abroad* encounters the new strangeness of visiting tourist mecca landscapes that were changing before Mark Twain's eyes under the pressure of the same publishing revolution that *A Tramp Abroad* was intended to exploit. In other words, this book is about the adventure of negotiating several imaginative predicaments and challenges at once: the overwhelming physical place, the new geographic and technological realities of European tourism, and the competing abundance of printed images and words concentrated on the experience that Mark Twain himself was struggling to achieve and forge into an entertaining narrative.

In the convoluted business relationship between Mark Twain and the American Publishing Company, the standard conclusion is that with regard to their first outing together, *The Innocents Abroad*, Elisha Bliss and his staff made most of the important decisions as to how this volume would be designed and marketed.[17] When Clemens came away from Hartford in January of 1868 with a signed contract to develop his *Quaker City* adventures into a full-scale travel book for the subscription trade, he was still an innocent himself about this business and about the professional challenge he was taking on. He was obligated now to double the length of his 1867 reportage to the *Alta California* from Europe and the Holy Land, assuming that the *Alta* could be persuaded to release copyright on the original material. When that release was secured after his trip to San Francisco in the spring of 1868, he still had to produce on a scale that he had not attempted before, if only to bolster and validate the welter of pictures that the APC intended to pour in.

Writing and editing *The Innocents Abroad* became a labor that Mark Twain grumbled about, and his other preoccupations at that time (including the courtship of Livy in Elmira and a couple of lecture tours, one of these in California and Nevada and the other through the midwestern prairies by rail) kept him away from sustained interference with the evolution of the product once the manuscript left his hands.[18] Seeing only a few of the proofs for illustrations, he apparently assented to them without quibble, second-guessing instead about advance publicity for the book and the timing of its release.[19] However, in the most detailed study we have on the construction of *The Innocents Abroad*, Robert Hirst makes a strong case that by supplying source material for many of the illustrations himself, including photographs and postcards collected on the *Quaker City* excursion, by labeling them to specify their location and relevance within the verbal text, and by reviewing at least some of the finished images passed to him by the APC, Mark Twain exerted palpable influence over the visual content of even his first real book. "Although the actual physical insertion of the 'electros' into the standing type was largely left to Bliss," says Hirst, "it is apparent that Mark Twain controlled the placement indirectly":

Not only did he specify where pictures should correspond with the text, he obviously consulted with Bliss when problems of this nature arose. Moreover, he must have seen at least some pictures in preliminary stages. For instance, in early March he mentioned to Mrs. Fairbanks that there would be an illustration of Jack Van Nostrand with his buckskin patch—a drawing that eventually appeared on page 610 of the book. . . . Thus Clemens must have seen the illustration, perhaps even before it was electrotyped: it would be months before the type for page 610 was set up. This is a typical example . . . of illustrations supplied by artists who had manifestly read the manuscript: the approximate position of all such text-related illustrations was controlled by the text to which they alluded.[20]

When *The Innocents Abroad* sold 89,502 copies in two years,[21] the success did much for Clemens's self-assurance as a player in the subscription leagues. As a famous writer now, not only of a substantial book but also of a new *kind* of book, and as a writer with uncommon background and interest in technologies of printing and publishing, Clemens began to zigzag his way into the particulars of APC operations. In the early 1870s, while he was still preoccupied with co-owning, writing for, and then selling his share of the *Buffalo Express,* and also with completing the text for *Roughing It* and doing lecture tours across the Northeast and Midwest, he remained a distant nuisance to his publisher rather than an effectual referee of whatever was released with his name on the cover. He proposed to Bliss a clandestine scheme to send a proxy named John Henry Riley on foreign travels and to concoct another book, or several more, from his reports. Though the plan collapsed when Riley fell ill and died before he could write anything, Mark Twain would resurrect him briefly as a name in a digressive joke in *A Tramp Abroad,* and the idea of travel-by-proxy would come back as well—also as a joke and as a pretext for ridiculing a literary style favored by some of the competition. From the early 1870s, there are other letters in which Clemens postured as an expert on publishing and marketing, offering Bliss advice about royalties and copyrights, the construction and release of London editions, the prose selections in the canvassers' prospectus for *Roughing It,* the disadvantages, as he saw them, of marketing an older book and a new one at the same time, and collaboration with Charles Dudley Warner on one of the first American novels sold by door-to-door subscription after the Civil War, *The Gilded Age.*[22]

In the interval between *Roughing It* and *A Tramp Abroad,* Mark Twain's leverage with the APC had continued to grow, along with his fame and his professional truculence. Having purchased $5,000 worth of APC stock, he was now a director with a seat on the board. With encouragement and editorial help from William Dean Howells, he had published "Old Times on the Mississippi" over several issues in the *Atlantic Monthly;* the experiment with Warner had made a profit, and a spin-off play of *The Gilded Age* was touring the country and bringing in a lot of money. Though *The Adventures of Tom Sawyer* wasn't selling as well as Mark Twain had hoped, it was still a fresh and visible presence in the literary marketplace. High on his own genius and reputation, he was thinking himself weighty enough to intrigue with other publishers. Later in the decade he released several volumes with the James R. Osgood Company, drawing Osgood into risky ventures in subscription selling and colluding with Frank Bliss, Elisha's son and business partner, to bring out *A Tramp Abroad* with a separate house that Frank was at that time maneuvering to establish. Apparently Clemens believed that by working with young Frank instead of the cagey father he could exert more control over the design and sale of new volumes and contract for more of the profits.

In that same year, 1878, Clemens had several other skillets on the fire. Dan Slote, the *Quaker City* companion who had lately sold Clemens nearly 80 percent of the stock in Kaolatype, approached him with a side-deal to publish another collection of sketches with a different house—"including," Slote suggested, "a few of the best selections of Innocents, Roughing it, Gilded age, Tom Sawyer"—and to market it conventionally rather than via subscription if things could be arranged so that "Bliss won't kick."[23] The plan was evidently for a follow-up to *Punch, Brothers, Punch! And Other Sketches,* released by Slote, Woodman, & Co. in the spring of that year. And although Frank Bliss's new company never took flight, and the new travel book, still unwritten, migrated back to his father's APC, Clemens had done enough advance planning at this point to ensure that among the four travel books he published in his lifetime *A Tramp Abroad* would be most thoroughly his own. We see here the height of his involvement in producing a complete textual and visual experience—and a new height of playful self-consciousness, as a very modern species of American tourist and as a teller and illustrator of adventures on the water and the road.

A Tramp Abroad catches an important technological and cultural moment in the history of the United States, a moment when much had been knocked into hazard as to what a "book" of reportage was and ought to be, what its obligations were to the intended audience and the literary marketplace and also to the cultures it accommodated or resisted. *The Innocents Abroad* had been about places. *A Tramp Abroad* would be more about the going, and it evolved into a narrative of transition, of walking and riding, drifting and climbing through varied landscapes and modes of representation. Instead of valorizing the romantic over the actual, or the other way round, or the elegant image over the crude cartoon, the volume that Mark Twain oversaw would tour many modes and levels of competence with exhilarating impartiality, escaping the clutches of any established way of seeing or representing.

In Chapters XIV through XIX, Mark Twain tells of a raft ride down the Neckar River, from legendary Heidelberg to the town of Neckarsteinach, accompanied as usual by "Harris" (the alias here for Joseph Twichell, already a close friend of the Clemens family) with layovers, as prescribed by the guidebooks, to visit the right ruins, castles, caves, and picturesque villages. Though the lumber raft is supposedly drifting with the slow current, the six-chapter narrative of this journey makes so many leaps and digressions that any motif of sitting peacefully and letting worldly experience roll gently by is thoroughly undercut. The sequence of ostensible subjects in these chapters runs as follows: a quick description of lumber rafts on the Neckar and how they move, and of landscapes and country folk glimpsed along the shore; a romantic-sentimental legend, told deadpan, of a haunted cave near Hornberg; a retelling of the legend of the Lorelei—which pertains to a different river and which is filched, with only a flicker of acknowledgment, from L. W. Garnham's "Legends of the Rhine"—followed immediately by the words and music of Heine's "Song of the Lorelei," spread out across two pages and printed sideways like a musical selection in a *Godey's Lady's Book*. Mark Twain's homemade complete translation of the song comes next, followed by a comparison of his text with Garnham's English version, also completely transcribed. The side trips keep coming: comments on the inept English labels affixed to pictures in a Munich art museum (also a considerable distance from the Neckar valley), and a burlesque medieval legend, involving a Sir Wissenschaft, a dragon, and a modern fire extinguisher. Chapter XIX finishes up with accounts of dynamite explosions along the shore and a preposterous storm at sea on this narrow and peaceful river, an episode spiced with the jargon of American sea dogs.

What to say about this mélange? Perhaps it suggests the unrestricted play of a mind at leisure, the caprice and free association of an artist-reporter with many and miscellaneous things to look at, and a trove of alternative voices and styles with which to regard and describe. Pilgrim, joker, cynic, gullible ingenue, aesthete, lyric poet, newsman, folksy yarn-spinner—as the subject or the inclination changes, so does the voice, loafing and shopping among the various competing discourses for "writing" Germany, and suggesting that the Germany along this shoreline is also a jumble of old and new, of vernacular and picturesque. The illustrations in these chapters vary accordingly—which is to say unpredictably and drastically. Sometimes they seem to suit the momentary mood of the narrative and sometimes not. Chapter XV opens with a casual cartoon, by Walter Francis Brown (soon to be a major contract illustrator for the APC), of Mark Twain and Harris sitting on the edge of the raft and dabbling their feet in the river; a few pages later, the legend of the cave is supported by a full-page rendering of a damsel in distress, also done by Brown, but in a tongue-in-cheek Pre-Raphaelite style. Though the next two quarter-page images continue in this mode, the chapter ends with a notebook doodle credited to Mark Twain himself, with handwritten annotations, purporting to show a crow's-eye view of this raft on its float through bends and reaches of the Neckar. Through the next two chapters, the numerous images folded into the verbal text continue to show no concern for stylistic or thematic consistency. *Faux* John Tenniel is followed by *faux* Edward Lear and even *faux* Gericault, along with those gratuitous pages of music, printed in a large font, perhaps so that owners of the book might pause here, balance it on the piano somehow, and give the tune a try.

In its original published form, *A Tramp Abroad* is an agglomeration of textual and visual experience with no continuity of mood, subject, or aesthetic principle—and the evidence is clear that Mark Twain was intending that kind of radical inconsistency even before he began any serious work on the verbal text. His 1879 correspondence with Frank Bliss makes clear that in this project literary and artistic fads and styles were intended to clash. Culturally conditioned expectations pertaining to mass-market travel books were to be fulfilled, yet also defied; and aesthetic coherence, and for that matter coherence or continuity of any sort, were values to be toyed with and subverted. From Switzerland, while he was still collecting the experience he wanted to write about, Clemens teased the younger Bliss with a "secret" running gag for the book he was planning: that these European adventures would include little in the way of actual tramping and a great deal of comfortable excursion by coach, rail, and steamboat—in other words, that *A*

Tramp Abroad would be in some dimension a burlesque of a popular mode of European travel adventure, the self-congratulating memoir of strenuous manly exertion.

Forget Byron and Shelley and other early-wave Romantics emoting solus like Manfred on the crags, finding in these alpine vistas, impossibly remote not so long ago, the perfect backdrop for exquisite (and exclusive) High Feeling. The railroads, the motorized packets on Lac Leman and the Thunersee, and a midcentury interlude of Continental peace have brought into this landscape regular seasonal waves of privileged Victorians, including the cadres who brought the word *mountaineering* into common usage in the 1850s,[24] naming a risky new sport for modern English gentlemen on holiday. Their own accounts of essentially pointless self-endangerment are finding a market in Britain and the United States and bringing in more tourists. The figure on the heights is no longer the tormented exile but a genteel and wholesome member of the London-based Alpine Club, the very British sporting society organized in 1857 to "conquer" the Swiss peaks that complaisant locals in the valleys below had never felt a call to assault—and then to ride the rails and steamers swiftly home to busy professional and social schedules in Piccadilly and South Kensington.

In 1871, when Sir Leslie Stephen (prominent Anglican minister, fellow and tutor at Cambridge, all-around man of letters, conqueror of several mountains heretofore unscaled, and, somewhat later, the sire of Virginia Woolf) collected some of the accounts he had written about his own exploits and published them, sparsely illustrated, with the respected house of Longmans, Green, & Co., Sir Leslie called his book *The Playground of Europe*—a name that self-promoting renegades of Wordsworth's generation would have found stunningly blasé as a way of referring to adventures in that terrain. With vivid prose and a handful of well-executed plates, Sir Leslie's book remained in print for more than forty years. When Alfred Wills, another Alpine Club member and accomplished "mountaineer," returned from his ascent of the Wetterhorn (an achievement that some historians of the sport call its true beginning), he told the story in a book that he coyly titled *Wanderings in the High Alps,* as if he had merely "wandered" up to a twelve-thousand-foot summit that no human being had reached before him. Famous as a founder of the study of eugenics, Francis Galton, a cousin of Charles Darwin, had in his youth explored on the Upper Nile and in the South African deserts, feats that had won him nomination as a fellow of the Royal Geographical Society. This same Galton eventually authored *Fingerprints,* the influential monograph from which Mark Twain would borrow heavily for the plot twists at the heart of *Pudd'nhead Wilson.*

In 1860, however, Galton took time off from his scientific research, mountaineering, and other pursuits to edit a series of volumes for the general public about the exotic travels of some of his friends, expeditions not only to the summits of the Alps but also far up the Amazon River, across the Pacific to Fiji and the Micronesian cannibals, and into uncharted and dangerous territory along the Niger. The London firm of Clay and Taylor issued the series for three years—and the name of it was *Vacation Tourists,* a title that may be unsurpassable as an expression of Victorian upper-class cool.

In Galton's annual volumes, there were typically about a dozen engraved maps and no other images. With regard to publishing true-life adventures on the edge, etiquette had taken shape among the gentleman-authors and respectable publishers in London, resulting in an array of strong-selling books, amid which Mark Twain's own effort, involving no significant risk of life and limb for its author, would need to achieve a place. British adventurers had led the conversion of the Swiss and French Alps into a strange sort of playland, and these austere books about their heroics implicitly put to shame, and sometimes scorned outright, the masses of ordinary tourists who had come so lately onto the trodden paths farther down the slopes—and any come-lately travel book that would tell of this country with no personal adventure at the core, and with recourse to a vulgar abundance of pictures.

Another club member and good friend of the above gentlemen, however, was Edward Whymper, whose own adventure book was a challenge of a different sort. A skilled artist in his own right and the son of the celebrated engraver Josiah Wood Whymper, Edward had nearly died in the 1865 assault on the Matterhorn—his eighth attempt at the peak. Achieving the summit this time, his team lost four men on the descent—and when he told that story he showed no hesitation in bolstering it with engravings based on harrowing firsthand experience. Like Wills, Stephen, and Galton, however, Whymper chose a title that was stunningly debonair. Published in England in 1871 from the house of John Murray, *Scrambles amongst the Alps* included more than a hundred illustrations by Whymper himself, with additional pictures from his accomplished father. This publication was a break from certain London habits of austerity in the telling and embellishment of alpine adventure, and Whymper had earned the right to make that move, for among his fellow mountaineers he was unique in having the proficiency to make vivid pictures of what he had seen, working from the sketch on the pad straight through to the engraving for the electroplate. His handsome and compelling text would figure significantly in *A Tramp Abroad* as both a source and an imaginative vexation.

The recurring joke in *A Tramp Abroad* involves a feigned inability or perverse refusal, by Mark Twain and Harris, to acknowledge how they are actually moving themselves from place to place, but also the outright loss of a quality that had intensified some of the travel in Mark Twain's previous books about travel—genuine and necessary risk and adventure. In 1867, Palestine and Syria were not the beaten track for Western tourists. In Damascus, Mark Twain had come down with cholera; in the desert, "sun-flames" had scorched him "like the shafts of fire that stream out before a blow-pipe." In *Roughing It* he had supped with gunslingers, endured mountain blizzards, and dodged forest fires; as a young pilot in *Life on the Mississippi* he had braved reefs and shoals that had wrecked other steamboats. But here in the Alps, the recent advent of these opposite varieties of "wandering"—high-risk mountaineering and easy, modern-style tourism—had transformed a rugged terrain into a peculiar play space where the visit could be accomplished with any level of exertion desired, including no real exertion at all. The nineteenth-century steam-powered "Rush to the Alps," as one historian calls it,[25] had been going on for decades when Twain and Harris showed up, and it had already established the mediated landscape and imaginative frustration that visitors encounter in those summer-thronged Swiss valleys today. Near the Jungfrau, in the heart of the Berner Oberland, Mark Twain offers a sigh about seasonal tourism and the end of exotic travel on the Continent:

> What a change has come over Switzerland, and in fact all Europe, during this century. Seventy or eighty years ago Napoleon was the only man in Europe who could really be called a traveler; he was the only man who had devoted his attention to it and taken a powerful interest in it; he was the only man who had traveled extensively; but now everybody goes everywhere; and Switzerland, and many other regions which were unvisited and unknown remotenesses a hundred years ago, are in our days a buzzing hive of restless strangers every summer. But I digress.[26]

The burlesque in Mark Twain's title seems mechanical, but it is also defensive, irony as self-preservation. Others before them and around them assault the heights and call it a "holiday" and a kind of "play"; these two middle-aged Americans will ride the rails and the boats and the rafts, stroll a few well-recommended valleys and lower slopes, and call their sedate experiences a "tramp," thereby reclaiming Switzerland from the Galtons, Stephens, and Whympers—and giving it back to everybody else, or at least to those real or vicarious ordinary tourists who will never climb with crampons and an ice axe. Mountaineering is an aberration, a reactionary and suicidal refusal of the present and the future. After that early incursion of hardy Romantics came the bourgeois critics and landscape painters in horse-drawn coaches and railroad carriages. Turner had done hundreds of sketches in Switzerland on four major excursions between 1801 and 1841; Ruskin made more than a dozen trips to the Alps between 1845 and 1870; in the spring of 1846, Dickens settled for several months in Lausanne and returned to Switzerland with his family in 1853. Tennyson and Thackeray and George Eliot and Matthew Arnold also came in search of the vistas; on their heels came the multitudes, and by 1875 Ruskin was telling his audiences of students and workingmen that the European rail systems and easy travel were ruining both the landscape and the art of looking at it.[27] The John Murray firm, which over the course of the century published personal accounts of many adventurers, including Whymper, Herman Melville, David Livingstone, and Charles Darwin, turned out its first edition of *A Handbook for Travellers in Switzerland,* written by the publisher himself, as far back as 1838, the year that the first inn for visitors opened in Zermatt. Forty years and many editions later, the Murray guide was facing formidable competition from a fresh Baedeker about the country, the latest overhaul of the skillfully translated English edition that had first reached the London shops in 1844.

At 456 pages in nonpareil, and with twenty-four handsomely engraved and tinted maps, seven annotated mountain panoramas, and ten city plans, the 1877 Baedeker gives a powerful impression that there isn't a quarter-acre of Swiss ground left for any kind of true imaginative discovery. A rail line had connected Zurich to Baden as early as 1847, and a nationwide system had been mapped out and begun in 1852;[28] in the 1870s, panoramic paintings of the Eiger, the Munch, and the Jungfrau region were on long-term exhibit around Leicester Square;[29] in Ruskin's *Modern Painters,* panegyrics to the vistas brought more artists in search of them, as did the alpine ecstasies in poems of Matthew Arnold. Around Interlaken and Zermatt there was a boom in hotels, restaurants, and of course postcards. Though ordinary tourism could not domesticate the dangerous crags, it could commodify a nation, muddling the borders between high adventure and book-guided excursion, between lonely exploration and packaged group holiday.

When Mark Twain and Joe Twichell venture out from their first hotel on their "tramp," the technology and media of modern tourism have already reached to almost anywhere they are planning to go or might possibly see on a whim. To sustain the narrative and keep it amusing, therefore, a single recurring joke about that saturation, and about all those other travel books on the market, will not suffice. As a meditation on firsthand and secondhand seeing, and also on writing amid a clutter of published texts about the same territory, *A Tramp Abroad* must engage resourcefully with imaginative and rhetorical dilemmas related to modern travel as a cultural practice, especially on these favorite tourist routes through the highlands of western Europe.[30] After Heidelberg and the ride on the Neckar, Mark Twain and Harris head for the crags—which is to say, for pleasant accommodations much farther down the slope, with agreeable vistas of the crags. What they find are places infatuated with the exploits of the mountaineer and this new dedication to going up as high as possible.

A standard explanation for this sudden interest in risky entertainment is the promulgation of Romantic sentiments, a popularized mix of Manfred-machismo and valorized sensibility that revised the central *massif* from a geographic impediment into a vast pantheistic temple of inspiration and heroic self-challenge. Another plausible reason, if less charming, is that with the advent of steamers and railroad lines and telegraphs to facilitate movement from one previously remote valley to the next, these alpine valleys grew so awash with sightseers that the robust elites who wanted to stay ahead of the mobs, or accomplish anything special on their own holidays, were virtually forced to the higher altitudes. After about 1855, getting away from the crowds in Switzerland meant going up.

In his *Playground of Europe* memoir, Sir Leslie Stephen derides this tourist onslaught with a mix of condescension and cavalier self-accusation, affecting an attitude and a voice born of his own life at the headier elevations of both Swiss topography and the English class system:

> I studied with a philosophic eye the nature of that offensive variety of the genus of *primates,* the common tourist. . . . The cause of his travelling is wrapped in mystery. Sometimes I have regarded him as a missionary intended to show by example the delights of a British Sunday. . . . This view is con-

firmed by the spirit in which he visits the better known places of pilgrimage. He likes a panoramic view in proportion to the number of peaks which he can count, which, I take it, is a method of telling his beads; he is doomed to see a certain number of objects, and the more he can take in at one dose, the better. . . . Some kind of lingering fetish worship is probably to be traced in these curious observances. Although the presence of this species is very annoying, I do not think myself justified in advocating any scheme for their extirpation, such as leaving arsenic about, as is done by some intelligent colonists in parallel cases, or by tempting them into dangerous parts of these mountains. . . . Or at least, let some few favoured places be set apart for a race who certainly are as disagreeable to other persons as others can be to them—I mean the genuine enthusiasts, or climbing monomaniacs. (152–54)

The gregarious instinct has doubtless been implanted in the breast of the commonplace traveller for a wise purpose. It is true that it leads migratory herds to spoil and trample under foot some of the loveliest of Alpine regions, such as Chamonix or Interlaken. But, on the other hand, it draws them together into a limited number of districts, and leaves vast regions untrodden and unspoilt on either side of the beaten tracks. . . . Shall I not in some degree be accessory to the intrusion of some detachment from that army of British travellers which is forcing its relentless way into every hole and corner of the country? Will not some future wanderer take up his parable against me and denounce this paper as amongst the first trifling hints which raised the sluices and let the outside world into this little paradise? (194–96)

Poor Sir Leslie: there can be no peace for the "climbing monomaniac," who by merely telling of his own exploits provokes the vulgar multitudes to come and see where the great man has been. And poor Mark Twain, for in this "little paradise" he must either achieve some *geste* of his own or be nothing more than a "migratory bird" or a throwback worshiper of fetishes. Even a travesty of an exploit is better than nothing, and that seems to be Mark Twain's cue for resolving to attack the heights. Late in *A Tramp Abroad,* and presumably from a hotel armchair in Zermatt, Mark Twain announces to the phlegmatic Harris that his "mind is made up" to "ASCEND THE RIFFELBERG!"—which, as most of Mark Twain's American readers would *not* know, and as Mark Twain does not explain until the "ascent" story that follows has come nearly to the end, is a joke about the height of this ridge and the next hotel where he and Harris will be staying. From Baedeker's 1877 *Switzerland* (because the Baedekers were edited biennially, this was the latest edition, and likely the one in Mark Twain's kit):

The **Hotel** on the Riffelberg (8429', 3114' above Zermatt, open from the middle of June to the end of Sept.) being often full, it is advisable to inquire beforehand at Zermatt if accommodation can be had on the Riffel, and if possible to procure a ticket entitling the holder to a bed. . . . In the height of the season the traveller should endeavour to reach the top at an early hour. . . .

The bridle-path, which ascends rapidly (3, descent 2 hrs.), cannot be mistaken (guide unnecessary). From the Hôtel du Mont Rose we follow the road straight on past the church.[31]

So the Riffelberg is not another daunting summit in the Zermatt neighborhood but an intermediate ridge so tame that a tourist hotel is situated at the top, and any amateur on a horse or a mule can do the excursion. In *A Tramp Abroad* these punchline facts are delivered about two dozen pages after the sketch commences—and at least a dozen pages too late. The incongruity of the mighty made-up expedition does not become clear. This troop of "198 persons, including the mules; or 205, including the cows" (419) and an overall length of "3,122 feet . . . —over half a mile" (420) is another joke too oblique to succeed; the point, apparently, is that Mark Twain's entourage extends farther than the elevation gain (according to Baedeker) from Zermatt up to the Riffelberg Hotel, another fact that Mark Twain fails to exploit, mentioning the distance only as "3 hours," and only in the wrap-up paragraph that opens Chapter XXXIX. In *A Tramp Abroad*, this embedded narrative seems to assume that readers will have the guidebook handy for cross-checking Mark Twain's travel account and discerning the humor. Though the Riffelberg sequence may be the only one in the book that seems so contingent on the idea that "now everybody goes everywhere," or at least that now "everybody" *reads* and *knows* about "everywhere," the muddled experiment runs long, another uncomfortable concession that all the trails Mark Twain can tramp here are too well marked, and old news.

Sensing perhaps that the sketch has already shriveled by the time it is halfway unfolded, Mark Twain takes a narrative break in the midst of it to make gratuitous fun of another sort of creature that easy travel has brought into the hotel lobbies, the American trust-fund showoff, a condescending young man who is calling himself an "old traveler" when barely out of his adolescence and who has nothing at all to do with the Riffelberg hike. A digression in a burlesque adventure: by this point in *A Tramp Abroad* Mark Twain's readers may be conditioned to expect discontinuity and even to enjoy it, but in the ten chapters that situate Mark Twain and Harris in the environs of Zermatt and Chamonix (Chapters XXXVI through XLVI) there is a good deal of uneasy shifting with regard to subject and mood, a back-and-forth motion between accounts of real, deadly mountaineering by others and travesty exploits by Mark Twain himself, overheated descriptions of tourism conducted in comfort and complete safety.

After the end of the Riffelberg joke, Mark Twain moves into a meditation on alpine glaciers—their enormous size and depth, their slow and predictable movement—and segues into a morbid account of the Glacier des Bossons, near Mont Blanc, yielding up, forty years later, the frozen mangled bodies of climbers who had fallen into a crevasse there in 1820. Immediately after this comes the extensive passage lifted verbatim from Whymper's *Scrambles amongst the Alps,* the first climb of the Matterhorn in July 1865, and the fall on the descent, losing four members of the team in a plunge of four thousand feet. Mark Twain's excuse for including these six pages (along with alpine-action engravings stolen from *Scrambles* and other sources, with signatures removed and titles altered) is that the details of Whymper's catastrophe "are scarcely known in America. To the vast majority of readers they are not known at all" (473). There are reasons to suspect that Mark Twain had something else in mind than a gratuitous advertisement for Whymper's book. It is possible that this is nothing more than piracy and padding, an attempt to remedy or dodge the problem that in writing *A Tramp Abroad* Mark Twain was running out of steam and that from the heart of the legendary Alps he had little more than armchair observation and mule-path experiences to offer his audience. In the context of these chapters, however, the inclusion of the British hero's memoir may signify a struggle by this American tourist to achieve at last some kind of authenticity, not "authentic" mountaineering but rather a genuine personal relationship to this alien landscape—made more so by the constant intervention of other people's pictures and words—to human mortality, and to time itself. Guided by Baedekers and picture books, and ushered forward by guides, train schedules, and hotel reservations, the modern tourist can visit a place without ever being in it or *of* it. Those dead explorers disgorged by the Glacier des Bossons forty years later had joined that landscape, tumbling out of the normal cadences and disconnectedness of modern human experience; and when Mark Twain thinks about that sea change, while describing the identification of a long-frozen body by an old friend, there is wonder in the voice, even a touch of envy:

There is something weirdly pathetic about the picture of that white-haired veteran greeting with his loving hand-shake this friend who had been dead forty years. . . . Time had gone on, in the one case; it had stood still in the other. A man who has not seen a friend for a generation, keeps him in mind always as he saw him last, and is somehow surprised, and is also shocked, to see the aging change the years have wrought when he sees him again. Marie Couttet's experience, in finding his friend's hand unaltered from the image of it which he had carried in his memory for forty years, is an experience which stands alone in the history of man, perhaps. (469–70)

Three of the dead from the Matterhorn assault, as Mark Twain tells us at the end of Chapter XLI, are buried "beside the little church in Zermatt" (482); the fourth, a young English lord, remains lost in the slow-time of the mountain ice. This discovery provokes a visit to the village graveyard and to the cellar ossuary where buried bones are moved after a suitable interval to make vacancies in the scarce graves carved into the rock. Places unpopular with the makers of engravings and postcards, to be sure; and Mark Twain has written about such places before, having included plenty of bones and bodies as lurid subjects for illustrations in *The Innocents Abroad.*

This morbid side trip shares an odd motif with what comes before and after, a theme of digging or plunging into stone or ice, of making a living or a life or a good death out of the penetration of hard surfaces. The chapter on the Zermatt graveyard also includes a vignette about Swiss farmers, whose "plow is a wide shovel, which scrapes up and turns over the thin earthy skin of his native rock—and there the man of the plow is a hero" (485). And two pages later, Mark Twain offers the most provocative aside in this set of ruminations on landscape and the representation of truth:

In Nevada I used to see the children play at silver mining. Of course the great thing was an accident in a mine, and there were two "star" parts: that of the man who fell down the mimic shaft, and that of the daring hero who was lowered into the depths to bring him up. I knew one small chap who always insisted on playing *both* of these parts,—and he carried his point. He would tumble into the shaft and die, and then come to the surface and go back after his own remains. (487)

Vicariously in these chapters, and even physically in the Zermatt ossuary, Mark Twain repeatedly goes back after the remains, doing what he can to enact a "star" part in these local histories of heroic death. Whatever he does here remains child's play, however; with his own body or his imagination, he cannot penetrate the rock of this otherness, that remaining measure of alpine reality that the Baedekers and picture books have not co-opted. More successful than the Riffelberg sketch, Mark Twain's last attempt at a comic narrative about these mountains is his tale of ascending Mont Blanc—by telescope. Renting one for three francs on a Chamonix street, he finds a team approaching the top of the mountain and joins up with them, imaginatively:

> Presently we all stood together on the summit! What a view was spread out below! Away off under the north-western horizon rolled the silent billows of the Farnese Oberland, their snowy crests glinting softly in the subdued lights of distance; in the north rose the giant form of the Wobblehorn, draped from peak to shoulder in sable thunder-clouds; . . . to the east loomed the colossal masses of the Yodelhorn, the Fuddlehorn and the Dinnerhorn, their cloudless summits flashing white and cold in the sun; beyond them shimmered the faint far line of the Ghauts of Jubbelpore and the Aiguilles des Alleghenies; in the south towered the smoking peak of Popocatapetl and the unapproachable altitudes of the peerless Scrabblehorn; in the west-south-west the stately range of the Himmalayas lay dreaming in a purple gloom. (519)

Satire about travel-book namedropping and credibility, and jokes about the presumption that most people on this planet, including most of Mark Twain's American readers, would know or care about the difference between one big legendary mountain and the next; but an unanswerable question lurks here as well. What really is the difference now between being there in the flesh and seeing it all "close up" but secondhand or from a safe distance? Demanding a certificate for having "climbed" the Mont Blanc by means of a refractor telescope, Mark Twain makes a fool of himself and is turned down; yet he follows this pseudoreport immediately with a solemn account of an actual 1866 tragedy on the mountain "witnessed through the Chamonix telescopes"—mountaineers in peril, and some of them dying, before the eyes of people miles below in the tourist town. "Being there," and the point and possibility of truly "being there"—these fundamental goals of tourism have become mysterious, problematic. Death-defying mountaineers are sharing the pathways and accommodations with legions of middle-class tourists; doing, seeing, bearing witness, and knowing have become concepts as treacherous as the glacial ice. The Mark Twain book about these places, and about this transitional moment in the history of

European travel, is a mysterious mingling too, of firsthand, secondhand, and made-up experience, of images homemade, commissioned, adapted, and stolen. This narrative veers without warning into playful meditations on the marvelous processes by which travel and mass-market publishing about travel are now accomplished.

The walk-a-little, ride-a-lot conceit of *A Tramp Abroad* emblematizes how this book was put together—a few judicious measures of original effort and interludes of imaginative cruising on the labor of others: other people's boats, rafts, railways, hotels, mountain assaults, artwork, and personal memoirs. On the *Quaker City* trip in 1867, Mark Twain had participated in the first grand-scale, steam-engine-driven American tourist incursion into Europe—but that was now a dozen years back in time, and tourism had changed, and to these coveted destinations much more had happened than easier access for visitors and bigger crowds of foreigners in the village square. The reality of the visited place, and even of the tourist visits as genuine firsthand experience, had been compromised by the "tramp" of multitudes and an abundance of media exposure.

Even before Switzerland became Europe's "playground" in the middle of the nineteenth century, it was already difficult to pretend that any Western segment of the Grand Tour could still be accomplished with some increment of originality. By 1877 the chances were closer to nil, for each panoramic view recommended in the Baedeker had now acquired its own engraved or photographic likeness; English, French, and German castles were retrofitted with resident ghosts that the tides of tourists expected *not* to see; old casemates and ruined chapels were suffering restoration in the operatic style of Violett-le-Duc, acquiring contingents of jaded tour guides and a courtyard café. The mechanized picturing of picturesque Europe had already achieved its clichés. Each conventionalized style of representation—melancholy panorama, dreamy Doré dreamscape, Daumier-naturalistic vignette—had plenty of competition in the shops, as mass-produced images made the visual experience of Europe a free market of styles and levels of competence.

The metamorphosis was beginning (now perhaps grown virulent) whereby destinations made popular by publishing would become simulacra of themselves, remade and "conserved" in lovely configurations they had never actually had before, to satisfy the expectations of paying customers and conform to mass-marketed illusion. In the latter half of the nineteenth century, chromos, panoramas, photo books, and travel guidebooks made quaintness and grandeur into economic imperatives for many tourist sites, imperatives that the advent of film and television has only intensified. The passenger trains that anticipated the spur-of-the-moment choices and limited stamina of Mark Twain and Harris also anticipate our fleets of jumbo jets loaded with conscientious idlers setting off to visit what most of them have already "seen" many times before in screened and printed images. Contemporary mass-market tourism requires that the reality of the visited "real place" (if it can still be called that) conform to the mediated encounter that precedes it—the brochure, television travelogue, screen-saver, and calendar photo on the office wall back home.[32] When the railroad and steamship lines grew numerous and popular and the Baedekers offered up Heidelberg to cohorts of outsiders, *Alt Heidelberg* would need to remain *Alt* until the last view-books and beer steins embellished with the *Alt Schloss* or the *Alt* Neckar bridge were peddled to the final busload of day-trippers.

The British public responded to *A Tramp Abroad* enthusiastically—it was Mark Twain's best-selling book in England during his lifetime[33]—perhaps because it offered those readers a relaxed and vicarious visit to places that in a sense they too already knew, or because it represented not just another excursion but also an unceremonious reconquest of an oversentimentalized part of the Continent. In *A Tramp Abroad*, Germany, Switzerland, northern Italy, and eastern France become more truly the playground that Leslie Stephen had called the Alps; scarred, sword-dueling undergraduates at Heidelberg University devolve into a show; pinnacles where Swiss and British climbers have recently died can be gawked at by ordinary folk in tweeds or browsed in retailed pictures and books. There were so many ways now to see and represent the sights of Europe without looking at them directly—and a witty self-conscious tramp abroad could be a tramp through the alternatives.

Writing to Frank Bliss from Paris on May 10, 1879, Clemens proposed to take charge of acquiring all the illustrations for the big book that he had only just begun to draft. Aside from demonstrating that he was once again conceiving a long manuscript with pictures in mind from the start, and that he wanted this hypothetical book's graphic artists to work for *him* and do what he wanted rather than report to Frank Bliss or anyone else in the APC organization, this letter announces that Mark Twain himself will join in producing the book's visual component by turning out several pictures on his own. His comic ineptitude as an artist had been played for laughs before, notably in the "Map of Paris" woodcut joke in the *Buffalo Express* and even as far back as a few barbarous images he made as a boy for the *Daily Journal.* But in a travel book about northern Europe, which would also be a book *about* travel, and a book with plenty of commissioned art by competent hands, what did Mark Twain really have in mind? As he gets down to business in this important letter, the Great American Rustic pitches his plan as an insider with regard to media technology as well as current Boulevard taste:

> Now as to illustrations. I remember your father telling me the artist's and engraver's work for the Innocents Abroad cost $7,000. Of course we can knock down a deal of that expense, now, by using the new photo-processes. I've got an artist, here, to my mind,—young Walter F. Brown; you have seen pictures of his occasionally in St. Nicholas and Harper's Weekly. He is a pupil of the painter Gerome, here, and has greatly improved, of late.
>
> He is willing to make the pictures for my book about as cheaply as the photo-people here will put them on the plates for. There are two or three of the processes suited to different styles of work, and I shall have occasion to use them all.[34]

In the spring of 1879, the processes that Clemens was thinking about included photo-electrotypes (on the market now from Paul Emile Placet and other Paris firms), photogravure (made famous throughout Europe by the local firm of Goupil & Co.),[35] rotogravure, photolithography, and photozincography, all of which were operational as production shortcuts, reducing or eliminating a need for professional engravers in the conversion of images, whether drawn or painted, to printable formats. Photolithography was a chemical-bath procedure by which a negative was used to produce a print, then a transfer sheet, and finally a workable image on a stone surface, effectively a lithograph.[36] Photo-electrotype, which made use of the electrotype technology and "chromatized gelatin" to produce a raised plate from a photograph, employed a different technique from photogravure, a process that had premiered in Paris just before the disastrous war with Prussia and that created a copper stereotype plate by means of a similar gelatin but enhanced with fine grit to produce an effect of grain in the printed image.[37] Evolving from experiments by the versatile British scientist William Henry Fox Talbot in 1852, rotogravure made use of a cloth screen pressed against a steel plate with a photosensitive coating so that the photographic image retained the impression of the mesh, allowing subsequent acid treatments to erode into the surface proportionate to the lines and shadings of the original photograph.[38]

All of these were intriguing new toys to exploit, and Clemens wanted to play. Later in the same letter, he discloses to Frank Bliss that he has already taken off on this vector, hiring Brown directly on a trial basis, paying for production of a few plates of his work, and collaborating with him in "smouching" from Gustave Doré:

> Brown agrees to submit all pictures to me and re-draw them till I approve of them. He also agrees to superintend the process business and see that the work is properly done. . . .
>
> I enclose proofs of plates made for this book by the processes, so that you can judge of their merit and of Brown's drawing.
>
> We meant the Matterhorn accident for a full-pager, but I had to guess at the size.

In her study of the illustrations in the first editions, Beverly David has determined that for the "full-pager" in question (which eventually became page 480 in the first American edition) Brown was adapting from two Doré lithographs, one of them of the Whymper team's ascent of the mountain and one of the catastrophe on the return.[39] Later in the construction of *A Tramp*, either Clemens or the APC would go back to Doré's Matterhorn-disaster print and steal it outright, retitling it "ASCENDING MT. BLANC" (evidently on the assumption that Mark Twain had joked about, that for an American audience one icy Alp was the same as the next) and printing it as half of a double illustration on page 517. Negotiations over who would make the plates and by which process and where continued in the correspondence with Frank Bliss for about six weeks afterward, with Bliss offering interesting details about the technical capabilities at his disposal in Hartford at that moment:

> Browns package of 35 drawings just arrived this a.m. all safe; will have them right in the works. Seems to me they should be reduced even more than you have marked them, in order to get them down to the proper degree of sharpness. I notice that some of the shading in the pictures has been produced by thinning the ink, so that it gives a sort of <u>brown color</u>, now <u>Mr B</u> will have to be careful about that & have every line & mark that he wants to <u>take</u>, a <u>jet black,</u> anything that is not <u>black</u> makes <u>white</u> in the picture. Shading can be accomplished by making the lines <u>coarse</u> or <u>fine</u> as is necessary. Brown

wants to know whether our process workers here can do a picture that has a <u>ruled</u> tint-paper for ground work. Please tell him <u>yes</u>, we can produce <u>anything</u> that shows a black mark, <u>stipple</u> or rule or anything, but as written in previous letter the stipple won't make a good plate to <u>print</u> from & therefore I would not use that, but some pictures on the ruled paper will look nicely. . . . What I've said about <u>black</u> ink you will want to bear in mind when you lay out any more of <u>your own</u> designs. I'll go over that donkey you sent & make the lines black so he'll take, as you used "mauve" Ink. —<u>India</u> Ink is the stuff to use, if you will tell Brown all this it will save my writing him.[40]

Though Clemens eventually gave up on the idea of selecting the specific production technology himself, he was firmer about the original art he wanted for his book:

If you will send me *Eleven hundred dollars, gold,* to Paris, you shall receive, in return for it,

10 full-page plates	@	$18	. . . .	$180.00
25 half-page do	@	$9.	. . . .	225.00
75 quarter-page do	@	$4.50	. . . .	337.50
100 sixth-page do	@	$3	. . . .	300.00
210 drawings.			Totals.	1,042.50[41]

Clemens was trying to establish that he would be the referee, deciding what would go into print, and in what sort of layout: "I may use only 6 or 7 full-page pictures," he added, "and split up the other 3 or 4 into smaller ones; I may use some 1/3-page ones, and fewer 1/4-page. And so on—but the amount of space covered by pictures will remain the same and cost the same."[42] It is right after this that Clemens springs the idea of playing artist himself: "*In addition* I propose to give several pages of space to *my own* pictures, but these will only increase the above picture-bill at the rate of $9 a page for processing the same (and duties)—I think I won't charge you anything for artist's work, although I've had a good deal of trouble with these things and thrown a world of mighty poor talent into them" (115). Thus a plan for sixty pages of pictures, in styles ranging from sublime to burlesque and from competent to crude, all for an as-yet imaginary book whose verbal text would veer from belles lettres hyperbole to parodies of that style and several others. Once the finished manuscript arrived in Hartford, however, and production deadlines loomed and the publishing company's local staff closed in, Clemens's Parisian master plans suffered the fate of expediency and a lack of follow-through on his part. The APC hired additional artists with varying levels of skill to fill the remaining blank spots; and postcards, commercial lithographs, tourist brochures, and other materials gathered by Clemens en route and possibly by others were copied by local talents such as Ben Day and True Williams and also by anonymous stringers. Thanks to the versatility of electrotypes, several pictures were folded in from other APC books—and thanks to legal loopholes and slipshod enforcement of international copyright agreements, Whymper and Doré were raided for the first American edition, as foreign copyrights were still essentially a joke, but were prudently left out of the London version.[43]

Mark Twain did not get precisely what he envisioned—and what writer ever does? But *A Tramp Abroad* did carry him considerably closer than before, or ever again in his career, to creating a word-and-image book whose contents were of his own making and choosing. The artifact reaching the American market in 1880, in tens of thousands of copies, probably from several printing plants and binderies under APC contract, was not Mark Twain's hand-fashioned and personal *Leaves of Grass* but inevitably a collective, bureaucratic production, and we may never determine (or need to) exactly who chose or contributed each and every image positioned within the verbal text, and with what measure of intervention or supervision from the author. Playful thwarting of expectations was Mark Twain's motive from the start, and we could regard the ongoing upheaval in printing and illustration technologies and the incorporation of American publishing as making their contributions to his cause by mucking up, here and there, the detailed reverie that Clemens had begun with.

However, the complex dilemmas that *A Tramp Abroad* engages and the cultural and artistic paradoxes that it represents as an illustrated narrative are richer than that kind of situational irony. The media-assisted imaginative conquest of other nations in the second half of the nineteenth century was illusory, of course, as millions of combat dead in Belgium and northern France would prove to later generations. But illusions of this sort are pernicious. Returning after the First World War and again after the Second, they have grown so strong that entire Swiss, Italian, and Cotswold hamlets have been embalmed to foster it, along with expanses of quaint real estate in the heart of the European metropolis. Europe as theme park: Ancient Glory, High Middle Ages, Quattrocento, Tudor, Regency; Rome, Chartres,

Bruges, Florence, Venice, Paris, London . . . in *A Tramp Abroad,* if some of the digressions from writing the mandatory tourist experience seem desperate, they may enact a yearning that prowls in the heart of the sight-besotted modern traveler. Mark Twain affirms a right, or a compulsion, *not* to look steadily and raptly at whatever must be wondered at, in the too-abundant company of everyone else.

We can try such a reading with *A Tramp Abroad*'s most famous imaginative excursion away from the main excursion. The "Blue Jay Yarn," often excerpted from Chapters II and III and anthologized as a short story, suffers when disconnected from that larger context—in which it crops up as a narrative outrageously *out* of context. One reason why the story still strikes American readers as funny within the flow of *A Tramp Abroad* is that there is no plausible excuse for it to be there. The "Blue Jay Yarn" comes early in the book, not as conspicuous padding like the final chapters of *Roughing It,* or the procedural, spiritless closing chapters of *The Innocents Abroad,* or the hypertrophic latter half of *Life on the Mississippi.* In the APC editions, the story of the blue jays turns up less than forty pages into a six-hundred-page tome, and the ostensible subject, just before this lurch in the narrative, is a travel book cliché: the haunted loveliness of *Alt Heidelberg,* the picturesquely ruined *Schloss,* on the hilltop by night. Mark Twain has quit his hotel and gone strolling alone on the castle grounds, in search (like a conscientious tourist) of what the pictures and the guidebooks about the place have promised to be "the last possibility of the beautiful" (31). On this pilgrimage he has encountered a raven:

> I eyed the raven, and the raven eyed me. Nothing was said during some seconds. Then the bird stepped a little way along his limb to get a better point of observation, lifted his wings, stuck his head far down below his shoulders toward me, and croaked again—a croak with a distinctly insulting expression about it. If he had spoken in English he could not have said any more plainly than he did say in raven, "Well, what do *you* want here?" I felt as foolish as if I had been caught in some mean act by a responsible being, and reproved for it. However, I made no reply; I would not bandy words with a raven. (32)

As other ravens show up, our pilgrim to the crepuscular sublime hears himself ridiculed in the universal raven language—and what follows this is the blue-jay story, supposedly as told by "a middle-aged, simple-hearted miner who had lived in a lonely corner of California, among the woods and mountains, a good many years, and had studied the ways of his only neighbors, the beasts and the birds, until he believed he could accurately translate any remark which they made" (36). The story is about a common American bird exhausting himself in trying to fill up with acorns a knothole he has spotted in a cabin roof; the implicit frame story is about a crazy (or crafty) frontiersman telling Mark Twain a ridiculous tale, either to inform him or to amuse or confound him.

The frame story encompassing *that* one, however, is a story about an imagination struggling in an environment that is both alien and imaginatively depleted: about a famous American, a professional writer, wandering these much-too-written-about Heidelberg hills and failing to achieve the emotional and rhetorical experience that swarms of other visitors have had (or counterfeited) in this same place. The moonlit walkway by the *Schloss* is sodden with other people's effusions and graphic representations. Finding no cue here for originality in perception or feeling, and humbled even by the mundane birds of this place, our narrator escapes his creative predicament by veering into a tale that seems brazenly random, about other sorts of birds in a wilderness halfway around the world, in territory that most American and British tourists, armchair and otherwise, would know much less about. The "Blue Jay Yarn" is more than a fable about compulsive behavior and ridicule by neighbors who have too little else to occupy their attention. The story of the story is the liberation of the teller from his own imaginative project. It celebrates a license to fill up the empty house of this book with acorns of Mark Twain's own choosing, with facts and relevant experiences, or impressions and whimsy, anything that defends the freedom of American travelers from locales made treacherous by mechanized tourism and publishing.

The Innocents Abroad subverts travel as pilgrimage. *A Tramp Abroad,* from the beginning, subverts *The Innocents Abroad,* for travel this time is not pilgrimage but defiant meander. This is an insurrection against conventions of seeing, conventions that threaten to grow even more rigid as "fine art" and masterpiece images are promulgated as such to the millions. In the British and American first editions there is a frontispiece joke that Clemens contrived himself by mutilating two lithographs with a pair of scissors, a bit of paste, and a careless or misleading caption. A commercial picture of a squalling brat is superimposed on a pious lithograph by Paul Delaroche—or, more precisely, on an engraving by Edmund Evans of a painting by Delaroche—and the violated picture of the picture is titled "Titian's Moses." In one of Marcel Duchamp's notorious art jokes forty years later—now in the hands of a private collector and probably worth millions—Leonardo's *Mona Lisa*, or rather a picture of that picture, is improved with a thick moustache and retitled *L.H.O.O.Q.*, which, as college art teachers love to point out, is a pun on an obscene French phrase. An implicit theme in Duchamp's *faux* desecration, about the tedium of seeing "great paintings" again and again in the same old way, is much the same as in Mark Twain's opening visual joke. The venerated (and mediated) masterpiece and its subject are both seen better, or at least more freshly, when the conventional mediation is transgressed. The *Tramp Abroad* frontispiece is a teaser and a foreshadowing. In the verbal and visual text coming after, "Art" and "Europe" will prove to be livelier experiences when glanced at casually, or on the fly, or out of the corner of the eye, than when viewed reverently, dutifully, and straight on. Occasionally the requisite Great Sights will be presented with moustaches drawn upon them—not to obscure the vista but rather to make them new.

So—a travel book about a newer kind of travel, tourism expanded and disrupted, mountain-track happy wanderings transgressed with quick, easy scene changes and mechanical dislocations. So also, a travel book loaded with illustrations bespoken by its author, verbal and visual text disrupted by person or persons unknown who shuffled in more pictures without consulting the author. For understanding *A Tramp Abroad,* what relationships are most worth looking at between the verbal narrative, blocked and boosted by all these images, and the *visual* narrative, or travesty of a narrative, created by the sequence of those images? A few basic perceptions, driven home by the pictures-and-words barrages that pour into daily life now, might roll us forward. For instance, an image self-evidently transcribed by a mechanical process is "art" in some dimension, yet also a kind of machine in its own right; and a book of printed pictures is a complex mechanism, a virtual-reality device constructed of all the pictures and the provocative intrusions of verbal text among them. More information for readers to negotiate—perhaps with collateral damage that media critics have learned to lament, all the more loudly (and ineffectually) as the assault compounds: more signifiers, less signified. In their range of subjects and styles, their dubious provenance and wavering connection to the verbal text, these pictures break up the book and preclude any fussing about narrative coherence. The visual experience of *A Tramp Abroad,* constantly interrupting the verbal text, seems to urge that we read this book any way we like, in bits and pieces or even backwards, pausing or quitting at any blank space, any anomalous narrow zone between the image and the word. What is *A Tramp Abroad* about? Excursions, of course—but among these a few of notable modernity: into landscapes altered and compromised by so much transcribed seeing and published telling, and into a kind of "writing" where the pictures came first, or nearly so, in the creative process, and where the printed story as never before, as memoir, reminiscence, and entertainment, is free.

But nothing is stable in *A Tramp Abroad,* not even a strategy of refusal or burlesque. In the APC edition, the page with the "Titian" travesty is faced with a solemn steel engraving of Mark Twain himself (as promised in the APC's advertisements for the new book): a profile of the eminent author, embellished with an engraved replica of his signature, "Yours truly, Mark Twain." No hint of laughter or self-parody is in evidence here. Visually as well as textually, *A Tramp Abroad* is a "text" in which narratives and illustrations seem to be positioned with scant concern for form, for thematic or tonal continuity of any sort. As a modernist fixation, however, form may have only slight relevance in a nineteenth-century word-and-picture book about a crisis involving words and pictures, a travel book about a moment in which travel and perception are caught in metamorphosis into something modern, something truly strange.

There is a connection between the Riley who turns up briefly in *A Tramp Abroad* and the John Henry Riley with whom Mark Twain colluded to produce a travel-by-proxy book about ten years before. A fellow correspondent from Clemens's brief stint in Washington in 1867–68, Riley returns to life here as a literary proxy of another sort, as "my odd friend," the designated teller of someone else's saga of doing nothing. This buffering of the story that Mark Twain calls "THE MAN WHO PUT UP AT GADSBY'S," in Chapter XXVI, goes beyond the usual ploy and pretexts involved in frame-tale narration: still at large in Lucerne, Mark Twain stops one day to watch people fishing in the gorgeous lake, a pause that supposedly brings back to his mind "very forcibly" this memory of Riley and every word of his narrative, at night on a Washington street, to a visitor named Lykins. We have three idlers on the street, two of them supposedly listening to the eccentric third—and the longer his story continues, the greater the mystery about its purpose—Riley's for telling it, Mark Twain's for including it in a book about travel in Europe. This is how the encounter ends:

"Is that all?"
"That is all."

"Well, for the *time* of night, and the *kind* of night, it seems to me the story was full long enough. But what's it all *for?*"

"O, nothing in particular."

"Well, where's the point of it?"

"O, there isn't any particular point to it. Only, if you are not in *too* much of a hurry to rush off to San Francisco with that post-office appointment, Mr. Lykins, I'd advise you to '*put up at Gadsby's*' for a spell, and take it easy. Goodbye. *God* bless you!" (270–71)

The story that leads up to this has standard-issue pathos at the heart: a young man grows old and poor from fruitless waiting, at Gadsby's hotel, for a government favor to come his way. As Riley's victim tonight, Mr. Lykins is freshly arrived from San Francisco, also to collect a favor, a position at a post office, and head straight home to California with thoroughly modern speed:

"When are you intending to leave?"

"For New York to-morrow evening,—for San Francisco next morning."

"Just so. . . . . . . What are you going to do to-morrow?"

"*Do!* Why, I've got to go to the President with the petition and the delegation, and get the appointment, haven't I?"

"Yes . . . . very true . . . that is correct. And then what?"

"Executive session of the Senate at 2 p.m.,—got to get the appointment confirmed,—I reckon you'll grant that?"

"Yes . . . . yes," said Riley, meditatively, "you are right again. Then you take the train for New York in the evening, and the steamer for San Francisco next morning?"

"That's it,—that's the way I map it out!" (264–65)

So a sad, unnamed protagonist has languished more than thirty years at Gadsby's Hotel, anticipating that tomorrow, always tomorrow, an old promise will be kept and a civil service post will come his way. The fable is comic insofar as it exploits the trope of human psychological rigidity and also sad as a narrative of wasted life and vain hopes. Two generations later, F. Scott Fitzgerald would tell much the same tale in his short story "The Long Way Out," in which a charming widow, who turns out to be delusional and permanently incarcerated in a mental hospital, packs up and preens herself every morning, to sit patiently alone in the asylum hallway, waiting for her dead husband to come and take her home. Deepening the strangeness in Mark Twain's version, or rather Riley's, are embedded ironies connected to recurring themes of *A Tramp Abroad*. Over the course of this nameless petitioner's life, the world has shrunk and travel has grown faster, yet with no apparent effect on anything more than details of his own pernicious fantasy of escape. At the fable's outset, this earlier visitor to Washington arrives in the Age of Jackson, with a slave and a fine carriage and four horses, a classic gentleman's conveyance. Over the course of his wait he sells the horses, driver, carriage, and even his dog, and so on until he becomes a penniless, pathetic man afoot in these streets. The "rough mountain roads" he had talked about, "where a body had to be careful about his driving," in 1834 made the trek from Tennessee to Washington a lengthy and risky expedition; thirty years later, when rails and steamboats can carry Lykins and other supplicants a very long way on a brisk schedule, human beings can still slip into limbo and never get out again.

Going on at such length, Riley evidently intends something like this as the moral of his story. Yet Riley is also (for the moment at least) a character in a larger narrative, and so is this Lykins, and this younger Mark Twain, all three of them idlers on a Washington street, apparently with little else to do than tell or listen to rambling tales. These two news correspondents, Riley and Mark Twain, are spending their days collecting and telling stories to the world that the world may not want or understand or that have no point at all. How different do they seem from the man that this tale is supposedly about? How different is the author who writes about them all in the midst of a rambling account of a ramble through the heart of Europe, wandering from one prescribed and picturesque setting to the next, and drifting away from them in his imagination, to fill a book about wandering, about "putting up" in a sequence of hotels and boardinghouses? And to take one pace farther back from all this: What of ourselves as readers of the book? To move through a narrative like this, after all, is to be only another idler, pausing at length for a range of stories about which we can also ask, "But what's it all *for?*"—and receive no plausible answer. "Everybody goes everywhere": as a people accustomed now to being where we don't belong, engaging in business that is often, in a strict sense, not our own, we might not find the existential distance between Mark Twain and ourselves and the lonely man at Gadsby's as wide and comforting as we might prefer.

As Mark Twain and Harris meander the environs of Lucerne, catching conveyances out to sights already measured carefully and sanctioned in the

Baedekers, Riley's fable can be read as a small ode and elegy to imaginative restlessness. Though this is the only appearance of a Riley in *A Tramp Abroad*, some echo of an abandoned plan may turn up as a joke somewhat later on when Mark Twain recovers the proxy-travel scheme as a burlesque—of his own laziness and desperation to deliver the goods, with regard to "seeing" Switzerland, and also of a gaseous cosmopolitanism that mars the prose of guidebooks and other travel writers. Harris is sent off on his own for a week to draft a report on the glacial environs of Furca (or Furka), where the Rhone River rises north and east of Visp. The description in the 1877 Baedeker (translated, but not quite completely, from the original German) seems to revel in names and phrases beyond the skills of most English-speaking visitors:

> The road slowly ascends the slope of the *Längisgrat,* enters after ¼ hr. the valley descending from the *Furca,* and crosses the *Muttbach,* the discharge of the *Gratschlucht-Glacier,* which flows under the Rhone Glacier and forms one of the sources of that river. . . .
> The track leads from the upper part of the Rhone Glacier up a steep snow slope and difficult rocks, and finally over a long arête of névé (rope and ice-axe required). Imposing view.[44]

Language like this may seem fitting and proper when it is also technical and indigenous and when the intended audience are proprietors of ice axes and special mountaineering know-how. Leslie Stephen, however, sometimes tosses it around to demonstrate the social-class crevasse between the aristocrat-adventurers of his Alpine Club and the "cockney" waves of British and Yankee tourists on their cheap and comfortable excursions. Describing the route of an earlier explorer, Sir Leslie tosses in a condescending pun about the machinery bringing these vulgar mobs into his paradise:

> From Lauterbrunnen he "contemplates with rapture" and astonishment part of the great central chain "of the Alps." He even reaches the *couvercle* on the *Mer de Glace,* and admires, though he does not visit the *Jardin.* . . .
> If we ask by what avenues the beauty of the Alps succeeded in first revealing itself to an unpoetical generation, we shall find two or three leading trains of sentiment which gradually became popular.[45]

Harris's report is a pastiche of Baedeker's earnest, redundant guidance and Sir Leslie's erratically playful affectations:

Near this point the footpath joins the wider track, which connects the Grimsel with the head of the Rhone *schnawp:* this has been carefully constructed, and leads with a tortuous course among and over *les pierres,* down to the bank of the gloomy little *swosh-swosh,* which almost washes against the walls of the Grimsel Hospice. We arrived a little before 4 o'clock at the end of our day's journey, hot enough to justify the step, taken by most of the *partie,* of plunging into the crystal water of the snow-fed lake. (313–14)

And so on for three more pages, after which Mark Twain cross-examines his proxy on the motives for writing in this style:

> "Why have you used all this Chinese and Choctaw and Zulu rubbish?"
> "Because I didn't know any French but two or three words, and I didn't know any Latin or Greek at all."
> "That is nothing. Why should you want to use foreign words, anyhow?"
> "To adorn my page. They all do it."
> "Who is 'all?'"
> "Everybody. Everybody that writes elegantly." (320–21)

Which triggers a homily from Mark Twain about the modesty and straightforwardness of true erudition and the "great cruelty to nine out of ten" (321) readers that rises from this flaunting of foreign expressions. The joke here may wear out before it is finished, and the extended admonition may bear down harder than we might prefer, especially from a writer famous for incisive understatement. What the Furka interlude amounts to, however, is a canvasser's sample for the European-travel book that Mark Twain did *not* write—but that "everybody" else, in his estimation, was pushing into the marketplace where *A Tramp Abroad* had to thrive.

In those chapters set (more or less) on the Neckar River, two illustrations represent a complex kind of signifying especially appropriate to that interlude. Within this ostentatiously "finished" first edition, the reader is suddenly offered a bit of holograph manuscript, of proof text, perhaps as an implicit commentary on the sequence of human and mechanical interventions that make the final artifact possible. We are also offered a glimpse into the construction of a "text" that continues to evolve through time and epistemological change. Nothing like this happens in *The Innocents Abroad* or in *Roughing It:* the electrotype reproduction of supposedly raw pages from Mark Twain's own notebooks, of phrases and crude drawings accomplished (again, supposedly) on the fly or on the Neckar raft or somewhere else on the tour. A naive drawing of a bird, an equally unskilled bird's-eye view of the long raft on the narrow winding river, the crude drawing of a china plate decorated with a cat—and on each of these pages there are also a few holograph observations about these things.

What are these raw materials doing in the published book? As "finished" reproductions of casual notes and drawings, these published images carry several implications. They assert the authenticity of the narrated moment—Look! I made these by myself! On the spot! I was there!—though they also suggest a *non*authenticity, a seductive dubiousness about those better-crafted pictures and also about the polished narrative text coming before and after, including the extended contrivance of the storm-at-sea joke that closes the Neckar sequence. These pages and some other ungainly personal cartoons that Mark Twain or his editors inserted at other places in *A Tramp Abroad* are subversive, as they seem to whisper that the mannered professional engravings that abound in this book, and in so many other travel books of the time—engravings of ruined castles in moonlight or alpine vistas or quaint country folk in quaint village byways—are emanating from the imagination of a stranger in a Paris studio or somewhere back home in the States, or from other drawings, paintings, engravings, and photographs purloined from the trove to which Mark Twain's public has access already. Seeing Germany and the Alps firsthand now means also seeing through the "eyes" of print.

Mark Twain's drawings of a bird, a china plate, and a raft on a river are egregiously no better than what most of his adult readers could do by themselves. Such pages may recall moments in *Tristram Shandy* where Sterne (as Shandy) pretends to give up for a moment on the writerly chores of describing and includes space where readers can finish the job however they like. Hamlet's words are (in his own words or something like them) no longer his own once he has said them; Mark Twain's experiences are also no longer his own once they have been received in some far-off editorial and engraving-shop tranquility and transformed by the hired Unseen. What Mark Twain's illustrations might imply is how little the excursion has yielded in the way of immediate and personal record and how craft and technical processes take over and determine what we think we see.

Does this kind of subversive reflexivity also inform the style of the telling or distinguish it from earlier travel books, even books by Mark Twain himself? Consider how *A Tramp Abroad* opens, compared to *The Innocents Abroad,* which begins with a long extract from the official announcement of the *Quaker City* excursion, bolstered with outbursts of enthusiasm from the narrator. Drum rolls of expectation: what a great event this voyage and this book about it are going to be!

> For months the great Pleasure Excursion to Europe and the Holy Land was chatted about in the newspapers everywhere in America, and discussed at countless firesides. It was a novelty in the way of Excursions—its like had not been thought of before, and it compelled that interest which attractive novelties always command. It was to be a picnic on a gigantic scale. The participants in it, . . . were to sail away in a great steamship with flags flying and cannon pealing, and take a royal holiday beyond the broad ocean, in many a strange clime and in many a land renowned in history! (19)

And so on for another half-page of flamboyant rhetoric and ostensibly innocent delight. Ten years later, the rhetorical fires are damped; a promise of exotic fun has been replaced with a flat recollection of logistics. With six perfunctory paragraphs and a sequence of declarative sentences in much the same cadence, *A Tramp Abroad* begins with a shrug:

> One day it occurred to me that it had been many years since the world had been afforded the spectacle of a man adventurous enough to undertake a journey through Europe on foot. After much thought, I decided that I was a person fitted to furnish mankind this spectacle. So I determined to do it. This was in March, 1878.
>
> I looked about me for the right sort of person to accompany me in the capacity of agent, and finally hired a Mr. Harris for this service.
>
> It was also my purpose to study art while in Europe. Mr. Harris was in sympathy with me in this. He was as much of an enthusiast in art as I was, and not less anxious to learn to paint. I desired to learn the German language; so did Harris.
>
> Toward the middle of April we sailed in the *Holsatia,* Capt. Brandt, and had a very pleasant trip indeed.
>
> After a brief rest at Hamburg, we made preparations for a long pedestrian trip southward in the soft spring weather, but at the last moment we changed the program, for private reasons, and took the express train. (17)

No book by Mark Twain opens more bluntly, and to account for the tone, and for the miscellaneousness of the whole book, much has been said about the mood and personal circumstances of the writer as he churned it out. Without a best-selling book in more than five years, he was balked in completing *Huckleberry Finn* as a sequel to *Tom Sawyer;* he was beginning his entanglements with the Paige compositor; he was busy, scattered, over-extended, and too frequently away from home.[46] The life and the career were in a phase of turmoil—but so was the world of print, the world in which he had been trained and in which he had flourished.

A Tramp Abroad responds to that situation in American publishing, and the response is a disorderly rush of resistance, for this book has achieved no victory over the imaginative challenges it faces. But in the summer of 1883, when Mark Twain returned to a pigeonholed sequel for *The Adventures of Tom Sawyer,* to a handful of chapters that, when he had quit them, were the rudiments of a potboiler detective story that had suddenly moved in an unexpected direction, he saw new possibilities in Jim and Huckleberry Finn and new possibilities in the world they would move through, a world disrupted by the rising dominion of the printed page.

'Huckleberry Finn'
and the American Print Revolution

"[I]f I'd a knowed what a trouble it was to make a book . . ."

Adventures of Huckleberry Finn

The opening page of *Adventures of Huckleberry Finn*—at least as far as the end of the first paragraph, where Huck stops alluding to Mark Twain and his telling "the truth, mainly," in *The Adventures of Tom Sawyer*—can be difficult if we want it that way. Huck's comments about that previous book and about the reliability of the man who wrote it complicate the problem of who is speaking now, and where and when, and what passes for "truth" in *Tom Sawyer*, or this new novel, or memoir, or whatever it is that begins here.[1] These are conundrums about authority and voice, and they grow worse if we try to keep several pages of this text in mind at once: this beginning of Huck's narrative, told in his own words, along with an interesting first try at devising a title for the book, on the first page of the manuscript, which turned up in a private home in Hollywood, California, in 1990. The questions that these pages incite together also have to do with historical time, and especially with the dislocations that printed documents can work *upon* time.

On the title page of the WebsterCo editions, two phrases are printed below the book's title and the parenthetical series hint "(TOM SAWYER'S COMRADE)" and just above the plug for the edition's "ONE HUNDRED AND SEVENTY FOUR ILLLUSTRATIONS":

SCENE: THE MISSISSIPPI VALLEY
TIME: FORTY TO FIFTY YEARS AGO

Since at this point the reader is coming up fast on the "NOTICE" by "G. G." about being prosecuted, banished, or shot for looking too deeply into any aspect of the tale that follows, why not just allow the scene-and-time advisories to settle, or at least to silence, any troublemaking about when this supposedly unfolds—the adventures that Huck tells about and the later adventure of Huck's telling? We know now that Mark Twain wavered in specifying the time of the novel's action. The "forty years ago" notation, along with the designation of the scene, was on the typescript he sent to Webster, but in the summer of 1884 Mark Twain decided to loosen up the temporal possibilities, notifying Webster to make the change to "forty to fifty." As to why Mark Twain changed his mind about the time of the action after completing the novel, the best guess, put forward by editors at the Mark Twain Project, is that as a media businessman he was thinking ahead to a possible sequel for this sequel—a next book in which Tom and Huck would be on the Oregon Trail in its early days, fifty years back rather than forty.[2]

Whether or not this was the motive, the change was retrospective fudging. The cultural predicament facing Huck on his trip down the river with Jim is particular to the middle and later 1840s and not ten years earlier. In any case, the title-page notation about the "time" of *Huckleberry Finn* is blindsided by that opening sentence of Huck's narrative: "You don't know about me, without you have read a book by the name of 'The Adventures of Tom Sawyer,' but that ain't no matter." On the chance that some American reader beginning this book would not know about *Tom Sawyer* or might miss a comic incongruity embedded here, Huck develops the connection: "That book was made by Mr. Mark Twain, and he told the truth, mainly"—and no contortions of logic are required to get lost in the implications. If "Mr. Mark Twain," as the "maker" of *The Adventures of Tom Sawyer* (published about a decade before the appearance of *Huckleberry Finn*), is an American celebrity, posing for the photographers and holding forth in leonine middle age, and if these opening lines are meant to signal the beginning of an impersonation—Mark Twain as Huck Finn this time, telling Huck's own story—then when and how, precisely or even vaguely, is Huck to be imagined as doing this work?

In other words, because *two* narratives begin here, the narrative of Huck's adventures and also the story of Huck recollecting them and struggling to understand the moral consequences of his own experience, Huckleberry Finn as the imaginary "maker" of this book requires a context for being an author. And since the time of the action is at least forty years in the past, is this Huck who speaks now also a man of middle age, looking back so long a way to the adventures of his youth? In the last pages of this novel, "his" novel, there are firm indications that this is a bad guess, for the final lines about "lighting out for the Territory" imply that Huck, in the moment of wrapping up his reminiscence, is still a boy, and that he is writing or saying all of this fairly soon after his exploits along the river are ended. He says, for example, that Tom Sawyer is still flaunting for local admirers the bullet that wounded him at the Phelps farm, that Jim is freshly free, and that the Widow Douglas is planning another campaign to domesticate Huck in her house in St. Petersburg. So if Huck has promptly taken up his pencil to write all this down, or has begun to dictate his adventures to somebody else soon after the boys and Jim have returned home, how can Huck know anything about a "Mr. Mark Twain," who "forty or fifty years ago" was a boy named Sam Clemens, apprenticed to a Hannibal printer?[3]

Time out. Does worrying about the imaginative logic of this narrative accomplish anything worthwhile? Or does it merely bother the straightforward enjoyment of a famous and pleasurable American novel? If Huck himself is to be thought of as constructing this book of his adventures when they are still green in his memory, then of course there will be discrepancies pertaining to the imaginary act of composition and to our own imaginative negotiation in the act of reading—the kind of metaphysical puzzle that is bothersome chiefly to pedants. One way out of it is to allow that the mediation of print can also bend and alter the implicit story of the *writing* of a text. As a formalizing process of indeterminate duration, the rituals of publishing can liberate written discourse from the real or make-believe historical moment of its origin. With regard to printed books: the production of manuscripts, copyedited texts, and corrected galleys obscures intervals of months or (in the case of this text, if we think of it as Mark Twain's rather than Huck's) several years between the author's completion of one chapter and his starting upon the next. And unless the publishing project is something truly perverse (like a scholarly "variorum" edition), the interceding editors, designers, and printers are supposed to obliterate the hints of cancellations, reshufflings, and other amendments and hesitations by which a sheaf of holograph material becomes a smooth and seamless printed artifact. *Huck's* novel? *Huck's* manuscript? As jaded consumers of modern printed books, do we even have a right to fantasize a keepsake snippet of Huck's scrawl as some kind of validation? Sorry, but Elvis is dead, and there never was a Huckleberry Finn. Stuck at the other end of a complex publishing process, readers are not entitled to authenticating pseudodocuments like those inept notebook-doodles of rafts and statues and hairtrunks that turn up in *A Tramp Abroad* and those cartoons flaunting the artistic clumsiness of Mark Twain as the real author out on the trail—as well as the intermediating dark magic of the bookmakers in other places far away. Indoctrinated in "the death of the author" as an imaginable soul mate in this media blizzard where we are supposedly lost, what business do we have conceiving of someone named Huckleberry Finn as writing or saying anything at all?

Nonetheless, such questions are difficult to keep at bay, regarding the circumstances in which Huck, as an autobiographical author rather than as "Tom Sawyer's comrade," inscribes or relates his own story, for they bear on a more important problem in the interpretation of this novel, the circumstances in which Huck supposedly achieves his moral perspectives about his experiences on the river with Jim. Does he do his growing up on the spot—or does it happen as all this is recollected in tranquillity? Because stable answers about these matters are impossible, we can, if we like, chalk up a few more inconsequential points against a book that millions of people, without the nuisance of commentary from literary critics, have enjoyed and regarded as some kind of American masterpiece.

Moreover, there might be actual advantages, for ourselves as modern readers, in Mark Twain's apparent indifference to this time-of-the-telling problem pertaining to a book that is implicitly *also* about Huck taking the "trouble," as he says on its final page, "to make a book." The interventions of the publishing process do much to liberate a text not only from a specific moment in time but also from the imprint of personal identity. Since a "real" author's name on a volume's spine, front cover, and title page constitutes an ascription of responsibility and a claiming of "intellectual property," the handsomely printed authorial (false) name, the engraved facsimile of his (fictitious) autograph, and the heliotyped tipped-in plate of his dignified bust (all of these accoutrements turn up in the front matter of the first edition of *Huckleberry Finn*) underscore the *un*reality of this book as a work by one hand only. Standing up for old-school New England aesthetic restraint in the arts of printing, a reviewer for the Boston *Evening Traveller* took umbrage at this showing off by the Webster artisans and regarded the text and the design as a collective exercise in corporate vulgarity. "The publication rejoices in two frontispieces, of which the one is supposed to be a faithful portrait of Huckleberry Finn, and the other an engraving of the classic features of Mr. Mark Twain as seen in the bust made by Karl Gerhardt. The taste of this gratuitous presentation is as bad as the book itself, which is an extreme statement."[4]

Modern book publishing, subscription or otherwise, brings many others into the production of "your" text. An author's words are engaged as artifacts for manufacture, and what is eventually created is a composite entity: lovelier and in some ways more precise than the original manuscript but also a thing displaced, awkwardly yet consolingly apart. Huck, as he says, has made a book, not "written" one, and his complete benediction for the process he has completed is this: "Tom's most well now, and got his bullet around his neck on a watch-guard for a watch, and is always seeing what time it is, and so there ain't nothing more to write about, and I am rotten glad of it, because if I'd a knowed what a trouble it was to make a book I wouldn't a tackled it and ain't agoing to no more" (362). The key phrase, in which Huck ultimately lays claim to his own narrative, is worth pausing over, for to "make a book" "forty or fifty years ago"—which turns out to mean around 1845 or a little later—was a different undertaking from writing and publishing in the 1880s, when print runs of a few hundred locally sold copies (a typical fate for a personal memoir, especially by an unillustrious young man in the latter days of handpress publishing) had given way to automated national and international production of thousands of volumes. When Huck draws attention to himself at the end as a bookmaker of some sort, he thickens the mystery about the historical moment and predicament of the creator. What exactly does Huck imagine he is making when he talks about making a book? If Mark Twain knew well the meaning and implications of the phrase, then what about his new hero, who seems to have joined or stumbled into the same line of work a generation before Mark Twain did—or perhaps in some time-warped way a generation after? We have been warned: "persons attempting to find a Plot in it will be shot"; persons attempting to fuss about Huck himself as the author of a book, or the very idea of a book in a specific time and place, will be hooted out of the conversation.

Once again, the physical brute fact of the novel as published by Mark Twain's company offers a pathway into this thicket. Regardless of whatever dimension it might be imagined as having come from, the printed text of the WebsterCo editions—available to the American public of 1885 (according to options listed in the canvasser's book) in blue cloth or green, in library leather or half-morocco, with a choice of plain, sprinkled, or marbled edges, and on the front cover of the cloth editions an embossed picture of an impish-looking boy—all of this artifice and manufacture participate in the launching of utterance into realms beyond geographic place and ordinary time. If Huck is to be imagined as about fourteen years old forty years before, and somehow still about the same age when he reminisces, or when Mr. Mark Twain performs the reminiscence through him, then perhaps that confusion itself is testament to the heady powers of the printed word.

Written, told, tell, make: these are vexatious terms, and we must stay a bit longer with these enigmas of "telling." They suggest the kind of authoring that this impersonated young author has accomplished and sources of our own capacity to conceptualize the text we are reading. To raise a question subtending from these others: Is *Adventures of Huckleberry Finn* to be engaged as a *spoken* book or as a written one? Mark Twain's notations about that are contradictory. On the first page of the manuscript he began in 1876 there is a heading, apparently amended to its present form a few years later, that did not appear on the pages he sent to Webster or in the published book:

Huckleberry Finn

Reported by

Mark Twain[5]

So in this first experiment with telling Huck's story the idea was apparently to position Huck as an oral informant and Mark Twain himself as a kind of stenographer, much like the "faithful and interested amanuensis" he called himself when he reminisced (in a dictated letter, much later in life) about the act of writing.[6] The evidence for that early plan not only validates an impression that the discourse of *Huckleberry Finn* is *oral* discourse rather than "writerly" or "literary"; it also finesses a question about Huck's reasons for settling down to make this book, given his impatience with closed rooms and disciplined labor. Talking in the company of others is easier for him than writing alone. And by avoiding the customary infinitive, *to write* a book, Huck allows the reader some additional leeway to assume that this narrative has been talked out in comfortable circumstances rather than laboriously inscribed by the boy himself. Mark Twain's early notation would fit the Huck we do "know about" if we have indeed read *Tom Sawyer* or have come to know Huck's temperament from earlier chapters in this sequel. Huck is not fond of hard work, but he is demonstrably fond of his own variety of the English language, and like most Americans he is more willing to say aloud at great length than to write anything down. Nonetheless, Huck discovers that such a long narration is a chore in its own right, and as he concludes it he tells us so.

Part of the pleasure of this text, therefore, lies in the uncertainty about its provenance, the way Huck's profoundly oral narrative heightens the peculiarity of this tale as a published book, and in how the compounded artifice of the printed editions, and especially the illustrated editions produced in Mark Twain's lifetime from the company he controlled, underscores the artifice of Huck's rusticity. In the front matter of the first edition there is also an EXPLANATORY, which asserts that various dialects to be perceived in the following narrative are there by design and are different from each other by design and that readers of *Huckleberry Finn* should not "suppose that all these characters were trying to talk alike and not succeeding." This short paragraph is from "The Author"—which has to signify Mark Twain rather than Huck writing "By Himself," the validating subtitle in the front matter of Frederick Douglass's *Narrative*. In other words, the front matter of *Huckleberry Finn* gives us a nudge to recognize that this is a crafted text, by an "Author" who is not Huck and who knows what he is doing, and that the prose here is not nearly as spontaneous and raw as it might seem. However, this same short paragraph also draws attention to the fact that Huck, or rather Sam-Clemens-as-Mark-Twain-as-Huck, will be so much "in character" in what follows that he will not stop along the way—whosoever "he" might be—to offer guidance as to which regional dialect is emanating from which personage. As the teller, Huck will maintain his innocence about the art of telling, an innocence founded in a delusion (or rather, a supposition *accurate* for the moment and context in which we should imagine him speaking or writing) that whoever may navigate "his" book will understand the cultural and historical milieu that it supposedly comes from and what it is fundamentally about. Here is an experience in strangeness, compounded by another "advisory," implicit rather than printed at the outset—that as our narrator and guide, and as the ostensible author of what follows, Huckleberry Finn will neither understand nor care about where, for his listeners or readers, the obscurities of his tale may lie.

To sum up: Sam Clemens as Mark Twain creates Huckleberry Finn, who "makes" this book, or who tells it for Mark Twain to write down, and who seems to make it for the sort of audience that such a book would have reached in the Mississippi River heartland of the later 1840s. If persona and author seem to contend here for imaginative dominion over a verbal text, there is nothing new or deleterious about that kind of conflict in Anglo-American literary history. Much of the fun of reading a narrative by somebody writing as somebody else lies in the indeterminacy as to where in the text which personality might be said to prevail and how a pretended author—Robinson Crusoe, Moll Flanders, Fanny Hill, David Copperfield, Lockwood, Jane Eyre, Esther Summerson, Nick Carraway, the Invisible Man, and so on—"takes over" the story, overwhelming or obliterating the personality of the other author, the one who collects the royalties. What is interesting about any such contest within *Huckleberry Finn* is not only that Huck is such a convincing personality and voice but also that Huck and Mark Twain are situated on either side of a forty-year cultural and technological divide, during which time the potential reach and importance of published narratives by American writers have drastically changed. In the imaginary moment of the making, the 1840s, what Huck creates is a free-wheeling, unpretentious narrative about his personal experiences, including his scrapes with new and rapidly encroaching national media. What Mark Twain, E. W. Kemble, and others affiliated with the Charles L. Webster Company created together is a commodity in and for those media, an illustrated book (on the front cover of the first edition, the word "Illustrated" appears in a large font right below the title) to be sold everywhere in the United States.

Where is the commonality between these two "made" books? Can it be said that *Huckleberry Finn,* as a narrative, as an imaginative construct, as an adorned and published book, as a cultural sensation, is faithful to the historical and technological circumstances of both the adventure and the telling—in other words, to an American media crisis of the 1840s? Where in this novel are the conspicuous interventions of others, including perhaps another voice, a "Mark Twain" voice, into what is supposedly Huck's book? To frame an answer, we need to look at the illustrations that Mark Twain commissioned and oversaw for this novel and then return to the verbal text as a commentary about print culture and the upheaval it caused in American rural life when Sam Clemens and Huckleberry Finn were both teenaged boys.

Much has been learned about the genesis of these illustrations, about E. W. Kemble as the principal artist for the book, and about Mark Twain's supervision of its visual dimensions. More than forty years later, reminiscing for the first issue of the book collectors' journal the *Colophon*, Kemble told a story of how his work had caught Mark Twain's eye:

> While contributing to *Life* I made a small picture of a little boy being stung by a bee. . . .
>
> Casting about for an illustrator, Mark Twain happened to see this picture. It had action and expression, and bore a strong resemblance to his mental conception of Huck Finn. I was sent for and immediately got in touch with Webster. The manuscript was handed me and the fee asked for—two thousand dollars—was graciously allowed. I had begun drawing professionally two years before this date, and was now at the ripe old age of twenty-three. . . .
>
> Now began the important job of getting a model. The story called for a variety of characters, old and young, male and female. In the neighborhood I came across a youngster, Cort Morris by name, who tallied with my idea of Huck. He was a bit tall for the ideal boy, but I could jam him down a few pegs in my drawing and use him for the other characters.[7]

Kemble's memory may be soft or self-serving here, as there are differing accounts of how he was brought aboard for this project.[8] There are also indications that Mark Twain's satisfaction with Kemble's work ebbed for a while and then recovered as Kemble reworked his pictures to please his mercurial client. In recent years, attention has also been paid to Kemble's habit of complacency and racism in depicting African Americans, especially in work published under his own name in the years after *Huckleberry Finn*. Because of the success of this novel, "My coons caught the public fancy," he said, and he made a good living as the waning century's most popular cartoonist of African Americans. And because there is no record of Mark Twain expressing discomfort about those caricatures, inferences have been drawn about the stability and limits of his own convictions regarding race and prejudice in the United States.[9] Speculations have also centered on a brief note to Webster on May 7, 1884, in which Clemens remarked that the first set of drawings portrayed Huck's mouth as "a trifle more Irishy than necessary,"[10] fueling debate as to whether Huck was meant by his creator to be "Irishy" in other ways—and if so, with what implications.[11]

Racist or not, the style of Kemble's illustrations for *Huckleberry Finn* is intricately rustic. The beaux arts elegance of Frank Merrill, who did many of the lush images for *The Prince and the Pauper*, or of Dan Beard, whom Twain would select for *A Connecticut Yankee*, is mercifully absent here.

Irishy

Twain changed illustrators

There are no disruptive incongruities between the cultural import of the pictures and the breezy vernacular of the verbal text. More needs to be said, however, about how these images are embedded within this text, how that fusion differs from previous illustrated books by Mark Twain, and how this visual experiment complicates the novel, as published by Mark Twain's own company and in the physical form that he oversaw. The Webster edition was an entertainment for, and from, a new era in American publishing; yet it was also an experience in imaginary quaintness, a book that pretended, in several ways, to come from a bygone time.

To begin with the start of each chapter: though the subscription editions of Mark Twain's work had always been lavishly illustrated, pictures in those earlier volumes were never merged so thoroughly into the verbal text that begins each chapter as they are in the WebsterCo *Huckleberry Finn.* In *The Innocents Abroad, A Tramp Abroad,* and *Life on the Mississippi,* if a chapter closes with a small image, the next chapter normally opens with a simple block-capital heading—something like "CHAPTER XXXIII"—and nothing else in the way of adornment. In *Huckleberry Finn,* however, each chapter opens with a Kemble drawing that includes both an image and a word of the verbal text of Huck's narrative rather than with anything in set movable type; and the font (if we can call it that) in each of these picture-and-word openings is never of a variety found in a type case. Often Kemble draws his letters as assemblages of twigs; spiderwebs turn up here and there; in the Chapter IV heading, a schoolmaster's spectacles, complete with his eyes, perch in the bottom curve of the expansive *C.* "Chapter V" features a slouch hat, evidently Pap Finn's, parked atop the same first letter. Mississippi River weeds are tangled up in "Chapter XVI" and several other headings; dark little birds sit on a cartouche *C* at "Chapter XXVIII." Each of the three *X*'s in "Chapter XXIX" pokes into a piece of paper, alluding to a handwriting test that the duke tries to bluff, and so on. Every chapter begins with a quarter-page illustration, encompassing the hand-drawn opening word of Huck's narrative.

With each new chapter, therefore, the reader of *Huckleberry Finn* negotiates an intervention by the artist, the compositor, the publisher, and implicitly also Mark Twain rather than Huck. Each of these pictures asserts a parsing of Huck's memoir by others, and each picture signals a way to imagine settings and characters in this segment of the story even before Huck begins to describe them. Indulged or perhaps challenged with these visual impressions in advance of the relevant verbal text, readers of the

Chapter IV.

!!!!!

WELL, three or four months run along, and it was well into the winter, now. I had been to school most all the time, and could spell, and read, and write just a little, and could say the multiplication table up to six times seven is thirty-five, and I don't reckon I could ever get any further than that if I was to live forever. I don't take no stock in mathematics, anyway.

At first I hated the school, but by and by I got so I could stand it. Whenever I got uncommon tired I played hookey, and the hiding I got next day done me good and cheered me up. So the longer I went to school the easier it got to be. I was getting sort of used to the widow's ways, too, and they warn't so raspy on me. Living in a house, and sleeping in a bed, pulled on me pretty tight, mostly, but before the cold weather I used to slide out and sleep in the woods, sometimes, and so that was a rest to me. I liked the old ways best, but I was getting so I liked the new ones, too, a little bit. The widow said I was coming along slow but sure, and doing very satisfactory. She said she warn't ashamed of me.

One morning I happened to turn over the salt-cellar at breakfast. I reached for some of it as quick as I could, to throw over my left shoulder and keep off the bad luck, but Miss Watson was in ahead of me, and crossed me off. She says, "Take your hands away, Huckleberry—what a mess you are always making." The widow

FIG. 6 Kemble's opening page for Chapter IV of *Huckleberry Finn.* (New York: Charles L. Webster Company, 1885).

Webster editions have no choice but to engage with this segment of the story by first engaging with an image, at least for an instant, to discern and decode the stylized word that sets this portion of Huck's narrative in motion. In Chapter XVII, the first word looms in white through a window of the Grangerford house at night; in Chapter XXI the *I* of the opening *It* is cut in half by a wooden sword wielded by Jim in a practice fight with the king; in Chapter XXVI the opening *Well* floats up against a roof beam; in Chapter XXXVII, the first word, *That,* turns up on a hand-lettered sign suspended from a tree.

Is this another step, then, in a cultural meander from the "illustrated novel" of the nineteenth century toward the "graphic novel" of our own time, a metamorphosis, happy or otherwise, made possible by slicker technologies for merging images into pages of letter-press type? From *Huckleberry Finn* onward to the end of his career, Mark Twain, his illustrators, and his publishers, with varying degrees of collaboration and influence over the final product, would experiment with the balance and mix of printed words with visual experience. In some of those later books the illustrations would take up literally half the space in the volume, nearly equaling the verbal text as a source of thematic content and tone. In the case of *Pudd'nhead Wilson,* Mark Twain's lean and puzzling story of murder and racial identity in Dawson's Landing, published by the APC in a large font with wide margins on octavo pages, would be teased toward a chaos of intention by flocks of incongruous little figures scattered down those margins. As an interpretive challenge, the accompanying images would matter even more in Mark Twain's books after *Huckleberry Finn,* and these chapter-top experiments in Huck's narrative are a moment in a protracted shift away from the verbal and toward the visual—perhaps foreshadowing a twenty-first-century culture, in which the mediated visual experience will overwhelm.[12]

Even so, the manipulation of the chapter headings in *Huckleberry Finn* is also in a sense a throwback, and a useful one in the organization and pacing of this particular narrative, for Kemble's strategy makes the Webster editions flamboyantly bookish. If the bastard posterity of these pages includes the modern graphic novel, then the ancestry zigzags back to the illuminated manuscript of the European Middle Ages, the hand-fashioned treasure in which each psalm and Gospel opens with a flourish of color and images, including ornamental first letters and words. There are also similarities with regard to the way that the ornamentation contributes to the pacing and shaping of the verbal text. Like the river he rides, Huck's verbal narrative

Chapter XVII.

"WHO'S THERE?"

In about half a minute somebody spoke out of a window, without putting his head out, and says:

"Be done, boys! Who's there?"

I says:

"It's me."

"Who's me?"

"George Jackson, sir."

"What do you want?"

"I don't want nothing, sir. I only want to go along by, but the dogs won't let me."

"What are you prowling around here this time of night, for—hey?"

"I warn't prowling around, sir; I fell overboard off of the steamboat."

"Oh, you did, did you? Strike a light there, somebody. What did you say your name was?"

"George Jackson, sir. I'm only a boy."

"Look here; if you're telling the truth, you needn't be afraid—nobody 'll hurt you. But don't try to budge; stand right where you are. Rouse out Bob and Tom, some of you, and fetch the guns. George Jackson, is there anybody with you?"

"No, sir, nobody."

I heard the people stirring around in the house, now, and see a light. The man sung out:

"Snatch that light away, Betsy, you old fool—ain't you got any sense? Put it on the floor behind the front door. Bob, if you and Tom are ready, take your places."

"All ready."

FIG. 7 Chapter XVII of *Huckleberry Finn*.

Chapter XXVI

THE CUBBY.

Well, when they was all gone, the king he asks Mary Jane how they was off for spare rooms, and she said she had one spare room, which would do for uncle William, and she'd give her own room to uncle Harvey, which was a little bigger, and she would turn into the room with her sisters and sleep on a cot; and up garret was a little cubby, with a pallet in it. The king said the cubby would do for his valley—meaning me.

So Mary Jane took us up, and she showed them their rooms, which was plain but nice. She said she'd have her frocks and a lot of other traps took out of her room if they was in uncle Harvey's way, but he said they warn't. The frocks was hung along the wall, and before them was a curtain made out of calico that hung down to the floor. There was an old hair trunk in one corner, and a guitar box in another, and all sorts of little knick-knacks and jimcracks around, like girls brisken up a room with. The king said it was all the more homely and more pleasanter for these fixings, and so don't disturb them. The duke's room was pretty small, but plenty good enough, and so was my cubby.

That night they had a big supper, and all them men and women was there, and I stood behind the king and the duke's chairs and waited on them, and the niggers waited on the rest. Mary Jane she set at the head of the table, with Susan alongside of her, and said how bad the biscuits was, and how mean the preserves was, and how ornery and tough the fried chickens was,—and all that kind of

FIG. 8 Chapter XXVI of *Huck Finn*.

meanders among incidents and ruminations, and textual cues that a discrete episode is either commencing or ending correlate poorly with where the chapter breaks fall. Sometimes, to be sure, the next chapter begins with a blunt announcement that a substantial interval of time has been jumped. "Well, three or four months run along" gets Chapter IV underway; "Two or three days and nights went by" opens Chapter XIX. Others begin with Huck waking upon a following morning or with a quick shift from one day's dawning to nightfall.

Often, however, the chapter breaks seem to slice Huck's narrative arbitrarily into digestible pieces. Opening with "They swarmed up the street, towards Sherburn's house," Chapter XXII merely continues Huck's on-the-fly reportage at the heels of the Bricksville lynch mob heading for Sherburn's house, the mob that has been "yelling, and snatching down every clothesline they come to, to do the hanging with," at the suspenseful close of Chapter XXI. Without the intrusion of the ornamented heading, the action and the narrative would move forward seamlessly. In the episode at the Wilks house, the motions of another rambunctious crowd are again intruded upon arbitrarily by the image that opens Chapter XXIX, and after the end of Chapter XXXIV the conversation between Huck and Tom seems to continue after only a pause for breath. In other words, Huck's memoir itself, as a screed of verbal recollection, shows no consistent strategy with regard to conventions for the parsing of a *literary* text. And when it does pause or alter its course, those changes cannot compare, in flourish, with Kemble's pictorial artifice in announcing each successive chapter of *Huckleberry Finn*.

These interventions of clever quaintness, therefore, much as they might influence the cadence and thematic content of Huck's narratives (including the implicit narrative of Huck's struggle to complete and comprehend the meaning of his own memoir somewhere around 1845), signal both the modernity and antiquity of the artifact before us, the physical book. For ultimately these evocations of handmade book production emphasize the reality of this book as a *machine*-made thing, underscoring the disconnection between whatever Huck, as the imaginary author, might have thought he was doing when he supposedly produced this outpouring of words and what Mark Twain and his collaborators in the complex production process and advertising blitz—forty years on from the supposed moment of the action and the relating—believed they were doing when they constructed a volume of prose and pictures for an international audience.

Moreover, with regard to these image-laden WebsterCo editions, there is this ungainly fact as well: worked into chapter heads or no, the abundance of pictures enforces an implication that this counterfeit personal history, as a physical, published book, must be negotiated by the reader in something other than a headlong way. In other words, when a narrative is profusely enhanced by visual experience, which both extends and complicates the imaginative experience fostered by the verbal text, then the reading process cannot be linear. As a published book in the form that Mark Twain himself oversaw, *Huckleberry Finn* is a visual-verbal text designed for double-back reading, a text to be revisited and reconsidered for these ramifying encounters between word-text and picture-text. Is that what Huck's Pap really looks like? Do Huck's words about Mary Jane Wilks induce us to imagine her as she appears in the accompanying picture? Back and forth rove the eyes, between the story Huck tells and the story told through the pictures, and the compounded reading experience evolves not merely from the number or nuisance of these images but also from something deeper, our knowledge that Mark Twain indeed intended to write an *illustrated* book, to imagine the complete text as an interconnected sequence of prose passages and arresting pictures, and to generate a story in prose compatible with abundant illustration.

In thinking about *Huckleberry Finn* as a contrast or quarrel among different eras in the history of American publishing, the design and embellishment of the Webster Company editions, as constructed under Clemens's supervision, offer much to consider. In several dimensions, this novel is both an artifact of a new information age and a meditation on what it meant to be an author amid the expansion of American publishing from the time of Huck's boyhood on to the summer of 1883, when Mark Twain apparently recovered his interest in this sequel, took up the manuscript again, and completed it. As commentary on the American print revolution's transformation of the published verbal narrative, and also its transformation of several forms of American identity—the literary protagonist, the imaginary narrator, and the living author—Mark Twain's best novel centers on a hero who tells his own story (inscribes it, perhaps) and then apparently plans to "light out." So Huck might be imagined as a recently returned adventurer launching with guileless enthusiasm into the making of this book or as an unhappy boy compelled by circumstance into speaking for himself (after all, since "Mr. Mark Twain" "stretched" some things in writing the Tom-and-Huck book that precedes this one, can he be trusted to get the facts right this time?). Either way, Huck as the creator of his own history wants to resist entrapment in the social and personal consequences of doing this kind of work, the identity of "author," with its attendant constrictions as an American profession and as a psychological fate.

Not literate in a Tom Sawyer sense, or even a Missouri schoolroom sense, Huck nonetheless reads his world intently in order to survive, which means that he also negotiates its excretions of print and a deluge of images published in cities far away. There is no indication that Huck has any special love for books and printed words. These things for him are part of the larger, treacherous cultural mix, hazards in a personal struggle to keep sane and grow up. The printed word and the printed image are important constituent forces in the culture that Huck sometimes lives in and often tries to escape, but one way or another he has to engage with them all. Though Huck can lapse into risky innocence and moral complacency when he encounters social affectations and other varieties of ritualized thinking and conduct from the people he meets (conduct borrowed from or encouraged by publications pouring into their world), one of Huck's saving graces is that he understands that words and pictures on paper must be kept at a psychological and moral distance, even when, or if, he should eventually turn author himself. The fantasy that blooms in the novel's final paragraphs about the way that Huck's story has come into our own hands is that Huck stops talking in Mark Twain's company, or leaves his written tale in someone else's custody, and lights out soon after—a phrase that generations of critics have latched onto, perhaps because it flatters a sometimes-concealed urge in bookish people to make their own clean getaway from print and the lonely self-discipline that goes with reading and writing. If some side of Huck wants to be an author, he also wants to be a fugitive or a wraith, and there is consolation in imagining that those drives might be one and the same.

Then why does Huck go to the trouble of generating this extensive memoir of harrowing personal experience? Archetypal Romantic or Victorian first-person narrators, after all, are clever at conveying, usually at the outset, some sense that the labor of telling is a kind of therapy, or a life-or-death sorting out of whatever has been traumatically lived or witnessed. In the second sentence of his personal history, David Copperfield describes the writing process as a quest to discover himself and what he loves and his own place in some greater scheme. Lockwood's account tests the truth and importance of what he thinks he has learned about Wuthering Heights; the nervous truculence of Jane Eyre's story marks it as an apologia for her own struggle for survival. Betraying no special pride in his previous adventures, as related in Mark Twain's mainly "true book" about Tom Sawyer, Huck begins his own narrative where the previous story of the two boys "winds up," with Huck in the protective custody of the Widow Douglas until he "couldn't stand it no longer" and (true to form) lights out. But Huck has not said all that we know about his own new outlook as *Tom Sawyer* ends, for in its last chapters Huck has to negotiate not only domesticity but also personal wealth and local celebrity, as one of the two heroes who has found a treasure in a dangerous cave, evading the vicious criminal Injun Joe and contributing to the villain's demise. If "sivilization" makes Huck squirm now, that social menace includes his own new identity as a rich and envied citizen of the town. The closing pages of *The Adventures of Tom Sawyer* make those new circumstances clear:

> Wherever Tom and Huck appeared they were courted, admired, stared at. The boys were not able to remember that their remarks had possessed weight before; but now their sayings were treasured and repeated; everything they did seemed somehow to be regarded as remarkable; they had evidently lost the power of doing and saying commonplace things; moreover, their past history was raked up and discovered to bear marks of conspicuous originality. The village paper published biographical sketches of the boys.
>
> The widow Douglas put Huck's money out at six per cent., and Judge Thatcher did the same with Tom's at aunt Polly's request. Each lad had an income, now, that was simply prodigious—a dollar for every week-day in the year and half of the Sundays. It was just what the minister got—no, it was what he was promised—he generally couldn't collect it. A dollar and a quarter a week would board, lodge and school a boy in those old simple days—and clothe him and wash him, too, for that matter.[13]

Composing a long narrative, however, as one of "sivilization's" classic and prestige practices, requires the maker *not* to light out but to settle down and work hard in isolated, self-scrutinizing ways that few other civilized activities require—and, if successful, to run a risk of additional public attention. The finished, packed narrative itself proves that Huck wants to tell all, and to tell it right, yet somehow not become ensnared in the consequences of having told. And if *Huckleberry Finn* enacts a spoken narrative, an "as told to" arrangement in which Huck speaks and Mark Twain writes down, then Huck's motives for all this saying become even harder to define. Because there is no implicit urgency in the voice, is this perhaps an authoring of an opposite sort, authoring as a kind of amusement, self-indulgence for Huck as a locally notorious idler who supposedly still comes and goes as he likes? In the previous novel, Huck was not presented as an artist *manqué,* or for that matter as a diligent creator of anything. So what is happening here, psychologically, as Huck begins to compose (or as the narrative pretends that he does), or at least to say "You don't know about me"? In other words, how to describe better the drama of the narrative's creation?

If Huck sounds uneasy as he begins his account, unsure of how to get it all said truthfully or how to present himself, his first unsteady words are also part of the first signature of a thick, decorated volume, and the egregious physicality of the finished book dampens any suspense about this narrative as a struggle to finish narrating. Either on his own or in some obscure and chronology-bending collaboration with Mark Twain and the modern publishing industry, Huck has run the gauntlet, and in the first edition there are about two hundred printed pages to prove it. By putting that issue to rest, however, the materiality of the embossed and illustrated first edition of *Huckleberry Finn* intensifies the question of what manner of book the imaginary author thinks he is creating. The media revolution that made Mark Twain possible was only just breaking when Huck's adventures, and his imaginary adventure in authoring, supposedly unfold, and if one can envision Huck as settled in for a while, perhaps somewhere in a Missouri village, to construct his personal history one way or another, it is impossible to imagine him as doing this work with any inkling of the production system and market that Mark Twain's *Huckleberry Finn* was being readied for in 1884–85. And so the two narratives coexist: a verbal text to be imagined as written or spoken essentially as a private document, or a document intended at most for a limited and regional audience; and the same verbal text yet very different, the text constructed for, and transformed by, another set of technological and economic circumstances, illustrated by commissioned artists, printed by fast machines, gilded or speckled at the edges, expeditiously bound in the customer's choice of blue or green cloth or morocco leather, and shipped to places farther away than any "territory" Huck imagines when he thinks about lighting out for the Territory as soon as his memoir is done. To make a book in Huck's time in the rural heartland was to produce for what was still essentially a cottage industry, and that difference compounds the richness of Huck's narrative. His words are heard, and the cultural context, including the media context, is overheard. Mark

Twain is writing an illustrated book; Huck is not. Mark Twain is writing for a vast market; Huck himself, as a boy making a book, can harbor no such intentions or dreams. This means that as readers we have two books for the price of one, a naive personal history written or spoken by a boy in his teens, fresh from a perilous experience on the Mississippi River and telling it all essentially for his neighbors, and a performance by the most celebrated humorist of the Gilded Age, crafted as a mass-market corporate enterprise.

What can be gained by reading both texts at the same time? One possibility is an experience of a special kind of American nostalgia, extending beyond the quaintness of steamboats and the bygone, midcentury heartland pastoral. Actually, that quaintness is invoked only intermittently in the verbal and visual text of *Huckleberry Finn,* but it is regularly exaggerated when the novel undergoes mass-media exploitation in Hollywood movies, television specials, soft-focus posters and calendar pictures, tourist brochures and miscellaneous souvenirs, all influencing how the novel is remembered by multitudes who have not reopened it for years or read it at all.[14] The other nostalgia has to do with the nature of narrative itself, a nostalgia for a simpler and more innocent relationship between the speaker and the listener, the writer and the reader, when the word *you* that commences the telling of this book, "You don't know about me . . . ," presumes a "you" that Huck himself would "know about" better than a middle-aged and world-famous Mark Twain could ever "know" his own potential readers when he was writing in either Huck's voice or his own. Huck's "you" implies an audience with the limited social variety and the shared cultural experience that a much younger Sam Clemens, a boy close to Huck's age, would have imagined when the *Hannibal Journal* or any other small-town paper he worked at resorted to pronouns of direct address: "you," our readers and neighbors in Marion County, you who negotiate the same culture and historical moment as "we" who write and print the *Journal* this day—or as "me," the actual, corporeal writer and printer of the issue you happen to be holding.

Huck's narrative frequently evokes that lost intimacy, the regionally privileged experience and discourse that an American media revolution is in the process of inundating at the moment of Huck's adventures. To listen to Huck is to encounter many indications that his story is indeed about a specific place and time and is a story addressed *to* that place and that time. Witness the offhandedness, the assumed commonality, with which he refers to the ordinary equipage and bric-a-brac of rural Missouri life at that moment in the first half of the nineteenth century. His account is littered with material that provokes footnotes now and would have puzzled many Boston- and London-bred readers even in the year of the book's first appearance: split-bottom chairs and case knives and sugar hogsheads, miscellaneous accoutrements of backwoods cabins and village parlors, "home-knit galluses," the impedimenta of farmhouse parlors and bedrooms, backwater village streets, wrecked boats and uprooted houses floating on the river. Such are the adornments of a narrative asserting its own moment and site, a past that is also in a sense a prologue, a world on the edge in several ways at once.

To position the narrative itself on that edge, Huck's omissions are even more interesting than his passing allusions to the everyday physical stuff of life in rural Missouri and Arkansas forty years before. As a traveling reporter, Mark Twain commonly takes care to resituate himself and his readers with each remove and each new visited locale. *The Innocents Abroad* explains where the great church of the Lateran is located in Rome, where in Sicily to find the Blue Grotto, where the Mars Hill in Athens lies in relation to the Acropolis; without recourse to maps, readers of *Roughing It* have clues to hypothesize the distance and general direction of Lake Tahoe and Mono Lake from Virginia City and which way the Placer mining district is from San Francisco. For the first edition of *Life on the Mississippi,* Mark Twain wanted to include an enormous chart of the river—apparently twenty pages long, according to one notebook musing in 1882,[15] and indicating every hamlet, bend, and reef that figured in the narrative. *Tom Sawyer* is full of details about the geography of the action.

Compared to the scene-setting information packed into those books, Huck's narrative is terse to a fault. He does tell us that Jackson's Island is "about two mile and a half down stream" from his father's cabin, which is somewhere on the Illinois shore across from St. Petersburg; but beyond that, the global positioning of Huck's adventures is generally blurry. Where exactly is Goshen, Missouri, in relation to Huck's hometown? Where are Pokeville and Pikeville and Bricksville, or the Grangerford place, the Wilks house, and the Phelps farm? Some of these places are barely mentioned by name, and although conscientious students of the novel have constructed maps locating all of them, guessing their distance from St. Petersburg and one another, these are not matters that Huck himself attends to. When steamboats or other watercraft happen by on the river, their architecture and visible operations are ignored by a narrator who seems to assume that whoever takes up his book will know quite enough of the picturesque details of what he is talking about. As a boy raised along this river and taking its geography and appearance pretty much for granted, Huck is telling his story for people who are assumed to know all that and who do not have to be told the particulars, just as veterans of World War II, listening to personal experiences of fellow soldiers, want no explanation as to what a BAR was, or a Lancaster or a Sherman or a *Panzerfaust* or a Bangalore torpedo, for in not saying such things, or not calling for them to be said, tellers and listeners can reaffirm a privileged connection, a special bond. Likewise, the omissions in Huck's account, its obliviousness with regard to telling locations, describing contraptions that were exotic or antique in other places even in the year of the novel's publication, or describing regional folkways and religious practices and backwater superstitions, sustain a similar impression of intimacy, a sense that we as readers are being allowed into reminiscences and confessions that many among us are not qualified to understand, accepted into a circle of cultural knowing where most American and British readers, even in 1885, and most of us who come after, did not and do not belong.

But *Huckleberry Finn* is also about a violent closing of cultural divides. This is a world in crisis; and when Mark Twain returned to the story to finish it after a three-year hiatus, he developed that crisis into an important dimension of the tale. We have seen that when Sam Clemens began his professional training as a printer in Hannibal, the town and its old-technology print culture were being rocked by industrialized publication, a disruptive pressure of documents floating and rolling into this region from St. Louis, Cincinnati, and the East Coast. Huck's world is essentially young Sam's world, and Huck's world is shaking from the same tremors. The adventure with Jim is more than a sequence of conspiracies and narrow escapes in which printed pages play a part, requiring Huck to exploit or evade predicaments that have their roots in books, magazines, handbills, wanted posters, and other artifacts of local and national-market publishing. It also portrays the struggle of a young author to construct, and at the same time to resist, the narrative of his own experience within and against an attack of verbal and visual texts mass-produced in places that to him and his neighbors are only mysterious and evocative names.

Huck's journey with Jim down the river is a voyage through sites of print-inflected cultural disruption. Tom Sawyer's bookishness, his expertise about "pirate books, and robber books," has been only a nuisance to Huck in the opening chapters and an early comic lesson that cheap popular fiction from the European and American metropolis is reaching youngsters in these Missouri riverside villages. The farther Huck flees with Jim, however, the more pervasive and insidious this incursion of print from other places seems to become.

The first and best-known direct encounter with its lethal implications is at the Grangerford farm, where a counterfeit gentility and a pseudochivalric family style borrowed out of books, magazines, and wall-hung lithographs are warping imaginations and getting people killed. At the climax of the episode, Buck Grangerford, who is a boy about Huck's age, and a cousin named Joe (about whom Huck says very little) are destroyed by their own subscription to these pretensions. Packing rifles, they go out to engage in a manly and chivalric *geste,* enacting a behavior absorbed from their pompous father and the publications in the farmhouse parlor. Intending to "fetch home a Shepherdson or bust," they are overwhelmed and shot by a gang of men from that family. The Grangerford who most thoroughly represents the destructive consequences of mass-market American publishing, however, is the dead daughter Emmeline, whose literary and artistic remains and morbid temperament Huck encounters in the young girl's consecrated bedroom. Oddly enough, Emmeline's verse and her pictures are the comic center of this episode, and much has been said about the dynamics of the humor here and the real-life analogues for her dismal poetry. Emmeline Grangerford has been paying too much attention to what her family makes available to read and gaze at in this isolated place, where big-city print is intruding like an exotic infection. Her imitations of these poems, engravings, and lithographs are now part of the permanent status display:

> This table had a cover made out of beautiful oil cloth, with a red and blue spread-eagle painted on it, and a painted border all around. It come all the way from Philadelphia, they said. There was some books, too, piled up perfectly exact, on each corner of the table. One was a big family Bible, full of pictures. One was "Pilgrim's Progress," about a man that left his family, it didn't say why. I read considerable in it, now and then. The statements was interesting, but tough. Another was "Friendship's Offering," full of beautiful stuff and poetry; but I didn't read the poetry. Another was Henry Clay's Speeches, and another was Dr. Gunn's Family Medicine, which told you all about what to do if a body was sick or dead. There was a hymn book, and a lot of other books. . . .
>
> They had pictures hung on the walls—mainly Washingtons, and Lafayettes, and battles, and Highland Marys, and one called "Signing the Declaration." There was some that they called crayons, which one of the daughters which was

dead made her own self when she was only fifteen years old. They was different from any pictures I ever see before; blacker, mostly, than is common. (137)

Hilarious and creepy, Emmeline's "crayons" recall a mystery that also pertains to Huck's own narrative, the mystery of how and by whose intervention this supposedly roughhewn text, Huck's text, has come into its final form. Because Emmeline "was only fifteen years old" when she made these drawings, and Huck is only about fourteen years old when he supposedly produces his memoir, they have something in common as artists, for both of them are adolescent amateurs experimenting in the professional work of adults. And though Emmeline's poems and pictures are terrible, even the worst of them can be understood, if not exactly excused, as ruins from an artistic process that was never lucky enough to be amended by the skilled intervention of others, the remedial powers of the same industrialized publishing system that scrambled her thinking in the first place. Like one of Mark Twain's notebook cartoons inserted for comic surprise in *A Tramp Abroad,* Emmeline's intended "masterpiece," her drawing of a distraught young woman who is about to jump to her death, is presented as an interrupted draft, unredeemed by options that modern grown-up picture printers have at their disposal:

> It was a picture of a young woman in a long white gown, standing on the rail of a bridge all ready to jump off, with her hair all down her back, and looking up to the moon, with the tears running down her face, and she had two arms folded across her breast, and two arms stretched out in front, and two more reaching up towards the moon—and the idea was, to see which pair would look best, and then scratch out all the other arms; but as I was saying, she died before she got her mind made up, and now they kept this picture over the head of the bed in her room, and every time her birthday come they hung flowers on it. Other times it was hid with a little curtain. The young woman in the picture had a kind of a nice sweet face, but there was so many arms it made her look too spidery, seemed to me. (138–39)

The APC's artists and technicians could begin with a Mark Twain chicken-scratch or a few lines of suggestive verbal text and produce plausible vistas of Swiss Alps or German rivers they had never seen. What might the unseen minions of American corporate publishing have done for Emmeline's "masterpiece"? Kemble's accompanying picture of Emmeline's picture is a skilled representation of a ludicrous deficit of skill but also of a step in those intermediate processes by which even the skilled artist works by stages toward whatever is finally transferred to the electroplate, or by which the imperfect picture is touched up and made presentable by others in a publishing organization. As a girl intoxicated by the printed page, Emmeline lives and dies too far from the hubs of the industry that nurtures and poisons her, an industry that already has the technological power to turn almost anything into passable, or at least salable, images and words.

At several places in *Huckleberry Finn,* Huck's memoir comes back to this theme of "art," literary and otherwise, coming straight from the hand of the artist working alone, in emulation of things seen in verbal documents and images printed somewhere else. We are treated to the clumsy "crayon" sketch, the one-shot draft of the poem nobody reads or remembers, the hackwork of writers in isolation. As for his own "scratch-outs," Huck almost never includes them in his narrative. He leaves out the remains of sentences or chapters drafted on paper or in his mind and then abandoned as intermediate stages in a creative literary process—where there might have been three pairs of arms, in a sense, before Huck did what authors usually do, settling on one best alternative. There are two exceptions, however, moments when Huck's narrative seems to stay "too spidery," like Emmeline's unfinished picture. In Chapter XXXI, the passage in which Huck tells of writing a short message to Miss Watson and ripping it up soon after has been highlighted by generations of readers as a key moment in a kind of Old Southwest *Stances du Cid,* a young hero's lonely struggle to achieve a noble and dangerous moral resolve. If the passage in question plays such a role in the novel, it does so with conspicuous variance from Huck's usual rhetorical style:

> So I was full of trouble, full as I could be; and didn't know what to do. At last I had an idea; and I says, I'll go and write the letter—and *then* see if I can pray. Why, it was astonishing, the way I felt as light as a feather, right straight off, and my troubles all gone. So I got a piece of paper and a pencil, all glad and excited, and set down and wrote:
>
>> Miss Watson your runaway nigger Jim is down here two mile below Pikesville and Mr. Phelps has got him and he will give him up for the reward if you send.
>> HUCK FINN. (269)

[handwritten marginal note: different crude writer]

In punctuation, syntax, and other niceties of writing, why is there such a discrepancy here between the crudeness of Huck's note and the comparative elegance of the lines introducing it? Describing the act of writing this message, Huck's periodic sentences are offered with commas in the proper places, dashes for flourish, a colon—and two semicolons! How many American college students understand the uses of a semicolon? Though these three introductory sentences assert once again that Huck (or whoever is copying all this down) needs no tutoring in the pacing and punctuating of English prose, the note itself shows no hint of that proficiency. This discontinuity in Huck's literacy connects to questions we began with, about when Huck is to be thought of as constructing this memoir and whether the prose on this or any page can be understood as truly and completely his own.[16] Do the outbreaks of semicolons and periodic sentences nudge "Huck" out of the way and reintroduce Mark Twain as the real writer implicit in this discourse? Or is the inference something else, that phantom editors lurk somewhere between the "piece of paper" and the finished book, transforming Huck's "real" voice into discourse appropriate to the printed page? One way or another, Huck's narrative flaunts here a contrast between his ineptitude as a note writer and his considerable literacy as an author, leaving a mystery as to how, or with what ghostly assistance, the young man's prose has changed. Why should Mark Twain create that problem at all? Why not punctuate—which is to say, why not let Huck punctuate—this crucial message to Miss Watson? If there is no reason to make an interpretive mountain out of a couple of missing commas, the incongruity here is part of a larger pattern whereby the narrative draws attention to differences between the raw and the cooked in the making of discourse and specifically in the making of discourse for the printed page.

Elsewhere in the novel, Huck's level of literacy surprises in other ways. In Chapter XXIII, only a page or two after the confidence men, with Huck and Jim in tow, flee the village of Bricksville to avoid ambush by an incensed audience at the third performance of the Royal Nonesuch, Huck delivers an extended chaotic lesson to Jim about the history of kings in Renaissance and Restoration England, spiced with random inclusions from the Middle Ages, the history of France and America, and fragments of Shakespeare and *The Arabian Nights*. As Huck tries to share with his friend what he thinks he knows about that history, he is funny and satiric without knowing it because his monologue cavorts innocently in treacherous zones among printed text, comprehension, and memory—between the content published in grammar school history textbooks and what this one boy has "learned" from being hauled through them. Huck is trying for comparisons between the supposedly royal folk that he and Jim are traveling with and the real thing:

"You read about them once—you'll see. Look at Henry the Eight; this'n's a Sunday School Superintendent to *him*. And look at Charles Second, and Louis Fourteen, and Louis Fifteen, and James Second, and Edward Second, and Richard Third, and forty more; besides all them Saxon heptarchies that used to rip around so in old times and raise Cain. My, you ought to seen old Henry the Eight when he was in bloom. He *was* a blossom. He used to marry a new wife every day, and chop off her head next morning. And he would do it just as indifferent as if he was ordering up eggs. 'Fetch up Nell Gwynn,' he says. They fetch her up. Next morning, 'Chop off her head!' And they chop it off. 'Fetch up Jane Shore,' he says; and up she comes. Next morning, 'Chop off her head'—and they chop it off. 'Ring up Fair Rosamun.' Fair Rosamun answers the bell. Next morning, 'Chop off her head.' And he made every one of them tell him a tale every night; and he kept that up till he had hogged a thousand and one tales that way, and then he put them all in a book, and called it Domesday Book—which was a good name, and stated the case. You don't know kings, Jim, but I know them; and this old rip of ourn is one of the cleanest I've struck in history." (199)

This is only about half the lesson, which rolls on through Henry VIII's involvement with the Boston Tea Party and the murder of his father, the Duke of Wellington, in a "butt of mamsey, like a cat." If we try to classify this monologue—one of Huck's longest in the novel—as a stock comic interlude, one ignoramus misinforming another, then what we have here is a borrowing from minstrelsy. For at least two reasons, however, such a description will not hold. First, Huck's quick tour through these monstrous kings and his jumbling of Henry VIII with King Shahryar are ludicrous on higher levels of sophistication than a minstrel act would normally reach for. Apparently Huck has been *reading*, and though he has a garbled memory of what he has read, the lesson he offers Jim is in some measure a satire about what it means to have read a miscellany of histories and tales, how they swap around in the mind like the juices in his favorite kind of American dinner, and how in a culture beset by print a new idiocy becomes possible, an idiocy in which names, facts, and fiction are whirled together, making a mess that can pass for cultural literacy.

What enriches the comedy here is that although Huck has most of the names and events wrong, he has the crude historical book-learned patterns right, and his glib allusions to various bloodthirsty or incompetent royals— Charles II, Edward II, Louis XIV, James II, and so on—might win him a passing score on some standardized test favored by state bureaucracies, a modern multiple-choice nightmare of randomness and disconnection. On his raft of inaccuracies, Huck has floated to the right shore with regard to the fundamental meaning of the history he misremembers, for at least he understands the depravity that comes of wielding absolute power. Moreover, because by this point in the novel Huck has demonstrated that affectation is not one of his vices, his explications to his friend Jim are nearly impossible to read as a glimpse of Huck showing off. His friend has asked a question, about the character of kings, and Huck in good faith is providing the best answer he can, not putting on airs like a fool in a minstrel act.

So what is the comedy here about? Huckleberry Finn is a boy who skips school whenever he likes, and whose idea of a happy home is an empty barrel on a riverbank, a boy whose father is an illiterate and vicious drunk; but Huck is also, or nonetheless, a boy who can sustain a monologue of sorts on the character of monarchs in the European Middle Ages and Renaissance. In a madcap way, Huck can historicize. And one way to situate this bizarre self-quotation within Huck's story of his own adventures and to construe the passage as *Huck's* words rather than an intervention by Mark Twain at the expense of his narrator's credibility is to historicize Huck. But how can we do that? Is it possible to envision him as curled up in that barrel or upstairs in his bedroom in the Widow Douglas's house, quietly consuming volumes of English history and the *Thousand and One Nights* or paying sustained attention to schoolroom lessons on these subjects? Expanding and revising the book in 1883, Twain added a few lines to the beginning of Chapter XIV on Huck's reading to Jim "about kings, and dukes, and earls, and such" out of the "lot of books" they had harvested from the floating wreck. But this casual inclusion is hardly enough to change the impression about Huck's relationship to the printed page. The Tom-and-Huck narratives provide too little to support a conception of Huck as an avid reader on the sly or as a conscientious cultural historian in the rough. What we do know about him is that he is a capable social observer: that he takes in what transpires around him and understands the culture from which he wants to keep his distance.

And consistent with that general impression of Huck, we can see him here as a participant or as a victim (willing or otherwise) within an American rural culture scrambling to reinvent itself or maintain its footing under a rapidly increasing accumulation of published discourse. Before the first Bricksville show, Huck learns to double-talk Shakespeare "easy enough," picking up a twenty-five-line hodgepodge of *Hamlet* and *Macbeth* with just a touch of *Richard III* simply by listening in as the duke tutors the king. Huck lives and writes from a kind of cultural literacy that seems appropriate even to an "illiterate" boy in a time when print is intruding into ordinary life as never before, and when print-centered learning can be acquired, at least in choice fragments, simply by keeping company with people who are negotiating print more directly, as naive enthusiasts (like Tom Sawyer), as undiscriminating back-country emulators of gentility (like the Grangerfords), or as unscrupulous exploiters, like the duke himself.

Huck's stint as a fill-in lecturer on European history becomes more than a comic interlude, for it suggests how knowledge can circulate through the American West in a time when print is haphazardly abundant and how knowledge molts into plausible nonsense when it travels by such pathways—into the consciousness of the reader, thence to a muddled remembering and an eventual impromptu retelling to listeners whose own experience and unsteady attention will make another puree of whatever text or body of facts we might have begun with. Huck's mangling of what he thinks he has read or heard is at least benign. His corrupted comprehension of possibly corrupted printed texts doesn't get people killed, like the books and images in the Grangerford house, or cheat a succession of downriver fools, like the duke's ridiculous but serviceable fragments of Shakespeare and English theater history.

But one more glance is required at this historical effusion from Huck, specifically at the aside about "all them Saxon heptarchies that used to rip around so in old times and raise Cain," for this seems a special oddity amid Huck's string of offhand references to bad monarchs. The allusion seems a jump beyond the plausible for Huck, even in the context of this passage. If we can imagine the boy tuning in, on his nontruant schooldays, to the lurid domestic mayhem of Henry VIII and a scattering of other royals, and violent incidents notorious enough to have some presence in the schoolbooks and popular print culture of his own time, these Saxon kingdoms and feuds of the eighth and ninth century are more difficult to rationalize as leftovers from grammar school lessons or something encountered in books, magazines, and lithographs available to a print-shunning boy in a Missouri village in the 1840s. Is Mark Twain exploiting his narrator's voice here to show off that Mark Twain himself, as the grown-up author operating behind the ostensible boy-author, has had his nose lately in Carlyle or has been boning up on the European Dark Ages? If a case can be made that this is a lapse in the construction of Huck's identity, there are reasons to keep that judgment tentative. For what Mark Twain might be *reconstructing* here is a moment of anarchy in the evolution of an American democratic culture of the printed word. Copyrighted or pirated, butchered or competently transcribed, narrative history and pseudohistory have escaped the dominion of New England and Middle Atlantic bookshops and printing offices, and cheap texts are now abundant, if randomly so, in the riverbank villages of the heartland, making "literacy" even in this place a dynamic concept, complicating generalities that Tocqueville had offered only a decade before the time of the action, about a dispersed American public that as yet had only a limited range of things to read and showed no effects, salutary or otherwise, from exposure to works of imagination:

> The citizens of the United States are themselves convinced that it is not for them that books are published, that before they can make up their minds upon the merit of one of their authors, they generally wait till his fame has been ratified in England; just as in pictures the author of an original is held entitled to judge of the merit of a copy. . . .
>
> The inhabitants of the United States have, then, at present, properly speaking, no literature. The only authors whom I acknowledge as American are the journalists. They indeed are not great writers, but they speak the language of their country and make themselves heard. Other authors are aliens; they are to the Americans what the imitators of the Greeks and Romans were to us at the revival of learning, an object of curiosity, not of general sympathy. They amuse the mind, but they do not act upon the manners of the people.[17]

In *Huckleberry Finn*, however, the technology of printing is present in more ways than as tidy inventories on the table in the parlor, printed pictures on household walls, and consequent psychological damage to friends and strangers. In Chapter XIX an actual printer shows up in this novel, and he is a con artist:

> "Old man," says the young one, "I reckon we might double-team it together; what do you think?"
>
> "I ain't undisposed. What's your line—mainly?"
>
> "Jour printer, by trade; do a little in patent medicines; theatre-actor—tragedy, you know; take a turn at mesmerism and phrenology when there's a chance; teach singing-geography school for a change; sling a lecture, sometimes—O, I do lots of things—most anything that comes handy, so it ain't work. (160–61)

For the duke and the king, a favored weapon of deception turns out to be the printing press, which they exploit several times for a quick profit and convincing documents for the promulgation of lies. In this neighborhood, to set something up in movable type and print it off is to confer credibility, even upon the abjectly ridiculous. The duke carries a miscellaneous set of printed flyers as basic tools for imposture:

> The duke went down into his carpet-bag and fetched up a lot of little printed bills, and read them out loud. One bill said "the celebrated Dr. Armand de Montalban, of Paris," would "lecture on the science of phrenology" at such-and-such a place, on the blank day of blank, at ten cents admission, and "furnish charts of character at twenty-five cents apiece." The duke said that was *him.* In another bill he was the "world-renowned Shaksperean tragedian, Garrick the Younger, of Drury Lane, London." In other bills he had a lot of other names, and done other wonderful things, like finding water and gold with a "divining rod," "dissipating witch-spells," and so on. (168–69)

In the Mississippi valley of forty years before, print in quantity has come suddenly, and the rural public here is naive with regard to sorting out nonsense from news or telling valid credentials from those that are cooked up on the spot, composed directly on the composing stone. A local handpress at that moment is an apparatus for both community enlightenment and fraud, for promulgation of truth, informed opinion, nonsense, and counterfeit. Fake news stories, fake licenses and deeds and bills of sale and warrants, fake credentials and plaudits of every sort—anyone with access to a serviceable print shop and the skills to use it can produce not just legible inked paper but enhancements and alterations of personal and professional identity, embellishments of history, and radical (if transitory) revisions of local myth and wisdom.

When Huck and Jim are drawn into the con game webs of the duke and the king, the first town they strike is Pokeville, remembered for the king's histrionics at the camp meeting, his outrageous, and monetarily successful, masquerade as a pirate recently returned to America after thirty years of pillage in the Indian Ocean. Just before that show, however, the duke and the king part company for a while: "The duke said what he was after was a printing office. We found it; a little bit of a concern, up over a carpenter shop—carpenters and printers all gone to the meeting, and no doors locked. It was a dirty, littered-up place, and had ink-marks, and handbills with pictures of horses and runaway-niggers on them, all over the walls. The duke shed his coat and said he was all right, now" (170). So while the king emotes, the duke prints; and while he is at it he fleeces a few of the visiting townsfolk:

> He had set up and printed off two little jobs for farmers, in that printing office—horse-bills—and took the money, four dollars. And he had got in ten dollars worth of advertisements for the paper, which he said he would put in for four dollars if they would pay in advance—so they done it. The price of the paper was two dollars a year, but he took in three subscriptions for half a dollar apiece on condition of them paying him in advance; they were going to pay in cord-wood and onions, as usual, but he said he had just bought the concern and knocked down the price as low as he could afford it, and was going to run it for cash. He set up a little piece of poetry, which he made, himself, out of his own head,—three verses—kind of sweet and saddish—the name of it was, "Yes, Crush, Cold World, this Breaking Heart"—and he left that all set up and ready to print in the paper and didn't charge nothing for it. Well, he took in nine dollars and a half, and said he'd done a pretty square day's work for it. (174)

All of this is action offstage, print-shop labor and gratuitous literary effusion as recollected proudly by the duke himself. The contribution to the plot is that the group comes away with an additional nine dollars of "stake," a convincing "wanted" poster describing Jim (which, when brandished by smooth-talking white people on a raft, will allow them to travel in the daytime as slave catchers), and competently executed handbills for their first scam on the local stage. In the duke's "pretty square day's work," however, there are whispers of Sam Clemens's boyhood experiences in rural print shops like this one and of his life as an entertainer, wandering the Midwest, selling himself with handbills testifying floridly to his own prowess. Starving county papers like Orion's *Western Union* had tried to survive by demanding payment in advance for subscriptions—two dollars was in fact an advertised annual rate for the *Hannibal Journal* in 1852, and its publisher had to fend off payments in onions and cordwood in lieu of the coin of the republic. For their part, the prepaid subscribers to papers that Clemens had worked for could find themselves deprived of their money and their promised issues if the "concern" went bankrupt in the great tradition of village four-pagers. In other words, the duke's adventures here are described as much the same as the daily working life of folk who would normally inhabit this printing office: a few odd jobs completed, a few dubious promises for a trickle of money—and this final item, the poem, "kind of sweet and saddish," dreamed up by this genuine "jour" (the literal meaning is single-day) author-printer-publisher and set up in the press for no charge as a burglar's calling-card but also perhaps as a compensation for usurping the shop and for the trouble that the real owners will have with angry customers later on.

Is the writing and setting of the poem to be understood as a *frisson* of conscience from the duke? Is it a glimpse of nervous exuberance in a dishonest man who finds himself, for the moment, engaged in the semihonest trade he might actually like doing? Though a thin case could be made for either of those possibilities, we should also note a three-way similarity between some of this con man's exploits and publications, the career of the author who penned this nearly gratuitous paragraph as a "little piece of poetry," and the novel itself as a commodity, an act of creativity, and the quid pro quo of an exuberant national sales campaign. Soon after the Pokeville camp meeting, the duke goes to a print shop again—only as a customer this time, apparently—to prepare for the foray into Shakespeare:

> The first chance we got, the duke he had some show bills printed; and after that, for two or three days, as we floated along, the raft was a most uncommon lively place, for there warn't nothing but sword-fighting and rehearsing—as the duke called it—going on, all the time. . . .

The duke he hired the court house, and we went around and stuck up our bills. They read like this:

SHAKSPEREAN REVIVAL!!!
Wonderful Attraction!
For One Night Only!
The World-renowned Tragedians,
DAVID GARRICK THE YOUNGER,
of Drury Lane Theatre, London,
and
EDMUND KEAN THE ELDER,
of the Royal Haymarket Theatre, Whitechapel,
Pudding Lane, Piccadilly, London, and the
Royal Continental Theatres,
In their sublime Shaksperean Spectacle entitled
THE BALCONY SCENE
in
ROMEO AND JULIET!!! (180)

Outrageous misrepresentation from beginning to end—but what if we compare the duke's handbills with those for another ballyhooed event, a forthcoming book about "Tom Sawyer's Comrade" marketed throughout the United States, payment due upon delivery, obligating scores of thousands of Americans to receive and remunerate for something that turned out to be an entertainment experience considerably different from what they were led to expect? From a Webster Company canvasser's prospectus, circulated with Mark Twain's approval, and perhaps even authored by Mark Twain himself:

> WRITTEN IN MARK TWAIN'S OLD STYLE.
> This book is simply irresistible, and is pronounced by an author of
> WORLD-WIDE reputation and HIGH AUTHORITY, who has read the
> manuscript: "The brightest and most humorous book
> that Mark Twain has ever written."
> A BOOK FOR THE YOUNG AND THE OLD,
> THE RICH AND THE POOR.
> **A cure for melancholy.**—Nine-tenths of our ills are due to an
> over-burdened mind, an overtaxed brain, or imaginary troubles
> that never come. An amusing book is a panacea more agreeable
> than medicine and less expensive than doctors' bills.
> A MINE OF HUMOR
> FULL of startling incidents and hair-breadth escapes.
> 366 PAGES and 174 ORIGINAL ILLUSTRATIONS, NEARLY
> ONE HUNDRED PAGES LARGER THAN "ADVENTURES OF TOM SAWYER,"
> *with fourteen* more illustrations, better printed
> and more attractively bound, yet afforded at the *same price.*
> SOLD ONLY BY SUBSCRIPTION.

Cure for melancholy, mine of humor: *Huckleberry Finn* has amused generations, but it has held its spot in the American canon for other qualities than these. And *Huckleberry Finn* is written in exactly which of Mark Twain's "old" styles? The intention of the advertisement might be to reassure buyers that this book would not be another dose of the genteel narrating that Clemens had tried in *The Prince and the Pauper,* that *Huckleberry Finn* would sound more like the Mark Twain they had known before the excursion into Ye Olde England. But Mark Twain had never before published a long narrative in a Missouri dialect, much less a book almost entirely in the voice of a country boy. For the subscription buyers of this novel—most of whom would not have seen the tidied and modulated excerpts published in the *Century Magazine* in December 1884 and January and February 1885[18]—there would be other surprises. After all, *Tom Sawyer* had a plot, but this sequel opens with a promise by "G. G." (long assumed to mean General Grant, but possibly an inside joke referring to the Clemens family butler)[19] to shoot anyone who tries to find so much as a plot in what follows. *Tom Sawyer* was narrated by an urbane omniscient voice; *Tom Sawyer* was about a child learning to be loyal to his Aunt Polly, loyal in love, and noble and stoic in the face of adversity. He learns to keep his mischief within the bounds of social custom, and when he plays by those rules he is ultimately rewarded. When it was published, *Tom Sawyer* was not widely banned from libraries or attacked in the press as corruptive to American youth. If subscribers were signing up to buy a book like *The Adventures of Tom Sawyer*, what they got for their money could not have been what they bargained for—for it was not even the novel that Mark Twain had intended to write when he began it. In conceiving the duke as a printer as well as a con man and in opening this "campaign" as a mix of honest work (in a "borrowed" print shop), fraud, and a stab at poetry, Mark Twain playfully revisits his own professional past and his current incarnation—as printer, performer, author, publisher, huckster. In the months before its release, *Huckleberry Finn* was recognized as one of the most heavily advertised new books in American publishing history,[20] and with Clemens as pilot of that campaign, the published advertisements to recruit sales agents were as dubious as the promises to the American reader: "In returning to his old style of writing, Mark Twain is certainly in his element, for his book, while intensely interesting as a narrative;— holding the reader's attention with a tenacity that admits of no economy of midnight oil,—is also at the top of the list as a humorous work. Interwoven in its text are side-splitting stories, sly hits at different weaknesses of society, and adventures of the most humorous description. All of its forty-three chapters are simply overflowing with interest and humor."[21]

Sometimes mischievous, sometimes not, handbill hype had been part of Mark Twain's career since his early outings as a stage performer twenty years before. His famous ads from a postwar San Francisco performance dish out thick-sliced baloney and satirize the practice at the same time:

A Splendid Orchestra
Is in town, but has not been engaged.
Also,
A Den of Ferocious Wild Beasts
Will be on exhibition in the next block.
Magnificent Fire Works
were in contemplation for this occasion, but the
idea has been abandoned.
A Grand Torchlight Procession
May be expected; in fact, the public are privileged
to expect whatever they please.

The duke's announcement of himself and the king as Garrick the Younger and Kean the Elder is fraud, with no implicit joke except on a credulous bumpkin audience. Compared to the playful excess in the announcement of Mark Twain's San Francisco performance, the duke's notice for this "Shaksperean Revival!!" indulges in a different sort of noise, an amusing cacophony in which places and names and pedigrees blend into a music strange and familiar at once, and if there is satire in this comedy of maladroit pretension and fraudulence, it is satire about more than the semi-barbarism of the duke's own cultural experience and the more complete barbarism of the locals he takes in.

The deeper joke may be about knowing what we think we know as participants in a culture that so successfully dissociates picture knowledge and print knowledge from the real thing. When *Adventures of Huckleberry Finn* rolled off the presses, most Americans who could read and write "knew" who Mark Twain was, probably knew the face and reputation and perhaps some of the witticisms—but they could not know Mark Twain. Thanks to the popularity of Dickens, Trollope, and Macaulay and illustrated travel books and newspapers and magazines and popular histories of England, they might know that Piccadilly, Haymarket, Whitechapel, Drury Lane, and Pudding Lane were legendary locales in London; and some might even be aware that "Royal Haymarket Theatre, Whitechapel, Pudding Lane, Piccadilly, London," was a travesty of an illustrious address, that Whitechapel and Pudding Lane were at the other end of town from the theater hub of the West End. However, if this moment in *Huckleberry Finn* is intended to flatter some segment of its American audience, for at least an instant, as having a better store of secondhand London-savvy than the handful of Bricksville culture hunters who show up for the "Shaksperean Revival," the duke's printed handbill, failing to draw a good crowd, carries other implications, other mysteries. Though the duke knows nothing about London except random names, what he assumes at this point—perhaps wrongly—is that even the rubes of Bricksville have been struck, here and there, by these fragments of cosmopolitan cultural shrapnel, the ballistic scrap that this media assault is lobbing even as far as the Old Southwest, allowing these two roving charlatans to be glib about far-off lands that they know nothing about and to exploit local delusions of knowing a wider world, delusions absorbed from exposure to magazines and books.[22] If there is no way of telling in what measure the duke's handbills are meant as a private joke on this town or a manifestation of his own ignorance, the poor attendance at the show proves that in this case he has overestimated (or underestimated) the locals, who are not yet at the level of pretending to each other that they know London or revere Shakespeare and who want from their entertainers neither balcony scenes nor soliloquies.

After the flop of the opening night, the duke's next advertisement, "drawed off" with black paint rather than printed with movable type, packs the house with what he now regards as "these Arkansaw lunkheads" by cutting out the hodgepodge of London place names and promising a racy show for men only, exploiting a style more in keeping with these environs at this moment in their history: the hand-painted sign. Knowing now that Shakespeare and letterpress publicity are too high-flown a combination to "fetch 'em," the duke makes his new handbill a different mess of incongruity. It still touts "GARRICK THE YOUNGER!" and "EDMUND KEAN THE ELDER!" "*Of the London and Continental Theatres*"—but the promised entertainment this time subverts any inkling of sophistication. The menfolk of Bricksville have no taste for paradox in what they read or what they will pay fifty cents to watch. As far as they are concerned, European high culture and celebrity, convincingly faked or not, are only noise. These patrons want their amusement raw, and the only discourse that matters on this new poster is "the biggest line of all: LADIES AND CHILDREN NOT ADMITTED." Left over from the previous campaign, the Garrick and Kean allusions are now merely decorative, like a pretentious marquee on a run-down pornographic theater, providing a little "class" and cover for a salacious revue. Playfully, yet more intensely than the Grangerford episode, the Bricksville chapters of *Huckleberry Finn* ponder the impact of published words and images as they arrive haphazardly along these Mississippi shores.

If print from the distant city is sometimes plentiful and fresh, the culture to receive it and understand it is as yet unformed and unready; and what flourishes is a comic, dangerous carnival of clumsy exploitation and showing off.

In Chapters XXXIV through XLII of *Adventures of Huckleberry Finn*—the chapters in which Jim is imprisoned in a shed at the Phelps farm and Tom and Huck conspire to break him loose—the American publishing revolution looms large, and for generations readers have complained that with this final sequence, pushed along by a book-dizzy Tom Sawyer, who turns up out of the blue to take over the action, the novel loses its vitality and turns claustrophobic. Huck degrades into a mildly resentful and ineffectual sidekick, and in the "hut down by the ash-hopper" Jim is reduced to a compliant voice. Because Tom has come down the river with his usual baggage, a head stuffed with romantic popular fiction, what transpires from this moment onward can be called a drawn-out, low-intensity skirmish between Huck as a realist and Tom as an embodiment of virulent romanticism, a good target for Mark Twain's rage at the South of his own youth, its infatuation with borrowed postures institutionalized without comprehension from books by Walter Scott, James Fenimore Cooper, Alexandre Dumas,[23] and a legion of imitators whose cheaply reprinted novels mesmerized a region and a generation, promoting self-delusions that contributed to the disaster of the American Civil War.[24] So the tyranny of romance closes in, with Tom Sawyer as its obnoxious avatar, and for the balance of the novel Huck and Jim are trapped in a narrative by somebody else, a narrative mediated and re-mediated too many times to keep track of, moving from French into English and thence to the new and wide-open world of large-scale, low-quality, no-royalty book publishing in the United States. For such a reading—not of Scott, Dumas, and company, but of *Huckleberry Finn*—there is no great fault other than incompleteness. The final chapters may or may not be satisfying or structurally consistent with the exuberantly unstructured narrative that comes before, but Tom Sawyer's return to Huck's life and the clutter of book-borrowed "wisdom" that Tom imposes on his friends carry the narrative into further media troubles, complicating the adventure that Huck is trying to survive, the verbal account he is trying to finish, and the impersonation that Mark Twain is laboring to bring to a close.

There is considerably more in Tom's carpetbag of literary experience than a few recognizable works of romantic fiction, lately available to readers in rural Missouri. Tom Sawyer's imaginative life has also been fueled by published histories that were popular and even sanctioned at that time in American schoolrooms. Casanova, Baron Friedrich von der Trenck, Cellini, Henry of Navarre, and Abbé Faria: these people, who turn up in Tom's mind and in the games he plays at the Phelps farm, are not figures borrowed from popular romance. In fact, the real-life adventures and incarcerations that Tom is reenacting were being circulated in sensationalized yet expurgated biographies as an *antidote* to popular romance, a tactic for luring mid-century American youth, and especially boys of Tom's impressionable age, into imaginative negotiation with something resembling actual history rather than fantasy.[25] About twenty years after the time of the novel's action, the *North American Review* lamented the disappearance of these editions from the common experience of school-age children:

> With this permanence of fascination, one wonders that any new children's books should be needed. Yet while Robinson Crusoe and his peers still survive immortal, it is pathetic to reflect what argosies of fancy and of fact have gone down into the abyss of "out of print," within easy memory. Whither is departed that boyish literature so precious, that once throve in the shelter of school-desks, and under safe coverts of benches? It was a literature in itself innocent of moral guilt,—unless, perhaps, enormous lying be held an offence,—which yet possessed in its use, by reason of surreptitiousness, much of the sweet savor of sin. Baron Trenck was there, with his imminent deadly breaches,—Rinaldo Rinaldini, the Three Spaniards, and the Scottish Chiefs,— four nations sifted to find sufficient heroes of romance for us. These books were cautiously transmitted from hand to hand, in little, thin, dingy volumes, suitable to the pockets of youth, in editions which each boy secretly supposed to have been printed, like the classics, "for the use of schools." Nobody knew whence they came, nobody had ever bought them, nobody owned them, everybody borrowed them. Among the older boys there lurked a tradition that certain boys still older had left them behind on going to college,—bequeathed them to their younger brothers, still in bonds. The same mystery, or deeper, yet hangs over them.[26]

Tom is abusing what he knows, but at least he knows *something*, and the history of American publishing makes clear that by the middle of the 1840s this body of knowledge would be neither a peculiarity nor a financial impossibility for enthusiastic, indiscriminate young readers from ordinary homes and schools in villages like Hannibal.

Sam Clemens himself wanted to see American children running around with a head full of lively facts, preferably as selected and inculcated by himself, to fill the place vacated by these "thin, dingy volumes"; while finishing *Huckleberry Finn,* he was near the midpoint of his long tinkering with the History Game, and in 1885, the year of *Huckleberry Finn'*s publication in the United States, he copyrighted a version called *Mark Twain's Memory Builder, A Game for Acquiring All Sorts of Facts and Dates,* intended to nurture, not "cultural literacy" in the modern sense of the phrase, but rather a wide-ranging knowledge of dates and facts, most of them connected to monarchies, battles, and revolutions. The game's flyer of instructions stresses the difference:

and Twain's Anthology of Am Lit

> The greatest histories are the reverse of lavish with dates, and so one is sure to get the order and sequence of things confused unless he first goes to a skeletonized school-history and loads up with the indispensable dates beforehand. This will keep him straight in his course and always in sight of familiar headlands and light-houses, and he will make his voyage through the great history with pleasure and profit. Very well, if he will gather his dates and play them on the game-board a while, he may then attack any history with confidence.

"The most conspicuous landmarks in history," says the flyer, "are the accessions of kings; therefore these events are given the first place in the game and allowed to count the most. Battles come next." So in this context *history* signifies mostly European history, and European history means kings and combat, and the game board accordingly divides the "facts" you can score with into three categories. "Accessions" are worth ten points; "Battles" are worth five; and "Minor Events," covering everything that isn't either a coronation or royal demise or a general slaughter, will bring one paltry point apiece.

When he shows up at the Phelps house, Tom Sawyer comes equipped with the kind of chaotic but expansive training that could make him a competent player of a game like this, recalling the lurid details and exempted by the rules from making any profound sense of what he remembers. Tom's mental inventory of "history" is less jumbled than Huck's, yet Huck uses what he knows to teach and to try to make sense of people and the world right here, which he and Jim must negotiate. For Tom, remembered or half-remembered episodes or facts are only raw material for self-indulgent dreams and sport. In that time and context, his indoctrination is plausible. In his head he carries miscellaneous gleanings from those yellow-cover, popularizing histories of notorious Europeans, juicy chunks of French romantic novels, and "factoids" from respectable big-selling textbooks of that decade—fragments, for example, from the enormous output of Samuel Griswold Goodrich, who under the pseudonym of Peter Parley started turning out informative books for young people in the early 1830s and dominated the American public schools of the 1840s with what his Boston publisher advertised as "wholesome" volumes, entertaining as well as educational: *Famous Men of Modern Times* (1843), *Lives of Celebrated Women* (1844), *Celebrated American Indians* (also 1844), *A Pictorial History of England* (1846), *Peter Parley's Common School History* (1848), *History of Europe* (1849), and *The Balloon Travels of Robert Merry and His Young Friends over Various Countries in Europe* (1855), which taught geography and history in an unusual way and which might also be an overlooked source for the plot of the next Tom-and-Huck sequel that Mark Twain would finish, *Tom Sawyer Abroad.* Some of these Goodrich books were published also in London; a few of them were even translated into French and sold in Paris. To end *Huckleberry Finn,* Tom Sawyer returns to the action as a menace constructed not entirely of pernicious historical romance but also of this storehouse of ostensibly moral and "improving" reading, which he spins into a gaudy fabric to decorate and encumber real life.

But here a distinction is required, for this "real life" that Tom besieges at Phelps Farm is obviously not real life at all but another artifice of make-believe, a fiction about an imaginary man in a shed and two made-up boys in a fantasy-addled conspiracy to achieve his escape. There is another level of complication here if we want it: eventually we learn that Jim has been legally free for weeks, that Miss Watson has emancipated him and that Tom knows it when he arrives at the farm, and that Huck and Jim have been caught up not only in Tom's romantic prisoner fantasy but in a basic misconception Tom perpetrates about Jim's legal status. Any reading of the end of *Huckleberry Finn* has to negotiate the dilemma that what we have is a mildly suspenseful narrative about imprisonment, coerced into shape by the imposition of *other* fantasies and an accumulation of historical facts about other imprisonments, an imposition, in other words, of romantic fiction, outright deception, and incompetently recollected truth upon a fiction that might seem more true but isn't.

If an intention of these final chapters is to condemn popular romance as an American cultural vice especially pernicious for the young, then such moralizing would be not only as derivative as Tom's play but also disingenuous. Derivative, because social critics and self-appointed moralists had been publishing tirades, in national-circulation children's magazines, against overheated unwholesome books and stories as far back as the 1840s, in which this novel is set. It was an established editorial practice when the *Youth's Companion,* one of the popular nationally circulated children's magazines of midcentury, founded and edited for a while by Goodrich himself, offered this explanation for the moral monstrosity of John Wilkes Booth, twenty years before Mark Twain completed *Huckleberry Finn:*

> Does any young man feel as if he would like to be educated to do as daringly and dexterously as did Booth? Let him keep on, then, reading the bloody tales of the weekly story papers, or the flashy, ten cent, yellow-covered literature sold in almost every book store. He will soon learn how to be a hero of the approved romantic type. But, young friend, if you have any regard for your character, your future standing in society, the credit of your families, your own peace and the *welfare of your souls,* let such reading alone! . . . God has better pastime for you; better literature than that for your leisure hours. There is no aliment for the mind in that reading. Rather never read a printed line. Such material stimulates only the bad in your nature.
>
> We know the difference between offal-fed meat and meat fed on solid corn. The first ill-grained, washy and deleterious, the second substantial and healthy. Mind fed on offal follows the same law as meat. Victims of this intellectual and moral debasement are seen dawdling through society in every city and town, communicating poison to all who touch them. They are found in every low resort where the slang of vice is spoken; gaping about play-houses, and taking the lead in street riots. The penitentiary and the insane hospital harvest every year some of the avails of this literary garbage. Avoid it, young men and women, as you would the plague; as you would murder and treason![27]

And disingenuous, in light of the sales pitch in the advertising for *Huckleberry Finn.* "A cure for melancholy . . . a mine of humor full of startling incidents and hair-breadth escapes": another sensational story, in other words, and whether Mark Twain's customers got what they bargained for is beside the point. The record is clear: *Huckleberry Finn's* thematic somersaults with regard to American romantic tastes and sensational reading extended a long way beyond the "THE END, YOURS TRULY HUCK FINN" that closes Huck's narrative. The Concord Public Library notoriously declined to acquire and circulate the novel because the book itself, rather than the books it critiqued, was sensationalist and immoral, and with Clemens's enthusiastic urging, a set of mass-market American periodicals sensationalized that ban and boosted his sales.

Huckleberry Finn was, is, a made-up adventure story that intermittently admonishes against the evils of made-up adventure stories, and the marketing campaign that Clemens approved for it made no promise of moral improvement. The obdurate truth about these final chapters is that if Tom shows the salacious effects of an education in the wrong sort of modern fiction, he also turns the story of a man locked in a shed into a livelier tale of conspiracy, noble suffering, and procrastinated escape. Jim's ordeal is in some dimension a travesty of Byron's *Prisoner of Chillon* or the miseries of Edmund Dantes, but Jim is nonetheless a prisoner in his own right, evidently facing a return to slavery and perhaps a worse fate if he is sold down the river, and whether or not Tom is in charge, Jim may be killed if he tries to get away. With respect to old tropes of imaginative literature: though these final chapters indict, they also exploit. Huck complains and complies with Tom, and tells, in his vernacular, his version of "what happened." And as Huck endures a tyranny of mass-market sensational fiction, Mark Twain pleases a national audience by giving sensation-loving readers a bitter but generous slice of what they want.

Even so, there are further ranges. Because *Huckleberry Finn* is about a culture in the midst of a disruptive infusion of print, the personality of the teller and the text of the narrative both embody and enact that disruption. It is Huck himself, rather than Tom, who is struggling to create a personal ethos and a personal identity fit for survival in a world that launches borrowed, misunderstood cultural novelties at Huck and Jim throughout their adventures along the Mississippi River. Huck is memorable for his masquerades, and memorable also are the masquerades of the world he negotiates. Huck hides his truth, but the world he moves through has lost track of where and how deep the truth is hidden. He encounters people who aspire to kill, and who actually murder, on the basis of what they see on the printed page or what they hear from others intoxicated by such reading and seeing. Structurally, does the novel fall apart? The fact that most readers of *Huckleberry Finn* don't seem to care about thematic or formal imperfections urges a different approach to the question of its cultural value. What about reading *Huckleberry Finn* as a narrative also deftly configured for the actual moment of its completion and publication? At work on his sequel to *Tom*

Sawyer, Mark Twain, at the middle of his life and the beginning of his financial travails, felt anxiety that his own career and fortunes were floating away on a tide of other people's words, and on a red-ink sea of dangerous investment in companies and devices to manufacture and promulgate words. Those anxieties are mirrored in the most interesting novel that he wrote. It is Huck who tells the story, a boy with only scattered and secondhand experience with the etiquette of stories, and thanks to his youth and ignorance his performance seems mercifully free from loyalty to conventions that Gilded Age narratives were supposed to respect in order to situate themselves on the ever-expanding booklist that guaranteed their oblivion. Huck is an author because he either tells or writes, yet Huck is not a professional who, as he tells, sacrifices his sense of the truth. He tells his adventures guilelessly, and if the "form" of his narrative seems as barbaric as his yawp, this disregard for conditioned expectations is one of the pleasures of "his" book, the book that he has made.

Huck's voice and story, then, resist the encroachment of the typographic. Movable type signified power to Samuel Clemens, but it also signified inhibition. In his boyhood, print had required him to turn himself and his professional thinking literally backwards in order to do his job. "THE END, YOURS TRULY HUCK FINN": in the novel's closing line, Huck lays his claim once again as this narrative's *author.* On the final page, as he grumbles about how hard it is to make a book, he underscores that this has been his project and nobody else's. But the cover of the book, the front matter, and the copyright all say otherwise, and once again the physical artifact and the text of this mass-market project keep alive the question of who is to be imagined as the maker. The structure and the embellishment of *Adventures of Huckleberry Finn,* as a novel and as a commodity, contradict the implications of the voice, challenging our own imaginative engagement with this narrative, physical object, cultural event, and work of art.

Chafing at pop-culture values that Mark Twain, as the author of the author, variously satirizes and indulges, Huck creates personal memoirs for an earlier phase of an American media crisis than Mark Twain wrote the novel for; and with this "YOURS TRULY," Huck passes away like a ghost, a voice from a generation that is also gone. But the "Territory" that he means to light out for has also (and long since) been conquered by print, and in announcing this last vain intention Huck grows quaint. The blank space at the bottom of the final page, below the final image, becomes the real ending, bearing a message that this engaging boy is grown up and gone away.

And who is, or was, "the rest" that the fleeing Huck would stay ahead of? Civilization, certainly—but also, by implication, the unstoppable westward push of books and magazines that would obliterate the culture he knows and thereafter, probably, this book that he has made. Yet "the rest" also participates in the making of Huck himself, as well as his book: their various crafts are redolent in the finished thing, and the verbal text closes with the movable-type signature of a young author who never was. Huck's narrative, as a creative act, can be imagined as a complex act of refusal, even of subversion; Mark Twain's impersonation of Huck is an act of subversion as well. Working together, what do they subvert? The etiquette and the ostensible reliability of the omniscient narrative voice, to be sure, but also the constrictive civilities of an industrializing American literary culture, orthodoxies of structure, form, plot, dictated by a publishing and marketing system that was acquiring the pathologies of an industry. They resist the disappearance of the author into the accumulation of his own printed words, the compounding perils of modern literary success.

FIVE

Mark Twain
and the Information Age

To be sure, not every one can be, like Mr. Clemens, his own
Harper & Brothers, and his own Edwin Booth.

EDMUND CLARENCE STEDMAN

Schizophrenia may be a necessary consequence of literacy.

MARSHALL MCLUHAN

In constructing a drama of Mark Twain's life, the last act has been skillfully
rewritten, many times, with different moods and themes in ascendance. So
much was going on—with his family, his circle of friends and assistants, his
finances, his interactions with admirers around the world, and his psychological and physical health. And though after 1895 the new work he
published grew sparse, in his final years an avalanche of writing heaped up:
journals, notebooks, autobiographical dictations, reams of business correspondence from him and to him; personal letters and private diaries by others, with Mark Twain as the center of attention; and a stack of imaginative
manuscripts, some of them nightmares and wish-dreams. Depending on
who reads all this, and when, and with what valuation assigned to each document, Mark Twain's biographers have given us many endings to the story.
We can have him as a victim of modernity, a casualty of new scientific and
social thought; as a tragic hero, undone by his own devices and desires; as
a shadow of his former self, weakened in his wits and his creativity; as a
lonely warrior, achieving some kind of ultimate victory over his own fears
and personal circumstances—or perhaps only a dignified armistice.[1] The
Mark Twain legend abides for many reasons, including the malleability of

the record. In every return to heroes from the American cultural past, to infuse them with our own imaginative blood and bring them back for whatever kind of kinship we might require, Mark Twain has been a wonderful subject for reanimation.

I have suggested that the life and the work of Samuel Clemens can also be understood as a mirror for a different sort of contemporary predicament, different from the treacheries of celebrity, debilitating age, loss of confidence and creative fire, or the great amorphous challenge we call modernity. Mark Twain's final years show us a media revolution absorbing an individual talent into a multidimensional turmoil, affecting the intention of literary texts, the connection of the writer to his own words, and the public identity that his own words had constructed. In the last twenty years of his life, Mark Twain struggled to achieve several kinds of dominance in American printing and publishing, while he also worked to maintain his own autonomy and fame. When he failed as an investor and a publisher, the price of defeat was loss of that independence and the ascendancy of others in the design, the marketing, and even the intention of literary texts that were still supposedly his. The visual component of these printed works often became more than embellishment, more than thematic enrichment. At times, these images would rival the verbal text for space in the book and for ascendancy in the establishment of tone and theme.

Though printed in his lifetime, and usually with his endorsement or at least his acquiescence, Mark Twain's books after 1895 were no longer under his dominion as they had been in previous years, when he had wielded extraordinary leverage with his publishers or had owned the house outright. When this ascending baron of the American media became one of the casualties instead, his imagination veered in new directions with regard to the cultural and psychological power of the printed page. He contemplated the triumph of the published image, and in one of his last long narratives he wrote about the rise of printing and the transformation of personal identity; the heady power and the ultimate futility of the printer and the author; and the transcendence, or dissolution, of the individual self in a sea change wrought by published words.

Between the first edition of *Huckleberry Finn* and 1890, Mark Twain came as close as he ever would to being both a media tycoon and an arbiter of American literary culture. He still had hopes that some version of a "history game" with his name on it would be for sale in the stores or featured in the newspapers;[2] in affluent American homes, three feet of shelf space would be filled by a uniform set of national literary masters, with his own work among them, published by his own company. In production plants where written words become printable, revolutionary equipment for that conversion would prove him right and make him rich. In its first year of release *Huckleberry Finn* had been a modest success, and by the end of 1886 his Charles Webster Company had an impressive array of titles either on the market or in the pipeline. *Personal Memoirs of U. S. Grant* had won critical acclaim and was selling better than any other nonreligious book in American subscription-trade history.[3] Grant's swashbuckling corps commander in the Army of the Potomac, "Phil" Sheridan, had also written a *Personal Memoirs* with WebsterCo, describing campaigns in the deep South, in the Shenandoah Valley, and out west in the Indian Wars. Closing with Sheridan's eyewitness report of Bismarck's 1870 destruction of the armies of Napoleon III, the two-volume 1888 edition featured twenty-seven well-executed maps and a comprehensive index. Meanwhile, *McClellan's Own Story* (1887), stopping with the Battle of Antietam in September 1862, was still thick enough for subscription sale: seven hundred pages, with fourteen illustrations and an extended biographical preface (McClellan had died in the fall of 1885) by Mark Twain's erstwhile satiric target W. C. Prime, whose *Tent Life in the Holy Land* he had ridiculed in *The Innocents Abroad.*

When famous generals (or *brevet* ones, as was true with Custer) had passed on without telling all in their own words, widows were brought under contract. After Second Army Corps Commander Winfield Scott Hancock died in February 1886, WebsterCo produced a haphazard *Reminiscences* (1887) compiled by his wife. Mrs. George Armstrong Custer's *Tenting on the Plains,* lionizing her impetuous late husband with 702 pages and twenty-nine illustrations, appeared in the same year. The company also had plans for both an autobiography and a *Life of Christ* by Henry Ward Beecher, who was still the best-known religious leader in America, even after the adultery trial in Brooklyn in 1875, or perhaps because of it. When Beecher died suddenly in March 1887, less than a month after signing the contract,[4] the company worked at high speed with his widow and son to produce an illustrated biography while the national memory was green, turning out seven hundred pages from Beecher's notes and drafts in less than a year. For an expanding and increasingly affluent community of American Catholics, WebsterCo was offering a Vatican-endorsed biography of Leo XIII, the reigning pope, a tome guaranteed to come with "Two colored plates, two steel plates, and twenty-two other full-page illustrations."[5]

Though typesetting machines competing with the Paige were moving into the market, Mark Twain still had hopes for his compositor's success, and the project's damage to his personal finances was not yet lethal. With Kaolatype in a coma, he was sporadically busy and buoyant about "Mark Twain's Memory Builder," whose development and marketing he had required Charles Webster to take on as an additional responsibility, with mercurial instruction from Clemens along the way. And through the balance of the 1880s, the "Memory Builder" project remained another bonanza in the pipeline—at least in the mind of its creator.

In cultural and literary importance, several of the books produced by Mark Twain's company in its single decade of operation moved bravely beyond the standard fare of his subscription-trade competitors, including the extensive lists of the APC.[6] Most of WebsterCo's books sold well enough to do no financial harm; the problem was that after Grant's *Personal Memoirs* there was no other smash hit to overcome the liability of the Paige and the other schemes. Among these publishing ventures, the only one that did serious damage was *A Library of American Literature from the Earliest Settlement to the Present Time,* which came into the firm, with Mark Twain's assent, in the late winter of 1887 but which did not reach the market as a complete set until 1895, the final year of the company's life.

In the history of American publishing, the *Library* is still a landmark achievement, and for reasons other than its role in sinking Mark Twain's house and bringing on its bankruptcy. In funding this project—ten volumes, octavo, with about six hundred pages per tome, including selections from about 1,100 authors from Captain John Smith to the present, with biographies of all and portraits of many, and with an additional volume containing a thirty-five page index, author biographies, and other apparatus—Clemens was moving into risky territory, in both the American book publishing business and the construction of a national canon. From conventional trade houses, individual volumes and extensive sets assembling prose and poetry by American greats were fairly common near the nineteenth century's end. Publishers in Boston and New York were turning out handsomely bound "standard editions" of famous authors and multivolume collections of Great Books, sometimes selected for the general public by a board of worthies[7] and garnished with expensive polychrome illustrations. But these projects seem modest when compared to WebsterCo's *Library.*

Needing a mastermind for the set, the company contracted with one of Clemens's old acquaintances, the brilliant, emotionally volatile Edmund

Clarence Stedman, who had first proposed and begun the project with a Cincinnati publisher. With blood connections to Boston Brahmins and Ivy League credentials of a sort (he had been expelled from Yale for misconduct but was invited back and honored many years later for turning out better than expected), Stedman came with a long list of high-toned publications: poems, belles lettres essays, criticism, biographies, editions and collections of other authors, and two respected historical surveys, *Victorian Poets* (1875), and *Poets of America* (1885). He offered the prestige and old-school literary connections that a project of this scope required, especially one coming from the wrong side of the publishing tracks, the subscription trade. Having made a name for himself on other fronts as well, including as a Civil War correspondent for the *New York World*, Stedman now had a seat on the Stock Exchange, where he had been doing well enough financially to attract Clemens's attention as a possible investor for the Paige.[8] Stedman and Clemens had mutual friends, including Howells, the late Bayard Taylor (with whom Stedman had corresponded warmly and frequently),[9] and Thomas Bailey Aldrich, who had collaborated with Stedman on an edition of poems by Walter Savage Landor. In an autobiographical dictation, Clemens remembered Stedman as part of "the gay company that used to foregather in Boston, thirty-five years ago, and more"—which implies that the personal relationship dated back to the 1870s.[10] To work with Stedman, the company also hired Ellen ("Nellie") McKay Hutchinson, a versatile young author with energy and common sense as well as a pedigree. Descended from Hutchinsons of the Bay Colony, she had published poetry in the *Century,* short fiction in the *St. Nicholas Magazine,* and a kindly reviewed collection,[11] *Songs and Lyrics,* issued in 1881 by Osgood, which in that year was also publishing *The Prince and the Pauper.* It is worth remembering that in this early experiment with a comprehensive American anthology, a woman writer, according to Stedman, had veto power over all selections for the *Library* and a major role in bringing these elaborate volumes together.[12]

Three years would pass between the signing of those agreements and production of the first segments of the *Library,* however, and as the heavy books rolled from the binderies, they entered the national subscription market as it began to falter. To cover the production expenses, they were priced at a frightening $33 for the set. For comparison: from the Sears mail-order catalogs of that time, a five-foot solid oak roll-top desk and a Singer sewing machine, complete with a stand and accessories, could be ordered together for less money, delivery included.[13] To make headway in selling at that price,

WebsterCo was required to offer *LAL* on an installment plan at payments of three dollars per month and with the company paying the full commission to the canvasser at the outset. The strategy was a recipe for up-front red ink, which time and luck would supposedly turn into profits someday.[14] As delays and expenses connected to *LAL* piled up in the early 1890s, Clemens, who may or may not have expressed initial reluctance about taking on this project,[15] agonized about the scope of the enterprise and the depth of his own liability: "We issue 50,000 general books & 24000 sets *LAL* a year & still no dividends & no reduction of debt," he scribbled in a notebook between August 1890 and June 1891. "How many of the two *are* required to produce a result?"[16]

As for Stedman, he remained a believer, which was part of the problem for Clemens and Fred Hall, who took over daily operations of the company from the ailing and demoralized Webster in 1888. The *Library*'s general editor did not concern himself with mundane matters like positive cash flow from sales or the financial survival of the issuing house. Sending the first seven volumes of the set to Walt Whitman (whose work was also represented in the *Library*), Stedman gushed to his friend about the cultural *gravitas* of the undertaking:

> [Y]ou of all men will take in, comprehend, the purpose, the meaning, of this compilation. *You* will justly estimate its significance, and this quite irrespectively of its literary or artistic qualities. There are masterpieces in it. But it is *not* a collection of masterpieces: it is something of more moment to you and me. It is *America*. It is the symbolic, the essential, America from her infancy to the second Century of her grand Republic. It is the diary, the year-book, the Century-book, of her progress from Colonialism to Nationality. All her health and disease are here: her teething, measles, mumps, joy, delirium, nuptials, conflicts, dreams, delusions, her meanness and her nobility. We purposely make the work *inclusive*—trying to show every facet of this our huge, as yet half-cut, rose-diamond.[17]

Stedman's hyperbole here seems Whitmanesque, but he wasn't far wrong about the uniqueness of what Mark Twain's company was out to achieve. In its contents, *A Library of American Literature* shows a comprehensiveness and diversity that put to shame even the bulkiest anthologies for college courses in "Am Lit," which began reaching captive audiences of American undergraduates a quarter-century later. The *Library*'s African American array, for example, includes not only Frederick Douglass but also selections from George Washington Williams, rarely remembered now as the author of *History of the Negro Race in America* (1883), the first African American graduate of the Newton Theological Seminary, the first black man to serve in the Ohio Legislature, and an early and outspoken critic of King Leopold II's Congo Free State. Several pages of "Negro Hymns and Songs" are also presented for their literary value. Women writers in *LAL* include many safe choices—Bradstreet, Rowson, Lydia Maria Child, Stowe, Sedgwick, Susan Warner, Lydia Sigourney, and Constance Fenimore Woolson—but some of the heretics are here as well, like Margaret Fuller and Elizabeth Cady Stanton; and there are dozens of women novelists, short-story writers, essayists, and poets who have subsequently dropped off the historical radar. Among these are Sarah Boyle, Edith M. Thomas, Esther Carpenter, Nora Perry, Arabella Eugenia Smith, Ella Wheeler Wilcox, and Virginia Wales Johnson. Emily Dickinson is absent, as very few of her poems had been published when *LAL* was being assembled, but Anna Elizabeth Dickinson is here for rediscovery, a Philadelphia playwright of Quaker upbringing who became famous in her time as a lecturer, actress, abolitionist, novelist, and feminist. There is a Native American presence in words from Black Hawk and Red Jacket's 1805 "Speech to the Iroquois Six Nations"; the Confederacy is represented with excerpts from John C. Calhoun, Augustus Baldwin Longstreet, Henry Timrod, Sidney Lanier, and Thomas Bangs Thorpe.

There are also selections from men that Mark Twain personally detested, including Bret Harte and Whitelaw Reid, and from some eccentric types who have not found their way back into the graces of American literary history. Conspicuous among these is Fitz Hugh Ludlow, who died at the age of thirty-three, in 1870. Having wandered out to California in the early 1860s in the company of Albert Bierstadt, Ludlow was in San Francisco and writing for the *Golden Era* when Clemens himself was working there, and there is speculation that the two might have crossed paths—especially since Ludlow had praised Mark Twain in the pages of that journal.[18] Originally published by Harpers in 1850, Ludlow's *The Hashheesh Eater* was a confession in the Thomas De Quincey mode, with self-indulgent descriptions of the drug's euphoria and some cautionary prose about the evils of falling under its power. In his short life, Ludlow had turned out an amazing range of material, including poems, accounts of travel in the West, short stories, and essays on many subjects, but Stedman and Hutchinson preferred the memoir of addiction.

Four Mathers, two Winthrops, Freneau, William Byrd, Emerson, and Thoreau—it is hard not to marvel at the *Library*'s range and at the labor and

expense of putting it together. In the winter of 1892, Clemens was propos-
ing to Fred Hall that they sell shares in the project to keep it capitalized;
when there were no takers, he scrambled for other ways to keep himself and
the company out of bankruptcy. On New Year's Day 1893, from a villa outside Florence, he wrote home to Hall, worrying over the continuing
financial burden of the series and the odds that a summer epidemic might
slam the public's doors on a canvassing campaign:

> Of course my friend declined to buy a quarter interest in the L. A. L. for
> $200,000. I judged he would. I hoped he would offer $100,000, but he
> didn't. If the cholera breaks out in America a few months hence, we can't bor-
> row or sell; but if it doesn't we must try hard to raise $100,000. I wish we
> could do it *before* there is a cholera scare. . . .
>
> How I wish I had appreciated the need of $100,000 when I was in New
> York last summer! I would have tried my best to raise it. It would make us
> able to stand 1,000 sets of L. A. L. per month, but not any more, I guess.[19]

Clemens also approached Andrew Carnegie for financial support for the
LAL around this time, but to no avail; and as sales remained slack, *A Library
of American Literature* became WebsterCo's noblest disaster. Though the
paper chosen for the set was not high quality, the design throughout was genteel, to the extent that it clashed at times with the daring of specific selections.
Among the engravings of the authors, the favored posture for women is stock
sentimental, while the men, regardless of their politics, their conduct, or the
degree of moral heat in the excerpts, are presented as dignified folk who
could keep company on some lofty Parnassus of civility and taste. Trying so
hard to be a publishing and cultural breakthrough, as well as a commodity for
middle-class American families, *Library* turned out to be too big and much
too expensive. When Mark Twain's company folded, the rights to *LAL* were
sold to the New York house of William Evarts Benjamin, a son-in-law of
Henry Huttleston Rogers, who had taken over the restructuring of Clemens's
finances, and the series remained in print for more than a decade after.

"HARK FROM THE TOMB FOR A DEAD NATION"

As Mark Twain involved himself in these and other perilous enterprises, he
completed only one new book before the end of 1890, a novel about a

resourceful man creating his own empire out of steam and lightning, dynamite, and printed words. It is also, appropriately, a story about borrowed ideas, manufactured words and images, and the disappearance of authenticity. Its hero, Hank Morgan, really invents nothing, thinks no new thoughts, and even inveighs against the delusion of originality. Trained in the factories of the Colt Arms Company in Hartford (which in the 1880s was turning out automated printing equipment as well as firearms) and in the middle-class values of New England, Hank Morgan rebuilds the world he knows in a "new" ancient setting—and his strategy in the Camelot of King Arthur parallels Mark Twain's in building the novel. *A Connecticut Yankee in King Arthur's Court* was a raid on a thriving fashion in popular literature; it was also a wish-dream of a print revolution in another time and place and entirely under one man's control. The novel is a milestone in Mark Twain's thinking about the enigma of the printed page—how it signifies, what it can risk, and what it can actually achieve.

As the first edition of *A Connecticut Yankee in King Arthur's Court* was reaching subscribers in the spring and summer of 1890, at least two reviewers of the book observed, rather tactfully,[20] that the decisive ruse early in the story, Hank Morgan's prediction of a solar eclipse to scare these Dark Age locals and establish himself as a great wizard, was borrowed from H. Rider Haggard's *King Solomon's Mines* (1885). In that best-selling adventure, Haggard's dauntless British narrator Allan Quatermain, his two stalwart White Hunter companions, and Ignosi, their mysterious Zulu guide, with his ominous tattoo and regal demeanor, use the same trick to terrify a duplicitous tribal chief and the populace of an uncharted kingdom, save themselves from being killed, and prove their supernatural talents in this African "lost land." Hank Morgan to Clarence the young page, when Hank learns that he is soon to be executed: "Go back and tell the king that at that hour I shall smother the whole world in the dead blackness of midnight; I will blot out the sun, and he shall never shine again; the fruits of the earth shall rot for lack of light and warmth, and the peoples of the earth shall famish and die, to the last man!"[21] Allan Quatermain to Twala, chief of the Kukuanas:

"Now, tell me, can any mortal man put out that sun, so that night comes down on the land at midday?"
The chief laughed a little. "No, my lord, that no man can do. The sun is stronger than man who looks on him."

"Ye say so. Yet I tell you that this day, one hour after midday, will we put out that sun for the space of an hour, and darkness shall cover the earth, and it shall be for a sign that we are indeed men of honor, and that Ignosi is indeed king of the Kukuanas."[22]

Mark Twain's raid on Rider Haggard's adventure stories was more extensive than these friendly reviewers observed. In *King Solomon's Mines,* the disgraced and treacherous ancient sorceress Gagool, gleeful at trapping the white intruders in a great cavern that turns out to be both King Solomon's legendary treasure house and the royal sepulcher of the Kukuanas, is crushed to death in a doorway by a massive stone as she tries to escape; gloating that Hank and his cadets are effectively buried alive in their Sand Belt cave, the old wizard Merlin roasts himself on an electrified line at his moment of triumph. In Haggard's *Allan Quatermain* (1887)—Haggard was quicker at pumping out sequels than Mark Twain was—the goriest chapter by far is "The Battle of the Pass," an apocalyptic clash between armies of two rival warrior princesses, a slaughter of thousands in another lost land (white people this time) in another uncharted corner of the Dark Continent. With Redcoat courage and know-how, Quatermain and his companions carry the day, but the aging hero's wounds and the exertion of battle ultimately cost him his life; and like Hank Morgan's narrative, Quatermain's account of his exploits must be completed "By Another Hand." As a beautiful, murderous queen, the Morgan Le Fay of *A Connecticut Yankee* descends from namesakes in Mallory and Tennyson, but one of her cousins might be Ayesha, still known to adventure-yarn lovers as "She-who-must-be-obeyed," the immortal and dangerous queen at the center of *She,* a Rider Haggard novel so durably popular that it spawned spin-offs, dramatizations, comic books, feature films, and parodies for almost a century after its release in 1886.

Haggard's novels are only the best-remembered works from a crowd of "lost race" and "lost land" stories that flourished at the end of the nineteenth century, especially in the years when Mark Twain was writing *A Connecticut Yankee.* In the popular fiction of that time, ancient unknown peoples were turning up regularly in out-of-the-way spots. Between 1880 and 1890, British and American boys could enjoy a flood of lurid new books about barbarous Celts thriving in remote English caves; remnants of Alexander's legions still acting like ancient Greeks high in the Himalayas or in secret valleys in Central Asia; giants and old Norse utopias concealed in the Arctic; more giants and races of superwomen in caverns deep under the earth;

Aztec mischief on modern Easter Island; Incan lost cities flourishing in the Andes; a race of pre-Incan midgets in a place called Itambez; Atlanteans, Hyperboreans, and other interesting folk living in exotic settings and fighting gory battles in the blank spaces on the globe.[23] When Hank Morgan titles his memoir "The Tale of the Lost Land" he is making a shrewd marketing decision, whether he knows it or not. Sam Clemens certainly knew it. Across the water, Haggard was getting rich; lost-land adventures were a publishing boom; and as usual, Sam was keeping an eye on how other people were making money as writers.

By transporting Hank to King Arthur's Camelot, Mark Twain could exploit two trends at once, for in satirizing chivalric romance and the Victorian love affair with things medieval, he could also play to those fads, telling a tale of narrow escapes, tournaments, treachery, love, war—the usual attractions in a chain-mail fantasy. In fact, the knights and damozels of *A Connecticut Yankee* make for a more satisfying romantic wish-dream than Tennyson's popular *Idylls of the King,* not only because Mark Twain's Camelot, before Hank's interventions, is more plausible than Tennyson's, but also because Hank's conquest is a plausible vicarious thrill. Any reasonably literate modern American dropped into this place could be like him, doing a little of what he does, playing a few tricks from a later time, and showing off modern knowledge to win worshipers. What was unusual about *A Connecticut Yankee,* however, was the temperament of the hero, the mysterious abruptness of his arrival in the strange place, and his pet projects in remaking this world. In a standard lost-land adventure story from the Gilded Age, the visitors find the unknown territory as explorers, gold seekers, hunters, missionaries—people who travel far and take risks in getting there. The struggle to arrive is part of the story. Hank Morgan, however, doesn't mountain-climb or machete his way into Camelot. He wakes up there as the result of a vaguely explained time-travel knock on the head; and after he figures out where he is, and when he is, and how to pass himself off as a wizard, he embarks on a quest for additional, powerful identities: inventor, industrialist, educator, and the first communications mogul in the history of the West.

Though *A Connecticut Yankee* doesn't center on a print revolution or a culture overthrown by print alone, one peculiarity of this novel is that most of the other components of Hank Morgan's empire—the bombs and fireworks, electric batteries, pistols and Gatling guns, high-wheel bicycles and soap and toothbrushes—are back-story developments, while the changes that Hank works on the media of Camelot are described in detail.

Hank's memoir is punctuated with boyish ecstasies, usually after wowing a crowd with a show of fire, thunder, or mechanical and ballistic prowess. But among these outbreaks of bliss, the oddest and most intense is this one, in a late chapter, "The First Newspaper":

> And might they take this strange thing in their hands, and feel of it and examine it?—they would be very careful. Yes. So they took it, handling it as cautiously and devoutly as if it had been some holy thing come from some supernatural region; and gently felt of its texture, caressed its pleasant smooth surface with lingering touch, and scanned the mysterious characters with fascinated eyes. These grouped bent heads, these charmed faces, these speaking eyes—how beautiful to me! For was not this my darling, and was not all this mute wonder and interest and homage a most eloquent tribute and unforced compliment to it? I knew, then, how a mother feels when women, whether strangers or friends, take her new baby, and close themselves about it with one eager impulse, and bend their heads over it in a tranced adoration that makes all the rest of the universe vanish out of their consciousness and be as if it were not, for that time. I knew how she feels, and that there is no other satisfied ambition, whether of king, conqueror or poet, that ever reaches half way to that serene far summit or yields half so divine a contentment.
>
> During all the rest of the séance my paper traveled from group to group all up and down and about that huge hall, and my happy eye was upon it always, and I sat motionless, steeped in satisfaction, drunk with enjoyment. Yes, this was heaven; I was tasting it once, if I might never taste it more. (344)

To set Hank's simile in context: in Chapters XL and XLI, about three years after this glorious presentation of Hank's newspaper, a few clues are offered, on the fly, about what has transpired in Hank's personal life. We learn that Hank has married the "perfect blatherskite" Sandy, whom he has somehow rebuilt from a scatterbrained ignoramus into a sentimental American-style middle-class wife, and that they now have an actual baby to cherish rather than a sheet of newsprint. There is a paragraph here describing Sandy as a cherished friend and companion, and another about Hank's acquiescence to her naming the baby "Hello-Central," misunderstood lingo from the dawn of the telephone in the United States. There are also a couple of sentences about the "little chap" as the "centre of the universe" for her parents. But that is the extent of it: Hank's memoir expends more words on his triumph in publishing a newspaper than on his own daughter or his three years of domestic life with Sandy.

This rhapsodizing about newspapers actually begins in Chapter IX of *A Connecticut Yankee*—added late in the course of composition. Hank witnesses a tournament and gets himself into trouble with Sir Sagramor over a chance remark. In a rambling paragraph, Hank's reminiscence slides from the day's events into a hymn to the working press as a force for democracy and civil progress:

> I not only watched this tournament from day to day, but detailed an intelligent priest from my Department of Public Morals and Agriculture, and ordered him to report it; for it was my purpose by and by, when I should have gotten the people along far enough, to start a newspaper. The first thing you want in a new country, is a patent office; then work up your school system; and after that, out with your paper. A newspaper has its faults, and plenty of them, but no matter, it's hark from the tomb for a dead nation, and don't you forget it. You can't resurrect a dead nation without it; there isn't any way. So I wanted to sample things, and be finding out what sort of reporter-material I might be able to rake together out of the sixth century when I should come to need it. (109)

An opportunity lurks here to make a distinction between Hank Morgan's sensibility and Mark Twain's, for Mark Twain was not always euphoric about the salutary value of journalism. In March 1873, for example, he spoke to the Hartford Monday Evening Club on the subject of the "License of the Press":

> It seems to me that just in the ratio that our newspapers increase, our morals decay. The more newspapers the worse morals. Where we have one newspaper that does good, I think we have fifty that do harm. We *ought* to look upon the establishment of a newspaper of the average pattern in a virtuous village as a calamity. . . .
>
> That awful power, the public opinion of a nation, is created in America by a horde of ignorant, self-complacent simpletons who failed at ditching and shoemaking and fetched up in journalism on their way to the poorhouse. I am personally acquainted with hundreds of journalists, and the opinion of the majority of them would not be worth tuppence in private, but when they speak in print it is the *newspaper* that is talking (the pygmy scribe is not visible) and *then* their utterances shake the community like the thunders of prophecy.[24]

Compared to Mark Twain himself (in a bad mood, and more than a dozen years before he wrote *A Connecticut Yankee*) Hank Morgan sounds like an innocent about the social and moral value of newspapers. A problem with enforcing this contrast between the author and his protagonist, however, is that Hank's innocence is not sustained in the novel. When "The First Newspaper" is hawked in the alleys of Camelot, Hank feels the rapture of a proud new mother; but in his appraisal of this first issue, the Colt Arms Company foreman lapses into the perspective, and the language, of a veteran from the newspaper trade:

> Yes, it was too loud. Once I could have enjoyed it and seen nothing out of the way about it, but now its note was discordant. It was good Arkansas journalism, but this was not Arkansas. Moreover, the next to the last line was calculated to give offense to the hermits, and perhaps lose us their advertising. Indeed, there was too lightsome a tone of flippancy all through the paper. It was plain I had undergone a considerable change without noticing it. I found myself unpleasantly affected by pert little irreverencies which would have seemed but proper and airy graces of speech at an earlier period of my life. . . .
>
> Of course it was good enough journalism for a beginning; I knew that quite well, and yet it was somehow disappointing. . . .
>
> However, take the paper by and large, I was vastly pleased with it. Little crudities of a mechanical sort were observable here and there, but there were not enough of them to amount to anything, and it was good enough Arkansas proof-reading, anyhow, and better than was needed in Arthur's day and realm. As a rule, the grammar was leaky and the construction more or less lame; but I did not much mind these things. (339–42)

Between Hank's first dream of a newspaper for Camelot and this arrival of the *Weekly Hosannah and Literary Volcano,* other moments indicate that a foray into print is very high on his list of improvements for medieval Britain. When Clarence, grown up, proves to the Boss that "there wasn't anything he couldn't turn his hand to," Hank pushes Clarence into journalism—and once again, Hank sounds like an insider: "[T]he time seemed about right for a start in the newspaper line; nothing big, but just a small weekly for experimental circulation in my civilization-nurseries. He took to it like a duck; there was an editor concealed in him, sure. Already he had doubled himself in one way; he talked sixth century and wrote nineteenth. His journalistic style was climbing, steadily; it was already up to the back settlement Alabama mark, and couldn't be told from the editorial output of that region either by matter or flavor" (121).

But these outbursts of Hank as print connoisseur could also signify something else: that as an ordinary Connecticut reader he has picked up the jargon and professional viewpoint of the commodity he consumes every day, that he has become media savvy, like a modern adolescent with the requisite ten thousand hours of growing up in front of video screens. What was Hank Morgan like when he was back in Connecticut? A printer and editor *manqué*? Because Mark Twain does not make Hank a psychologically coherent center for this novel, these perorations about printed media, and the telephone, and the telegraph, are all as much Mark Twain's voice as they are Hank Morgan's. When Hank makes a feint into the joys of "chromos," this blurring of voices is apparent once more. Dropped suddenly into a somewhere else, Hank has astonishing things to look at all around him—yet chief among the missing "conveniences" he complains about, at the outset of Chapter IV, and so soon after his triumph with the eclipse, is no chromo-lithographs on the castle walls:

> There was no soap, no matches, no looking-glass—except a metal one, about as powerful as a pail of water. And not a chromo. I had been used to chromos for years, and I saw now that without my suspecting it a passion for art had got worked into the fabric of my being, and was become a part of me. It made me homesick to look around over this proud and gaudy but heartless barrenness and remember that in our house in East Hartford, all unpretending as it was, you couldn't go into a room but you would find an insurance-chromo, or at least a three-color God-Bless-Our-Home over the door; and in the parlor we had nine. But here, even in my grand room of state, there wasn't anything in the nature of a picture except a thing the size of a bed-quilt, which was either woven or knitted, (it had darned places in it,) and nothing in it was the right color or the right shape; and as for proportions, even Raphael himself couldn't have botched them more formidably, after all his practice on those nightmares they call his "celebrated Hampton Court cartoons." Raphael was a bird. We had several of his chromos; one was his "Miraculous Draught of Fishes," where he puts in a miracle of his own—puts three men into a canoe which wouldn't have held a dog without upsetting. I always admired to study R.'s art, it was so fresh and unconventional. (83–85)

For Hank, at least at this moment, the chief comfort of the modern home is colorful images all over the walls. The perspective here is slippery. The phrases about the Morgan house, in modest East Hartford (the other side of town from the posh Nook Farm neighborhood where Sam and Livy had built their mansion), suggest that Hank represents the new middle classes of southern New England. But in his meandering segue, from absent chromos through a critique of the tapestry that stands in for them, and then to commentary on Raphael, there is a peculiar ventriloquism: the source of the voice cannot be told for sure. From one perspective, Mark Twain seems to be speaking, not Hank, for this sounds more like the Mark Twain who wanders the galleries and churches on his European travels, bluntly telling what he sees and challenging the pieties of tour-book art appreciation. By responding here as Mark Twain would to these revered, implausible representations of fishing boats and fishermen, or anything else that looks and operates differently in actual life, Mark Twain, through Hank, can air out his commonsense judgments once again and play one of his old comic games.

The funniest, trickiest phrase in this paragraph, however, "We had several of his chromos," seems to break in a different direction—toward Hank Morgan's personality rather than toward Mark Twain himself, and also toward the way in which modern *East* Hartford Americans, people of Hank's new and rambunctious social class, come to know Fine Art, via these chromos. Mark Twain may have actually seen the Raphael in question, but Hank has not. His commentary, therefore, might intend a glimpse into his own barbarities as a critic, his possibly appalling indifference with regard to knowing the original artist and painting from the modern mass-produced copy. Or there might be a playful, subversive theme here: that with the triumph of high-resolution duplicate images discriminations of that sort, between the original and the copy, are on their way to irrelevance.

In the East Hartfords of America at the century's end, ordinary people can indeed "know" these Old Masters as the public has never known them before and even have them to look at every day, a luxury denied to all previous human beings except the keepers of the original paintings. In the world Hank knows best, a whole flock of "Raphaels" can be bought retail and hung all over the house. Moreover, this new multitude of patrons of the arts neither understands nor cares about problems of authenticity or whatever nuances of the original work might have been lost in the transcription. After all, the tapestry that demoralizes Hank in his new parlor, his "grand room of state," is an original work. In a modern museum it would be insured for millions, perhaps even accorded a gallery wall of its own, though "nothing in it was the right color or the right shape." So much for the advantages of originality.

For Hank Morgan and his cohorts back home, any problem with a

Raphael chromo lies not with the chromo but with Raphael. The problem with "art" in an age of duplication is not the competence of the duplication or the compromise of the "aura" but rather the mimetic failures of the real thing. As a member of this new audience, educated by printed pictures and words, Hank has learned—on his own, yet like millions of others—to desire color and an impression of truth, or a lively, well-upholstered illusion, regardless of its provenance or "originality," whether it comes straight from an Old Master or through a succession of fabricators in the employ of Prang's or Currier and Ives. Do similar values apply with regard to modern printed narrative? Jules Verne, H. Rider Haggard, Mark Twain: if, as Hank Morgan says later, "we have no thoughts of our own, no opinions of our own," and if "[a]ll that is original in us . . . can be covered up and hidden by the point of a cambric needle," and if mechanized publishing now belea-guers the world with texts in such profusion that each "original" artifact vanishes in a heap of copies of copies, then whose story is this, anyway, and what does it matter who is really speaking? For Hank, the chromos in his Connecticut home are Raphaels; *A Connecticut Yankee* is Hank Morgan's story, and Mark Twain's too, and also another chromo on the wall, color-ful, skillfully engraved, and muddled in its provenance.

Two illustrations by Dan Beard complicate the passage. Near it, Beard offers a smoking oil lamp, described in the text as "a bronze dish half full of boarding-house butter with a blazing rag floating in it"; and Hank, in a ridiculous hat (Gilded Age in style but garnished with a plume), standing forlorn in a stony medieval hall. The last time he appeared in this novel's sequence of images, Hank was naked, but now he looks like a motley lord of an empty domain. Hank's (Mark Twain's) ode to chromos is enhanced, therefore, by these accompanying pictures. While the narrative toys with the prospect that full-color duplication makes authenticity obsolete, the qual-ity of Beard's reproduced work, here and elsewhere in the novel—these illus-trations were made expressly for reproduction in this book—supports the same point. Moreover, thanks to the beaux arts proficiency of Beard's draw-ings, this mercurial subversion of chivalric romance novels can advance in a sheep's clothing of chivalric romance. Many of Beard's larger pictures here, of men at arms and knights on plunging stallions, of village streets and bat-tlements, and the climactic panorama of the assembled chivalry of England marching on Hank and the cadets in the Sand Belt cave, would seem at home in Charles Reade's *The Cloister and the Hearth* (1861) or an ambitious reprint of Scott's *Ivanhoe*. The key anomaly of the verbal text, therefore, echoes in the visual text as well: To what extent is this sumptuously illustrated narrative a "real" medieval adventure, as well as a travesty of the mode? In after-dinner remarks to the Society of Illustrators in New York, a few days before Christmas 1905, Mark Twain described *A Connecticut Yankee* as a collaborative work between its author and its illustrator. However, because Dan Beard was not only an honored guest in attendance but also a previous speaker, Mark Twain's comments, which rattle a bit in attributing thematic responsibilities, might not be a last word on the dynamics of that relationship or on the chemistry between words and images in the book that they made together:

> Now, Beard got everything I put into that book and a little more besides. Those pictures of Beard's in that book—oh, from the first page to the last is one vast sardonic laugh at the trivialities, the servilities of our poor human race, and also at the professions and the insolence of priestcraft and kingcraft—those creatures that make slaves of themselves and have not the manliness to shake it off. Beard put it all in that book. I meant it to be there. I put a lot of it there and Beard put the rest.[25]

In this banquet-hall tribute to Beard there is a measure of uneasiness. It simply isn't true that Beard's images for *A Connecticut Yankee* are social satire "from the first page to the last," and the praise seems to falter and prevaricate just as Mark Twain breaks it off and switches to another subject. But if the words tell us only a little about the making of this novel, the tone may say more: with regard to mode, to narrative voice, to theme, there is thematic restlessness in the novel itself, and the images that accompany and even invade Mark Twain's verbal text help to sustain that mood.

This invasion of the verbal text by these illustrations is a matter of special interest. Praised often for their elegance of execution and satiric import, Beard's images also gain from the finesse with which persons unknown situated them on the page. On the plates of the Webster editions, these images are sometimes merged into the lines of type much more skillfully and ostentatiously than on any page in *Huckleberry Finn*—sometimes to the point of hindering a straightforward encounter with the verbal text alone. On page 109 of the first edition of *Yankee,* for example, an elongated figure of a sour-looking priest, sitting cross-legged on a plinth, obtrudes into the middle, breaking the lines of the narrative in half, and requiring the eye to hop from left to right across the image, searching for the rest of the sentence. An armored knight on a charger causes the same sort of trouble on page 179; a stork and a terrier invade the lines on page 421; and there are several other instances where the eye has to dodge around the pictures to recover the track of the prose.

Rules of etiquette with regard to typesetting, layout, and reading are being played with and transgressed. When the accompanying illustration is at the top or bottom of the chapter, or set off by itself on a facing page, or tucked discreetly into a margin, then the image keeps its customary place, and the reader can either ignore it or negotiate it before or after dealing with the words. When pictures break into the lines, however, they can become a different kind of enrichment, or a nuisance—or an intimation that our readerly habits, with regard to printed books, are growing quaint, that printed discourse now encompasses and includes the printed image, and that our attention, or consciousness, must alter accordingly, keeping pace with these designers and publishers. Dropped into sixth-century England, Hank takes on the task of waking it up, jolting a civilization out of destructive rituals of thinking and seeing. I have found no evidence that Clemens involved himself in the layout of pages for *A Connecticut Yankee*. But if some of these stunts with situating Beard's illustrations seem an excess or an annoyance rather than an enhancement of the reading experience, some deeper assonance might be here with regard to this narrative's themes.

Equally interesting are certain pages in *A Connecticut Yankee* where the verbal text and a different kind of illustration—not from Beard's hand but from some other—make a reflexive mix that outdoes the chapter headings of *Huckleberry Finn* or these tricks in constructing the plates. When Hank talks about his newspaper, the reader is treated to replicas of what Hank is supposedly looking at, facsimiles of Camelot news items, riddled with errors from the composing stone: misspellings, wrong fonts, inverted type, broken type, faulty alignments, uneven inking, and nearly everything else that could go wrong in setting up and printing off a sheet of news in a primordial shop. Obviously part of the comedy, this incompetence clashes with the "pert little irreverencies" that Hank chafes at in the prose. What is presented, then, is a text that for a moment becomes both verbal text *and* illustration, a verbal text subverted by its own appearance, satirizing others, yet stumbling as it does so. This is a variation on a kind of barbarous clowning that goes back to Aristophanes—an unkempt rube, laughable as he ridicules others—except that in *A Connecticut Yankee* the counterfeited medium is a part of the message.

In these episodes where fragments of supposedly actual newspapers are revealed "as is" to speak and posture for themselves, the implications are a delight. There is celebration here of the printed word as well as playful nostalgia for simpler times in printing, hand-labor adventures in shaking the world with movable type. There might also be a touch of nostalgia for the vanishing world of village newspapers, where Sam learned his trade and committed his own howlers as an apprentice. But beyond all that, paradoxes flourish: the contrast between the comically bad typesetting of these first newspapers and the show-off production of this Webster Company edition affirms the triumph of *A Connecticut Yankee* as an achievement of industrialized corporate publishing—yet with that triumph there is also a whisper of fatality. The presentation of these two artifacts of printed discourse as one, an error-ridden first try amid a bravura demonstration of doing it right, allows these two enterprises to be understood as not just comparable but also in a sense equal. Hank Morgan's own first newspaper, crude as it is, is still a sheet of paper with a measure of eloquence; and as apocalypse brews in Hank's updated Camelot, one set of printed words, in any legible form, might ultimately be as potent, and as transient, as any other.

The entanglements and interconnections that Clemens supported, or acquiesced to, making his bankruptcy such a mess to litigate and resolve, followed a familiar pattern in Gilded Age finance: when in doubt, add layers of complication. It would be easy to get lost in the paperwork legacy of the Connecticut Company (a principal holding company for the Paige), the Traction Syndicate (a builder of the machine), the feints and gambits to save WebsterCo, and the welter of special arrangements with Frank Bliss, Harpers, the Mount Morris Bank, Chatto and Windus, and a succession of law firms. After 1890, Mark Twain's dream of glory in American publishing decayed into gloomy monthly reports mailed to wherever he was and highheat responses from the Boss, urging Hall and others to try one desperate stratagem after another. Having failed to see that the Linotype and Monotype were dooming the Paige, Mark Twain also failed to see that the railroad network, which had brought the subscription-book trade into primacy, was now bringing it down. Not nearly so isolated as before, small-town Americans could order their reading by mail-order catalog or connect with commercial districts where inexpensive trade books were in ample supply. Too often, Mark Twain had fancied himself an expert with regard to every major dimension of the publishing business, and too frequently he had been wrong.

As late as 1893, for example, with the Paige project pulling the Webster Company toward ruin, and with *A Library of American Literature* burdening the business rather than helping, Clemens was telling Fred Hall to start up a new national magazine called the *Back Number,* which would reprint articles from the early days of American serial publishing. Clemens wanted initial print runs of twenty thousand copies.[26] Mark Twain's outbreaks of micromanagement, his reveries of long-range success, and his harassment of managers, hired artists, engineers, and anyone else who had professional dealings with him can be assembled into one long tale of personal unhappiness, with enough character flaws in evidence to suit a Eugene O'Neill. But that same body of evidence can be read differently, and with stronger relevance to the present. Mark Twain knew publishing; he knew printing; he knew what it took to be a first-magnitude American author. With energy and prodigious experience, he tried to dominate and was overwhelmed— and what figured most in bringing him down, I think, was not some mythological Wheel of Fortune or tragic flaw, but an onward rush of innovation so strong and treacherous that a man who had known movable type and presses and writing since childhood could not keep up with it all or stay out of its way.

In books that Mark Twain published after *A Connecticut Yankee* there is new turbulence in the relationship between the text and the accompanying visual experience and between both of these and the popular image of this celebrity author. As his money dwindled, so did his authority over the design and visual content of his own books. With the Charles Webster Company in trouble, Mark Twain went back to the APC to publish *The Tragedy of Pudd'nhead Wilson and the Comedy of Those Extraordinary Twins*—a couple of loosely connected narratives, each too short for separate release in book form. Bound into the same covers, they would still have been too lean as verbal text, so APC opted for wide margins on all sides and a jamboree of small images around the words. For the first time in more than twenty years, the American public received an imaginative experience of language and illustrations with Mark Twain's name on it but with half the printed material created by others and inserted without his review. What results is the most difficult novel that Mark Twain published in his lifetime, for these obtruding little pictures not only aerate the reading of the APC edition but distort and disrupt significant themes and intentions in the narratives.

The peculiarity of this reading experience cannot be matched in any edition from which these pictures by C. H. Warren and F. M. Senior, these hundreds of cartoons, have been excised or thinned. Stunningly different in mood and style from the sparse, melodramatic illustrations by Louis Loeb that accompanied the serialized *Pudd'nhead Wilson* in the *Century* in 1893–94, the figures on each page of the APC first edition sustain an impression that what unfolds in this narrative is not a human drama but a battle of frogs and mice: antics in a Mississippi River neverland, not a story of full-scale characters. In 1899, when Rogers had negotiated a transfer to Harpers of most of Mark Twain's literary assets and the great trade house was pushing the APC for control of reprint rights, the APC produced an "Edition de Luxe" of *Pudd'nhead Wilson* and other Mark Twain works, adorning *Pudd'nhead Wilson* with a whole new set of illustrations, this time all by Kemble. Scarce this time around—befitting a dignified book—these pictures still alter the impact of the text dramatically, and not for the better. Meanwhile, Harpers put out an edition of its own, also with a small number of full-page images—including a couple of thematically crucial ones by Kemble from the "Edition de Luxe."

In both of these, the most egregious conflict between picture and verbal text is Kemble's portrait of Roxy, which appears early in each book. To develop a theme that in Dawson's Landing blood is preposterously construed as the source of character, Mark Twain emphasizes that Roxy is one-sixteenth African—and that the "blackness" that she sees in herself, and that others see in her, is a cultural construct. But Kemble ignores this all-important theme and draws Roxy as a caricature, the "Mammy" from the molasses jar and the chicory coffee can. His full-page picture blindsides the verbal narrative's meditation on race and identity. In each of these editions, the illustrations carry unprecedented thematic weight, and no Mark Twain narrative before *Pudd'nhead Wilson* was so muddled by its own pictures as it reached the American public. And after his death, no novel by Mark Twain has been altered so much by the scholastic versions from which it is usually taught, books from which all or most of the pictures from any source have been excised.

In that first APC edition, the story of Roxy and the two Tom Driscolls, a story that engages uneasily with questions about heredity and nurture, a tale about greed, desperation, and ruined lives, cannot become a "tragedy" because the illustrations jam the attention of anyone who looks at the entire artifact that he or she is reading. As drawn by Warren and Senior, most of the black characters are stereotypes; most of the images of white people are so small that their facial expressions have no complexity, no

FIG. 9 Louis Loeb's version of Roxy, from the *Century Magazine* serialization, January 1894. The same picture appeared in the first London edition of *Pudd'nhead Wilson*.

interest—with the implication that time invested in thinking about any of them, or about any big, disheveled theme in Mark Twain's verbal narrative, is time spent on the wrong book.[27]

This first edition is important, therefore, because it underscores a dilemma related to printed texts in an age of "new media." In situating *Pudd'nhead Wilson* within its own historical moment, should Senior and Warren's illustrations, done for the most widely circulated edition in Mark Twain's lifetime, be construed now as part of the essential and original text? Or have the college editions been wiser to cut these pictures out because Mark Twain was *not* the arbiter of the visual experience in what was ostensibly "his" book?

Though these questions can seem pedantic, a larger, underlying problem reverberates in our daily encounter with so many other distracting and compelling artifacts, texts and images raining down from indeterminate sources, ramifying an interpretive dilemma that in American culture traces back at least as far as *Pudd'nhead Wilson:* sound bytes, re-edits, and corporate interventions, special effects by machines and armies of autonomous wizards—and no way of knowing which "artists" or intermediaries are morally or aesthetically responsible for whatever it is that steals our attention. As the closing credits swarm by, the *auteur* becomes only another CEO or perhaps nobody at all, only another myth invented and buffered by agents and technocrats. Market forecasts and film studio demands can influence a "literary" work even before it is written, as the contemporary media company—publishing houses, film studios, newspapers, magazines, and television and radio networks all under one roof—values synergy in the making of the "cultural event." In its first release *Pudd'nhead Wilson* was a corporate production, more so than any novel that Mark Twain had written before, and because so much of the cultural experience that we live with now is corporate in its birth and clockwork, the interpretive experience is frustrating, yet familiar. Because the problematic text cannot be reduced to elemental particles of intention, perhaps the best recourse, or the only one we really have, is to negotiate this book as we cope with so much else that comes at us now: as an experience of dynamic connections with mysterious provenance and purpose. From the perspective of our own moment, the most relevant theme of *Pudd'nhead Wilson* could be this: that its aesthetic and moral turmoil, the visual and verbal reality of this printed book, signify together—the conflicted, moment-to-moment adventure of reading now, and seeing now, and pondering the uncertainties that close in from every margin—long after the book itself is closed.

By 1900, American readers who wanted fresh editions of *The Innocents Abroad* or *Roughing It* or *Huckleberry Finn* could find them from Harpers, perhaps with a frontispiece and a tipped-in plate of The Author, but not much else in the way of visual embellishment. Losing most of their pictures, Mark Twain's travel books acquired the look of classics; but in doing so they also ceased to be American travel books. In the Harpers *Pudd'nhead Wilson* editions, similarly bereft of images, the lean, lonely verbal text drifted toward a somber high seriousness that (properly or not) had gone largely unnoticed in 1895. *Huckleberry Finn* ceased to be read with its portfolio of Kemble head-pieces, tail-pieces, and borderless illustrations along the way— a loss that diminished its eloquence as a novel about the cultural influence of print and pictures. The American publishing industry was building for Samuel Clemens his "whited sepulchre," conferring dignity at the expense of vitality, even sometimes at the expense of meaning.[28] The arrangements that Henry Huttleston Rogers negotiated with Harpers allowed the firm to do pretty much what it wanted with its Mark Twain titles. With the departure of Fred Hall and the end of WebsterCo, Sam's business responsibilities came under the stewardship of Rogers and his son, or Isabel Lyon and Ralph Ashcroft, or Albert Bigelow Paine, and eventually Clara Clemens, all of whom made decisions on his behalf. And as Sam lost his businesses, his grip on his own mythic legacy also slackened. "Mark Twain" was growing estranged from the human source.

In the reinvention of printing and publishing, there was no lull during the final fifteen years of Mark Twain's life. The annual production of books and periodicals in the United States continued its exponential climb, while new modes of communication opened a contest with the printed word for the attention and the dollars of the American audience. By 1900, the airspace above New York and Chicago streets was an anarchy of telephone lines, stock-ticker cables, telegraph wires, and electric service; steam had given way to dynamos and electric motors as basic components of production; wood pulp had taken dominion as the material of choice for newsprint and cheap books; and the promulgation of images had been revolutionized again, intensifying the pressure of visual experience upon the domains of the verbal. In the United States, the output of new book titles spiraled upward: 3,520 in 1888, 5,134 in 1893, 6,356 in 1900.[29] To an aging man who had mastered traditional printing when American publishers were turning out fewer than a hundred new titles per year, these changes must have been astounding—and not a little unsettling. From the perspective of Mark Twain's career and strongest interests as a writer, three areas of development, in this last phase of his life, seem especially important.

First was the widespread adoption of the Linotype technology and the declining importance of movable type. By the middle of the 1890s, Mergenthaler's cast-on-demand strategy was establishing itself as the American system of choice for efficiency and cost reduction in typesetting. For decades after, there would be strikes and job actions, a secret "Brotherhood" of typographers, and plenty of miscellaneous difficulty before the publishing industry and the International Typographers Union worked out a truce with regard to automating this work.[30] The conversion was relentless, however, and where there were Linotypes, typesetting for newspapers—and eventually for books as the equipment was refined for that work[31]—was accomplished quickly, and production costs went down.

Though the economic impact of the Linotype is clear enough, it is harder to document the imaginative consequences of this defeat for hand-assembled movable type as a physical and symbolic step in producing the printed word. Though the Paige compositor was a contrivance to eliminate the journeyman printer, it was also a scheme to conserve the cultural weaponry he worked with. Humans were to disappear from the composing process, but the process itself, in its classic essentials, was meant to live on. The Linotype not only diminished the power of a guild that had been at the center of Western culture for the previous four hundred years but also threatened the aesthetics of printing as Mark Twain had known them all his life.

Earlier in this book I speculated about the psychological and imaginative effects of setting words in movable type—as an art, a meticulous creating that attributes authority and consequence to the reified verbal text. Even today, and especially in a moment when a little work with a keyboard can yield printed copy in any font and format that one might desire, writers feel honored when some skilled enthusiast with a handpress and the old accoutrements of the craft sets up and prints off a few keepsake pages of their work or chapbooks made in the traditional way. From the earliest models onward, the Linotype also operated with a keyboard, and though successive versions of the machine before 1910 required more effort and skill from their operators than merely tapping the right keys, the new production process sacrificed much of its kinship to the art and homage of printing as generations had known it. When Hank Morgan revels in seeing and reading his first newspapers in Camelot, he is imagining his own protégés in the thrall of a professional activity that, when they have mastered it, will require them to temper their irreverent high energy with poised attention to detail—like the mix of free spirit and professional competence that Hank hopes for in his corps of cadets and his "man factory" of modern Englishmen. What will happen, however, when the art and the drudgery alike are expelled from the professional life, made redundant by faceless intervening powers? In an automated world, the liberated body and mind might possibly float away, lost in exotic and dangerous contemplations. When the medieval print shop in Mark Twain's final draft of "The Mysterious Stranger" undergoes a supernatural automation, the crisis that ensues, as Mark Twain imagines it, is no longer about good production, hours worked, and fair pay received. It becomes a crisis for the soul.

A second development was the American ratification of international copyright agreements. When the U.S. Congress passed the Chace Act in 1891,[32] it ensured, at long last, the security of literary property and the professional environment of American authors. The act fostered the development of bilateral agreements with England and various members of the Commonwealth and with France, Germany, Norway, and other countries where literature of interest to Americans was being produced and where markets were possible for American writers. In these new arrangements there were still kinks and complications. One provision, which endured for decades after, centered on electroplates for books by foreign authors: U.S. statutes required that all such plates be produced here rather than shipped in from foreign sources. There were also complex special arrangements with Canada and Australia; but as a longtime proponent and high-profile advocate for this kind of legislation, Mark Twain could now breathe more easily with regard to publication of his own work in major markets abroad. He could also curtail the foreign travel necessitated by older covenants: to be present on English or Canadian soil, for example, on the precise day when one of his books was officially released there. This normalization also did much to ease tensions within the extended family of authors writing in the English language and to improve the status of Americans in this clan.

As a participant in the culture of the English-speaking world, the United States was finally legitimate, and the door was open wide for the internationalization of publishing companies and the easy transatlantic flow of texts and royalties.

After 1891, Mark Twain's political and moral interests became international as never before. *The Innocents Abroad* and *A Tramp Abroad* had been written from the perspective of a hard-core American sensibility, displaced for a while to foreign settings and strange folk; his books after *Pudd'nhead Wilson* often favored the viewpoint of a cosmopolitan, a voice disconnected from a homeland, disconnected at times even from time itself. Perpetual voyagers, strangers without national affiliation, and figures from Scripture and myth and legend attracted his interest: as Mark Twain's words circulated more freely than ever, so did his creative imagination.

A third development was the emergence of new possibilities and challenges pertaining to the published image. In the final years of Mark Twain's career, there were developments that stand apart from technologies mentioned thus far. Each of these involved photography: the adoption of halftone and rotogravure techniques for reproducing photographs in newspapers and inexpensive books and the advent of the Kodak portable camera, utilizing rolls of comparatively high-speed film, thus freeing the photographer from tripod and studio, freeing the subject to breathe and even to move—and liberating photography from control by professionals. These years also saw the first successful experiments with motion pictures. As far back as the 1870s, heliotype and kindred technologies had allowed publishers to include photographic likenesses as features in expensive books. The newspaper and the magazine remained largely beyond reach, however, until about 1895, when the photographers of the celebrity could move literally into the streets, catching the famous man or woman on the move. No surprise, then, that Mark Twain eventually adopted the summer white suit as year-round public wear, matching his fine, wild mane of hair, or that he was known to time his New York and London outings and promenades so as to encounter the crowds and the daylight photographers.

For newspaper and magazine photographs, Mark Twain was happy to cut a striking figure. But the portable camera loomed as more than a convenient device for disseminating the visage of an author. The new Kodak could be taken anywhere—smuggled in, if necessary—to record the truth, even when the little box was wielded by amateurs. In representing truth, it could validate, or rival, or overthrow the efforts of the literary artist. Though

Edison would eventually send a motion-picture team to catch Mark Twain fidgeting on the porch at Stormfield, his final American home, cinema was as yet only a distant, gathering disturbance in the new media climate. For the time being, the printed page remained the arena for the contest between words and image, a contest that grew fiercer in the final years of Mark Twain's life. In Mark Twain's new books after 1895, the illustrations continue to compete with the verbal text, for the space between the covers, and for control of intention.

As Clemens struggled with bankruptcy and creative dry spells, he was assisting (whether he knew it or not) in the rise of a new species of narrative. One reason for this intensified competition between the verbal and the pictorial within his own work was the brevity of most of the manuscripts that Clemens finished and submitted for publication before his death. In his younger days he had padded some of his APC best-sellers to achieve the bulk that the trade required, but as he aged the job and the indulgence of fattening his volumes fell to the illustrators. The APC and the Webster Company could not have sold volumes as meager as *Extracts from Adam's Diary* (1904), *Eve's Diary* (1906), or *Extract from Captain Stormfield's Visit to Heaven* (1907), but as a media powerhouse of the time Harpers could exploit Mark Twain's stardom, build interest in new literary work from him with its monthly magazine, and push his thin books into the retail stores. Moreover, editors at Harpers had another advantage that the APC staff and Mark Twain himself had never acquired: an astute understanding of recent trends in the visual arts. This cosmopolitan company, which by 1894 had a thriving London branch, publishing books and essays by Walter Pater, Arthur Symons, Henry James, H. G. Wells, and Thomas Hardy, understood that printed pictures were evolving not just in the technology of their production but also in their aesthetic range and vocabulary. The APC's first edition of *Following the Equator* (1897) had experimented with halftone, and photographs reproduced by this process are mingled with rotogravure images and conventional engravings. When the pictures in this book derive from drawings or paintings, however, the presentation is not markedly different from styles favored in Mark Twain volumes of twenty-five years before. In Mark Twain's last travel book, the visual component is sometimes gaudier but not fresh, and it does little to change the image of the author or his association with a cultural moment slipping into the past. The management at Harpers, however, understood that as the twentieth century began, the experiments of the Aesthetes, the Impressionists, and the Decadents were no longer beyond the pale as models for illustrating trade books for the general public. When the APC, Osgood, and WebsterCo had poured pictures into the discourse of Mark Twain, they had sometimes complicated and muddled the intention of that discourse. When the pictures were commissioned and selected by Harpers, however, those images helped to rejuvenate "Mark Twain" as an American icon—and even restyle him to pass as a modern.

EVERY FACING PAGE

In 1904 and 1905, Harpers published two short books by Mark Twain, each of which, in its own way, nudged the balance of thematic power between his words and the pictures printed with them. Each of these books is as much a visual text as a verbal experience, and there are dramatic differences between them in the style of the illustrations and in the processes by which they were reproduced. To look at these Mark Twain books together is to come upon an old friend sporting a fresh style and a modern attitude—dressed up in new clothes that might look better on someone else.

Off and on for about ten years, Clemens had been experimenting with personal accounts supposedly by Adam and Eve. Some of the Adam pages had appeared as amusing filler in the London edition of *Tom Sawyer, Detective,* and in a small volume by several hands called *The Niagara Book,* from a firm in Buffalo, which provided the verbal text that Harpers worked with in 1904 to pump up a new book of its own. Soon after, Clemens went back to this material, changing it extensively, and sent it to Frederick Duneka at Harpers. Duneka ignored the author's wishes and rearranged things as he saw fit, producing a different "Adam's Diary" to fill out *The $30,000 Bequest and Other Stories* and borrowing some material to finish out *Eve's Diary,* which Clemens had been working on in the wake of Livy's death.[33] This companion work, which Clemens had thought of only as a "booklet" at most,[34] first appeared in the 1905 Christmas issue of *Harper's Monthly Magazine* as a short story, with no illustrations. When Harpers made a book out of it, however, they poured on the pictures, fattened it up, brought it to life, and changed dramatically its look and its implications.

For *Extracts from Adam's Diary,* Frederick Strothmann's cartoons of Adam and Eve could be described as caveman-Egyptian, and engravers for Harpers made expert use of rotogravure to enhance the impression of figures

FIG. 10 From *Extracts from Adam's Diary*, one of Strothmann's Stone Age–Egyptian cartoons of Eve.

chipped into stone. There are as many pages of images here as there are of verbal text; and the artistic style, the special effects of the rotogravure process, and the presentation of each illustration as a separate page, facing a page of "Diary," give the visual half of *Adam's Diary* an importance beyond that of the scores of pictures in *Pudd'nhead Wilson*. As the strangest-looking volume bearing Mark Twain's name and produced in his lifetime, *Adam's Diary* seems to uproot the American heartland humorist and storyteller and drop him into Continental bohemian company, for Strothmann's images recall the artistic action in Montmartre studios and cabarets after the collapse of the Second Empire,[35] a fierce and gleeful irreverence that reinvented the *affiche,* the journal cover, the set design for revolutionary satire and drama. As far back as thirty years before *Adam's Diary,* radical coteries in Paris, including the *Hydropathes* and the *Incohérents* in Montmartre, followed by the Aesthetes, the Decadents, and other insurgencies, had been breaking the rules of drawing, outraging the tastes and pieties down the hill in the fashionable districts. Outcault's *Yellow Kid* (1896), Dirks's *Katzenjammer Kids* (1897), and other newspaper comic strips (which first appeared at the turn of the century) are plausible sources for Strothmann's style in *Adam's Diary;* but so are some fin de siècle experiments that were too hot, in themselves, for ordinary American tastes: the crude *Ubu* woodcuts by Alfred Jarry; "shadow-theater" lithographs and photo-reliefs by Henri Rivière and Pierre Bonnard; bizarre covers by Georges Lorin and his friends for renegade Paris magazines; the South Seas woodcuts by Gauguin.

In other words, there is a gratifying resonance between Strothmann's images for this whimsical Mark Twain book and a fin de siècle stir in the arts that was picking up a following in New York and Boston studios and gaining favor with sophisticated American consumers. There are no indications that Clemens himself wanted to take a cue from either comic strips or the Montmartre gang; but whether he wanted that or not, the Harpers edition of *Adam's Diary* confers upon "Mark Twain" the cachet of an early modernist, and in the company of these pictures the benign sentimental comedy in Clemens's verbal text acquires a heretical edge. Compared to this book, the 1906 companion work, *Eve's Diary,* seems a step backward in currency—again, an effect created not only by the tone of the verbal narrative but also by the illustrations, which once again account for half the pages in the published book. When Clemens complained to Harpers that Strothmann would be the wrong artist to do the pictures for *Eve's Diary,* he was listened to, and Lester Ralph replaced Strothmann. What Harpers and the

FIG. 11 From *Eve's Diary,* Lester Ralph's Eve, an aesthetic Pre-Raphaelite nymph.

author got from Ralph were illustrations in a hybrid style that reinforced the sentimentality but kept it under control with a dose of imported Aestheticism. Clemens expressed his satisfaction with that strategy in a subsequent letter to Frederick Duneka:

> We all think Mr. Ralph's pictures delightful—full of grace, charm, variety of invention, humor, pathos, poetry—they are prodigal in merits. It's a bonny Eve, a sweet & innocent & winning little lassie, & she is as natural & and at home in the tale as if she had just climbed out of it. <u>Now</u> do you think draperies are indispensable to picture women?[36]

Though Clemens read these pictures as celebrating Eve's innocence, in Lester Ralph's use of line and shading the wry and ominous style of Aubrey Beardsley is also in evidence. In Mauve Decade books and magazines, the truculent austerity of the Beardsley line and the merciless blackness of his shadows could insinuate a netherworld just beyond the margins: enclaves of absinthe, opium, and other modes of excess open exclusively to Those in the Know. But the young, mercurial Beardsley could play it both ways. When illustrating medieval poems or emulating Pre-Raphaelite experiments of William Morris or Burne-Jones, those same strong lines and austerities could also convey a simplicity and purity not quite gone from the world. In doing his pictures for *Eve's Diary,* Lester Ralph seems to borrow from this Beardsley as well, and the advantage to the verbal text is potent. Finishing the manuscript soon after Olivia's death, Clemens was working under the terrible pressure of personal grief; and if the story had begun somewhere farther back as a companion piece to the *Adam's Diary,* as another celebration of all obtuse men and the women who housebreak them, *Eve's Diary* evolved into a sanctification of Olivia Clemens and more than thirty years of their married life together. Bathos is a threat here—to contain it, Clemens compresses the final years of Eve and Adam into fewer than 150 words from Eve, which are followed by the one short sentence of elegy from Adam—which Duneka or someone else at Harpers borrowed from the revisions to "Adam's Diary." But Ralph's illustrations help pull the book through. Within their firm rectangular borders, floating in a field of blank white on the verso pages, these pictures can suggest exquisite bookplates from the library of Oscar Wilde or Arthur Symons—tight, enigmatic provocation, not program music for a heartbreaking tale.

Situating the reader somewhere between voyeurism and connoisseurship, the stylized nudes of Eve recall the "decadent" nineties but also some imaginary sexual innocence—and the "Art for Art's Sake" ancestry of these pictures enhances the impression of *Eve's Diary* as an artistic experiment in itself, the sort of "beautiful" and "useless" dream that Oscar Wilde celebrated as perfect art in his preface to *The Picture of Dorian Gray*. These intimations and effects circumscribe the emotions of Mark Twain's story; moreover, they move "Mark Twain" once more into new aesthetic territory. *Extracts from Adam's Diary* links him, for a moment, to Montmartre; this sequel connects him to 1890s London rather than Paris. Either way, this is Mark Twain as we haven't seen him before, and either way, a little more at home at those fashionable New York and London addresses (Fifth Avenue, Tuxedo, Tedworth Square, Dollis Hill) where he enjoyed showing off in his later years.

BOMBAST AND SILENT WITNESS

When the plight of new colonies elsewhere in the world attracted Mark Twain's attention in 1904, the narrative he wrote was provoked by an entirely different kind of visual experience, the Kodak photograph; and when his narrative was subsequently conjoined with photographs, the impact of the images upon the verbal text was catastrophic. As another short book from these later years, published not by Harpers this time but by a small Boston house on behalf of a struggling international rights group, *King Leopold's Soliloquy* was a minor project and in at least one significant way a wrongheaded one, for Mark Twain wrote it under an enraged misapprehension that Theodore Roosevelt and the American government were somehow endorsing the murderous exploitation in the Congo Free State.[37]

That confusion has an excuse. In the fall of 1904, when Mark Twain was first contacted in writing by Edmund Dene Morel and the Congo Reform Association (CRA), Leopold II, king of the Belgians, was sponsoring a media blitz in the United States to defend the operations of his privately owned company in Africa. The king's lobbyists were conspicuous on Capitol Hill and even in the White House, and the New York *American* had run incendiary columns about payoffs to several high-profile writers to portray the Congo Free State as a philanthropic mission.[38] The organized opposition to Leopold had arrived in the United States as well, with scant finances and weaker access to the media. In service of his cause, however,

Morel was energetic and eloquent. After many pamphlets and short books on colonial exploitation in sub-Saharan regions, Morel had just published *King Leopold's Rule in Africa* with the London house of William Heinemann. The 450-page chronicle included shocking, unprecedented Kodak snapshots, reprinted by the halftone process, of women and children mutilated by paramilitary thugs on Leopold's payrolls. But Morel's book would not be published in the United States until the following year,[39] and photographs of these atrocities were reaching only scattered audiences via slide shows at gatherings sponsored by the CRA and allied groups. When Morel came to the United States to expand support, he was also looking for a celebrity to help spread the word.

On October 10, from the Lake Mohonk Mountain House while on a speaking tour in upstate New York, Morel sent a note to Mark Twain in Manhattan to enlist his "sympathies in the question of Congo misrule."[40] When the message was received Clemens was at low ebb, four months after the death of Olivia, but when the grieving celebrity expressed interest Morel followed up quickly, this time from the Murray Hill Hotel in New York City (about a mile uptown from where Clemens was, at the Grosvenor), also sending over "by express messenger" a packet that included newspaper articles, "various pamphlets and leaflets," and "a special copy of the Memorial,"[41] referring to an extensive memorandum that Morel had presented to President Roosevelt in September, a document endorsed by the CRA, the British and Foreign Anti-Slavery Society, the Aborigines Protection Society, and the International Arbitration and Peace Association.[42] Evidently, the packet reached Mark Twain before Morel's letter did, and "the Memorial" had the greater impact—because of its photographs. Replying on October 16, Mark Twain attached this postscript to a short letter he had drafted the day before:

Dear Mr. Morel:

The Senate Memorial (<u>Mem</u>, I want another copy of it, & some terrible illustrations. reached *[sic]* me early this a. m., & I have remained in bed to read it.

If anything can be done—but come & let us talk about it.[43]

The letter to which this was appended cautioned Morel to "not trouble to write— . . . use the telephone: All days are alike to me in these black days of bereavement—I do not go anywhere." In November, Morel wrote to a colleague, Robert E. Park, a leader at the Boston headquarters of the American CRA: "Mark Twain. You are not likely to hear anything from him unless you write to him. . . . You must not ask him to join your Committee—only interest him and send him stuff. He is writing on the subject for Harpers."[44] Clemens indeed had the *Harper's Monthly Magazine* in mind for his satire, but when the final product was turned down,[45] and when the *North American Review* demurred as well, it found its way to the small house of R. P. Warren. No evidence has turned up that Mark Twain took an active role in choosing the photographs that made such a difference in this book, but there is no question that photographs had forced him out of the torpor of grief and into literary and political action.

Leopold's empire was fueled by profits from rubber and ivory, raw materials for a Europe of manufacture and luxury. The forces that eventually conjoined to bring disgrace on his enterprise emanated from a rising industrial enterprise of a different sort. In 1880, as Henry M. Stanley (the celebrated finder of Doctor Livingstone, and another star that Mark Twain had courted for a book with WebsterCo) was leading a corps of Leopold's agents up the Congo River to map a strategy for exploitation, George Eastman, in Rochester, New York, began commercial production of photographic dry plates, as crucial a breakthrough for professional photographers as oil paint premixed in tubes had been for the roving Impressionists. Before the dry plate, an operator of a camera was required to apply a gelatin surface to a sheet of glass, take the picture while the material was still wet, and produce the positive in a darkroom immediately after the exposure. With horse-drawn laboratories equipped for this purpose, Mathew Brady's teams had followed the Army of the Potomac. But Eastman's new plates came camera-ready, and once exposed they could be stored in a box for several days before processing. A lone photographer could now colonize in a different way, ranging farther and bringing home sights that had been unavailable to most of the world.

In the next ten years, the Eastman Company rapidly improved this mobility. In 1888, the first Kodak box cameras reached the market, advertised with the motto, "You push the button, we do the rest"—which meant that customers had to ship the entire camera back to the Rochester factories to recover the pictures. Only two years after, however, Eastman released the first camera with removable film on a roll, allowing the operator to reload on the spot and keep shooting. The exposed rolls could be stored for weeks before developing. As a technological breakthrough, this was equivalent to the breach-loading "needle guns" with which Bismarck's Prussians had routed the armies of Napoleon III. By the end of 1898, the Pocket Kodak was on the market—easier to use, easy to transport—and, when circumstances required, easy to conceal. A convenience and an amusement for millions, the Pocket Kodak was also a weapon, capable of acquiring evidence whose truth was considerably more difficult to controvert than verbal reportage. Clemens himself had been ambushed in this way as early as the winter of 1892. When he resisted doing an interview with "Luke Sharp" (a pen name for Robert Barr) for the *Idler Magazine,* a London "Illustrated Monthly," Sharp reportedly came at him with "several estimable gentlemen to assist me in this hazardous adventure" and one "small but industrious Kodak" that "'Held him with its glittering eye.'"[46] The piece was published with eight candid snapshots of Clemens in an overcoat, wandering around the deck of a ship. In a twenty-first-century wilderness of studio and desktop special effects, a conditioned skepticism can loom when we gaze at a photographic image; at the turn of the last century, however, in those earliest years of mobile and democratized photography, trust was stronger. As a result, in sites of colonial exploitation, forces of authority, legitimate or otherwise, clashed with raiders from this new power, vanguards of international witness.

When Mark Twain drafted his *Soliloquy,* he was launching a verbal text into a zone contested in more ways than one. His portrait of Leopold II is extravagant, so much so as to have little bite as an attack on either the king or the excesses of imperialism. This ranting Leopold occludes any insight into realities of colonialist thinking or the actual decisions and policies that worked such mayhem in central Africa. Moreover, for Mark Twain's projected audience of Anglo-American Protestants, this tirade was also safely and gratuitously anti-Catholic. Kissing his crucifix, Leopold is a caricature of murderous piety, a Borgia in an Edwardian suit. As a satire on modern-style villainy, the problems run deeper: the old trick of a soliloquy (as overheard by whom?) only underscores the artificiality of the rant. But because the dramatic situation is ludicrous, Leopold's speech calls attention to a new ineffectuality of merely speaking. This *Soliloquy* becomes an elegy for rhetoric itself, whether private or overheard, spoken or printed, in a moment when the relationship between the writer and the world is in a state of disruption:

In the early years we had no trouble in getting the press to "expose" the tales of the mutilations as slanders, lies, inventions of busy-body American missionaries and exasperated foreigners who had found the "open door" of the Berlin-Congo charter closed against them when they innocently went out there to trade; and by the press's help we got the Christian nations everywhere to turn an irritated and unbelieving ear to those tales and say hard things about the tellers of them. Yes, all things went harmoniously and pleasantly in those good old days. . . . Then all of a sudden came the crash! That is to say, the incorruptible *kodak*—and all the harmony went to hell! The only witness I have encountered in my own experience that I couldn't bribe. Every Yankee missionary and every interrupted trader sent home and got one; and now— oh, well, the pictures get sneaked around everywhere, in spite of all we can do to ferret them out and suppress them. Ten thousand pulpits and ten thousand presses are saying the good word for me all the time and placidly and convincingly denying the mutilations. Then that trivial little kodak, that a child can carry in its pocket, gets up, uttering never a word, and knocks them dumb![47]

Seek for affinity between the passionate satirist and the ostensible target of the satire, and troublesome possibilities turn up. Mark Twain's Leopold, after all, is another Gilded Age high roller, another entrepreneur with far-flung financial entanglements; and also like Mark Twain, this king has no patience with professional disappointment or incompetence and interference by others. Leopold pours indignation into the empty air, as Mark Twain had poured his own rage into notebooks and letters when embarrassment impended and debts and legal problems were closing in. The author and this persona may share this predicament as well: having constructed their respective empires out of language, they are beset now by the same problem—a fundamental change in the nature of printed discourse.

In the sequence of Mark Twain publications, *King Leopold's Soliloquy* marks a moment when images no longer merely enhance a verbal text or stretch it to publishable length or heighten or complicate the effect of the words. In this book, the images call into question the fate of satiric writing and even the continued relevance of the author. In the two Adam and Eve diaries, different as they are, the verbal impersonations are enriched and inflected by the visual experience, making it easier for the reader to imagine Adam as a good-natured, clueless American boy and Eve as a fin de siècle dream of a perfect sensitive wife. The pictures are half the pleasure and the emotional impact of each of these lean books—yet no more than half.

In *King Leopold's Soliloquy,* however, Mark Twain's impersonation of the king becomes a bombastic overture to a stunning silence. The Warren edition of the book is only forty-one pages, and in the first sixteen the maledictions of Leopold and the excerpts from missionary reports are enhanced with only four pedestrian graphics: three partial-page engravings of pen-and-ink drawings and one full-page portrait of Leopold fuming in his office, apparently a rotogravure of a likeness done in pencil or charcoal. There was nothing remarkable about the visual experience in the first half of this new work. On page 17, however, the intensity changes and the balance of power begins to shift. Leopold's screed of words is suddenly embarrassed by a full-page picture of a young African man, sitting on the edge of what seems to be a stone veranda, contemplating a severed hand and a foot lying just in front of him. The caption indicates that these are remains of his child, "dismembered by soldiers." The authority of the image, however, has as much to do with the medium as with the subject. This is an engraving of a photograph, and a small-font, block-letter caption at the bottom of the page tells us the provenance: "FOOT AND HAND OF CHILD DISMEMBERED BY SOLDIERS, BROUGHT TO MISSIONARIES BY DAZED FATHER," says the caption. "FROM PHOTOGRAPH TAKEN AT BARINGA, CONGO STATE, MAY 15, 1904. SEE MEMORIAL TO CONGRESS, JANUARY, 1905."

Everything that comes before this now seems fallacious, including the banal full-page portrait of the raging king and the verbal indignation—and also the imaginative contrivance of *creating* such a king. Suddenly the narrative itself seems forced into the presence of a kind of testimony that shames both the imperialist villain and any verbal intervention to reveal or revile him, any mode of indictment other than additional stark photographs like this one. Because the picture seems spontaneous and naive, compared to the cliché melodramatics of Mark Twain's Leopold shaking his fist at nothing in his private office, this Kodak picture of Nsala (for that was the father's name) sitting awkwardly, brooding over fragments of his own child, radiates an unspeakable repose.

Actually, this first image of mayhem in *King Leopold's Soliloquy* had been toned down compared to the photograph from which it was adapted, the picture facing page 144 of *King Leopold's Rule in Africa.* The resolution is higher there, the outlines of the figures and the body parts are harsher. Even the caption in Morel's book is more detailed and stark: "(Photographed by Mr. John H. Harris in May, 1904, with the hand and foot of his little girl of five years old—all that remained of a cannibal feast by armed rubber sentries.

FIG. 12 From *King Leopold's Soliloquy,* the cropped and softened image of a father with the remains of his child.

FIG. 13 From Morel's *King Leopold's Rule in Africa* (New York: Funk and Wagnall's, 1905), the original photograph of Nsala and the remains of his child.

The sentries killed his wife, his daughter, and a son, cutting up the bodies, cooking and eating them. See letter from Mr. Stannard in the Appendix.)"[48] There is no mention of cannibalism in the *Soliloquy* and no mention of an entire family killed. If this is airbrushing of the truth, the alteration of the image and the caption in the *Soliloquy* shifts the meaning in other ways as well, emphasizing the wordless grief of the survivor rather than specifics of the crime. There is an experiment here in the effects of not saying all, not showing all—and the result is another collision between silence and noise, between a literally unspeakable moment on a faraway veranda and a European prince unloading too many words in an opulent, empty room. Morel and his editors at Heinemann also knew how to pace and modulate the visual testimony. In *King Leopold's Rule in Africa* the first grisly photograph, of a group of men with a couple of severed hands, turns up facing page 48; before that, the interruptions of the verbal text are a few dignified studio portraits, photographs of an India-rubber shed, and a frontispiece of a Bangala woman and her child—not a photograph from life but an engraving adapted from a statue cast in bronze. Even atrocity requires an aesthetic, a cadence in the presentation.

McLuhan was among the first to observe that with the advent of the published photograph (as opposed to the one-off daguerreotype) physical posture became an important mode of public discourse, capable of embarrassing printed verbal discourse as "biased toward the private and individual,"[49] like Leopold solus in his rage. Because the photograph since the end of the nineteenth century constitutes an expansion of the central nervous system and collectivity of humankind, suppression of the photograph would be, in his view, a kind of amputation—which is precisely the metaphor that McLuhan exploits:

> The technology of the photo is an extension of our own being and can be withdrawn from circulation like any other technology if we decide that it is virulent. But amputation of such *extensions* of our physical being calls for as much knowledge and skill as are prerequisite to any other physical amputation.
>
> If the phonetic alphabet was a technical means of *severing* the spoken word from its aspects of sound and gesture, the photograph . . . *restored* gesture to the human technology of recording experience. (193)

When Leopold closes raging against "the trivial little kodak," the source of all the photographs that shame his pieties and the ostensible missions of his empire, this is what he yearns to do: amputate this technological extension of human capability like his agents chopping off limbs of the Congolese. The version that appears in *King Leopold's Soliloquy* is, as the caption confesses, an engraving of a drawing made from the photograph, and comparison with the original published form of the image, which appears in Morel's *King Leopold's Rule in Africa,* demonstrates that somewhere along the line the picture was cropped. On the right side, three bystanders and a potted plant on the porch have been taken out.[50] Nonetheless, the arrangement of this picture and especially the pose of its living human subject emanate from a different galaxy of visual discourse than the engraved drawings in the text preceding, all of them conventional in their blocking and theatrics and flaunting their aloofness from photographic reality. Awkward on the pavement, with one leg over the edge of the paving, the father seems puzzled as much as bereft. The reader is required to look at the picture with care to interpret the small thick objects on the surface to the left of the man as the severed limbs of a child, and then to interpret the face, searching there for signs of the grief and rage of the universal parent.

The sudden shift from the fuming, imaginary Leopold to the actuality of this porch, therefore, is a move into twentieth-century ways of seeing, straight from clichés of the nineteenth. To modern eyes pictures of grief-stricken fathers and fragmented children may be too familiar, so much so that the shock value for readers in 1905 has to be imagined rather than experienced. In the intervening decades, images of this kind have become the stuff we grow up with, holocausts regularly broadcast from far-flung places into the family room. More than a hundred years ago, however, these photographs published by the CRA and circulated by missionaries and activists in the years before *King Leopold's Soliloquy* introduced a visual experience that was almost pornographic in its starkness. With their cumbersome apparatus, Brady's and Timothy O'Sullivan's photographers had brought the Civil War dead to downtown galleries in Northern cities; but those dead, from battlefields already famous from news coverage, were not mutilated children turning up unexpectedly before our eyes from places unseen before and essentially unknown. The final full-page illustration in *King Leopold's Soliloquy* is a composite of nine photographs: nine Africans, mostly women and children, in formal poses, showing the stumps of their amputated hands. Previously printed and circulated individually by Morel and the CRA, these pictures are assembled here into one ghastly mosaic, one blow against the euphemisms and deceit that the ventriloquized "soliloquy" intends to caricature.[51] The collateral damage, however, is to the efficacy of the kind of satire that Mark Twain attempts here, ultimately routed by a handful of photographs, hideously serene. When the king's rage finally pounces upon "that trivial little kodak," the voices blend. We hear Leopold's fury, and perhaps also Mark Twain's bewilderment, at the rise of a new power for representing experience.

Behind the mask of Leopold, Mark Twain may have understood that the carnages of his own time could now be literally caught in a box, and their transference to paper would put to shame all other varieties of description, much as the corrupting corpses at the Sand Belt spelled the end to Hank Morgan's empire of words and to his verbal testament.

Rhetoric collides here with silence, with the photographic image as a variety of ultimate silence—and rhetoric fails. For written and printed utterance leads almost always to more utterance. Each sentence worth the reading carries within it a germ of suspense: What shall follow from this, which way will the thinking veer now? These photographs, in contrast, are each a dead end, and each is presented as such: a man or woman standing or sitting with a fixed stare, caught by a snap of a shutter—there is no intimation of a moment after, or anything to say. When Eve considers her own love for Adam, she finds no deep mutuality to base it on. Rarely do they talk, and rarely do they understand each other. She loves, yet she is alone: "Yes, I think I love him merely because he is *mine* and is *masculine*. There is no other reason, I suppose. And so I think it is as I first said: that this kind of love is not a product of reasonings and statistics. It just *comes*—none knows whence—and cannot explain itself. And doesn't need to."[52]

And when Eve dies, Adam faces the world not as a bereaved patriarch but as a man alone. King Leopold is presented as a man in a closed room, with nobody to talk to but himself—and even there, he cannot be honest even with himself. These three books make a set: two diaries and one soliloquy about people who must talk to themselves or write only for themselves: chronicles of loneliness and of the possible futility of saying—printed in books where the image matters as much as, or even more than, the word.

PRINTER'S DEVIL

In the final version of "The Mysterious Stranger"—the longest and best of his three explorations of the general idea—Mark Twain finally hit upon the "strangeness" that had compelled him to try telling the story again and again, each time with a shift in characterization and setting. What was he after? In the decades since William Gibson published an authoritative text of the story, building on the work of John S. Tuckey,[53] "No. 44, The Mysterious Stranger" has been read as Mark Twain's valediction, an American Prospero's farewell to the art—and also his farewell to hope.[54] There is much in the story to support that kind of reading. In the last version, as in the earlier ones, we have a supernatural being that comes as a kind of redeemer to lift a few human beings out of ignorance. In each version, cruelty is seen as endemic to the human breed; innocence is persecuted, and saintliness is a lethal mistake. And in that final famous conclusion, which Albert Bigelow Paine chose to ignore, and which Gibson argued was the intended ending to the "Print shop" version of the tale, everything becomes a dream, pointless motions of one "homeless Thought, wandering forlorn among the empty eternities!" (405). There is enough darkness here to satisfy any high modernist and to qualify Mark Twain, in his last years, as company for Beckett and Sartre, another pioneer in our adventures into despair.

But "No. 44, The Mysterious Stranger" is much more interesting than its ending—which was apparently written out of sequence, more than four years before Mark Twain's final work on the tale, and cannot be said, with absolute certainty, to be the ending that he ultimately intended.[55] "No. 44" has a different beginning and setting from its predecessors, and Mark Twain works hard to establish the time and details of this new context: a print shop in a place called Eseldorf, a small town in Austria, in the year 1490. This is a radical change, and there are more reasons for it than a chance for Mark Twain to reminisce about his own youth in a shop like this one, mastering the rituals of the Gutenbergs. His attention to detail here and his accounts of daily life in the composing room make the story's final version more energetic and vivid than the first try, which was set in the same town but diffusely described and in the year 1702, or than the abortive later manuscript, "Schoolhouse Hill," in which the Stranger drops into the world of Tom and Huck.

The Eseldorf print shop comes alive, and the breakthrough in this final telling was Mark Twain's recognition that his own anxieties about personal identity, the authenticity and transcendence of consciousness, and the truth of perception were deeply connected to, and even symbolized by, the technology in whose presence he had constructed his life. The story turns out to be his most daring engagement with the psychological and epistemological implications of printing and the impact of the first publishing revolution on the construction of consciousness and the very fabric of reality. This last version of "Mysterious Stranger" is in many dimensions *about* printing and a meditation upon printing as a cultural force. This shop is not only a setting but also a primary subject, and the themes explored there include three that can be summarized easily and one whose complexity and currency warrant special attention.

With regard to culture and belief in the West, "No. 44" contemplates the transmogrifying powers of the press. The story dwells on the machinery and procedures of the Gutenberg revolution just as it begins its contest with medieval hierarchies of class and intellect, the centralization and restriction of knowledge, caste systems, and the suppression of literate inquiry. There is also an ambivalent description here of the guild to which Sam Clemens had once belonged. The story describes the political and psychological liberation, as well as the alienation and hubris, experienced by people initiated into the arcana of print and publishing. Skill and experience as a "jour printer" had freed Sam from poverty and a circumscribed life in Hannibal; mastery of the trade had set him loose in America, confident that he could support himself anywhere that the publishing revolution of his own time was underway. His competence and independence as a printer had also allowed him to become a published writer, setting his own first literary efforts and turning out the pages. Those skills had given him credibility when he broke into the newspaper business in Virginia City, San Francisco, and Buffalo. Later, when he grew into an author of books, interacting with modern publishers, his insider's knowledge of production gave him leverage in the design of his own volumes and continuing authority, for better or worse, in the dynamic world of printing. That kind of knowledge was power—and Mark Twain idealizes that condition in the character of a fearless, truculent "wandering comp" named Doangivadam, who becomes for a while the hero of "No. 44," rescuing Stein, the young narrator August Feldner, and the homeless mysterious boy from a variety of disasters. Though 44's supernatural powers eventually overwhelm this story, this ascendancy happens later, *after* the young Stranger has learned the craft of printing, after the wandering comp, like a fearless hired gun, has faced down the treacherous strikers in Stein's shop—and after 44's own magic has been augmented, and liberated, by the magic of the printer's trade.

A related theme in the story, therefore, is Mark Twain's impatience with the retrograde conduct of modern printers and apprentices and with the fact that a professional life centered on letters and language may neither educate nor humanize the people in the trade. Mark Twain's frustration with American blue-collar practices, especially in the modern printing industry, had figured in his support for the Paige, which had promised to replace these fallible, recalcitrant creatures that Sam and his publishers had to contend with. The wish-dream of a supernatural shop where wraiths and "Duplicates" could get the work done properly and on time when ordinary human labor would not is a dream of transcendence, yet also a fantasy of revenge.

This brings us to one of the most provocative themes of "No. 44." Though his story at the end is a nightmare, along the way it is also a comedy and a fantasy. There is laughter here, and playfulness, about professional and psychological alienation, the dissolution of the self, and liberation from the confinements of ordinary psychological and physical identity— and in this narrative, all of these troubles and whispered consummations are connected to the advent of the printing press. Over the past forty years, speculations have heaped high about the impact that movable type and printing had on European life, ranging far beyond tallies of disruptions in political and religious practice. Consciousness itself is now counted as one of the casualties. The printed page signified a valorization of one sense, one mode of perception, above all others, a narrowing and a regimentation of seeing. The cultural trauma of innumerable and identical discourses challenged traditional assumptions about the originality of thought and the uniqueness of the thinker; the new rituals of printed discourse also brought the triumph of the paragraph, of logical exposition—and a devaluation of speech as an authoritative medium and of listening as a mode of attention.[56] About all this, Mark Twain was not a lonely sage decades before such perceptions came into full intellectual bloom. But in "No. 44" he did collide with these consequences, bravely and head on, exploiting a special understanding of what "printing" really meant, an understanding as firm as metal type or the workroom floor.

"It was 1490, winter." The so-called "Chronicle of the Young Satan," which Mark Twain never completed, had opened two hundred years later, in 1702; the "Schoolhouse Hill" experiment had moved the action forward another century and a half to the "forty or fifty years ago" of *Huckleberry Finn.* But the time *this* time is the opening years of the first information age, in the town of Eseldorf, where Heinrich Stein and his staff in the shop are agents in a subversion of culture and consciousness. Herr Stein's trade is new and radical and must be kept under wraps:

> Very few persons in our secluded region had ever seen a printed page, few had any very clear idea about the art of printing, and perhaps still fewer had any curiosity concerning it or felt any interest in it. Yet we had to conduct our business with some degree of privacy, on account of the Church. The Church was opposed to the cheapening of books and the indiscriminate dissemination of knowledge. Our villagers did not trouble themselves about our work, and had no commerce in it; we published nothing there, and printed nothing that they could have read, they being ignorant of abstruse sciences and the dead languages.[57]

Herr Stein is described by August Feldner as "a scholar, and a dreamer or a thinker, . . . [who] loved learning and study, and would have submerged his mind all the days and nights in his books and been pleasantly and peacefully unconscious of his surroundings, if God had been willing" (230). August's hesitation here is notable: "a dreamer or a thinker," implying that this young narrator cannot yet distinguish one sort of mental activity from the other, or perhaps that Stein himself is confused about what he is doing— or that the distinction between these two pursuits, dreaming and thinking, is arbitrary in any case. There would be no point belaboring such a quirky moment, were it not for the fact that Stein's trade is "dissemination of knowledge," publication of texts, and that so much space is given over to introducing him and his shop as otherworldly. What is the product of this factory—thinking or dreams? Knowledge or reverie? Stein's press is "hidden in an upper section of a round tower" (234) of an atmospheric old castle reminiscent of Monk Lewis or Bram Stoker:

> —prodigious, vine-clad, stately and beautiful, but moldering to ruin. The great line that had possessed it and made it their chief home during four or five centuries was extinct, and no scion of it had lived in it now for a hundred years. It was a stanch old pile, and the greater part of it was still habitable. . . . As a rule the spacious chambers and the vast corridors, ballrooms, banqueting halls and rooms of state were bare and melancholy and cobwebbed, it is true, but the walls and floors where in tolerable condition, and they could have been lived in. In some of the rooms the decayed and ancient furniture still remained, but if the empty ones were pathetic to the view, these were sadder still. (229)

On Stein's payroll is a wizard named Balthazar Hoffman, who "clothed himself as Egyptians and magicians should, and moved stately, robed in black velvet starred and mooned and cometed and sun'd with the symbols of his trade done in silver, and on his head a conical tower with like symbols glinting from it" (231). So from the opening of the "print shop" chapters of "No. 44," printing, dreaming, and magic are introduced as a mix. The earliest version of the Stranger tale had launched "young Satan," as a creature of relentless logic, into an Austria beset by ignorance, a sleepy, superstitious Austria still in the Age of Faith and terrorized by the likes of witch-hunting Father Adolf. The neighborhood is replete with ghosts or stories of ghosts. The Tom-and-Huck variation centers on the familiar, happy barbarism of the Missouri village.

In this final rendition, however, the action unfolds in a place apart from both the larger landscape and the time, a setting withdrawn from a village withdrawn from the world, magical before any supernal being arrives there. Stein's print shop is not a refuge from the naive imagining that overshadows the castle and the world beyond; there is no tidy arrangement here, aligning print and fact against illiteracy and superstition. In these early days of publishing, the thinking and the dreaming have not been centrifuged apart. And one incipient theme of "No. 44" is that they never will be.

With the opening "I" of Chapter 2, Mark Twain abandons the omniscient narration of "Schoolhouse Hill" and returns to the viewpoint of a young man in the thick of the action, puzzled to the last about what is going on here and even, as it turns out, about who it is that does the telling. For at that end of the story, an absolute kind of omniscient narration is reaffirmed: August apparently turns out to be everyone, which is to say the one lonely vagrant thought that dreams us all. In the meantime, however, he seems to have a personality, and his mix of empathy and decency conflicts with his conformist urges and a normal human measure of cowardice. Without a Missouri drawl or backwoods common sense, August still seems like a kindred spirit for Huckleberry Finn. But August is schooled in a prestige dialect—Austrian German, assumedly—as well as the esoteric new arts of the print shop and the social craft of fitting in with a crew of others with whom he has little in common. Inclined to let these others have their own way, August has not lost his belief in fairness and justice, despite the vulgarity and bullying that characterize most of his peers in Eseldorf. He improvises his way through his daily life as Huck might, confining his moral judgments mostly to the narrative he writes (or dreams that he writes), keeping his mouth shut when others are ventilating and imposing their will, and doing acts of kindness now and then, on the sly.

Even so, August's life is more complex than Huck's—which is to say that the various identities that August must assume ramify in ways that Huck's do not. To survive, Huck has to impersonate—Sarah Mary Williams, George Jackson, an English valet, and eventually Tom Sawyer—and none of these masquerades complicates his own sense of who he really is. But as a boy not much older than Huck, August has embedded himself in a trade, working and writing his way toward a momentous transition. When the narrative opens, he is already on a track to a psychological and moral condition whereby this trade shall become *him*. Working as an apprentice in the trade, he has yet to become a true professional printer in either skill level or mentality, but he is risking that kind of petrifaction. Raised in Eseldorf, he has never wandered from home or yearned to do so; as far as his personal aspirations go, he seems to want only a quiet mature prosperity, local social acceptance, marriage perhaps, and a daily routine with as little as possible in the way of trouble or challenge. He offers no reasons for taking up the trade of printing. Apparently he has come to the shop as Sam Clemens did in his own adolescence, responding to an opportunity for work and a livelihood or sent into the trade by his elders.

Mark Twain's first experiment with the Mysterious Stranger idea centered on one plot. A rational and omnipotent young man arrives from a World Beyond to teach a young Austrian boy named Theodor Fischer and his two playmates, Seppi Wohlmeyer and Nikolaus Baumann, a sequence of brutal lessons about human nature—the depravity of the "moral sense," the ludicrousness of human solipsism, the indifference of higher powers. The final version, however, becomes an array of stories with looser connections to one another. The first chapter is a repeat of the opening of "The Chronicle of the Young Satan," in which a Father Adolf, as a power-hungry priest, exploits superstition to terrorize the neighborhood and expel a rival cleric, Father Peter, whose Christian values include too much joy and forgiveness. Next comes a tale of the stoic suffering of 44, who at first seems a hapless waif, persecuted by bullies in the shop. Discerning that this new boy can read minds, August helps him learn the intricacies of the trade via mental telepathy but shies away from standing with him against the others on Stein's payroll.

At Chapter 9, the narrative veers in new directions. Rising tension between these workers and Stein brings a strike to the shop and a crisis in meeting a production deadline. Doangivadam, the "wandering comp" whose name summarizes his personality, arrives as a savior of sorts, a good swordsman and a proprietor's dream of professional dedication around the cases and forms; and this knight-errant printer joins with Stein, August, Katrina, and 44 in a struggle to keep the place in operation. The other apparent force for the good is the wizard Balthazar, whom August assumes is the power behind 44's increasingly frequent exhibitions of miraculous skill. When eight invisible ghosts turn up in the middle of the night to complete a backlog of work, the magician gets the credit, and by Chapter 14 the mild-mannered 44 seems a harmless mascot and amanuensis, even to Doangivadam and August:

> It turned me sick and faint, the way the men plunged at 44, crying "Kill him, kill him!" but the master and Doangivadam jumped in and stood them off and saved him. Then Doangivadam talked some wisdom and reasonableness into the gang which had good effect. He said—
> "What's the use to kill the boy. He isn't the *source;* whatever power he has, he gets from his master, this magician here. Don't you believe that if the magician wants to, he can put a spell on the boy that will abolish his power and make him harmless?"
> Of course that was so, and everybody saw it and said so. (295)

In the next chapter, however, 44 breaks out in an ecstasy of omnipotence, and the narrative becomes an account of his caprices and manipulations, with the frightened, exasperated August struggling to keep him in check. The first sustained havoc that 44 wreaks is his union-busting creation of the Duplicates, an extended motif in the narrative that will require some special attention. Later he vanishes in a burst of white fire, and everyone believes him dead; he reappears to August in his room after midnight, straight from a hedonistic romp in America, with roasted duck, a pipe full of New World tobacco, and lessons about Workaday-Selves and Dream-Selves—and the print-shop story fades away in a welter of fables about love, identity, time, belief, fate, banjos, talking cats, the absurdities of earthly life. Stein, the shop, the other printers, the urgencies and the bric-a-brac of publishing: these subjects drop out of sight.

After so much development, why are they dismissed? Does Mark Twain's last try at telling this tale lose direction and collapse? Is all the early attention to printing and publishing only a digressive reminiscence that slips out of control? Though "No. 44" is a messier narrative than "The Chronicle of the Young Satan" and "Schoolhouse Hill" fragments that preceded it, this last try is also the liveliest, and the energy rises from Mark Twain's rediscovery of the particulars of ordinary experience, their importance in bringing a narrative to life. Even so, it also rises from a recognition or intuition that pervades the tale to the end, that typesetting, printing, creative power, spiritual liberation, and unnerving imaginative possibilities are intertwined. "Young Satan" had no plausible reason for showing up and remaining in the company of the generic Theodor and his indistinguishable friends, but when 44, resembling a "singed cat," appears at the door of Stein's establishment, he has come to the right place, a place where a species of magic is already afoot, transforming the world and the self by radically altering the epistemology of words. Stein and his journeymen may have no idea of the power and implications of their own trade or the limits of that power, but 44 ultimately reveals that he does.

Before and after the Paige and the other machines that drove it from the market, the work of small-shop printers was mechanical assembly and disassembly: at the end of each press run, every line in the chase had to be broken down again into particles and distributed back into the case, an inevitable, conscientious dissolution of words. In a print shop working with traditional movable type, one truth is clear every day—discourse is a putting together and then a taking apart. The one "vagrant Thought" at the core of all dreams and stories dreams a printing shop and a boy named August Feldner at the center of it and dreams another boy, miraculous, to visit this place and change the life and mind of August himself. The dreamed-up stranger eventually delivers a homily about dreaming and thinking, a homily that offers us the mind as a compositor, or as a jour printer, and reality as only a contrivance, as transient as a chase full of type:

> "A man *originates* nothing in his head, he merely observes exterior things, and *combines* them in his head—puts several observed things together and draws a conclusion. His mind is merely a machine, that is all—an *automatic* one, and he has no control over it; it cannot conceive of a *new* thing, an original thing, it can only gather material from the outside and combine it into new *forms* and patterns. But it always has to have the *materials* from the *outside,* for it cannot make them itself. That is to say, a man's mind cannot *create*—a god's can, and my race can. That is the difference. *We* need no contributed materials, we *create* them—out of thought. All things that exist were made out of thought—and out of nothing else." (332–33)

So human beings can never be truly authors, but only compositors? Parallels, then, between the print-shop tale and the emergent theme about the human predicament? No surprise that Stein is described as "a thinker or a dreamer," since in the mind of 44—which is to say the mind of August thinking or dreaming the mind of 44—with human beings there can be no difference; no surprise that the books pouring from his enterprise have taught the makers nothing; no surprise that this shop includes a resident ineffectual wizard, a counterfeit creator. The anomaly that is publishing becomes the anomaly of existence. Publishing gratifies a drive to tell the world, to make telling permanent, to bring the teller fame, a "Duplicate" identity, which like the Duplicates of the story knows neither fatigue nor hunger nor death. But publishing is also an illusion of creation, a counterfeit of thought, a dream of an alternative existence, a mechanical process as alienated from who we are and what we think or dream as any other process in a mechanized information age.

At moments like this, the narrative seems eager to convince us that the dream-stuff we are reading is an outcome of technology and collective effort, more muscle and craft than imaginative genius. What other canonical American writer invested so much imaginative energy in subverting the imaginative construct of a commonalty between himself and his readers, or for that matter between any modern author and any public, except perhaps the resentful workforce that sets the manuscript in type and produces the imprint? This vigorous return to detail, to the complexity of ordinary experience, suggests that Mark Twain had rediscovered an essential virtue of American realism: the achievement of the fabric and feel of life through presentation of hard facts and respect for the ordinary daily doing that sustains and re-creates the world.

But something more is engaged in passages like this one. Unanswerable questions are touched on here, questions about the ontological nature of a printed text, the meaning of authorship, and how imagining, saying, writing, and publishing are propelled into paradoxical relations by the advent of the print shop, the transformation of the written word from a scriptorium artifact into a mass-produced commodity given alien form by alienated labor and transported to places and readers unknown. The last half of the story centers on 44 as whim incarnate, an omnipotent innocent who can be checked and sobered only by sharp words from one trusted human friend—and never for long. What relationship is there between this manic wizard-child and the gentle outcast who endures abuse through so many chapters at the start? There doesn't seem much point in contriving a case for 44 as a rounded character, especially since the final chapters of the book militate against the proposition that anyone achieves genuine individuality or that such a concept matters in understanding the human condition. If 44 evolves into an allegory for the imagination, then it comes in two configurations: Imagination Bound and Imagination Unbound. In Stein's house of printing and pain, the boy suffers without complaint. But when 44 cuts loose, creating the Duplicates, turning Katrina into a singing house cat, capering across ages and dimensions, changing shape, changing anything he wants to, the gear and procedures of handpress publishing vanish from the story. What takes over is a euphoria related to creative power, an anxiety about the loss of absolutes and the loss of belief in the worth and integrity of the self. What relationship can there be between the opening chapters of the story, centered so strongly on printing, and these heady themes later on?

Some connections are simple enough: in the Duplicates, created by 44 to labor tirelessly and for no pay in the print shop, there are remnants of the dream of the Paige. The invisible ghosts whom the Duplicates supersede, the spirits summoned to save the firm from a lethal strike by resentful human printers, are also, perhaps, ghosts of machines that never became what Mark Twain wanted—mechanical supermen to do the hardest, slow-est work of the jour printers. In the first half of the story, we have the successive arrival of four sources of hope, at four levels of force and sophistication, all of them related to wish-dreams about printing and publishing. 44 himself turns up from nowhere as a perfect quick study, throwing himself into every task, learning each skill on the first try, and performing a miracle now and then to pull the shop through in emergencies. When Stein's lazy crew organizes a strike after failing to intimidate the boy and drive him off, along comes Doangivadam, friend of oppressed proprietors, foe of shop stewards and thugs. And then come the ghosts, invisible, known only by their speed and expertise and a cold breeze when they pass. The Duplicates appear in Chapter 16—copies of every union worker in the shop, but better because they "did not need to eat or drink or sleep," and "got no pay for their work in the shop, and didn't care for it and wouldn't ask for it" (307). Even better than the ghosts, who appeared only in a crisis, did what needed to be done, and went away, the Duplicates are permanent. Comedy and interpersonal problems flourish as the workers and their Duplicates settle into life together, quarreling over women, puzzling over the nature of identity—but around Stein's presses all hereafter goes well, or at least well enough that the narrative suspends its interest in all of that.

Recurring reveries, perhaps, from Sam Clemens's younger days. There is no problem historicizing the first eighteen chapters of "No. 44" as a fantasy of revenge, a fantasy of triumph over every rascal who abused Sam as a junior worker or stood in his way later on, and as a Tom Sawyer dream of ease and comfort in which one innocent child, one roving hero, eight printer-ghosts, and finally a nonunion force of superprinters get all the hard work done.

But who or what is 44?

He is, we are ultimately told, August Feldner himself, and by implication all of us, as permutations of the one vagrant, lonely Thought, "wandering forlorn among the empty eternities," that has generated and sustained 44, August, and this whole tale, and all tales, as well as anyone who writes, prints, or reads them. Whether or not these closing pages make philosophical sense, their interpretation must countenance the possibility that 44 also represents the technology that he and August have in common. With the Stranger in charge, the revolutionary work of the print shop becomes the revolutionary play of overhauling the people who work there and the town, the historical moment, and time itself. In other words, the cosmic catastrophe of August Feldner, caught up in the antics and power of his supernatural friend (who turns out to be himself), is grounded in the actualities of his working life: the "reality" of the print shop where he lives and works becomes one dimension of an anywhere-anytime thrill-ride, not a place and a time separate from either history or a dream. They all begin here: these adventures in manic and terrible contemplations; the liberation and disintegration of the self; the overthrow of every basic expectation regarding daily work, human relationships, culture, and reality. 44 transforms the new arts of printing and publishing into another sort of dark magic, performed by ghosts and artificial beings, which confound and challenge these supposedly real tradesmen whom they counterfeit and replace.

But "No. 44" is also a dream of achieving something sublime, a bond between the imaginative faculty and the finished artifact, between the dream itself and the worldly deed, the word chosen or spoken and the world rediscovered or remade. From waif, to printer, to wizard, to god—it is not difficult to look at the shape-shifting evolution of 44 as paralleling Sam Clemens's professional history and aspirations as well as his fears. First, a difficult trade must be mastered. In the story's historical setting, the early decades of the Gutenberg revolution, Mark Twain can portray that trade as a radical newness, a power yet to be understood even by its wielders, like the print revolution that had taken hold in the American big city when Sam Clemens came to the shop in Hannibal. In both histories—of 44 and of Sam himself—practicing the printer's craft eventually gives way to dangerous outbreaks of sheer imagination; but these at first remain within the world of print, complicating one's own professional identity, challenging the cultural status and function of the trade. Does the "printer's devil" become a devil incarnate, and does the one incarnation lead to the other?

After Chapter 19, the plot of "No. 44" gambols off in several directions, and nothing is gained by trying to assemble all of these vectors and blind leads into some intricate grand design. But even a skeptic about the thematic depth or coherence of this story can observe its progressions: from order into disorder; from an archetypal plot—a fable of an ugly duckling or unpromising superhero—into plotlessness and a welter of speculations with regard to who or what anyone really is. In "The Chronicle of the Young Satan," the Mysterious Stranger appears, works miracles, and takes credit for them, all in a single chapter. In the last version of the tale, the gradual emergence of this boy-god is the essential story. Supposedly helpless when he shows up at Stein's castle, 44 reveals himself in glimpses and stages as a wonder boy and then as a shape shifter and a time traveler. Their Duplicates and their own Dream-Selves confound the local printers, including August himself, and in those controversial final pages the whole shebang turns out to be a dream. As special powers are revealed after a time of suffering, and as a boy's concealed wizardry remakes the world, personal identity becomes everything and nothing, and the narrative somersaults into a burlesque of narrative.

Much of this story is about printing, and printing is duplication, the transformation of the identity of the author, and also a kind of traveling through space and time. Words become substance and refuse to keep still. Stein's shop occupies a corner of an old castle, "near the centre of the mass," and the printers keep their heads down while participating in the rise of a new kind of power, the kind that Hank Morgan believed would conquer every castle in medieval England. Printing and disseminating a text is circulation of a Dream-Self, perhaps deathless and even timeless, bearing the writer's name, a thing like the author, perhaps, yet different and with a will of its own. Print re-creates, empowers the imagination, makes the dream real, or rather transforms the dream into a cultural force that might possibly rival whatever it is that passes for reality. Dream and dreamer are conjoined in widening spirals of euphoria and alienation. These are my words, my works—or so the author might imagine—yet when artifacts of that imagination hold sway in other minds they are in a sense no longer his own. What if "No. 44, The Mysterious Stranger" is read as a Mark Twain dream of Sam Clemens, reimagining the fate of his "real" self, rising by ambition and luck from small-town apprenticeship to dominance in the Vulcan forges of the new media, then losing that power and losing even his grip on his own public identity? From anonymity and innocence in an abode of printers, 44 transforms into a prodigy, then a master of revels, then a shape-shifter and time-shifter, and finally a disembodied voice, a figment of everyone's and no one's imagination, shrouding all imaginings in perfect doubt.

To sum up: the final version of the "Mysterious Stranger" can be understood as about the threatened disintegration of personality and belief under one specific pressure of modernity, the accelerating production and alienation of printed words. The shop is 44's chosen point of entry into the human world. It is where the Stranger learns about human nature; or, if we require the last pages of the narrative to explain its earlier chapters, it is where August, only dreaming all the while that he is a printer's devil, dreams a truer devil to turn his own dream of deadening routine into a dream in which routines, times, life, and death are taken up and dropped at will and whim. Why a print shop? Because in this place was the stuff that Mark Twain's dreams were made of, the earthly locale where aspirations took shape and were transcended. Print shops made possible the transfiguration of a backwoods boy into a new kind of author and a new kind of American life, translated *into* print by the treacherous dynamics of media celebrity—an identity transcended, immortalized, and menaced with obliteration by tides of words.

In the Old Ram sketch in *Roughing It,* a "symmetrically drunk" and free-associating Jim Blaine mentions a man named William Wheeler who worked in an automated carpet factory, where a powered machine transformed him in an instant from a human being into fourteen yards of three-ply carpet. The maker of the commodity becomes the commodity, and Mark Twain tells this grisly, ludicrous tale as a tale of a tale. As a manifestation of the unbelievable future of the printed word, 44 sweeps a printer's apprentice away, by stages, to a dizzying recognition or delusion that the rules of existence are dreams and delusions, that the only "real" thing out there in the boundless emptiness is thought woven by its own artifice into endless narrative.

As it turns out, however, August, or rather the homeless Thought that thinks August, has originated 44, or has combined him out of "observed things" that are *not* exterior things but *created* things, created by a mind more powerful than either a god's or 44's imaginary superior race. Consider too deeply and the confusion will only get worse: the intention of this text is regressing illusions, dreams within dreams within dreams. There may be no way to sort this out—and no need to do so if the dislocation created by moments like this, which grow frequent in the closing chapters, is what really matters. Everything in this narrative—including the ultimate subversion of narrative, of author, of reader, of reality—is created by *text,* by written language that in printed form might wander "forlorn" long after the end of Sam Clemens and Mark Twain, Dream alienated from Dreamer, Thought from Thinker. The final chapters of "No. 44" complicate story itself rather than the mere meanings of one story. These chapters throw into question the reality of the text we are reading, the reality and significance of the shapes of ink on the page. This published document denies the existence of all such documents—and we can complicate that paradox further by noting that Mark Twain did *not* send this document to a publisher.

When it finally emerged from the press, half a century after his death, it was something else, transformed more radically than any Mark Twain manuscript had been transformed by editors and print when he was alive. Out of a scattering of private writings it became supremely public, and many people have read it as a kind of Last Testament. From one holograph copy, the words have become legion and scattered across a planet. And because the tale is enigmatic or muddled in so many ways, it gathers interpretations like dust on an asteroid—interpretations like this one, which inevitably widen the distances between the teller and the tale.

No other Mark Twain story expresses such hope for the printed word as a kind of transcendence, an escape from time, from the confinements of sense, from illusion into truth; no other Mark Twain story raises such doubts about the power of the printed word to do any of these things. The text addresses the reader about the end of text, a vanishing of text as all texts vanish in the moment of transition from reading to having read, and as the encounter with printed or written words dissolves into vagrant thoughts wandering the eternities of mind. "No. 44" is indeed about the weakness and triviality of human nature, the limitless universe, and the futility of aspirations on this one random planet. But it is also about texts—how they are made and why, and with what constrictions in the thinking, imagining, and producing, and about their own epistemology as transient experiences, for all their illusory permanence.

The ending of "No. 44" is a multidimensional self-immolation—the mysterious companion goes away; August himself disappears in the instant he recognizes his own self-delusion; the narrative self-destructs as well because this ending makes everything that comes before it illusory and impossible *as* narrative, as an act of composition and publication. What all this comes to, then, may depend on what we imagine Sam Clemens thought he was doing when he wrote it. If this was private discourse, one aging author's closed conversation with his own existential dread, then the "appalled" fade-out at the end might signify a lonely mind reaching a dead end in a reverie that had begun safely and conventionally enough—a mysterious boy revealing himself gradually through a series of scrapes and marvels—and evolved or drifted into a contemplation that called everything into doubt. But when "No. 44" is read as a published literary text or merely as a text finished and intended someday for print, then everything changes. In a story about the dawn of printing in which a free imagination embarks from empirical truth about how stories are made real in the modern world, something new emerges: a text that becomes more than a text because it engages the making of texts, *and* the collateral *re*making of the writer, printer, and reader alike, a story that leaps boundaries among dream, text, truth, and individual human minds. In an age of print, when even the wildest dream must be contrived and promulgated with printed language that inevitably alienates and objectifies the dream, escape *from* the self and escape *into* text can be one.

Afterword

Mark Twain for the Next Fifteen Minutes

This book has been about Sam Clemens's professional and imaginative engagement with America as a rising information superpower. As a high-stakes player in the reinvented production and dissemination of printed discourse, as a casualty of those changes, and as a body of writing about them, what "Mark Twain" can signify now depends on where we suppose we are, in this accelerated process, when we seek that perspective. This kind of orienteering has never been more difficult. Every fresh wave of information technology seems to have its impact upon daily experience and the motions of the mind, including engagements with cultural history. Things are really up for grabs now, and drawing parallels to the adventures and writings of an author from another century, even an icon like Mark Twain, is a hard game to play, with the technological "now" shifting treacherously, at very high speed. To the media storm itself, what relevance can be ventured for a Mark Twain legacy?

With so many gurus to choose from for guidance, we can start with words from a prizewinner—and with an uncanny echo of "The Mysterious Stranger." In a 1990 Romanes Lecture in the Bodleian Library at Oxford, Saul Bellow spoke of the electronic obliteration of coherence—on video screens and between the ears. He warned of a generation growing up like the flesh-and-blood progeny of 44, child gods of mouse and remote—out of control and controlling all:

> Mastery belongs to the holder of the switch who diverts himself with inconsequence, and his willful switching is something like an assertion of independence, or a declaration of autonomy, or supreme immunity. Each sepa-

rate intelligence at its separate command post declares itself free from all influence. The kid with the clicker is the Boss. He can cope with any amount of randomness or inconsequence—with anything you can throw at him. This is clowning, of course, but it is also a sort of triumph for personal consciousness. Here, consciousness emptily asserts itself. The emptiness of the assertion makes it akin to autism, a word defined in my dictionary as a state of mind characterized by daydreaming, hallucinations, and disregard of external reality.

Of course, the ceaseless world crisis, otherwise known as the chaos of the present age, is not the work of the communications industry and its Information Revolution; but for our peculiar pseudoknowledge of what is happening, for the density of our ignorance, and for the inner confusion and centerlessness of our understanding, for our agitation, the communicators are responsible. Intellectuals and universities, from the ideological side, also have much to answer for.[1]

Bellow saw all this before the advent of broadband, before WiFi, flash drives, cell phones, and pocket computers, before satellite dish lines were punched into millions of family homes like fiber-optic IVs, and mainframe computers reached cruising velocities measured in teraflops, trillions of floating point operations per second. "That's faster than God thinks," said a physicist friend, not entirely in fun, when the Lawrence Livermore Laboratory put the first of these on line—outclassed and outmoded within months by something quicker, as he foretold. As we cartwheel onward in this fashion, the prospect is real that even the quickest human thinkers will have considerable trouble maintaining an imaginative grip amid an apocalypse of discourses, calculations, and synthesized dreams.

So—Saul Bellow and Mark Twain as a matched pair of visionaries, gazing together at a future overwhelmed by strange toys and media-besotted kids with no attention span at all. One problem, however, is that the prevailing mood of Mark Twain's last great story is not nearly so grim as it seems at the end, or as Bellow sounded in the gothic halls of the Bodleian. Moreover, Bellow may have missed, or underestimated, a certain resiliency that seems common among ordinary people in the West, especially among people much younger than himself: an intuitive knack for negotiating the continual chaos in this cognitive environment. Like Bellow's archetypal Anglo-American kid, Mark Twain's 44 has certainly learned to cope. With his "centerless understanding," his happy insouciance about whatever is being pitched at him as reality, 44 is at peace within his romp. Though plenty of existential despair can be found in this sprawling story about him, the young Stranger's festivity must also be reckoned with as a center of meaning. Exuberance, adaptability, playfulness, even hope: think of Hank Morgan with a cache of fireworks, ready for action at the Sacred Well, or Tom Sawyer on a new morning with a fresh fantasy in his head, or the young Mark Twain himself, happily out on his own in Paris and Rome in *The Innocents Abroad* or in his exuberant early sketches.

Steadily or otherwise, Mark Twain understood this redemptive human power to improvise and adapt amid disheveled circumstances, moving on to the next appalling recognition of one's own precarious or hopeless circumstances, the futility of one's own discourse, improvising transient good times and skeins of lively words along the way. Through much of his life he exemplified this power and celebrated it, even as he feared for our collective moral and psychological future in the opening years of Bellow's "ceaseless world crisis." In a rambling unfinished "dark" story from 1905, "Three Thousand Years among the Microbes," Mark Twain once again satirizes the pathological desire of the human race to see itself as consequential. In the middle of this tale, however, there is an outbreak of euphoria about a dreamed-up ultimate media device: a mind-recording machine, the literal last word in information technology, all the way out, beyond print and writing, even beyond words. The narrator of the tale is a cholera germ; his "universe," as he knows, is the filthy body of a tramp. But what difference does that make when all the obstacles between reverie and text can be transcended?

> You do not dictate *words,* you understand, but only thoughts—*impressions*—and they are not articulated; that is to say, you do not frame the impressions into words, you deliver them in *blocks,* a whole chapter in one blast—in a single second, you know—and the machine seizes them and records them and perpetuates them for time and eternity in that form; and there they are, and there they glow and burn forever; and so luminous are they, and so clear and limpid and superbly radiant in expression that they make all articulated speech—even the most brilliant and the most perfect—seem dull and lifeless and confused by comparison. Ah, if a person wants to know what an intellectual aurora borealis is like, with the skies all one tumultuous conflagration and downpour of divine colors and blinding splendors, let him connect-up a Recorder and turn on one of those grand poems which the inspired Masters of a million years ago dreamed into those machines![2]

Certainly, the kids with the clickers have more to click with each succeeding hour, downloadable empty eternities spawning before them like string-theory universes, no end of virtual space to wander, plenty of options for distraction from the void within, a consummate and appalling loneliness. Even so, for Sam Clemens, writing this strange story in his final years, after the deaths of Susy and Livy, there could still be ecstasies, as well as terrors, in the apparatus acquired along the way and in potent toys, yet to come, for the expression and amusement of the mind. As a prophet of media troubles and technological transcendence, Mark Twain has strong credentials.

On the multilane speedways of postmodernity, these supposedly autistic new legions that Bellow worries about seem to be managing no worse than the American populace half a century ago, and the Mark Twain who speaks to them has a voice more buoyant than doctrinaire. Despite their daily immersion in *guignols* of print, video, and cyberspace, a great many British and American college students can still talk and write coherently (at least when they have to) about the thematic thickets of *Pudd'nhead Wilson,* *Huckleberry Finn,* and *Connecticut Yankee,* though what they seem to enjoy and remember best is the vitality of these novels rather than the high-serious issues raised in the appendices by solemn professors. 44 delights and consoles them for his what-the-hell good humor, his indifference to puzzlement and explanations, and his serene acceptance of the futility of trying to make sense of it all. To these fresh legions with flip-on gadgetry in their pockets, and in their boudoirs a jumble of bulkier high-tech gear (instruction manuals, as they confess, are rarely glanced at), the supernatural boy's good cheer strikes deeper chords than August Feldner's panic or Saul Bellow's ceremonial funk. Shaken by a globalizing information culture, elders in our moment may prefer a Mark Twain of forebodings, a mustachioed Missouri Virgil in a sepulchral white suit leading a morose cortege into the postmodern dark. But in the Mark Twain legacy there is also this mercurial joy, this volatile faith that free, self-confident, barbarous new people will somehow learn to live, even happily, wherever they are, ignoring the instruction manuals and improvising as they go.

Bellow fears for the fate of the attention span, and among the endangered tribes of the printed word who doesn't? For psychological and cultural survival under a planetary information blitz, however, a good attention span might not always be such a blessing. Crossing the high deserts of central

Peru on the way from Puno to Arequipa, I rode a bus recently with about two dozen Aymara-speaking women, *campesinas* from adobe and concrete-block villages above ten thousand feet, near the shores of Lake Titicaca. These were subsistence farmers with small fields they worked by hand, untouched as yet by the full wattages of modernity. As a delegation to lobby the central government for better medical care in the hinterland, the women were going to Lima, and this was the longest journey that some of them had ever taken. To keep them amused and in their seats, the bus company had shut the side curtains and turned off the cabin lights to launch Hollywood movies at them from monitors on brackets in the aisles.

In one of these productions, Jim Carrey, as a latter-day postpubescent Tom Sawyer, an ambitious prankster working for a Buffalo television station, exploits a loan of divine powers to get himself a flashy new car, a prime-time audience, and better sex with his girlfriend—three basic ambitions of the wired North American male. In the second feature, Tom Cruise, as a sexy American army officer from the Gilded Age, turns up in Meiji Japan for a jumble of adventures echoing *A Connecticut Yankee.* Mr. Cruise shoots armored knights with a pistol, is knocked silly by a blow to the head, is taken prisoner and almost executed; he meets and woos a lovely, tradition-bound, submissive woman, teaches modern warfare to sword-wielding nobility, organizes a climactic and suicidal slaughter—yet somehow he survives all this to teach the emperor how to be a high-tech militarist and a better monarch. Some of the Aymara women seemed to be paying attention, but what they were thinking I preferred not to imagine. As another Yankee out of place, I yearned dutifully for a clicker, a long stick, anything to turn this off. But that was absurd: these media assaults on other people's values and sensibilities go on everywhere, unavoidably: the daily globalized business of trampling national and cultural borders. Part of the Mark Twain legacy, whether we like it or not, is that old stories he told about us, and for us, are pumped up now with light and magic and inflicted on the rest of the world. As representations of who we are, they help to extend an imaginative empire far beyond anything Mark Twain thought possible. In those hours, on that mountain road, the scions of Sawyer and Morgan were Carrey and Cruise.

An abiding subject of this book has been the historical situation of one author and a set of literary texts, and the impact of new information technology on the cultural and epistemological predicament faced by that author as he wrote. A closely related question is how to read *any* literary text, by Mark Twain or anyone else, amid these media challenges to processes of interpretation and to the old imperative to understand. For provocative thought about such matters, Roger Chartier is one of the masters, and his writings on the history of print media, culture, and consciousness have influenced my thinking about Mark Twain.[3] Cooler-headed than Bellow about the prognosis for the individual consciousness in an electronic information age, Chartier has been scrupulous in updating and refining his insights with each new ramification he encounters. Reviewing the interpretive environment again recently, he proposed that the absorption of literature into cyberspace has already changed every important dimension of our negotiations with the literary—and also with whomever, or whatever, we choose to hold accountable for this cognitive trouble. He suggests that on this journey into bewilderment the postmodern West has already passed a point of no return:

> The originality and the importance of the digital revolution must therefore not be underestimated insofar as it forces the contemporary reader to abandon—consciously or not—the various legacies that formed it. This new form of textuality no longer uses printing (at least in its typographic sense), it has nothing to do with the *libro unitario,* and it is foreign to the material nature of the codex. It is therefore a revolution that in the same period in time, and for the first time in history, combines a revolution in the technical means for reproducing the written word (as did the invention of the printing press), a revolution in the medium of the written word (like the revolution of the codex), and a revolution in the use of and the perception of texts (as in the various revolutions in reading). This no doubt explains the confusion of the contemporary reader who must transform not only the intellectual categories he or she has employed to describe, structure, and classify the world of books and of other written materials but also his or her most immediate perceptions, habits, and gestures.[4]

Emerging into this new textuality, disembodied and dis-empaged, Mark Twain tumbles and shape-shifts, along with every other unforgotten writer, in gigabytes and pixels. The interesting difference, as we have seen, is that Clemens himself, almost alone among his literary peers in the nineteenth century, sought to crack this metaphysical barrier himself and actually did break through. Writing about machineries of apotheosis, he pondered their implications and maneuvered to be one of the oligarchs. As a result, no other American writer gone so long is so widely known; and no other is so widely and variously exploited. Even so, to try to move beyond Chartier's "confusion of the contemporary reader," how useful are the brute facts of Mark Twain's complicity in this upheaval or his literary engagement with its consequences? The biographical record and several of his best narratives (stabilized, at least for the time being, as *libri unitarii*) show us an American author, and characters of his invention, stunned and transformed by a massive outbreak of published texts—magazines, pictures, cheap books, and printed pages in unprecedented configurations and quantities. Several of Mark Twain's stories, especially some of the later ones, seem to recognize and even at times to embrace the prospect of an American culture overwhelmed by images and verbal discourses mechanized, electrified, incorporated, and omnipresent. Sometimes these narratives whisper the redundancy of a cherished American idea, of a sacred discrete self, amid new and boundless powers of duplication extending to personalities as well as pictures and words.

But if Chartier is correct about where we find ourselves now, are we thereby obligated to reconstruct Mark Twain as a martyr from an earlier stage of this hermeneutic confusion, wandering ahead of the rest of us on a brave or ridiculous drive into uncharted cognitive territory? About these media meltdowns of the West and their consequences for the act of reading, Chartier's limitation might be that as a cultural and literary historian he is too responsible to cut loose like this himself or to be exploited as grounds for such disjunctions. For such a cue we need to look elsewhere. If the context is mad, then homeopathic drams of interpretive outlandishness might be worth a try—if not for a cure, then at least for understanding and enduring the symptoms.

With regard to the impact of modern information technology, other cultural historians are grimmer than Chartier and more daring. For possible connections among the situation of written discourse precisely at the turn of the last century, Mark Twain's crises of faith at that time, and a hermeneutics of skepticism more than a hundred years after, Friedrich Kittler's historical study of what he terms "discourse networks" is a compelling source. Much of Clemens's work on "No. 44, The Mysterious Stranger" was done around 1900—one of Kittler's turning-point years in the intellectual and aesthetic history of the West. At the very close of the nineteenth century, according to Kittler, another wave of technology for transcription and storage of utterance (including the gramophone, the motion picture, and the chronograph and tachistoscope for tracking movement of the reading eye) forced the author and the literary text through another violent metamorphosis, further complicating the relationship among writer, text, and reader, sabotaging the old truth (or delusions) of discernible context and authenticity. Discourse hereafter runs wild, obliterating even the imaginative and intellectual bond between the author and the word:

> Literature in the discourse network of 1900 is a simulacrum of madness. As long and insofar as someone writes, his delirium is protected from the loss of the word. Distinguished from madness by a nothing named simulacrum, by a foil named paper, writing traverses the free space of eternal recurrence. Literary writing is its own justification precisely in its empty self-referentiality. Whereas the claim of not being delirious necessarily leads, under the discursive conditions of brain physiology, to the delirium of originality and authorship, the reverse claim achieves discursive reality. A delirium written down coincides with what sciences and the media themselves were doing.[5]

Though Kittler never discusses Mark Twain, the relationships that are possible here between his apocalyptic, disheveled narratives at the century's end and Kittler's technological apocalypse for writing and reading ever after are too big to miss:

> A completely different God stands over the discourse network of 1900 and its inkwells. He has gone mad. In him the simulators of madness have their master. When the insane God drinks, it is not in order to sublate fantasies in a threefold sense. Where in 1800 there was a function of philosophical consumption, one hundred years later there is bare annihilation. Writers who drown in the inkwell of the insane God do not achieve the immortality of an author's name; they simply replace anonymous and paradoxical analphabets who are capable of writing down a whole discourse network from the outside. For that reason there are no authors and works, but only writers and writings. (335–36)

Play with this for a moment: as 44 vanishes into the absolute, inescapable blackness or madness of Kittler's 1900, taking with him the last chance that this obstreperous story might finally reveal a clear intention, Mark Twain gives in to the Everlasting No, an apocalypse of mechanical duplication, a perpetual high-tech Dark Age in which everything can be nothing more than a copy of everything else. Degraded from "author" into paltry "writer" by the very technology he has loved, he embraces the moment, constructing a delirium that also signifies the doom of the literary text and the ship-wreck of the interpretive enterprise. If so, then the rest is silence and we can all go home.

Extreme as Kittler sounds here, the core of the argument is provocative, the possibility that wax cylinders, wires, and armatures were the real end of the innocence and that intellectual verbal discourses did not wreak the epistemological havoc by themselves. Nonetheless, if Mark Twain's late writings, reopened with Kittler's assertions in mind, can be construed as pushed to the edge of an abyss by technological change, they can also be read as resisting the fatal plunge. Mark Twain's penchant for exuberance, which turns up even in those years when the so-called Great Dark Writings were taking shape, was part of a lifelong intellectual and emotional rest-lessness that never allowed him to settle down in either despair or belief. Whether or not any or all of his final works "drown in the inkwell of the insane God," some of them might be understood as prescient in a complex way, creatively and evasively responsive to this proffered catastrophe for the printed word and for every intelligence engaged with writing and reading.

Kittler offers a totalizing formulation, a vista of "annihilation," of epis-temological chaos, from which it seems there can be no turning away. As a thinker, Mark Twain was by most estimations a different sort, nihilistic at times, yet also suspicious of repose in absolutes, including absolute zeroes. In that turmoil there could be additional relevance for us, perhaps even a lesson about psychological survival, about keeping afloat in a rising tide. Amid our own media nightmares, one option is to stay loose, polymor-phously provoked and not committed to any one perspective. Like Simon Suggs, the frontier con man created by J. J. Hooper and popular in Clemens's boyhood, today's American rovers should weigh the advantages of keeping "shifty in a new country," ideologically unattached and ready for anything, when there is no way to know what will come up next—includ-ing, possibly, some unforeseen escape from the inevitable next ambush.

Because Mark Twain as a cultural icon has stayed shifty, thanks to his wit, impetuousness, and playfulness, we can compare him to temperaments from our own moment, cultural observers who, like himself, prefer to jolt complacency rather than evangelize for one stable point of view. In a spate of short essays for *Libération,* Jean Baudrillard, on the general subject of cyberspace and the destruction of personal privacy, intellectual coherence, and everything that formerly passed for truth, cuts loose in ways that can cut us loose as well, with a take-it-or-leave-it polemic in the tradition of

Carlyle, Emerson, or Aristide Bruant, or Mark Twain in his later years—outrageous, yet also curiously consoling, even restful:

> *But this time we seem to have the final solution, the definitive equivalent: Virtual Reality in all its forms*—the digital, information, universal computation, cloning. In short, the putting in place of a perfect virtual, technological artefact, so that the world can be exchanged for its artificial double. A much more radical solution than all the others, this, since it will no longer have to be exchanged for some transcendence or finality from elsewhere, but for itself, by the substitution of a double which is infinitely "truer," infinitely more real than the real world—thus putting an end to the question of reality, and to any inclination to give it a meaning. An automatic writing of the world in the absence of the world. Total equivalence, total screen, final solution. Absolutely consolidating the idea of the network as niche, into which it is so easy to disappear. The Internet thinks me. The Virtual thinks me. My double is wandering through the networks, where I shall never meet him. For that parallel universe has no relation to this one. It is an artificial transcription of it, a total echoing of it, but it does not reflect it. The Virtual is no longer the potentially real, as it once was. Non-referential—orbital and exorbital—it is never again intended to meet up with the real world. Having absorbed the original, it produces the world as undecidable.[6] [emphasis in the original]

To Mark Twain's readers, such a "final solution" to arguments about literary meaning and the moral relevance of printed texts might come as a relief: an excuse, at least, to stop debating whether the Mysterious Stranger stories are theological and philosophical nonsense or whether other Mark Twain narratives suffer some kind of structural or thematic breakdown. With help from Baudrillard, structural and thematic confusion are reborn as festive commentary on writing as a cultural practice, estranged by the technological transfiguration of discourse. As a patriarch of the postmodern condition made over in this way, a "perfect virtual" Mark Twain would also be more cool than most of the Mark Twains we have now. He would be not another victim of fin de siècle writerly delirium, but a cagey, prophetic, one-man avant-garde, experimenting with Dadaist and Situationist playfulness twenty or fifty years ahead of schedule.

If there is any truth in this, then how early might Sam Clemens have recognized that literature was becoming a crazy enterprise? And when and how can we catch him happily at it, joining in the craziness? "My double is wandering through the networks," says Baudrillard, "where I shall never meet him." If so, Sam Clemens's double got there first, lighting out for the global-virtual territory about twenty years ahead of 44 and several generations before everyone's wandering double could be morphed into everyone else's. Baudrillard's *hélas* relieves us from interpretive drudgery. From his "parallel universe" perspective it would not matter, and perhaps never did, that we cannot say how Hank Morgan, in Connecticut, is transported back to Mark Twain's King Arthur's Court. For if "the virtual thinks us," then a parallel-universe "lost land" of Camelot becomes only another VR, obliterated and reconstructed over and over, even before the fatal year 1900, by so many other skilled imaginers—Mallory, Tennyson, William Morris, Burne-Jones, Wagner, Rossetti, Waterhouse, Mark Twain, Hank Morgan (as Mark Twain's virtual imaginer)—not a realm ever governed by classical laws of space and time.

With momentum on this vector, one can spin out quite a way: *Huckleberry Finn* as a text about an intuitively cool young man resisting an encroaching empire of printed texts oppressing the independent imagination; *A Tramp Abroad* as a story of two subversive Yankee travelers rebelling against the organized impossibility of immediate experience, contending with landscapes systematically polluted by verbal and graphic simulacra. Dubious—yet an excursion into *rive gauche* hyperbole does help us recover some wilder implications of Mark Twain's thematic shiftiness, his taste and talent for heretical bon mots and intellectual skydives, some of which could hold their own with Baudrillard's aerobatics.

Beyond the literary texts and the famous wisecracks there is also the lingering wraith of the celebrity, and that too must be countenanced as a source of meaning or some variety of moral companionship. The Mark Twain biography delights for its incongruities, its defiance of psychological profile. Small-town wayward boy, apprentice and journeyman printer, steamboat pilot, militiaman, gold-rush prospector, Wild West correspondent, anonymous prankster, traveling stand-up comic, international tourist: all of these incarnations preceded Sam Clemens as literary artist. As a genius in the craft of media celebrity, he was also the first American master of the international public image, getting his pen name and his remarkable face known to millions of people who really did not know him at all. Transforming Mark Twain into a brand and a trademark, Clemens was notoriously jealous of his own intellectual and artistic property and careless about the rights of others.[7] Dedicated at times to his art, he also churned out potboilers and collaborations and spin-offs, authorized package deals, tie-in sales, and mediocre stage productions based on his best-sellers. He was a source of misery for nearly every partner and subordinate who worked with him directly. Unpredictable in his moods and his politics, he held fast to his rank as a front-page icon, complete with chemical dependencies (nicotine in prodigious quantities, irrigations of Scotch now and then), notorious friends, financial disasters, and toward the end a disturbing interest in populating his private house with other people's little girls.

For a "makeover" of Mark Twain as a contemporary superstar, the gross components are there to exploit, and with only the usual brutality they can be cobbled into the sort of pop-culture presence that America now seems to crave. As we have seen, however, there are twists in such a story: about this fame (still full-blown without agents and sponsors) Mark Twain himself could be thoughtful and eloquent. In his stardom, this is a paradox that sets him apart, this literary engagement with technological and cultural forces that made him famous, made him rich, ruined him, then remade him, over and over.

But a case like this can also be beneficially turned on its head. It's quite easy, in fact, to imagine Sam Clemens as someone not so different from a modern general public, another American struggling, perhaps in vain, for some measure of sanity as the words and the images rain down. Trend-watching psychologists are marketing a new category of pathological behavior supposedly brought on by the electronic obliteration of privacy and psychological repose, a numbing of traditional values by overloads of stimulation. In a couple of recent books, we are told that the United States is in a pandemic of "hypomania," and with zest the symptoms are laid out: erratic outbreaks of starry-eyed optimism; intermittent crashes of anxiety and despair; episodes of profligate investing and egregious material self-indulgence—all reflecting a deep-seated confusion about the purpose of modern life, about personal identity and what we really need and want.[8]

As one might expect, these studies blame a video-fueled craving for material luxury, mouse-click financial booms and busts, and our incessant exposure to bewildering cues for desire. To anyone familiar with the life and work of Sam Clemens, however, items on these checklists of twenty-first century psychosis will ring a bell. For negotiating such a present, perhaps nothing and no one in the cultural past can provide much guidance, beyond the dull fact that every culture caught in a crisis of values must invent its own reasons for carrying on. In a quest for collective agency, these histories must be created: narratives of old friends from the national past whom we can imagine as caught up in troubles not unlike our own—improvising a life and struggling against the madness of the everyday.

Various incarnations to choose from—and one of the best choices we have is not to choose. When Sam Clemens invented Mark Twain he also invented a process for continual *self*-reinvention, and when Clemens died he left behind a virtual identity with a capacity to regenerate as cultural contingencies might require. I have said that Sam Clemens may have understood—as many people now seem to understand—that value, and even a kind of solace, can be found in merely taking what comes, amid cultural upsets of endurable strength, and keeping faith in possibilities of self-renewal. From the perspective of the biographical record as well as the literary work, what is the heresy in summoning up an appropriate Mark Twain for moral support in whatever cultural emergency comes along? After all, this has been a useful practice for several decades. But that question leads to another: What can "Mark Twain" signify in the escalating confusion between the authentic and the false, even within one's own mind?

For this second question, an oblique answer: someone long ago, remembered as Aesop, is credited with the fable of a mountebank whose counterfeit pig noise humiliates a farmer from the audience at a public test of skill—until the farmer reveals the actual squealing piglet he has concealed under his cloak and gets the last laugh. Aesop must have lived in simpler times: as the simulation and the genuine article grow harder to tell apart, so also the mountebank and the truthful yeoman. So also Mark Twain the realist, Mark Twain the humorist, social chronicler, dreamer, businessman, liar, prophet, fool, and genius. And for that matter, Aesop's fable may come down not from anyone named Aesop, but from some unknown fabulist instead, a counterfeit Aesop in a long succession, much as Mark Twain's trove of memorable lines and adventures is regularly enhanced with new accounts of things that Sam Clemens never said or did. There is no question that Clemens worked to embellish and complicate his own history, that he often adulterated his writings with plots, pictures, and verbal texts "borrowed" from somebody else. Even so, behind his stubborn enthusiasms and passing interests there was much more than an infantile or professional need for attention, more than a Gilded Age craving for riches or modern-style pathological self-evasion. Closer to the core was a drive to transcend all normalized and limiting constructions of being. One seductive promise of the information age that dawned in his time was, and possibly remains, the intimation of wider possibilities, of escapes into other times and identities.

Millions of contemporary Americans now expend appalling quantities of their time on earth being someone else, constructing ersatz personalities in cyber-nightmares and virtual play-spaces, sharing intimate thoughts of these made-up selves with virtual "friends," proximate or faraway strangers, also in masquerade. On that pathless journey as well, Mark Twain was only a little ahead of the rest.

Still, the most reliable truth about information revolutions is the fool-hardiness of summary judgment from the thick of the action. Three years before Sam Clemens was born, the ever-anxious Carlyle was warning that those Fourdrinier and Gilpin machines, pouring out paper cheap and abundant, would spell the collapse of English literary culture under tides of mediocre publication, a disaster from which higher material prices and slow production methods had heretofore protected the public.[9] Ignoring the fact that cheap paper had made periodical essays financially possible, essays like the one that included this tirade, Carlyle had no inkling of what was around the next bend—a technological clean sweep, exposing the innocent reading multitudes to an eruption of other English public intellectuals (Macaulay, Ruskin, Arnold, Newman, Pater, Huxley, Wilde), some of whom would prove sharper than Carlyle as cultural prophets, and better writers to boot.[10]

With that in mind, a turn toward home makes more sense than another veer into grandiose speculation. The story told here began with a picture, a face, a three-letter name put together backwards by a boy with a handful of movable type. Returning to the beginning at the end is an old charade of symmetry. Even so, that first image, contemplated now in the context of a long life in the world of type, printed words, and published images, takes on added significance. The picture may seem fresher now than when we first looked at it. From a small, one-off daguerreotype, this inverse likeness of the boy gazes out from many books and gallery walls, many sites on the World Wide Web. Liberated from uniqueness and physicality, the media remains of an American cultural icon are also transformed as moments in time. Because everything that is left behind is of the past, "then" achieves a treacherous parity with "after," and even with "now." Sequence implodes, and when we contemplate a life and a literary achievement, the first pictures and words collide with the last.

In *Writing and Difference,* Jacques Derrida pauses in an essay about Emmanuel Levinas to ponder the difficulties of interpreting a printed human visage, of negotiating transcribed faces that seem to gaze back into our own eyes, like the anonymous backwards "SAM" boy and all those iterations of the mustached, wild-haired famous man. "The face is not only a visage which may be the surface of things," says Derrida. It is also not only "that which sees things—a theoretical relation—but that which exchanges its glance." But the brief meditation ends in a quandary: "the face does not signify," he observes. "It does not incarnate, envelop, or signal anything other than self, soul, subjectivity."[11] A discrete, wordless encounter with the single inanimate visage is finally an interpretive blind alley. Even so, these passing observations seem poignant as a glimpse into Derrida himself and relevant to that enormous sequence of Mark Twain likenesses that begins with a boy and a type stick. By avoiding photographers through much of his career, vetoing the portentous, meaningless authorial pout for the dust jackets of his books, Derrida sought an unusual purity—incongruous and even reactionary in our image-besotted culture—for the relationship between his verbal texts and the intellect and imagination of the reader. Why engage in the disruptive practice that Sam Clemens loved in his prime? Why muddle a carefully constructed sequence of printed words by eliciting dead-end readerly inferences about an imagined look in the eye? This first likeness of Sam Clemens does seem to look back, and the exchange of glances may indeed be essentially without meaning.

Nonetheless, from the nineteenth century, no American author gazes back at us so fervently and frequently as these published faces of Mark Twain; and for modern Americans who wisely or compulsively interrogate these images for clues about personality and literary intention there is a strangeness in these encounters, especially when numbers of these photographs are brought together as a random array or a chronological sequence. A boy in a daguerreotype; a photograph of an ailing old man lying in bed, apparently peering in our own direction, or into the encroaching dark; a snapshot of a gentleman somewhere in between, in the prime of life, at ease on a summer veranda; a white-maned literary lion in his cherished academic getup; an itinerant opera-house performer in a publicity portrait; a world-class celebrity, posed at the rail of an ocean liner or before the dark portal of an ancient church: for such fantasies of connection across time and circumstance, these Mark Twain faces seem full of psychological and thematic possibilities, and many of his photographers were skilled at catching them.

But what can one say is the cultural or literary importance of these images in profusion, so many different glances exchanged with one long-dead American author? Because Mark Twain is a phenomenon of such pervasiveness, for millions of adults in the early twenty-first century there can really be no innocent reckoning with a discrete likeness of the man. When the face is recognized it conjoins in the mind with other pictures from other moments in the amazing career. Transported vicariously into the wilderness of his adventures and incarnations, we try to get our bearings. Where is he, and *what* is he just now, in this picture before us? What imaginative and professional fires within him are hot at this particular moment, or have yet to kindle, or might have gone to embers? The striking raiment, the wild hair, and the intensity in the eyes are probably not the key reasons why this accumulation of Mark Twains refuses to drift out of sight. The stories we tell ourselves about them do much to ensure their cultural longevity. As we fray into the future, we hold these images in the light as eloquent keepsakes, fragments of another narrative of incessant becoming. From the Mark Twain legacy, every generation has constructed the kind of companion it has required, and that process of renewal may be accelerating. The instability of our technological and cultural life extends into the private and collective processes of reading, the signification and fate of the printed word, and the encounter with the published human face.

Twenty years ago, writing about the imaginative challenge of photographs, and especially of images of the dead, Roland Barthes waxed lyrical and elegiac. In his view, the narratives we construct, compulsively, from these encounters with the transcribed face are not illusory, not meaningless. Contemplating the photograph is an imaginative collision between an enigmatic "now" and some unrecoverable "then." The viewer recalls the moment of the taking, possibly long before, and the intervening remembered experience between that moment and the now of the seeing. The living and the absent, or the dead, come together almost supernaturally across space and time: "The photograph is literally an emanation of the referent. From a real body, which was there, proceed radiations which ultimately touch me, who am here; the duration of the transmission is insignificant; the photograph of the missing being, as Sontag says, will touch me like the delayed rays of a star. A sort of umbilical cord links the body of the photographed thing to my gaze: light, though impalpable, is here a carnal medium, a skin I share with anyone who has been photographed."[12]

To gaze again at that first likeness of Sam, as Barthes might have gazed at it, is not only to be reminded of how much would come after, the spectacular overbrimming life that even this imaginative boy could not have fantasized. It is also to apprehend a future that *was* in a sense imaginable but that young boys refuse to think about—middle age, waning powers, loss of loved ones, old age, mortality. No interpretive blind alley, then, but really a kind of séance, a sharing of *humanitas* across great divides. Times have changed. To encounter *this* picture, now, is also to apprehend media transfigurations that befell after the death of the old famous man that this boy eventually became: the long amazing journey of this single image from a village daguerreotype parlor into a world of print and ultimately into a kind of hyperspace, where verbal discourses and photographs are altered in form, and deracinated from time and physical place, by technologies that Barthes did not live to see.

To put it another way, the epistemological negotiation of transcribed images may now have grown too complex and volatile for wistful ruminations about one old photograph, or a whole stack of them printed on antique material, glass and paper. For Baudrillard, what impends for us all is a fate wilder than a few more incremental complications in the psychological encounter with pictures, tame enigmas about authenticity, the reading of visual and verbal texts, and the imaginative reification of the past. "Reality" has run its course: compared to what we face now, even "the society of the spectacle" that exasperated Guy Debord in the 1960s seems like a trivial interlude. Every uploaded image, even of trusted companions like Mark Twain, is part of the same disaster:

> But we are no longer in the society of the spectacle, which has itself become a spectacular concept. It is no longer the contagion of spectacle which alters reality, it is the contagion of the virtual which obliterates the spectacle. With its diverting, distancing effects, Disneyland still represented spectacle and folklore, but with Disneyworld and its tentacular extension, we are dealing with a generalized metastasis, with a cloning of the world and of our mental universe, not in the imaginary register, but in the viral and the virtual. We are becoming not alienated, passive spectators, but interactive extras, the meek, freeze-dried extras in this immense reality show. This is no longer the spectacular logic of alienation, but a spectral logic of disembodiment; not a fantastic logic of diversion, but a corpuscular logic of transfusion, transubstantiation of each of our cells. An undertaking of radical deterrence of the world, then, but from the inside this time, not from outside, as we saw in what is now the almost nostalgic world of capitalist reality. In virtual reality the extra is no longer either an actor or a spectator; he is off-stage, he is a transparent operator.[13]

The picture of the boy, and all these other vexatious images of Sam Clemens ascending into Mark Twain, posturing for the cameras, aiding and abetting the vanguard of a technological catastrophe: for Baudrillard, all such remains are absorbed into a leaderless, multimedia conspiracy to degrade the publics of the world into one vast and clueless audience. The illusory power that we toy with now, clicking and jump-cutting from each visual encounter to the next on a whim, only confirms our own status as extras in a "reality show" that no one can escape. And if Mark Twain can be only another "freeze-dried extra," another ghost in this "spectral logic of disembodiment," like the genial, plastic-skinned robot resembling him at the theme park in Florida or the Hollywood impersonations with gray fright-wigs and pasted-on moustaches, then we have reached the kind of omega point that Sam himself wondered about in his final years, and contemplations of his relevance can go no farther.

Obviously I pull up short of such an abyss, preferring to believe, as I think Mark Twain unsteadily believed to the end of his life, that we still have some agency in our cultural and psychological fate and that in our struggles with "the contagion of the virtual" some of us have not forgotten (not yet, anyway) that one button on every control panel will actually turn the damned thing off. In a sense, every generation has been right about the Mark Twain they have re-created—not just from the plenitude and the thematic restlessness of what he wrote but also because his passionate restlessness extended to his conception of what writing was, what a literary text is, what it means to print and publish, and the marketplace and culture into which his words were launched. Printing and publishing changed more drastically over the course of his career than they had for the four hundred years preceding his birth, and in his lifetime an unfinished revolution began in what it means to read. Yet nothing grows stale faster than sonorous wisdom about the future of the printed text, electronic communication systems, or this culture that evolves at a pace commensurate with the sophistication of its own technological powers. And because the meaning of the Mark Twain legacy remains as unsettled as everything else in our culture, no stable truth about the future of any of those things seems possible—other than a recognition that our own condition is also an adventure in change and that no other classic American author exemplifies so thoroughly that kind of adventure, in which identity and the meaning of text and literary art are so linked to drastic transformation in the processes of telling and showing. The Young Satan in the first version of the Stranger story was a supernatural bore because he moralized deadpan about everything. The final iteration of the Stranger, from what he himself calls the "New Series," was an improvement, supremely facetious and supremely wise.

Most people alive in the West have no firsthand experience of a time when art and literature and mass-marketed fashion were not so whirled together as to make distinctions among them pedantic. One certainty: whatever we think now about our own situation will devalue quickly, like the electronic gear on this desktop, acquired when I got serious about this project a couple of years ago. Passé already, it amuses some of my students, who swing by the office in their spare time to play a quaint round of an endangered sport, conversation face to face. Occasionally, for fun, we compare notes about this technological and cultural circus they were born into, this encircling turmoil that seems to bother them so little. Going out the door, all they may take with them is a puzzling reminder that people from obsolete generations can still be bothered by any of this: the velocity with which every new media toy and weapon is deployed and junked for something faster and stronger; these ever-morphing challenges to culture and consciousness; and this stubborn, blessed human capacity to "Dream other dreams, and better!" improvise fresh values and hopes on the fly, and spin away into the unimaginable. In more dimensions and at greater depths than ever before, Mark Twain is a companion on their adventure.

ONE. SAMUEL CLEMENS AND THE PRINTED WORD

1. The original daguerreotype is in the Mark Twain Papers and Project at the Bancroft Library, at the University of California at Berkeley, hereafter abbreviated as MTP.

2. From Marion County records, Terrell Dempsey has determined that the population of the county in 1840 was 7,239 white people and 2,342 slaves. See Terrell Dempsey, *Searching for Jim: Slavery in Sam Clemens's World* (Columbia: University of Missouri Press, 2003), 9. For Hannibal itself, a population of three thousand by the late 1840s is a conventional estimate in the Mark Twain biographies. See, for example, Edward Wagenknecht, *Mark Twain, the Man and His Work* (Norman: University of Oklahoma Press, 1961), 7; and Fred Kaplan, *The Singular Mark Twain* (New York: Doubleday, 2003), 19. However, Mark Twain's biographers have not offered estimates for the African American population in the village during Sam Clemens's adolescence, and in his letters and autobiographical writings there are no indications that African Americans worked in skilled or semiskilled jobs in the print shops where he was employed.

3. In his *Dictionary of the Art of Printing* (London: Longman, Brown, Green, and Longmans, 1841), William Savage described cast-iron chases as "coming greatly into use" (168) as an improvement over wrought iron and wood. For a good contemporary description of the gear of a print shop before steam power and automation, see C. H. Timperley, *A Printer's Manual, Containing Instructions to Learners, with Scales of Impositions and Numerous Calculations, Recipes, and Scales of Prices* (London: H. Johnson, 1838), 79–95.

4. Thomas F. Adams, *Typographia, or The Printer's Instructor: A Brief Sketch of the Origin, Rise, and Progress of the Typographic Art, with Practical Directions for Conducting Every Department in an Office* (Philadelphia: Peck & Bliss, 1853), 240–41. Adams's book pirates the main title and (with updating here and there) much of

the contents of John Johnson's two-volume *Typographia, or The Printer's Instructor, Including an Account of the Origin of Printing* (London: Longman, Hurst, Rees, Orme, Brown & Green, 1824). The similarity of these two manuals, thirty years apart, suggests how little had changed in English and American handpress printing offices in the first half of the nineteenth century.

5. William Vincent Byars, *A Century of Journalism in Missouri* (Columbia: State Historical Society of Missouri, 1920), 63.

6. The St. Louis telegraph line remained east of the river until October 1850, when a wire encased in gutta-percha made the transit. See William Hyde and Howard L. Conard, *Encyclopedia of the History of Saint Louis* (New York: Southern History Co., 1899), 1630, 2231. See also Byars, *Century of Journalism,* 63.

7. Hyde and Conard, *Encyclopedia,* 1846. See also Thomas Clarke et al., *The American Railway: Its Construction, Development, Management, and Appliances* (New York: Scribner's, 1897), 430–31.

8. Walter B. Stevens, *St. Louis: The Fourth City, 1764–1909,* 3 vols. (St. Louis: S. J. Clarke, 1909), 2:633–34.

9. "The St. Louis Type and Stereotype Foundry and Paper Warehouse, A. P. Ladew and Company," on Locust Street, is advertised in the *Hannibal Tri-Weekly Messenger* for January, 27, 1853, 3; the R. P. Mogridge Stereotype Foundry announced itself as "The Only Stereotype Foundry in the West" in William M. Montague's *St. Louis Business Directory for 1853–4* (St. Louis: E. A. Louis, 1853). For an account of the rivalry between the *St. Louis Republican* and the *St. Louis Democrat* in the early 1850s, see James Allee Hart, "An Historical Study of the *St. Louis Globe-Democrat,* 1852–1958" (PhD diss., University of Missouri, 1959), 14–27. Hart also notes that a smaller paper, the *St. Louis Union,* was operating with a "Hoe patent power press worked with a steam engine" when it was purchased by the *Democrat* in 1852 (14).

10. In the early 1850s, older-model powered presses capable of twenty-five hundred impressions per hour were already being sold off as new and faster machines came west from the Hoe factory in New York. In the *St. Louis Daily News,* July 6, 1852, Kemble and Hagen, a "Job Printer" on Olive Street, advertised for sale a used cylinder press: "Hoe's manufacture. Nearly new. Will throw 2500 impressions per hour" (2). When the *St. Louis Union* was purchased by the *Missouri Democrat* in 1852, the assets in the sale included "one Hoe patent power press worked with a steam engine, four iron hand peoples, one Card case, one standing press, one paper cutter, about 200 cases, a lot of chases, stains, lead sticks, three composing stones, and a large lot of type. In the job room were one medium press, one Ruggles press, and one Hoe card press" (Hart, "Historical Study," 14). In 1853, when Clemens left Hannibal to try his skills in St. Louis, the state-of-the-art paper there was the *Republican,* a four-page daily paper running ten columns per page and organizing its classified advertisements into categories like a modern newspaper. The sheet dimensions of the *Republican* were nearly twice those of the papers that Orion and Sam were producing in Hannibal.

11. Steamboats apparently stopped in Hannibal about three times per week in

the early 1850s. In Chapter IV of *Life on the Mississippi*, Mark Twain remembers these arrivals:

> the magnificent Mississippi, rolling its mile-wide tide along, shining in the sun; the dense forest away on the other side; the "point" above the town, and the "point" below, bounding the river-glimpse and turning it into a sort of sea, and withal a very still and brilliant and lonely one. Presently a film of dark smoke appears. . . . [I]nstantly a negro drayman, famous for his quick eye and prodigious voice, lifts up the cry, "S-t-e-a-m-boat a-comin'!" and the scene changes! The town drunkard stirs, the clerks wake up, a furious clatter of drays follows, every house and store pours out a human contribu-tion, and all in a twinkling the dead town is alive and moving.
>
> *Life on the Mississippi* (New York: Oxford University Press, 1996), 64–65

12. See Floyd Calvin Shoemaker, *Missouri and Missourians: Land of Contrasts and People of Achievements*, 2 vols. (Chicago: Lewis, 1943), 1:751.

13. See Robert Karolevitz, *Newspapering in the Old West* (New York: Barrage Books, 1965), 19–20; see also Howard Allen Rader, "Newspaper History of Calla-way Co. Missouri, 1839–60" (PhD diss., University of Missouri, 1961), 37–45.

14. *Mark Twain's Letters*, vol. 1, *1853–1866*, ed. Edgar Marquess Branch, Michael B. Frank, and Kenneth M. Sanderson (Berkeley: University of California Press, 1988), 1.

15. For a detailed description of the daguerreotype process, see Helmut Gerns-heim and Alison Gernsheim, *The History of Photography: From the Camera Obscura to the Beginning of the Modern Era* (New York: McGraw-Hill, 1969), especially 71–74. See also Robert Taft, *Photography and the American Scene: A Social History, 1839–1889* (New York: Macmillan, 1938), 98–100.

16. John Seelye briefly discusses this "visual trick" by a "camera sly" Sam in *Mark Twain in the Movies: A Meditation with Pictures* (New York: Viking Press, 1977): "Duplicity depending on technology, old and new, it was but the first of Sam's sev-eral schticks . . . the flourishes of a man who wishes to be remembered if not entirely known" (3–4). See also Linda Haverty Rugg, *Picturing Ourselves: Photog-raphy and Autobiography* (Chicago: University of Chicago Press, 1997), 29–32. Arguing that this boyhood photograph demonstrates Mark Twain's "ambivalent attitude toward photography and its representational powers" (30), Rugg asserts that throughout his life Clemens maintained essentially the same attitude toward photographic processes, though they transformed over the run of those years from these long-exposure daguerreotypes on glass plates to pocket Kodaks and motion pictures on rolls of celluloid.

17. In *The Literature of Labor and the Labors of Literature* (Cambridge: Cam-bridge University Press, 1995), Cindy Weinstein reads *A Connecticut Yankee in King Arthur's Court* and "Number 44, The Mysterious Stranger" as expressions of Mark Twain's moral ambivalence about American labor and his yearning for the enhancement or automation of his own literary productivity to mirror somehow the rising productivity of an industrializing nation. See especially 128–72. Jeffrey Steinbrink looks at *The Innocents Abroad, Roughing It,* and other Mark Twain proj-

ects as experiments in "an elegant refinement of the industrial model, in which *lots of people* contribute to the writing of the book, just as lots do to the construction of a steamboat or a dynamo" (81). See Steinbrink, "Mark Twain's Mechanical Marvels," in *Constructing Mark Twain: New Directions in Scholarship*, ed. Laura E. Skandera Trombley and Michael Kiskis (Columbia: University of Missouri Press, 2001), 72–86. The standard portrayal of Mark Twain's interest in technology, and the thematic and structural consequences for his literary work, is still exemplified by James M. Cox's famous essay, "*A Connecticut Yankee in King Arthur's Court:* The Machinery of Self-Preservation," *Yale Review* 50 (1960): 89–102.

18. A comprehensive inventory of Mark Twain's involvements with new machines and patents is Thomas Grant, "The Artist of the Beautiful: Mark Twain's Investment in the Machine Inventor," *Publications of the Missouri Philosophical Association* 4 (1979): 59–68.

19. Kent Rasmussen reports that the model at the Mark Twain Memorial was built in 1887. See Rasmussen, *Mark Twain, A to Z* (New York: Oxford University Press, 1995), 350.

20. The exact weight and dimensions of the Paige compositor are variously reported. Lucien A. Legros and John C. Grant described it as "eleven feet in length, three and one half feet wide, and six feet high," weighing "about 5000 pounds" and requiring a power source of approximately one-quarter to one-third horsepower to operate. See Legros and Grant, *Typographical Printing Surfaces* (London: Longmans, Green, 1916), 386. The estimate of 7,500 pounds and the parts count in my text are supplied by the Mark Twain Memorial.

21. Ibid., 381.

22. Ibid., 371.

23. Judith Yaross Lee notes that in the fall of 1881 William Hamersley, a Hartford attorney, brought in Clemens's opening investment of $5,000 and that the direct subvention ballooned to more than $150,000 in subsequent years—apparently not including the liability Clemens assumed in 1886 for the company's "patent, manufacturing, and promotion costs, in exchange for half the profits," which were never forthcoming. Lee, "Anatomy of a Fascinating Failure," *American Heritage of Invention and Technology* 3 (Summer 1987): 59. In *Mark Twain: A Biography* (New York: Harper and Brothers, 1912), Albert Bigelow Paine calculated the total investment at $190,000 (914). Justin Kaplan found that Twain had poured in "$150,000 or so" by the end of 1889; see Kaplan, *Mr. Clemens and Mark Twain* (New York: Simon and Schuster, 1966), 301. The most comprehensive recent account of Clemens's involvement with the Paige, and of his other bad investments and financial problems in the 1880s and 1890s, is Charles H. Gold's *Hatching Ruin: Mark Twain's Road to Bankruptcy* (Columbia: University of Missouri Press, 2003).

24. Roger Burlingame estimates the total cost of the Paige project as between $1,300,000 and something over two million dollars. Burlingame, *Engines of Democracy: Inventions and Society in Mature America* (New York: Scribner's, 1940), 146.

25. Untitled, incomplete MS, probably dated about 1887, comprising 21 leaves numbered 9 through 29, pp. 10–11, in Folder 1, Paige Typesetter, 1885 Documents, MTP.

26. Among the Paige compositor's American competitors in the 1880s and early 1890s, a standard strategy in working with movable type was either to build the distributing machine as a separate unit or to leave the problem to others. Lorenzo Dow's keyboard-operated "Composing Machine" (1885) was joined by a freestanding distributing machine in the following year; the Empire Composer and Distributor were two separate devices; the Thorne Typesetter and the Munson Automatic Typesetter (1882) had no distributor at all; the McMillan system, which Clemens saw as a significant rival, consisted of an upright typesetting machine and a distributing system resembling a big round table. See Richard E. Huss, *The Development of Printers' Mechanical Typesetting Methods, 1822–1925* (Charlottesville: University Press of Virginia, 1973), 112–46.

27. Untitled, incomplete MS, probably dated about 1889, comprising 2 leaves, p. 1, in Folder 1, Paige Typesetter, 1885 Documents, MTP.

28. See, for example, the contract between Clemens and Paige for "inventions and improvements in and relating to Electro Magnetic Motors," executed August 16, 1887, MTP. According to Colin Clair, 1891 was the first year in which electric power was used to drive printing presses. See Clair, *A Chronology of Printing* (London: Cassell, 1969), 163.

29. "The Paige Type-Setting & Distribution Machine," probably dated 1885– 86, comprising 13 leaves, pp. 1–5, in Folder 1, Paige Typesetter, 1885 Documents, MTP.

30. J. Ashworth, *Operation and Mechanism of the Linotype and Intertype,* 2 vols. (London: Staples Press, 1955), 1:41.

31. See Carl Schlesinger, ed., *The Biography of Ottmar Mergenthaler, Inventor of the Linotype: A New Edition, with Added Historical Notes Based on Recent Findings* (New Castle, DE: Oak Knoll Press, 1989), 22–41.

32. The *Inland Printer,* for example, offered consoling words about these new machines as late as May 1892 and worried instead about another technology:

> No fear may be entertained, I think, that the typesetting machine will affect job composition further than as to bookwork. . . . But another art is menacing the job compositor, and that is the art of photo-engraving or zinc etching. More and more will the products of the pen and ink designer and artist, assisted by the etcher, take the place of curve line and "fancy" job composition. Soon the job printer will rely more upon the zinc etchings for attaining pleasing effects than he will rely upon rule twisting, bending, or whatever you may term it. . . . The process of zinc etching has already revolutionized some branches of the trade, . . . and it will affect them to a still greater extent, and its circle of influence will constantly increase.
>
> Reprinted in Maurice Annenberg, *A Typographical Journey through the Inland Printer, 1883–1900* (Baltimore: Maran Press, 1977), 406

33. From the incomplete MS cited in note 25:

The Thorne, the Burr & the Macmillan are the latest additions to that process which I have spoken of, & are much the best of the column. Type-setting can be done upon them at the rate of about 4,000 ems an hour, corrected matter, all day long. But there is no great saving of money as a result; in each case wages must be paid to three persons on each 1000 ems produced: to a setter, a justifier, & a distributor. The three do not quite do four men's work.

There are two other candidates in the composition-field, the "Linotype" or Mergenthaler machine, & the "Matrix." But these two are jokes, & not to be taken seriously.

34. Basil Kahan, *Ottmar Mergenthaler: The Man and His Machine* (New Castle, DE: Oak Knoll Press, 2000), 91.

35. Ibid., 105.

36. From the later 1880s there are quires of unpublished notes, calculations, publicity drafts, and other materials projecting the Paige's chances for survival in a tightening market and speculating on the selling price of the machine once it was ready. For example, from MS page with subheading "No. Needed," meaning "number needed," in Folder 2, Paige Typesetter, 1885 Documents, MTP: "There are 60,000 city compositors. If but one size of type were used, we could replace these with 10,000 machines; but several sizes are used, & so the 10,000 men will each use 1 machine & a half. So the requirement to-day is 15,000 machines: $180,000,000." An 1885 "CIRCULAR OF JAMES W. PAIGE & CO. THE PAIGE COMPOSITOR" gives a price of $9,500. Folder 11, Paige Typesetter, 1885 Documents, MTP.

37. Karolevitz, *Newspapering*, 114.

38. For an overview of the importance of type-founding to American printers and the impact of the Linotype in altering that industrial structure, see Robert Darnton, "What Is the History of Books?" in *Books and Society in History*, ed. Kenneth Carpenter (New York: R. R. Bowker, 1983), 3–28.

39. A letter about this project from Samuel Langhorne Clemens (hereafter abbreviated as SLC) to Fred Hall (May 7, 1888) is quoted in chapter 3 of this book.

40. Paine tells the story of Kaolatype briefly in *Mark Twain*, 726–28. Describing the process as "ingenious," he attributes its failure to a host of competing technologies and patent infringements. Working from extant letters and notebook entries, Fred Kaplan reads the Kaolatype failure as an outright fraud by Charles Sneider (who had invented the process), possibly assisted by Dan Slote himself. Kaplan emphasizes the suspicious fire at the Kaolatype plant on the night before Mark Twain was scheduled to visit it and a gloomy 1881 report from Webster that the whole process was fraudulent. See Kaplan, *Singular Mark Twain*, 361–65.

41. SLC to Orion Clemens, February 26, 1880. Samuel Charles Webster, *Mark Twain, Business Man* (Boston: Little, Brown, 1946), 142.

42. Ibid., 148.

43. *Mark Twain's Notebooks and Journals*, vol. 2, *1877–1883*, ed. Frederick Anderson, Lin Salamo, and Bernard L. Stein (Berkeley: University of California Press, 1975), 390–93.

44. Marjorie Stafford, "Subscription Book Publishing in the United States, 1865–1930" (MA thesis, University of Illinois at Urbana-Champaign, 1943), 48–49. Stafford's thesis, though quite old, remains one of the best sources for details on the trade during the latter half of the nineteenth century. As Amy M. Thomas has observed, there is a stunning "paucity of scholarship on this topic. Although hundreds of thousands of subscription books were produced in the nineteenth century, and even though this method of bookselling was so successful that traditional booksellers feared they could not compete, not a single monograph has been written about the history of the subscription book trade." "'There Is Nothing So Effective as a Personal Canvass': Revaluing Nineteenth Century American Subscription Books," *Book History* 1, no. 1 (1998): 140.

45. At the MTP, Victor Fischer notes that the records of the American Publishing Company, Osgood, and WebsterCo indicate that only one set of electroplates was produced for each Mark Twain book they published. However, an 1895 unauthorized edition of *The Innocents Abroad,* produced briefly by the Joseph Knight Company of Boston, obviously made use of a set of original electroplates, possibly a stray or discarded set from the American Publishing Company. This would indicate that duplicate sets were indeed manufactured, at least for that one Mark Twain book from the APC. I am grateful to Robert Hirst for pointing out this additional interesting detail of publishing history.

46. Greeley's *The American Conflict* was the champion in subscription-book sales before 1870: 225,000 copies in the five years after the Civil War. Books about the war constituted the mainstay of the subscription business from 1865 to 1870. *The Innocents Abroad* came along just as the public was wearying of war books and hungering for other fare. See Stafford, "Subscription Book Publishing," 35–39. See also Jeffrey Alan Melton, *Mark Twain, Travel Books, and Tourism: The Tide of a Great Popular Movement* (Tuscaloosa: University of Alabama Press, 2002), 18–19.

47. On October 8, 1889, Fred J. Hall wrote to Clemens to caution him about this insistence and reassure him that *A Connecticut Yankee* skillfully avoided offending the main customer base that he and WebsterCo had in mind (MTP):

[T]he majority of the people heretofore had bought your books for the humor that was in them; that this book had a double advantage; that while it was as humorous as any work you had written, it was written with an object and a very noble one; that it taught lessons that would sink deeper into the public mind, in the way you taught them, than in any other way. . . . They said the sale of the book will go better after it is published than before. In this view I do not think you will agree, because you said some time ago that the book sale must be way previous to publication, but the general agents all said that it would go better after it was out, from the fact that people would then see that it was something infinitely more than a work of humor: That the more the book was read the better it would be liked; and that the church could not possibly hurt it; that it was the Catholic church that would principally attack, and that they were not book buyers anyway. Of course the Church of England, which is the Episcopal church in this country, may be a little sore, but that nothing is to be feared from the churches, and that the longer the book is out and the better it is known, the better it will sell.

48. For a recent discussion of Clemens's importance to American participation in international copyright laws, see Siva Vaidhyanathan, *Copyrights and Copywrongs: The Rise of Intellectual Property and How It Threatens Creativity* (New York: New York University Press, 2001), 35–80.

49. With regard to *A Connecticut Yankee,* Fred Hall for the Webster Company wrote to Chatto and Windus, indicating Clemens's willingness to tone down or delete passages that might offend an English audience and injure sales. See FJH to Chatto and Windus, August 5, 1889, MTP. In an October 8, 1889, letter, Hall advises Clemens not to worry about the novel offending American Catholics, since that constituency did not include substantial numbers of book buyers. See FJH to SLC, October 8, 1889, MTP. A week later, Hall wrote to Clemens to confirm a plan to eliminate Hank's antichurch tirades from the canvasser prospectus and the advertising of the novel. See FJH to SLC, October 16, 1889, MTP.

50. According to Gernsheim and Gernsheim, *History of Photography* (550–52), the adoption of halftone technology by daily newspapers required a bold move by a major publisher. This came about with the debut of the London *Daily Graphic* in January 1890 and the decision of the *Illustrated London News* to copy this strategy in the months following. Major market American papers took up the practice soon afterwards. See also Albert A. Sutton, *The Design and Makeup of the Newspaper* (New York: Prentice-Hall, 1948), 218–19.

51. Epigraphs: *Fulton Telegraph* quoted in Rader, "Newspaper History," 45; the plea in the *Hannibal Daily Journal* was run by Orion Clemens, its editor and publisher, less than a month before the *Journal* ceased publication; William Charvat, *Literary Publishing in America, 1790–1850* (Amherst: University of Massachusetts Press, 1993), 23.

See Shoemaker, *Missouri and Missourians,* 1:614. The telegraph network reached the Mississippi River at what is now East St. Louis in December 1847. See Robert I. Vexler, *St. Louis: A Chronological and Documentary History* (Dobbs Ferry, NY: Oceana Publications, 1974), 11.

52. The name Orion gave his weekly, a wishful and prescient choice, anticipated the nationwide telegraph news service that would take this name in 1856—five years after Orion's papers in Hannibal had all failed. Wire service did not reach Hannibal while they lingered.

53. *Hannibal Daily Journal,* May 31, 1853, 2.

54. *Hannibal Journal,* November 16, 1848, 3. However, as was true for advertisements in the *Hannibal Courier,* this picture could be a "dingbat" rather than a representation of any press in the shop. The *Courier's* similar advertisements, also with a Washington press dingbat during the period when Sam was working with Ament, appear regularly on p. 4. I am indebted to Robert Hirst for these and other insights about the Hannibal papers.

55. *Hannibal Journal,* July 13, 1848, 2.

56. After the Hoe Company acquired the Washington press patents and trade-

marks from Samuel Rust in 1835, they manufactured the Washington in seven different sizes. See James Moran, *Printing Presses: History and Development from the Fifteenth Century to Modern Times* (Berkeley: University of California Press, 1973), 79–81.

57. J. Luther Ringwalt, ed., *American Encyclopaedia of Printing* (Philadelphia: Menamin and Ringwalt, 1871), 140.

58. The Washington press (1827), constructed of iron, rugged and long lasting, was by the 1840s the biggest-selling machine for small-output printing operations. Manufactured first in Cincinnati, and eventually purchased by the Hoe Company and sold internationally as late as 1890, the Washington had clean modern lines compared to the Columbian, which was also of cast iron but was notable for filigree ornamentation and an iron American eagle atop the upright frame. In the heartland of Clemens's boyhood there was also the lightweight Ramage press, the ungainly wooden Ruggles, and some other designs—but all of these were hand-operated bed-and-platen machines, the essential workings of which Benjamin Franklin or even Caxton and the Gutenbergs would have understood readily.

59. In accounts of handpress operations the estimates of hourly output vary, but not dramatically compared to the output of steam-powered rotary or bed-and-platen machines. See, for example, Henry Mayer, *All on Fire: William Lloyd Garrison and the Abolition of Slavery* (New York: St. Martin's Press, 1998), 195. One year after Clemens left his brother's shop, a British history of printing calculated that two men operating a modern conventional handpress were capable of producing one thousand double-sided sheets in an eight-hour workday, or 250 single-side impressions per hour. See Charles Knight, *The Old Printer and the Modern Press* (London: John Murray, 1854), 253. In W. W. Pasko's *American Dictionary of Printing and Bookmaking* (New York: Lockwood, 1894) there is a calculation that "during the lifetime of Fox, Burke or Pitt" it was possible to print 6,000 impressions for a newspaper (one side only) in twenty-four hours, with "constant movement of the press during the entire time" and a team of six or eight men (445)—which is 250 impressions per hour. For comparison, Ringwalt's estimate of nineteenth-century handpress output, "under the favorable conditions of a busy season," is 156 impressions of one form in one hour (*American Encyclopaedia of Printing*, 360–61).

60. Moran, *Printing Presses*, 94.

61. Neither of the two extant Imperial handpresses that I have been able to locate (at the University of California at Riverside and at the University of Adelaide, in Australia) has a bed size larger than about fifteen inches by twenty, and I have found no listing of models with a larger bed size.

62. *Mark Twain's Letters*, 1:42.

63. *Official Catalogue of the New-York Exhibition of the Industry of All Nations, 1853* (New York: George P. Putnam, 1853), 20. See also Ezra Greenspan, *George Palmer Putnam: Representative American Publisher* (University Park: Pennsylvania State University Press, 2000), 323–31.

64. *Official Catalogue,* 33–34.

65. *Scientific American* 8 (July 30, 1853): 362.

66. *The New York City Directory, 1851–1852* (New York: Doggett and Rode, 1852), 259.

67. *Mark Twain's Letters,* 1:13. On the basis of specifics in Clemens's report to his sister, the editors conclude that "Clemens probably wrote this letter in the early hours of 3 September, having visited the Crystal Palace the previous evening" (14).

68. *Official Catalogue,* 31–41, 62–64, 99, 145, 150–51.

69. See Michael Schudson, *The Power of News* (Cambridge, MA: Harvard University Press, 1995), 38.

70. *Morning Intelligencer* (Columbia, TN), June 21, 1849, quoted in Guy Harry Stewart, "History and Bibliography of Middle Tennessee Newspapers, 1799–1876" (PhD diss., University of Illinois at Urbana-Champaign, 1957), 38.

71. In *Beyond the Lines: Pictorial Reporting, Everyday Life, and the Crisis of Gilded Age America* (Berkeley: University of California Press, 2002), Joshua Brown offers a general history of illustration in American journals. Brown observes that illustrated newspapers were scarce as late as the mid-1840s and that *Gleason's Pictorial Drawing Room Companion,* which began publication in 1851, was the first of many, made possible in part by the development of mass production in wood engraving (14–21, 35–40).

72. The "Soleleather" contributions to the New Orleans *Crescent,* in 1859, were discovered more than a century after by Edgar M. Branch. See Branch, "A New Clemens Footprint: Soleleather Steps Forward," *American Literature* 54 (1982): 497–510.

73. Albert Bigelow Paine is the source for the report that Orion set up his print shop in the Clemens home and kept his operations there for two years. See Paine, *Mark Twain,* 1:91–92. Dixon Wecter, however, observed the discrepancy between Paine's account and the evidence in the *Journal* itself that Orion maintained a regular place of business for his newspapers for most of their brief lives. Wecter, *Sam Clemens of Hannibal* (Boston: Houghton Mifflin, 1952), 243. For a recent, detailed reconstruction of dates and specific locations of Orion's newspaper offices, see Dempsey, *Searching for Jim,* 158.

74. Wecter, *Sam Clemens of Hannibal,* 256.

75. These events are summarized in Philip Ashley Fanning, *Mark Twain and Orion Clemens* (Tuscaloosa: University of Alabama Press, 2003), 27–31.

76. For a detailed history of the national controversy and federal legislation related to postal rates for newspapers and other publications between 1847 and 1852, see Richard Kielbowicz, *News in the Mail: The Press, Post Office, and Public Information, 1700–1860s* (New York: Greenwood Press, 1989), 86–90.

77. *Godey's Magazine and Lady's Book* 40 (June 1850): 421.

78. Greenspan, *George Palmer Putnam,* 331, 333.

79. Quoted in Ronald J. Zboray, "Antebellum Reading and the Ironies of Technological Innovation," in *Reading in America: Literature and Social History,* ed. Cathy N. Davidson (Baltimore: Johns Hopkins University Press 1989), 180–81.

80. See Charvat, *Literary Publishing in America*, 38–55. See also Michael Winship, *American Literary Publishing in the Mid-nineteenth Century: The Business of Ticknor and Fields* (New York: Cambridge University Press, 1995). Winship demonstrates that the average print run for a new work produced by this house in the 1840s, including textbooks and children's books, was about 1,500 copies (77). In the period 1850–59, the average for new works from Ticknor rose to around 2,000 copies (78).

81. For a useful summary of the marketing and distribution of books in the United States before the Civil War, see Zboray, "Antebellum Reading," 16–34. Winship (*American Literary Publishing*, 150–51) notes that Ticknor and Fields, as late as the 1850s, had no wholesale network in Delaware, New Jersey, Florida, Arkansas, Texas, or Pennsylvania beyond Philadelphia and that it reached the Midwest and South via small shipments to correspondents in a scattering of large and small cities. Additional detail is available in Henry W. Boynton, *Annals of American Bookselling, 1638–1850* (New York: John Wiley, 1932), and James Gilreath, "American Book Distribution," *Proceedings of the American Antiquarian Society* 95 (1985): 501–83.

82. John Tebbel chronicles the expansion: "Between 1830 and 1842, before the great leap forward of mass distribution, an average of about a hundred books a year had come from presses in America. This figure increased to 879 in 1853; 1,092 in 1855; and 1,350 in 1859–1860. Perhaps even more impressively, the value of books manufactured and sold in the United States increased from $2.5 million in 1820 to $3.5 million in 1830, to $5.5 in 1840, and . . . $12.5 in 1850." Tebbel, *A History of Book Publishing in the United States*, vol. 1, *The Creation of an Industry, 1630–1865* (New York: R. R. Bowker, 1972), 221.

83. Charvat, *Literary Publishing in America*, 54.

84. In *A Fictive People: Antebellum Economic Development and the American Reading Public* (New York: Oxford University Press, 1993), Ronald J. Zboray advises caution in the interpretation of these striking changes. Finding that histories of American publishing in the first half of the nineteenth century suffer from an "overemphasis on innovations in printing" (4), he notes that the new abundance of inexpensive printed material took time to find its way from the major cities to the heartland and that "if the democratization of literature means the equal participation of all in a unified print culture, the antebellum years witnessed a distinctly undemocratic trend" (15). By the time Sam Clemens reached his majority, however, many of these obstacles had been overcome; moreover, in understanding his response, the complications of the evolving American publishing system matter less than the viewpoint of a young man seeing these new possibilities firsthand.

85. *Littell's Living Age* 34 (January–March 1850): 274.

86. For a contemporary description, from the inside, of Harpers operations as reconstituted after the fire, see Jacob Abbot, *The Harper Establishment; or, How the Story Books Are Made* (New York: Harper and Brothers, 1855).

87. Andrea C. Pearson, "*Frank Leslie's Illustrated Newspaper* and *Harper's Weekly*: Innovation and Imitation in Nineteenth-Century American Pictorial Reporting," *Journal of Popular Culture* 23, no. 4 (1990): 81. Commencing publication in 1855,

Frank Leslie's Illustrated Newspaper achieved a national weekly circulation of more than two hundred thousand after the outbreak of the Civil War. See Brown, *Beyond the Lines,* 7, 48.

88. Ringwalt, *American Encyclopaedia of Printing,* 223.

89. See Annenberg's *Typographical Journey,* an excellent one-volume compilation of articles, advertisements, and editorials from this journal.

90. See Clair, *Chronology of Printing,* 145. Clair notes three separate, similar inventions advancing the process in 1839.

91. See, for example, Winship, *American Literary Publishing,* 119.

92. See Patricia Okker, *Our Sister Editors: Sarah J. Hale and the Tradition of Nineteenth Century American Women Editors* (Athens: University of Georgia Press, 1995), 13.

93. The Godey promise of "four times as many steel engravings" as its competitors appears in a repeating advertisement in the *Hannibal Journal* in the spring of 1853, on p. 3 of each issue, and includes this expression of scorn for older technologies: "What is the disappointment of the duped subscriber when he receives the numbers of a magazine thus advertised, to find his fine engravings are but common wood-cuts,—as poor in design as in execution!"

94. The APC's advance publicity for *The Innocents Abroad* is extensively quoted and analyzed by Anne Cook in "Finding His Mark: Twain's *The Innocents Abroad* as a Subscription Book," in *Reading Books: Essays on the Material Text and Literature in America,* ed. Michele Moylan and Lane Stiles (Amherst: University of Massachusetts Press, 1996), 155–77.

95. When halftone technology (for transcribing photographic images) was adopted for American book and magazine publishing in the later decades of the nineteenth century, etchings created by that process could be soldered into the plates. See C. S. Partridge, *Electrotyping: A Practical Treatise on the Art of Electrotyping by the Latest Known Methods* (Chicago: Inland Printer, 1908), 184.

96. George Kubler illustrates the difference with regard to sheer size:

> The first set of stereotype casts of a Bible sent from England to Philadelphia . . . may be remembered by the older printers as occupying the entire side of a moderate-sized room; and if the stereotype plates at present in the large cities were to be stored in this old-fashioned way, entire blocks of warehouses would be needed for the purpose. Packed in boxes, as they now are in the compact American method [i.e., the electrotype] . . . , a cellar or a vault suffices for the accumulated plates of a large publishing-house or an extensive printing office.
>
> *A New History of Stereotyping* (New York: Little and Ives, 1941), 173

97. In a comprehensive 1902 treatise, *The Practice of Typography* (New York: Century), Theodore Low De Vinne concludes his discussion of electrotyping by observing that now, at the opening of the twentieth century, "In the United States all books that may be reprinted are electrotyped" (41).

98. Quoted in Charles Asselineau, *André Charles Boulle, Ebeniste de Louis XIV,* 3rd ed. (Paris: P. Rouquette, 1872), 42. My translation.

99. *Mark Twain's Letters,* ed. Albert Bigelow Paine, 2 vols. (New York: Harper and Brothers, 1917), 2:472. The draft comes from a set called "Unmailed Letters," p. 1 of sequence 2. The assigned date is September 8–October 1887.

100. In *The English Book Trade* (London: Allen and Unwin, 1965), Marjorie Plant concludes that steam power was the crucial innovation in revolutionizing the publishing industry in the nineteenth century (see 272–73) and observes that steam-powered presses were in operation at the London *Times* as early as 1814.

101. Between about 1830 and the Civil War, *powered* did not always mean connection to a steam engine. Even at larger New York establishments in the 1840s and 1850s, automatic equipment was often driven by horses, with an apparatus of gears, armatures, and leather belts transferring the power (often in the basement of the establishment) upstairs to the pressroom.

102. Pasko, *American Dictionary of Printing,* 9.

103. Petition from Isaac Adams "for an extension of the patent," granted February 20, 1850, Schedule of the Letters Patent, 23, in Special Collections Department, Alderman Memorial Library, University of Virginia, Charlottesville.

104. Moran, *Printing Presses,* 115.

105. Ringwalt, *American Encyclopaedia of Printing,* 22.

106. *Mark Twain's Notebooks and Journals,* vol. 3, *1883–1891,* ed. Robert Pack Browning, Michael B. Frank, and Lin Salamo (Berkeley: University of California Press, 1979), 208–9.

107. For a general history of the Fourdrinier and Gilpin processes and their adoption and further development by American manufacturers, and illustrations of other machinery in the production process, see Dard Hunter, *Papermaking: The History and Technique of an Ancient Craft* (New York: Dover Books, 1974), 341–73. For more detail about regional development and economic and social impact, see Judith McGaw, *Wonderful Machine: Mechanization and Social Change in Berkshire Paper Making, 1801–1865* (Princeton: Princeton University Press, 1987). For an account from Mark Twain's lifetime, see Charles T. Davis, *The Manufacture of Paper* (Philadelphia: n.p., 1886), 46–51, 99–143.

108. Hunter, *Papermaking,* 366–68.

109. Julius Grant, *Wood Pulp and Allied Products* (London: Leonard Hill, 1947), 22–25.

110. According to one history, *Chicago's Accomplishments and Leaders,* ed. Glenn A. Bishop (Chicago: Bishop, 1932), a rail link opened between the city and Galena on the Mississippi River as early as November 1848; but the track for this connection ended several miles south of town. The completion of the line to Rock Island in February 1854 was more important in establishing the city as a commercial hub; by 1860, Chicago was the center of the largest railway network in the world. See Howard B. Furer, ed., *Chicago: A Chronological and Documentary History, 1784–1970* (Dobbs Ferry, NY: Oceana, 1974), 9–11.

111. Michael Hackenberg, "The Subscription Publishing Network in Nineteenth Century America," in *Getting the Books Out: Papers of the Chicago Confer-*

ence on the Book in Nineteenth-Century America, ed. Michael Hackenberg (Washington, DC: Library of Congress, 1987), 45–75. Stafford ("Subscription Book Publishing," 159) makes a case that the decline of the subscription-book trade was also hastened by a decision of regular publishers to develop their own subscription and mail-order operations.

112. For a summary of relevant innovations in illustration, see Budd L. Gambee, "American Book and Magazine Illustration of the Later Nineteenth Century," in *Book Illustration: Papers Presented at the Third Rare Book Conference of the American Library Association in 1962* (Berlin: Gebr. Mann, 1963), 45–55. Gambee highlights two developments in the years from 1830 through the 1850s: the utility of the electroplate for combining text and pictures on the same page (46) and the divided woodblock, a production shortcut that allowed several engravers to work simultaneously on one illustration, allowing the work to be finished more quickly—an advantage for periodicals like *Harper's Weekly* (51).

113. In their edition of *Adventures of Huckleberry Finn* (Berkeley: University of California Press, 2002), Victor Fischer and Lin Salamo offer an illustrated review of the process by which a drawing by E. W. Kemble became an image on an electroplate for the book (718–19, 721–25). See also Mason Jackson, *The Pictorial Press: Its Origins and Progress* (London: Hurst and Blackett, 1885; reprint, Detroit: Gale Research, 1968), 315–25.

114. From Beverly R. David's project to chronicle in detail the illustration of Mark Twain's books and periodical publications, *Mark Twain and His Illustrators,* two volumes have thus far appeared: (Troy, NY: Whitston, 1986 and 2001, respectively). For her survey of originality and piracy with regard to illustrations in *A Tramp Abroad,* see 2:70–196. In each volume of the Oxford Mark Twain reprinting an illustrated first edition, Beverly David and Ray Sapirstein offer useful commentary on pictures in that edition.

115. The letter is reprinted in *Mark Twain's Travels with Mr. Brown,* ed. Franklin Walker and G. Ezra Dane (New York: Russell and Russell, 1940), 157–58.

116. Peter C. Marzio, *The Democratic Art: Chromolithography 1840–90, Pictures for a Nineteenth Century America* (Boston: David Godine, 1979), 131–33.

117. For a summary of Prang's career and achievement, see Larry Freeman [Graydon LaVerne], *Louis Prang: Color Lithographer* (Watkins Glen, NY: Century House, 1971).

118. Quoted in Marzio, *Democratic Art,* 9.

119. Ibid., 3–21.

120. Ibid., 62.

121. Freeman, *Louis Prang,* 54–69.

122. The letter is reprinted in *A Connecticut Yankee in King Arthur's Court,* ed. Bernard L. Stein (Berkeley: University of California Press, 1979), 578–79.

123. Walter Benjamin, "The Work of Art in the Age of Mechanical Reproduction," in *Illuminations: Essays and Reflections,* ed. Hannah Arendt, trans. Harry

Zohn (New York: Schocken Books, 1968), 217–51. The essay was originally published in *Zeitschrift für Sozialforschung* in 1936.

124. Guy Debord, *The Society of the Spectacle* (New York: Black and Red, 1970), originally published as *La société du spectacle* (Paris: Buchet-Chastel, 1967).

125. One of these embossed and lithographed signs is in the collection of the Smithsonian Museum of American History. In the MTP, no indication has turned up that Clemens authorized anyone to commercialize his face in this particular way.

TWO. THE MISCHIEF OF THE PRESS

1. SLC's first experiments in Orion's paper and other places have been collected in Mark Twain, *Early Tales and Sketches, 1851–1864,* ed. Edgar Marquess Branch and Robert H. Hirst (Berkeley: University of California Press, 1979). The editors make a strong case for SLC's authorship of all the "Rambler" and "Grumbler" material in May 1853 (92–93).

2. As he recalled in a 1906 dictation, the most outrageous violation of a text for convenience in printing, during his time in the Hannibal shops, was a prank led by another of Ament's apprentices, Wales McCormick, who inserted a middle initial "H" into "Jesus Christ" to fill out a line because a minister had insisted on last-minute changes in a sermon that Wales and Clemens had already set up for the press. See *Mark Twain's Autobiography,* ed. Albert Bigelow Paine, 2 vols. (New York: Harper and Brothers, 1924), 2:279–82. See also Twain, *Mark Twain's Notebooks,* 3:305.

3. Twain, *Early Tales and Sketches,* 99.

4. Ibid., 159.

5. For discussion of "Petrified Man" as a comic text, see Bruce Michelson, *Mark Twain on the Loose* (Amherst: University of Massachusetts Press, 1995), 14–18.

6. Mark Twain, *Collected Tales, Sketches, Speeches, and Essays, 1852–1890,* ed. Louis J. Budd (New York: Library of America, 1992), 124.

7. Louis J. Budd, "Mark Twain's 'An Encounter with an Interviewer': The Height (or Depth) of Nonsense," *Nineteenth-Century Literature* 55, no. 2 (2000): 226–43. "An Encounter with an Interviewer" first appeared in *Lotos Leaves,* released by the small Boston house of William F. Gill as a fund-raiser for a New York dinner club to which Clemens belonged. It appeared in Dan Slote's collection *Punch, Brothers, Punch!* in 1878 and in Osgood's *The Stolen White Elephant* in 1882.

8. Schudson, *Power of News,* 48.

9. See Christopher Sylvester, introduction to *The Norton Book of Interviews,* ed. Christopher Sylvester (New York: W. W. Norton, 1996), 4–5.

10. Schudson, *Power of News,* 49.

11. Twain, *Collected Tales,* 583.

12. The story is summarized in Hyde and Conard, *Encyclopedia,* 4:1915.

13. Henry David Thoreau, *Walden,* ed. J. Lyndon Shanley (Princeton: Princeton University Press, 1971), 52.

14. Though Paine is oblique about the real causes, Paul Fatout makes it clear that Clemens was entangled in hostilities and impending duels, stemming mostly from a tasteless joke about a local charitable initiative. For a detailed account of this trouble, see *Mark Twain's Letters,* vol. 1, *1853–66,* 287–99. See also *Mark Twain of the Enterprise,* ed. Henry Nash Smith (Berkeley: University of California Press, 1957), 189–205. See also Paine, *Mark Twain,* 357–60, and Paul Fatout, *Mark Twain in Virginia City* (Bloomington: Indiana University Press, 1964), 196–212.

15. Stewart, "History and Bibliography."

16. *Republican* (Shelbyville), November 6, 1868, as quoted in Stewart, "History and Bibliography," 48–49.

17. Twain, *Collected Tales,* 313.

18. Ibid., 416–17. The story was originally published in July 1870.

19. Ibid., 108.

20. For a list of *Harper's Weekly* stories attributed to Alger, see Bob Bennett, *Horatio Alger, Jr.: A Comprehensive Bibliography* (Mt. Pleasant, MI: Flying Eagle Publishing, 1980).

21. "The Heart of Miriam Clyde," *Harper's Weekly,* February 27, 1864, 125.

THREE. "BUT NOW EVERYBODY GOES EVERYWHERE"

1. *Mark Twain's Letters,* vol. 6, *1874–1875,* ed. Michael B. Frank and Harriet Elinor Smith (Berkeley: University of California Press, 2002), 262–63.

2. Fred J. Hall to SLC, August 5, 1889, MTP.

3. Tebbel summarizes the nineteenth-century American subscription book trade:

> People who were hungry for books had not yet learned to discriminate. They bought volumes which had been blown up by publishers to twice the size actually required, tricked out in flamboyant bindings, printed on thick, cheap paper, with pictures badly printed—in general, the tasteless products of hucksters. A book of this kind might cost $5, while at the same time the identical text could have been bought, in a well-produced book of moderate size sold at a regular bookstore, for $1.50. Most people did not know about regular trade books, since the largest part of the population was not served by bookstores; consequently, they thought the cheap quartos were bargains, when in reality they could have bought Carlyle for ninety cents a volume, [George] Eliot for seventy-five cents and Dickens for a variety of prices.
>
> *A History of Book Publishing in the United States,* vol. 2, *The Expansion of an Industry, 1865–1919* (New York: Bowker, 1975), 512

And about agents and sales strategies:

> Book agents were roundly abused by virtually everyone in the business . . . and their legendary persistence was a subject for humor in and out of the trade. . . .

Much more serious were the questionable methods of selling subscription books which plagued the business and gave it a bad name among many people in and out of publishing. (2:513)

Alan Nevins observes, however, that on occasion even the genteel publishers of the Gilded Age, houses like Appleton and Lippincott, sold books by the subscription method and that in an era with a general dearth of decent bookstores (three shops in Chicago in 1867 and one good store in San Francisco) and lending libraries, the subscription trade provided millions of Americans with their only access to books. See Nevins, "The Broadening of American Culture," in *The Emergence of Modern America, 1865–1878,* vol. 8 of *A History of American Life,* ed. Mark C. Carnes and Arthur M. Schlesinger Jr. (New York: Macmillan, 1955), 228–63, esp. 236–44. For nostalgia about Mark Twain and the subscription book's presence in ordinary American life, see George Ade, "Mark Twain and the Old Time Subscription Book," *Review of Reviews* 41 (1910): 703–4.

4. J. Walter Stoops, *The Art of Canvassing, or, the Experience of a Practical Canvasser* (New York: "Printed for the Author," 1857), 7.

5. For an amusing account of the adventures of a canvasser working for WebsterCo in the sales campaign for *Mark Twain's Library of Humor,* see the article "A Book Canvasser's Woes," by one Margaret Gorman, *New York World,* April 21, 1889, 27. Though the *World,* under Joseph Pulitzer, was known for sensation and contentiousness rather than sobriety and accuracy, there may be some truth in Gorman's tale of misadventure in trying to sell a Mark Twain book in Pittsfield for Mark Twain's publishing house. Selected for the job by a Mr. Perry, at WebsterCo, because he preferred brunettes to blondes, Gorman reports that she went to Pittsfield on a promise of a salary of $3 per day and covered expenses for travel and hotels. She spent weeks at the 14th Street office, memorizing and practicing an extended pitch for the book. When she hit the road, however, the promises evaporated, and she spent several fruitless days trying to talk local citizens into signing up for the volume. She charmed a doctor, briefly, "But when I began to talk book he rose promptly from his chair and moving towards the door, minus the smile, opened it and stated that he had one of Mark Twain's books and he considered that enough. The name of the book he has is 'Roughing It,' which reminded me very forcibly that I was doing the same thing in earnest." Coming home without a single sale, Gorman summed up her WebsterCo experience this way: "My adventure has cost me $18.27 in cash; five weeks solid time given up to the Webster Publishing Company . . . besides wear and tear mentally and physically."

6. As the agents for *The Innocents Abroad* were fanning out across the nation, the Buffalo *Commercial Advertiser,* on August 17, 1869, offered an overview, and a lament, about the scope of subscription bookselling:

One of the most profitable branches of the book-publishing business in this country is that of publishing books which are sold only by subscription; though if the work is valuable and popular, stray copies can always be found on the counters and shelves of the bookstores. Hartford, Conn., is the principal seat of the subscription book-publishing business, and several large rival establishments are engaged therein. The books are generally octavos of seven hundred pages, printed in pica type, profusely illustrated, and sold at from $3.50 to $5.50 the copy, according to the binding. . . .

These subscription books are pushed everywhere by agents, whose main business is to make people buy books which they do not want; and the success of some of these agents is surprising. Large numbers of young men who work on farms in summer, and who would be idle in winter but for this business, become book-agents, and derive much profit thereby, some of them making as much as $5, $10, or even more dollars a day. (1, 7)

As James A. Madison observes, however, the American book trade of the 1870s and 1880s had other problems to face besides the subscription business, which favored thick books at padded prices. The national market was hit with a glut of very inexpensive poorly produced paperbacks that reprinted popular American and Continental fiction with no royalties to the authors or original publishers. When competition among these cut-price publishers grew severe, a consolidation of sorts was achieved with a "book trust" engineered by John W. Lovell, bringing a measure of peace to the dime-novel trade. See Madison, *Book Publishing in America* (New York: McGraw-Hill, 1966), 49–58.

7. To document the boom in subscription-book sales in the decade after the Civil War, James D. Hart offers the following statistics:

In seven years Greeley's *American Conflict* sold 250,000 copies; Joseph T. Headley's *The Great Rebellion* and T. P. Kettell's *History of the Great Rebellion* respectively sold 150,000 and 120,000 copies in nine years; and one of Albert D. Richardson's books, *The Secret Service,* sold 100,000 copies in six years, while his other, *Beyond the Mississippi,* sold 90,000 copies in four years. These were tremendous sales for a period of poor economic conditions.

The Popular Book: A History of America's Literary Taste
(New York: Oxford University Press, 1950), 151

8. The exhaustive history of Beadle's book company is Albert Johannsen's three-volume *The House of Beadle and Adams and Its Dime and Nickel Novels: The Story of a Vanished Literature* (Norman: University of Oklahoma Press, 1962). For a crisp overview of the heyday and consequences of the American dime novel, see Emory Elliot et al., *The Columbia History of the American Novel* (New York: Columbia University Press, 1991), 291–97.

9. The WebsterCo edition of the Right Reverend Bernard O'Reilly's *Life of Pope Leo XIII, from an Authentic Memoir* (1886) was a lavish production, scrupulously assuring American readers of its official status and factual accuracy. Opening with photoengraved copies of holograph letters of authorization from Cardinal Gibbons of Baltimore, Archbishop Corrigan of New York, and two cardinals at the Vatican, the book also includes attestations that "ALL the illustrations in this work are full-page engravings executed by the BEST AMERICAN ENGRAVERS from original photographs sent expressly for this book. None of them have ever before appeared in

print" (30), an important variation from the dubious provenance of illustrations in other subscription books, especially from the APC. Also unusual for a WebsterCo volume was the inclusion of two chromolithographs—one of the pope himself, the other of "Officers and Attendants of the Pontifical Court" (facing p. 304).

10. For sheer density of images, *Bible Lands Illustrated,* by Henry C. Fish, DD (New York: A. S. Barnes, 1876), with "six hundred engravings and maps," beat any travel book that Mark Twain wrote with the APC, Osgood, or WebsterCo. The Reverend D. A. Randall's *The Handwriting of God in Egypt, Sinai, and the Holy Land* (Philadelphia: John E. Potter; Chicago: J. W. Godspeed, 1862), used by Clemens while he was writing *The Innocents Abroad,* was a popular subscription tome, as was *Holy Land with Glimpses of Europe and Egypt,* by S. Dryden Phelps, DD (New York: Sheldon; Boston: Gould and Lincoln, 1863), with only twenty-two engravings. J. T. Barclay's *The City of the Great King of Jerusalem as It Was, as It Is, and As It Is to Be* (Philadelphia: James Challen and Sons, 1857), written by a medical missionary to the Holy Land, was bolstered with five steel engravings, three "illuminations," nine lithographs, ten chromolithographs, and more than forty woodcuts, and sold by an American direct-mail publisher. Conventional trade houses joined the trend as well: in 1881, Lippincott published *Lands of the Bible, a Geographical and Topographical Description of Palestine with Letters of Travel in Egypt, Syria, Asia Minor, and Greece,* by J. W. McGarvey, "Professor of Sacred History in the College of the Bible, Lexington, Kentucky." McGarvey's volume had about 150 illustrations. But *The Holy Land and the Bible: A Book of Scripture Illustrations Gathered in Palestine,* by Cunningham Geikie, a British vicar (New York: James Pott, 1888), was a two-volume work with only one map and no illustrations at all.

11. SLC to Fred J. Hall, May 7, 1888, Berg Collection, New York Public Library.

12. See Jeffrey D. Groves, "Judging Literary Books by Their Covers: House Styles, Ticknor and Fields, and Literary Promotion," in *Reading Books: Essays on the Material Text and Literature in America,* ed. Michele Moylan and Lane Stiles (Amherst: University of Massachusetts Press, 1996), 75–99.

13. Writing to Clemens about the design of *Huckleberry Finn,* Webster sought Clemens's consent about the appropriate font, paper thickness, and cover:

> What I want to know about, is: What color shall we have it? You said some time ago we would have several colors but in that case agents will be continually changing, and customers shilly-shallying between two colors.
>
> It seems to me we had better decide on some <u>one</u> color. Tom Sawyer is blue, but there is a growing dislike to that color. We are continually getting orders on different books, "<u>Any color but blue.</u>" Do you consider it necessary to have the <u>color</u> the same as Sawyer?
>
> Webster to SLC, April 17, 1884, MTP

14. James D. Hart estimated that in the busiest years of the subscription trade after the Civil War, "outside of school books and periodicals, more than three

fourths of all the money expended in the United States for books each year passed through the hands of agents" (*Popular Book*, 151).

15. Benjamin, *Illuminations*, 221.

16. For an overview of the connection between Royal Academy painters and the London market for engraved reproductions in the later eighteenth century and the Romantic period, see Gillen D'Arcy Wood, *The Shock of the Real: Romanticism and Visual Culture, 1760–1860* (New York: Palgrave/St. Martin's Press, 2001), 67–97.

17. In *Mark Twain and Elisha Bliss* (Columbia: University of Missouri Press, 1964), Hamlin Hill reports that Clemens "heard little about the book and did nothing to assist its publication" from August 1868 into the winter of 1869 (29) and became "unbelievably docile" (34) in the fall of 1869 after Bliss responded harshly to accusations that Twain had launched in an imprudent letter. However, Robert Hirst and Brandt Rowles have made a persuasive case that Clemens had personal access to a set of photographs taken on the *Quaker City* excursion and that these photographs were subsequently used by illustrators of *The Innocents Abroad*. See Robert Hirst and Brandt Rowles, "William E. James's Stereoscopic Views of the *Quaker City* Excursion," *Mark Twain Journal* 22 (Spring 1984): 15–33.

18. Paine (*Mark Twain*, 1:356–81) offers a fairly detailed account of Clemens's other adventures while writing *The Innocents Abroad*. More recently, in *Inventing Mark Twain: The Lives of Samuel Langhorne Clemens* (New York: William Morrow, 1997), Andrew J. Hoffman accepts at face value Clemens's personal recollection, many years later in the autobiographical dictations, that the writing process had been six weeks of relentless work from midnight until dawn (137–38).

19. For a history of Clemens's specific interactions with Bliss regarding the design and production of *The Innocents Abroad*, see Hill, *Mark Twain and Elisha Bliss*, 21–31.

20. Robert Hart Hirst, "The Making of *The Innocents Abroad*: 1867–1872" (PhD diss., University of California, Berkeley, 1975), 211–12. Hirst was also the first scholar to observe that in generating printable images of landscapes and portraits the APC made use of a "recently-invented photographic technique which permitted them to project an exact image of the picture card onto a photo-sensitive wood block, which was in turn developed and the resulting image engraved."

21. See *Roughing It*, ed. Harriet Elinor Smith et al. (Berkeley: University of California Press, 1993), 891. See also Everett Emerson, *Mark Twain: A Literary Life* (Philadelphia: University of Pennsylvania Press, 1999), 62.

22. Many of these letters are gathered in Mark Twain, *Mark Twain's Letters to His Publishers, 1867–1894*, ed. Hamlin Hill (Berkeley: University of California Press, 1967), 40–89. In North America in the eighteenth century, before the rise of the East Coast trade publishers, almost all publication was by subscription, with volumes from small print runs going to customers who had signed up in advance. In the mass-market subscription-book business after 1865, *The Gilded Age* was apparently the first novel to be marketed in this way.

23. Dan Slote to SLC, March 4, 1878, Scrapbook 10, p. 39, MTP.

24. The *Oxford English Dictionary,* compact ed., ed. James H. Murray et al., 2 vols. (Oxford: Oxford University Press, 1971), traces *mountaineering* to an edition of Southey's *Letters* in 1856 and gives the date of its first use in a book title as 1861 (p. 1863).

25. From Paul Bernard, *Rush to the Alps: The Evolution of Vacationing in Switzerland* (New York: Columbia University Press, 1978):

> By playing out a grand drama, by confronting death on the rock faces . . . [the mountaineers] attracted general interest to themselves; and with this interest came the hordes of spectators and hangers-on who are to be found in the vicinity of all spectacles that seem to promise the spilling of blood. . . . To be sure, the great climbs were beyond both their abilities and courage. . . . But a good scramble among the rocks, a climb to the top of some lesser, more attainable eminence, particularly with the secure knowledge that a good meal and a feather bed await one in the evening, also bestow a sense of having accomplished something, of having returned to older, saner, and presumably healthier pursuits. It was these not-quite-mountaineers who made up an important segment of the clientele of the Swiss Alpine resorts in the second half of the century. (43)

26. *A Tramp Abroad* (1880), ed. Shelley Fisher Fishkin (New York: Oxford University Press, 1996), 345. All subsequent page references to *A Tramp Abroad* refer to this widely available reprint of the APC first edition.

In *Mark Twain, Travel Books,* Melton notes the importance of this passage as indicating Mark Twain's uneasiness at finding himself in the midst of a "Tourist Age" and his recourse to vicarious experience in a place where the chances of adventure are slim (78–94).

27. As early as vol. 3 of *Modern Painters* (1856), Ruskin was complaining that "[g]oing by railroad I do not consider as traveling at all; it is merely 'being sent' to a place, and very little different from being a parcel; the next step to it would of course be telegraphic transport." *The Works of John Ruskin,* ed. E. T. Cook and Alexander Wedderburn (London: George Allen, 1904), 5:370. A quarter-century later in the *Deucalion* lectures, he laments that modern technological travel is affecting even the high-born, high-climbing mountaineers: "I spoke with sorrow, deeper than my words attempted to express, . . . of the blind rushing of our best youth through the noblest scenery of the Alps, without once glancing at it, that they might amuse, or kill, themselves on their snow" (*Works of John Ruskin,* 26:154).

28. For a summary of Swiss railroad and hotel development in the middle years of the nineteenth century and the concurrent tidal rise in British tourism, see Jim Ring, *How the English Made the Alps* (London: John Murray, 2000), especially 149–85. See also G. R. de Beer, "The Flowing Tide of Tourists," in his *Alps and Men: Pages from Forgotten Diaries of Travellers and Tourists in Switzerland* (London: Edward Arnold, 1932), 88–112. For a summary of rapid developments in steam-powered transport on the Swiss lakes and in the Alpine rail system from 1847 to

1870, see Karl Dändliker, *A Short History of Switzerland,* trans. E. Salisbury (New York: Macmillan, 1899), 291–94.

29. At his Leicester Square gallery, the painter Robert Burford exhibited at least two panoramas of the Alps in the middle years of the century: *A View of Mont Blanc* (1837) and *A View of the Bernees [sic] Alps* (1852). For an overview of the panorama craze and the popularity of alpine landscapes as subjects for these huge paintings, see Ralph Hyde, *Panoramania! The Art and Entertainment of the "All-Embracing" View* (London: Trefoil/Barbican Art Gallery, 1988).

30. In the past twenty years, tourism and travel narratives have become an important academic subject, and considerable attention has been paid to the cultural power of the visitor and the impact of touring on the imagination and constructions of cultural literacy. Among the best of these studies are Christopher Mulvey, *Anglo-American Landscapes: A Study of Nineteenth-Century Anglo-American Travel Literature* (New York: Cambridge University Press, 1983); James Buzard, *The Beaten Track: European Tourism, Literature, and the Ways to "Culture," 1800–1918* (New York: Oxford University Press, 1993); and Mary Louise Pratt, *Imperial Eyes: Travel Writing and Transculturation* (New York: Routledge, 1992). Nina Baym has pointed out that much of "the recent outpouring of theoretical and analytical work on travel and touring has created an all-male discourse" that ignores some important women writers, especially American women of the early and middle nineteenth century. See Baym, *American Women Writers and the Work of History, 1790–1860* (New Brunswick: Rutgers University Press, 1995), 290. Baym's volume does much to set the record straight.

31. Karl Baedeker, *Switzerland, and the Adjacent Portions of Italy, Savoy, and the Tyrol,* 7th rev. ed. (Leipzig: Karl Baedeker, 1877), 287.

32. For incisive discussion of this supposedly contemporary predicament, in which imaginative demands of the tourist or visitor transmogrify the culture under scrutiny, see Jonathan Culler, "The Semiotics of Tourism," in his *Framing the Sign: Criticism and Its Institutions* (Oxford: Blackwell, 1988), and John Urry, *The Tourist Gaze: Leisure and Travel in Contemporary Societies* (Thousand Oaks, CA: Sage Publications, 1995). See also Barbara Korte, "Julian Barnes, *England, England:* Tourism as a Critique of Postmodernism," in *The Making of Modern Tourism: The Cultural History of the British Experience, 1600–2000,* ed. Hartmut Berghoff et al. (New York: Palgrave, 2002), 285–304.

33. In *Mark Twain in England* (Atlantic Highlands, NJ: Humanities Press, 1978), Dennis Welland notes that *A Tramp Abroad* sold more than 174,000 copies in England in Mark Twain's lifetime—twice as many as *The Adventures of Tom Sawyer* and four times as many as *Adventures of Huckleberry Finn.*

34. SLC to Francis E. Bliss, May 10, 1879, in Twain, *Mark Twain's Letters to His Publishers,* 114.

35. Pasko, *American Dictionary of Printing,* 435.

36. Ringwalt quotes a publication from the American Photo-Lithographic

Company: "Line engravings, wood-cuts, pen-drawings, engraved and drawn maps, manuscripts, architectural and mechanical drawings, music, printed matter, plans, etc., are copied full scale, reduced, or enlarged, as may be required. Each class of work will be a perfect facsimile of the original copy, and possess all its peculiar characteristics. If, for instance, a wood-cut be reproduced, no one would venture to assert that the reproduction was anything else than a wood-cut, every detail being so accurately preserved" (*American Encyclopaedia of Printing*, 348).

37. Pasko, *American Dictionary of Printing*, 435.

38. For brief explanations of the various new photographic processes available in the 1870s, see Ringwalt, *American Encyclopaedia of Printing*, 346–50, and Pasko, *American Dictionary of Printing*, 435, 464–66. The variance in the names assigned to specific strategies is suggestive of the dynamic condition of the technology from the Civil War to the end of Mark Twain's career.

39. David, *Mark Twain and His Illustrators*, 2:140–43.

40. Frank Bliss to SLC, June 27, 1879, MTP.

41. Twain, *Mark Twain's Letters to His Publishers*, 114.

42. Ibid., 115.

43. For an extensive account, see David, *Mark Twain and His Illustrators*, 2:71–183.

44. Baedeker, *Switzerland*, 142.

45. Leslie Stephen, *The Playground of Europe* (1871; reprint, London: Longmans, Green, 1910), 42–43.

46. For a concise account of Clemens's struggle to complete *A Tramp Abroad*, see Emerson, *Mark Twain*, 112–16. Paine (*Mark Twain*, 2:636–48) reports that the writing was "always a chief source of gratification" (638) after Mark Twain worked through a spate of self-doubts about having "somehow lost the knack of descriptive narrative" (636). Andrew Hoffman (*Inventing Mark Twain*, 264–71) retells the story with emphasis on personal distractions that Twain was coping with at the time.

FOUR. "HUCKLEBERRY FINN"
AND THE AMERICAN PRINT REVOLUTION

1. See Michelson, *Mark Twain*, 95–101.

2. Victor Fischer and Lin Salamo review these title-page developments and variations and the possible reasons for them in their most recent edition of *Adventures of Huckleberry Finn*, 560–65.

3. Tom Quirk summarizes the time problems in *Huckleberry Finn* this way: "Huck's story as novel is impossibility followed by implausibility and linked together by unlikelihood." *Coming to Grips with Huckleberry Finn: Essays on a Book, a Boy, and a Man* (Columbia: University of Missouri Press, 1993), 100.

4. *"Huckleberry Finn," Boston Evening Traveller*, March 5, 1885, 1, quoted in

Louis J. Budd, *Mark Twain: The Contemporary Reviews* (Cambridge: Cambridge University Press, 1999), 267.

5. For facsimiles of these holograph pages, see *Adventures of Huckleberry Finn,* 562–65.

6. Mark Twain, *Mark Twain in Eruption: Hitherto Unpublished Pages about Men and Events,* ed. Bernard DeVoto (New York: Harper and Brothers, 1940), 196. For provocative discussion of Clemens's interest in automatic writing, inspiration, and the creative process, see Randall Knoper, *Acting Naturally: Mark Twain in the Culture of Performance* (Berkeley: University of California Press, 1995).

7. E. W. Kemble, "Illustrating *Huckleberry Finn,*" *Colophon: A Book Collector's Quarterly* 1, no. 1 (1930). The *Colophon* in these early numbers was not paginated. A notation at the end of the essay indicates that it was written for the journal in December 1929.

8. Beverly David and Ray Sapirstein find that Mark Twain was drawn to Kemble by the young artist's illustrations in *Life,* and specifically by a cartoon called "Some Uses for Electricity." See "Reading the Illustrations in Huckleberry Finn," in *Adventures of Huckleberry Finn,* 33–34. Kent Rasmussen observes that Clemens may have known about Kemble from interactions with his father when the two were contributing to the *Alta California* twenty years earlier. See Rasmussen, *Mark Twain,* 269.

9. The best commentary on this subject is Earl Briden, "Kemble's 'Specialty' and the Pictorial Countertext of *Huckleberry Finn,*" *Mark Twain Journal* 26 (Fall 1988): 2–14.

10. SLC to Charles Webster, May 7, 1884, in Twain, *Mark Twain's Letters to His Publishers,* 174.

11. For example, in "The Ethnicity of Huck Finn—and the Difference It Makes" (*American Literary Realism* 30, no. 2 [1998]: 1–14), Hugh J. Dawson argues that Mark Twain "stigmatized the Finns as Irish-Americans and made what could be perceived as Huck's racial legacy a means of identifying him with the black" (14).

12. For an astute meditation on the inadequacy of systematic literary theory to negotiate texts that are both verbal texts and images, see W. J. T. Mitchell, *Iconology: Image, Text, Ideology* (Chicago: University of Chicago Press, 1986), especially 157–63. Mitchell laments a debilitating Puritanism in his peers, a reluctance to accept the mingled aesthetic and semiotic experience of words and pictures brought together through authorial intention or acquiescence: "The major stumbling block in the way of this sort of study has always been, in fact, the hope for some master trope, some structural model, that would allow the kind of scientific, comparative formalism to proceed under the umbrella of a 'true theory' of the relation between image and text. The familiar excesses of comparative criticism of texts and images . . . are best understood as expressions of this desire for a master theory to unite the arts" (157).

13. Mark Twain, *The Adventures of Tom Sawyer,* ed. John C. Gerber and Paul Baender (Berkeley: University of California Press, 1982), 254–55.

14. For a playful recent survey of *Huckleberry Finn's* permutations in American popular culture, see Shelley Fisher Fishkin, *Lighting out for the Territory* (New York: Oxford University Press, 1997), 17–37.

15. For a description of Mark Twain's plans for a "standard work," including the multipage map of the river, see Horst Kruse, *Mark Twain and "Life on the Mississippi"* (Amherst: University of Massachusetts Press, 1981), 15–19. In *Mark Twain's Notebooks,* the editors establish that the map Clemens had in mind was a massive chart produced by the War Department (see 2:455–56).

16. Quirk notes a similar discrepancy in the way that "Jackson" is spelled in the Grangerford episode—correctly when Huck says the name for the first time in response to a challenge, but "J-a-x-o-n" later on, when Huck has to spell it aloud. See Quirk, *Coming to Grips,* 100.

17. Alexis de Toqueville, *Democracy in America,* trans. Henry Reeve, 2 vols. (New York: Vintage Books, 1945), 2:59 (Book 1, Chapter XIII, "The Literary Characteristics of Democratic Times").

18. For a thorough discussion of the convoluted process by which excerpts from *Huckleberry Finn* appeared in the *Century Magazine*, see Fisher and Salamo's introduction to *Adventures of Huckleberry Finn,* 744–57. See also Stephen Railton, "Prepublishing Huck," 1996, retrieved November 22, 2005, from http://etext.lib.virginia.edu/railton/huckfinn/hfcentry.html.

19. The case for George Griffin as the "G. G." mentioned in the novel's front matter is made by Victor Fischer and Lin Salamo in their 2001 edition. See *Adventures of Huckleberry Finn,* 376.

20. In reviewing *Huckleberry Finn,* two San Francisco publications, the *Bulletin* and the *Alta California,* made note of the special vigor of the sales campaign. "No book," said the *Bulletin,* "has been put on the market with more advertising" ("Current Literature," *San Francisco Bulletin,* March 14, 1885, 1, quoted in Budd, *Mark Twain,* 269). The *Alta* called *Huckleberry Finn* "probably the best advertised book of the present age, through publication of extracts in magazines, dissensions among publishers and threatened injunctions from the author against enterprising firms, who have desired to forestall . . . the publication of the book. As a self-advertiser, Mark Twain has become more of a success than as a humorist" ("Recent Publications," *San Francisco Alta California,* March 24, 1885, 2, quoted in Budd, *Mark Twain,* 273).

21. Advertisement for agents, included in the canvasser's circular for *Adventures of Huckleberry Finn* (San Francisco: Occidental Publishing, 1884).

22. In the forty years between Huck's adventure and Mark Twain's prime, the situation had deteriorated. Twain and his publishers and business associates had to fend off a long succession of Mark Twain impersonators and forgers stealing his name and reputation to exploit audiences and book buyers in America and overseas.

23. *The Count of Monte Cristo* was first published in book form in Paris in 1845, after serialization during the previous year in *Journal des Debats.* The Boston house of H. L. Williams published an American edition "with elegant illustrations" in

1846. If this chronology in itself does not establish anything about the time of the action in *Huckleberry Finn,* it harmonizes with other evidence in the novel. Drawing conclusions about Tom's borrowings from *The Man in the Iron Mask* is more difficult. Though Dumas did not publish his famous semifactual tale in Paris until 1850, he had written an essay in 1841 speculating that the notorious prisoner was the brother of Louis XIV. Commenting about the pathologies of French justice, Voltaire had mentioned the Iron Mask almost a century before that. In the United States, an early gothic romance called *The Royal Captives: A Fragment of Secret History* (Philadelphia: Robert Campbell, 1795) made use of the Iron Mask legend. Therefore, if we want to imagine that Tom Sawyer, who is about ten years old, has been reading in Voltaire, French periodicals, or Federal-period gothics along with contemporary popular romances and histories, perhaps the time of the action can be nudged back if substantial indications to the contrary are ignored.

24. Mark Twain indicts Walter Scott's fiction as a root cause for the psychological maiming of the South, and for the Civil War, in Chapter XVI of *Life on the Mississippi* (New York: Oxford University Press, 1996): "He did measureless harm; more real and lasting harm, perhaps, than any other individual that ever wrote. Most of the world has now outlived good part *[sic]* of these harms, though by no means all of them; but in our South they flourish pretty forcefully still. Not so forcefully as half a generation ago, but still forcefully" (467). Among recent discussions of the relevance of this hostility to *Huckleberry Finn,* see Lawrence Howe, *Mark Twain and the Novel* (Cambridge: Cambridge University Press, 1998), 54–57. For an earlier commentary on this theme, see Walter Blair, *Mark Twain and Huck Finn* (Berkeley: University of California Press, 1960), 220–21. In his study of Mark Twain and the sentimental tradition, Gregg Camfield finds that the Tom Sawyer who dominates the end of *Huckleberry Finn* is a "fraternal caricature of genteel, sentimental morality." See Camfield, *Sentimental Twain* (Philadelphia: University of Pennsylvania Press, 1994), 148.

25. Olin Harris Moore's "Mark Twain and Don Quixote" cites passages. *PMLA* 37 (1922): 324–46.

26. "Children's Books of the Year," *North American Review,* January 1866, 238–39.

27. "Booth and Bad Literature," *Youth's Companion,* May 11, 1865, 74.

FIVE. MARK TWAIN AND THE INFORMATION AGE

Epigraphs: Stedman's remarks come from a speech to the American Copyright League on March 17, 1888, in Laura Stedman and George M. Gould, *Life and Letters of Edmund Clarence Stedman,* 2 vols. (New York: Moffat, Yard, 1910), 2:411. McLuhan's quotation comes from Marshall McLuhan, *The Gutenberg Galaxy* (Toronto: University of Toronto Press, 1962), 22.

1. The darkest portrait to date is Hamlin Hill's *Mark Twain: God's Fool* (New

York: Harper and Row, 1973). Hill portrays Clemens as caught up in grief, loneliness, illness, misanthropy, artistic failure, and a contest among others for control of him and his fortunes. In *Dangerous Intimacy: The Untold Story of Mark Twain's Final Years* (Berkeley: University of California Press, 2004), Karen Lystra centers on Jean Clemens's diaries and finds that the father was "a more fortunate, less tragic Lear, who betrayed his own daughter but got her back—almost miraculously" (272) and that much of his late writing is a brave and lucid engagement with problems of personal identity, "a head-on collision with reality that was his greatness as a writer" (232). In *Mark Twain* (New York: St. Martin's Press, 1997), Peter Messent finds that the Clemens after 1890 was "not quite sure of his direction, . . . but fetching up, despite, as one of the most productive, important, and interesting writers of his time" (176). Andrew J. Hoffman (*Inventing Mark Twain,* 432–505) tells the story as an ironic contrast between a deteriorating personal life and soaring international fame. Justin Kaplan's narrative of Clemens's last years, as a psychological tragedy of alienation as well as family misfortune and old age, is well known (*Mr. Clemens and Mark Twain,* 312–88).

2. The notebooks indicate that Clemens's interest in developing a game of "Ages & deaths of great men—dates of great events" dates back at least to December 18, 1878. *Mark Twain's Notebooks and Journals,* vol. 2, *1877–1883,* ed. Frederick Anderson, Lin Salamo, and Bernard L. Stein (Berkeley: University of California Press, 1975), 252. The name for the game, and its configuration, went through many changes over the next fifteen years. Justin Kaplan, in *Mr. Clemens and Mark Twain* (253), indicates that WebsterCo brought out "Mark Twain's Memory Builder" as a board game in 1891; according to an explanatory note in *Mark Twain's Notebooks,* a version of the board game was patented in 1885 but never marketed (2:252).

3. For an account of the grand scale on which *Personal Memoirs of U. S. Grant* was produced and sold, see Tebbel, *History of Book Publishing,* 2:524–26.

4. William C. Beecher, Samuel Scoville, and Mrs. Henry Ward Beecher, *A Life of Rev. Henry Ward Beecher* (New York: Charles L. Webster, 1888), 673–75.

5. Canvasser's circular for O'Reilly, *Life of Pope Leo XIII,* MTP.

6. The Webster Company's list for 1892, for example, included Whitman's *Selected Poems* and his *Autobiographia,* a collection of stories by Tolstoy, a commentary on Herbert Spencer by Henry George, and a volume of the writings of Columbus to mark the four hundredth anniversary of the Discovery.

7. See, for example, the twenty-five-volume "Aldine Edition" of *The World's Greatest Books,* selected by William Rainey Harper, Edward Everett Hale, and others (New York: Appleton, 1898–99).

8. A notebook entry from August 1885 to March 1886: "Go to Stedman for a sub. to type setter." *Mark Twain's Notebooks,* 3:193.

9. Bayard Taylor, *The Unpublished Letters of Bayard Taylor,* ed. John Richie Schultz (San Marino, CA: Huntington Library, 1937), includes eighteen garrulous letters to Stedman from 1860 to 1875.

10. Henry Nash Smith and William Gibson, eds., *Mark Twain–Howells Letters* (Cambridge, MA: Harvard Belknap, 1960), 824.

11. "Miss Hutchinson's *Songs and Lyrics*," *Century: A Popular Quarterly* 23, no. 4 (1882): 626.

12. Stedman and Gould, *Life and Letters*, 2:140.

13. Fred L. Israel, ed., *1897 Sears Roebuck Catalogue* (reprint, New York: Chelsea House, 1968), 653, 698.

14. Twain, *Mark Twain's Notebooks*, 3:612–13, n. 141.

15. The evidence is contradictory. In a manuscript dated June 2, 1906, Clemens remembered the *LAL* project as a maneuver by Webster:

> Stedman, the poet, had made a compilation, several years earlier, called *The Library of American Literature*—nine or ten octavo volumes. A publisher in Cincinnati had tried to make it succeed. It swallowed up that publisher, family and all. If Stedman had offered me the book I should have said "Sold by subscription and on the installment plan, there is nothing in this book for us at a royalty above four per cent, but in fact it would swamp us at any kind of royalty, because such a book would require a cash capital of several hundred thousand dollars, and we haven't a hundred thousand."
>
> But Stedman didn't bring the book to me. He took it to Webster. Webster was delighted and flattered. He accepted the book on an eight per cent royalty, and thereby secured the lingering suicide of Charles L. Webster and Company.
>
> Twain, Mark Twain in Eruption, 191–92

However, Twain's reminiscences in his final years are notorious for tilting the facts to exonerate himself and assign blame to others. When he wrote to Webster directly about all this on March 1, 1887, he said, "I think well of the Stedman book, but I can't somehow bring myself to think *very* well of it. My notions are too long to write; but you look in here, on your rounds, & we will swap ideas." SLC to Charles Webster, Vassar College Library, quoted in Webster, *Mark Twain, Business Man*, 377.

16. Twain, *Mark Twain's Notebooks*, 3:612.

17. Stedman and Gould, *Life and Letters*, 2:121.

18. See Hoffman, *Inventing Mark Twain*, 92. For Clemens's January 1864 letter to his mother about Ludlow, see Twain, *Mark Twain's Letters* (Branch ed.), 1:268.

19. SLC to Fred J. Hall, January 1, 1893, in Twain, *Mark Twain's Letters to His Publishers*, 331–32.

20. See "New Books," *Charleston Sunday News*, January 5, 1890, 5, and "*A Yankee in King Arthur's Court*," Quincy [California] *Plumas*, July 2, 1890, 2, both reviews reprinted in Budd, *Mark Twain: The Contemporary Reviews*, 298–99, 318–19.

21. Mark Twain, *A Connecticut Yankee in King Arthur's Court*, ed. Shelley Fisher Fishkin (New York: Oxford University Press, 1996), 67–68.

22. H. Rider Haggard, *King Solomon's Mines*, in *Five Adventure Novels of H. Rider Haggard* (New York: Dover Books, 1951), 335.

23. The year 1889 was especially busy for lost-land adventure fiction, culminating a decade of lively business in this game and spurring Clemens and Fred Hall

to get *A Connecticut Yankee* out to the public while the trend was still hot. Examples include Julian Corbett's *Kophetua the Thirteenth* (London: Macmillan, 1889), about a lost civilization of Christian knights in some other unexplored African neighborhood; C. J. Cutliffe Hyne's *Beneath Your Very Boots* (London: Digby Long, 1889), about a lost race of ancient Celts thriving in a maze of deep caverns; Charles Lotin Hildreth's *The Mysterious City of OO* (Chicago: Conkey, 1889), about a civilization of ancient Greeks in the Australian outback; and Artegall Smith's *Sub Sole, or Under the Sun* (London: James Nisbet, 1889), about a great civilization hidden under the African desert.

24. In Twain, *Collected Tales,* 551–53.

25. Mark Twain, *Mark Twain Speaking,* ed. Paul Fatout (Iowa City: University of Iowa Press, 1976), 473–74.

26. SLC to Fred J. Hall, July 26, 1893, in Twain, *Mark Twain's Letters to His Publishers,* 352–53.

27. For a recent commentary on the moral and political challenge of reading *Pudd'nhead Wilson* as an illustrated text, see Werner Sollors, "Was Roxy Black? Race and Stereotype in Mark Twain, Edward Windsor Kemble, and Paul Laurence Dunbar," in *Mixed Race Literature,* ed. Jonathan Brennan (Stanford: Stanford University Press, 2002), 70–87.

28. Into the opening years of the twentieth century, Chatto and Windus continued to publish Mark Twain editions featuring most of the illustrations that had previously appeared in their imprints.

29. Tebbel, *History of Book Publishing,* 2:25–28.

30. For a concise history of typographers' unions and labor-management relations in the trade of typesetting, see Seymour Martin Lipset, Martin A. Trow, and James S. Coleman, *Union Democracy: The Internal Politics of the International Typographical Union* (New York: Free Press, 1956), 17–21. Lipset et al. note that the first "great strike" of printers against management took place in Lyons in 1539 and that restrictive rules demonstrating the power of guilds and unions were on the books in London by 1587. In other words, the job action that shuts down Herr Stein's shop in "No. 44, The Mysterious Stranger" has some basis in historical fact (26, n. 10).

31. As late as 1894, Pasko was reporting that the most advanced Linotype on the market was not yet suitable for book work: "It has scarcely been tried by the book men on account of these various defects, which appear magnified when an impression is taken on hard paper; but it has been much used in newspaper composition" (*American Dictionary of Printing,* 376).

32. For a thorough account of Mark Twain's central role in a long struggle (1870–91) for enforceable international copyright agreements, and the baroque maneuvers that he and his publishers engaged in to protect their works, see Vaidhyanathan, *Copyrights and Copywrongs,* 55–80.

33. Everett Emerson offers concise histories of the complex evolution of these two narratives. See *The Authentic Mark Twain* (Philadelphia: University of Pennsylvania Press, 1984), 189–90, and *Mark Twain,* 278–82. See also William R. Mac-

naughton, *Mark Twain's Last Years as a Writer* (Columbia: University of Missouri Press, 1979), 218.

34. Clemens refers to the project as a "booklet" in a letter to Rogers on July 13, 1905. *Mark Twain's Correspondence with Henry Huddleston Rogers, 1893–1909*, ed. Lewis Leary (Berkeley: University of California Press, 1969), 591.

35. An overview of these experimental artists and movements can be found in Phillip Dennis Cate and Mary Shaw, eds., *The Spirit of Montmartre: Cabarets, Humor, and the Avant-Garde* (New Brunswick: Rutgers University Press, 1996).

36. SLC to Frederick Duneka, March 20, 1906, Berg Collection, New York Public Library.

37. Hunt Hawkins observes that Mark Twain's mistake may derive from his reading of Morel's book and the Memorial, both of which emphasized that the United States had not ratified the 1884 "Berlin Act," an international treaty to regulate imperialist practices in Africa. See Hawkins, "Mark Twain's Involvement with the Congo Reform Movement: 'A Fury of Generous Indignation,'" *New England Quarterly* 51, no. 2 (1978): 147–75.

38. Leopold's American public-relations campaign is summarized in F. Seymour Cocks, *E. D. Morel: The Man and His Work* (London: Allen and Unwin, 1920), 106–7. The fall of 1904 was an especially intense season for controversy over the Congo Free State, and many famous Americans were drawn in on either side. When the matter of African atrocities was looming as an issue at a September "Peace Congress" organized by the Massachusetts Commission on International Justice, Cardinal Gibbons had written to the group to oppose its inclusion on the agenda. See Catherine Ann Cline, *E. D. Morel, 1873–1924: The Strategies of Protest* (Belfast: Blackstaff Press, 1980), 45. See also Adam Hochschild, *King Leopold's Ghost* (Boston: Houghton Mifflin, 1991), 242–49.

39. Funk and Wagnalls, New York, published an American edition of Morel's book in 1905.

40. Edmund Dene Morel to SLC, October 10, 1904, MTP.

41. Edmund Dene Morel to SLC, October 17, 1904, MTP.

42. Cocks, *E. D. Morel,* 107.

43. SLC to Edmund Dene Morel, October 15 and 16, 1904, British Library of Political and Economical Science.

44. Morel to Dr. [Robert E.] Park, November 26, 1904, British Library of Public and Economical Science.

45. Isabel Lyon, "Notes on the Duneka Letters," April 2, 1938, Berg Collection, New York Public Library.

46. Luke Sharp [Robert Barr], "A Conglomerate Interview with Mark Twain," *Idler Magazine* 1, no. 1 (1892): 80–81.

47. Mark Twain, *King Leopold's Soliloquy,* in *Following the Equator and Anti-imperialist Essays,* ed. Shelley Fisher Fishkin (New York: Oxford University Press, 1996), 37–38.

48. Edmund Dene Morel, *King Leopold's Rule in Africa* (New York: Funk and Wagnalls, 1905), facing 144.

49. Marshall McLuhan, *Understanding Media: The Extensions of Man* (New York: McGraw-Hill, 1964), 193.

50. Beverly R. David and Ray Sapirstein, "Reading the Illustrations in *Following the Equator* and *King Leopold's Soliloquy*," in Twain, *Following the Equator*, 27.

51. No evidence has turned up to establish who selected these photographs as the culminating experience in *King Leopold's Soliloquy* or arranged them in this collage, or whether Mark Twain had significant involvement in this phase of the book's design and production.

52. Mark Twain, *Eve's Diary*, in *The Diaries of Adam and Eve*, ed. Shelley Fisher Fishkin (New York: Oxford University Press, 1996), 103.

53. Mark Twain, *The Mysterious Stranger*, edited by William M. Gibson (Berkeley: University of California Press, 1969). All page citations of "No. 44, The Mysterious Stranger" refer to this edition. See also John S. Tuckey, *Mark Twain and the Little Satan: The Writing of "The Mysterious Stranger"* (West Lafayette: Purdue University Press, 1963; reprint, Westport, CT: Greenwood Press, 1973).

54. As one of the first critics to give careful attention to the final version of the Mysterious Stranger story, Sholom Kahn made a vigorous case for the thematic appropriateness of the ending and the philosophical earnestness of the entire text. See *Mark Twain's Mysterious Stranger: A Study of the Manuscript Texts* (Columbia: University of Missouri Press, 1978), 172–97. In contrast, James M. Cox regarded the Paine-Duneka version, which included a forged transitional passage connecting this same ending to most of the earlier "Young Satan" narrative, as the best representation of Mark Twain's intentions. See James M. Cox, *Mark Twain: The Fate of Humor* (Princeton: Princeton University Press, 1966), 270–72.

55. For the writing sequence and its implications, see Tuckey, *Mark Twain*, 76–78, and Gibson's introduction to Twain, *Mysterious Stranger*, 4–11.

56. For provocative speculations on the impact of print upon Western configurations of memory and consciousness, see Walter J. Ong's chapter "Print, Space, and Culture" in his *Orality and Literacy: The Technologizing of the Word* (New York: Routledge, 1988), 117–38.

57. Twain, *Mysterious Stranger*, 229–30.

AFTERWORD

1. Saul Bellow, "The Distracted Public," in *It All Adds Up: From the Dim Past to the Uncertain Future* (New York: Viking Press, 1994), 160–61.

2. Mark Twain, "Three Thousand Years among the Microbes," in *Mark Twain's Which Was the Dream? and Other Symbolic Writings of the Later Years*, ed. John H. Tuckey (Berkeley: University of California Press, 1967), 490.

3. For another overview by Roger Chartier of the unprecedented cultural challenge of the electronic text, see "Representations on the Written Word," in *Forms and Meanings: Texts, Performances and Audiences from Codex to Computer* (Philadelphia: University of Pennsylvania Press, 1995), 6–24.

4. Chartier, "Languages, Books, and Reading from the Printed Word to the Digital Text," *Critical Inquiry* 31, no. 1 (2004): 142–43.

5. Friedrich Kittler, *Discourse Networks, 1800/1900*, trans. Michael Metteer with Chris Cullens (Stanford: Stanford University Press, 1990), 304–5.

6. Jean Baudrillard, *Impossible Exchange*, trans. Chris Turner (New York: Verso, 2001), 14–15.

7. In *Authors Inc.: Literary Celebrity in the Modern United States, 1880–1980* (New York: New York University Press, 2004), Loren Glass discusses Mark Twain as "[p]art protomodernist genius, part populist icon" (59), and as the prototype of the commodified modern author: "Twain's attempts to trademark his pen name . . . [signal] a new model of U.S. authorship—one that legitimates literary property less as a mark of intellectual labor than as an index of cultural recognition" (59).

8. Peter C. Whybrow, *American Mania: When More Is Not Enough* (New York: W. W. Norton, 2005); John D. Gartner, *The Hypomanic Edge: The Link between (a Little) Craziness and (a Lot of) Success in America* (New York: Simon and Schuster, 2005).

9. From Carlyle, "Biography" (1832): "Ship-loads of Fashionable Novels, Sentimental Rhymes, Tragedies, Farces, Diaries of Travel, Tales by flood and field, are swallowed monthly into the bottomless Pool: still does the Press toil; innumerable Paper-makers, Compositors, Printer's Devils, Book-binders, and Hawkers . . . and still, in torrents, rushes on the great array of Publications, unpausing, to their final home; and still Oblivion, like the Grave, cries Give! Give!" *The Works of Thomas Carlyle* (London: Chapman and Hall, 1899), 28:58.

10. In *Reading, Writing, and Romanticism: The Anxiety of Reception* (Oxford: Oxford University Press, 2000), 33–48, Lucy Newlin describes the anxiety shared by many English writers and critics as publishing in England industrialized and output soared. See also Jonathan Rose, "Education, Literacy, and the Victorian Reader," in *A Companion to the Victorian Novel*, ed. William Thesing and Patrick Brantlinger (Oxford: Basil Blackwell, 2005), 31–47. See also Patrick Brantlinger, *The Reading Lesson: The Threat of Mass Literacy in Nineteenth Century British Fiction* (Bloomington: Indiana University Press, 1998).

11. Jacques Derrida, *Writing and Difference*, trans. Alan Bass (Chicago: University of Chicago Press, 1978), 98.

12. Roland Barthes, *Camera Lucida: Reflections on Photography*, trans. Richard Howard (New York: Farrar, Straus and Giroux, 1982), 80–81.

13. Jean Baudrillard, *Screened Out*, trans. Chris Turner (New York: Verso, 2002), 152–53.

BIBLIOGRAPHY

Abbot, Jacob. *The Harper Establishment; or, How the Story Books Are Made.* New York: Harper and Brothers, 1855.

Adams, Thomas F. *Typographia, or The Printer's Instructor: A Brief Sketch of the Origin, Rise, and Progress of the Typographic Art, with Practical Directions for Conducting Every Department in an Office.* Philadelphia: H. Johnson, 1857.

Ade, George. "Mark Twain and the Old Time Subscription Book." *Review of Reviews* 41 (1910): 703–4.

Annenberg, Maurice. *A Typographical Journey through the Inland Printer, 1883–1900.* Baltimore: Maran Press, 1977.

Ashworth, J. *Operation and Mechanism of the Linotype and Intertype.* 2 vols. London: Staples Press, 1955.

Asselineau, Charles. *André Charles Boulle, Ebeniste de Louis XIV.* 3rd ed. Paris: P. Rouquette, 1872.

Baedeker, Karl. *Switzerland, and the Adjacent Portions of Italy, Savoy, and the Tyrol.* 7th rev. ed. Leipzig: Karl Baedeker, 1877.

Barclay, J. T. *The City of the Great King of Jerusalem As It Was, As It Is, and As It Is to Be.* Philadelphia: James Challen and Sons, 1857.

Barthes, Roland. *Camera Lucida: Reflections on Photography.* Translated by Richard Howard. New York: Farrar, Straus and Giroux, 1982.

Baudrillard, Jean. *Impossible Exchange.* Translated by Chris Turner. New York: Verso, 2001.

———. *Screened Out.* Translated by Chris Turner. New York: Verso, 2002.

Baym, Nina. *American Women Writers and the Work of History, 1790–1860.* New Brunswick: Rutgers University Press, 1995.

Beecher, William C., Samuel Scoville, and Mrs. Henry Ward Beecher. *A Life of Rev. Henry Ward Beecher.* New York: Charles L. Webster, 1888.

Bellow, Saul. *It All Adds Up: From the Dim Past to the Uncertain Future.* New York: Viking Press, 1994.

Benjamin, Walter. *Illuminations: Essays and Reflections.* Edited by Hannah Arendt. Translated by Harry Zohn. New York: Schocken Books, 1968.

Bennett, Bob. *Horatio Alger, Jr.: A Comprehensive Bibliography.* Mt. Pleasant, MI: Flying Eagle Publishing, 1980.

Bernard, Paul. *Rush to the Alps: The Evolution of Vacationing in Switzerland.* New York: Columbia University Press, 1978.

Bishop, Glenn A., ed. *Chicago's Accomplishments and Leaders.* Chicago: Bishop, 1932.

Blair, Walter. *Mark Twain and Huck Finn.* Berkeley: University of California Press, 1960.

"Booth and Bad Literature." *Youth's Companion,* May 11, 1865, 74.

Boynton, Henry W. *Annals of American Bookselling, 1638–1850.* New York: John Wiley, 1932.

Branch, Edgar M. "A New Clemens Footprint: Soleleather Steps Forward." *American Literature* 54 (1982): 497–510.

Brantlinger, Patrick. *The Reading Lesson: The Threat of Mass Literacy in Nineteenth Century British Fiction.* Bloomington: Indiana University Press, 1998.

Briden, Earl. "Kemble's 'Specialty' and the Pictorial Countertext of *Huckleberry Finn.*" *Mark Twain Journal* 26 (Fall 1988): 2–14.

Brown, Joshua. *Beyond the Lines: Pictorial Reporting, Everyday Life, and the Crisis of Gilded Age America.* Berkeley: University of California Press, 1992.

Budd, Louis J. *Mark Twain: The Contemporary Reviews.* Cambridge: Cambridge University Press, 1999.

———. "Mark Twain's 'An Encounter with an Interviewer': The Height (or Depth) of Nonsense." *Nineteenth-Century Literature* 55, no. 2 (2000): 226–43.

Burlingame, Roger. *Engines of Democracy: Inventions and Society in Mature America.* New York: Scribner's, 1940.

Buzard, James. *The Beaten Track: European Tourism, Literature, and the Ways to "Culture," 1800–1918.* New York: Oxford University Press, 1993.

Byars, William Vincent. *A Century of Journalism in Missouri.* Columbia: State Historical Society of Missouri, 1920.

Camfield, Gregg. *Sentimental Twain.* Philadelphia: University of Pennsylvania Press, 1994.

Carlyle, Thomas. *The Works of Thomas Carlyle.* 30 vols. London: Chapman and Hall, 1899.

Cate, Phillip Dennis, and Mary Shaw, eds. *The Spirit of Montmartre: Cabarets, Humor, and the Avant-Garde.* New Brunswick, NJ: Rutgers University Press, 1996.

Chartier, Roger. *Forms and Meanings: Texts, Performances and Audiences from Codex to Computer.* Philadelphia: University of Pennsylvania Press, 1995.

———. "Languages, Books, and Reading from the Printed Word to the Digital Text." *Critical Inquiry* 31, no. 1 (2004): 133–52.

Charvat, William. *Literary Publishing in America, 1790–1850.* Amherst: University of Massachusetts Press, 1993.

"Children's Books of the Year." *North American Review,* January 1866, 236–49.

Clair, Colin. *A Chronology of Printing.* London: Cassell, 1969.

Clarke, Thomas, et al. *The American Railway: Its Construction, Development, Management, and Appliances.* New York: Scribner's, 1897.

Cline, Catherine Ann. *E. D. Morel, 1873–1924: The Strategies of Protest.* Belfast: Blackstaff Press, 1980.

Cocks, F. Seymour. *E. D. Morel: The Man and His Work.* London: Allen and Unwin, 1920.

Cook, Anne. "Finding His Mark: Twain's *The Innocents Abroad* as a Subscription Book." In *Reading Books: Essays on the Material Text and Literature in America,* edited by Michele Moylan and Lane Stiles. Amherst: University of Massachusetts Press, 1996.

Corbett, Julian. *Kophetua the Thirteenth.* London: Macmillan, 1889.

Cox, James M. "*A Connecticut Yankee in King Arthur's Court:* The Machinery of Self-Preservation." *Yale Review* 50 (1960): 89–102.

———. *Mark Twain: The Fate of Humor.* Princeton: Princeton University Press, 1966.

Culler, Jonathan. *Framing the Sign: Criticism and Its Institutions.* Oxford: Blackwell, 1988.

Dändliker, Karl. *A Short History of Switzerland.* Translated by E. Salisbury. New York: Macmillan, 1899.

Darnton, Robert. "What Is the History of Books?" In *Books and Society in History,* edited by Kenneth Carpenter. New York: R. R. Bowker, 1983.

David, Beverly R. *Mark Twain and His Illustrators.* Vol. 1. *1869–1875.* Troy, NY: Whitston, 1986.

———. *Mark Twain and His Illustrators.* Vol. 2. *1875–1883.* Troy, NY: Whitston, 2001.

David, Beverly R., and Ray Sapirstein. "Reading the Illustrations in *Following the Equator* and *King Leopold's Soliloquy.*" In *Following the Equator and Anti-imperialist Essays,* by Mark Twain, edited by Shelley Fisher Fishkin. New York: Oxford University Press, 1996.

———. "Reading the Illustrations in Huckleberry Finn." In *Adventures of Huckleberry Finn,* edited by Shelley Fisher Fishkin. New York: Oxford University Press, 1996.

Davis, Charles T. *The Manufacture of Paper.* Philadelphia: n.p., 1886.

Dawson, Hugh J. "The Ethnicity of Huck Finn—and the Difference It Makes." *American Literary Realism* 30, no. 2 (1998): 1–14.

De Beer, G. R., ed. *Alps and Men: Pages from Forgotten Diaries of Travellers and Tourists in Switzerland.* London: Edward Arnold, 1932.

De Vinne, Theodore Low. *The Practice of Typography.* New York: Century, 1902.

Debord, Guy. *The Society of the Spectacle.* New York: Black and Red, 1970. Originally published as *La société du spectacle* (Paris: Buchet-Chastel, 1967).

Dempsey, Terrell. *Searching for Jim: Slavery in Sam Clemens's World.* Columbia: University of Missouri Press, 2003.

Derrida, Jacques. *Writing and Difference.* Translated by Alan Bass. Chicago: University of Chicago Press, 1978.

Elliot, Emery, et al. *The Columbia History of the American Novel.* New York: Columbia University Press, 1991.

Emerson, Everett. *The Authentic Mark Twain.* Philadelphia: University of Pennsylvania Press, 1984.

———. *Mark Twain: A Literary Life.* Philadelphia: University of Pennsylvania Press, 1999.

Fanning, Philip Ashley. *Mark Twain and Orion Clemens.* Tuscaloosa: University of Alabama Press, 2003.

Fatout, Paul. *Mark Twain in Virginia City.* Bloomington: Indiana University Press, 1964.

Fish, Henry C. *Bible Lands Illustrated.* New York: A. S. Barnes, 1876.

Fishkin, Shelley Fisher. *Lighting out for the Territory.* New York: Oxford University Press, 1997.

Freeman, Larry [Graydon LaVerne]. *Louis Prang: Color Lithographer.* Watkins Glen, NY: Century House, 1971.

Furer, Howard B., ed. *Chicago: A Chronological and Documentary History, 1784–1970.* Dobbs Ferry, NY: Oceana Publications, 1974.

Gambee, Budd L. "American Book and Magazine Illustration of the Later Nineteenth Century." In *Book Illustration: Papers Presented at the Third Rare Book Conference of the American Library Association in 1962.* Berlin: Gebr. Mann, 1963.

Gartner, John D. *The Hypomanic Edge: The Link between (a Little) Craziness and (a Lot of) Success in America.* New York: Simon and Schuster, 2005.

Geikie, Cunningham. *The Holy Land and the Bible: A Book of Scripture Illustrations Gathered in Palestine.* New York: James Pott, 1888.

Gernsheim, Helmut, and Alison Gernsheim. *The History of Photography: From the Camera Obscura to the Beginning of the Modern Era.* New York: McGraw-Hill, 1969.

Gilreath, James. "American Book Distribution." *Proceedings of the American Antiquarian Society* 95 (1985): 501–83.

Glass, Loren. *Authors Inc.: Literary Celebrity in the Modern United States, 1880–1980.* New York: New York University Press, 2004.

Gold, Charles H. *Hatching Ruin: Mark Twain's Road to Bankruptcy.* Columbia: University of Missouri Press, 2003.

Gorman, Margaret. "A Book Canvasser's Woes." *New York World,* April 21, 1889, 27.

Grant, Julius. *Wood Pulp and Allied Products.* London: Leonard Hill, 1947.

Grant, Thomas. "The Artist of the Beautiful: Mark Twain's Investment in the Machine Inventor." *Publications of the Missouri Philosophical Association* 4 (1979): 59–68.

Greenspan, Ezra. *George Palmer Putnam: Representative American Publisher.* University Park: Pennsylvania State University Press, 2000.

Groves, Jeffrey D. "Judging Literary Books by Their Covers: House Styles, Ticknor and Fields, and Literary Promotion." In *Reading Books: Essays on the Material Text and Literature in America,* edited by Michele Moylan and Lane Stiles, 75–99. Amherst: University of Massachusetts Press, 1996.

Hackenberg, Michael. "The Subscription Publishing Network in Nineteenth-Century America." In *Getting the Books Out: Papers of the Chicago Conference on the Book in Nineteenth-Century America,* edited by Michael Hackenberg, 45–75. Washington, DC: Library of Congress, 1987.

Haggard, H. Rider. *Five Adventure Novels of H. Rider Haggard.* New York: Dover, 1951.

Hart, James Allee. "An Historical Study of the *St. Louis Globe-Democrat,* 1852–1958." PhD diss., University of Missouri, 1959.

Hart, James D. *The Popular Book: A History of America's Literary Taste.* New York: Oxford University Press, 1950.

Hawkins, Hunt. "Mark Twain's Involvement with the Congo Reform Movement: 'A Fury of Generous Indignation.'" *New England Quarterly* 51, no. 2 (1978): 147–75.

Hildreth, Charles Lotin. *The Mysterious City of OO.* Chicago: Conkey, 1889.

Hill, Hamlin. *Mark Twain and Elisha Bliss.* Columbia: University of Missouri Press, 1964.

———. *Mark Twain: God's Fool.* New York: Harper and Row, 1973.

Hirst, Robert Hart. "The Making of *The Innocents Abroad:* 1867–1872." PhD diss., University of California, Berkeley, 1975.

Hirst, Robert, and Brandt Rowles. "William E. James's Stereoscopic Views of the *Quaker City* Excursion." *Mark Twain Journal* 22 (Spring 1984): 15–33.

Hochschild, Adam. *King Leopold's Ghost.* Boston: Houghton Mifflin, 1991.

Hoffman, Andrew J. *Inventing Mark Twain: The Lives of Samuel Langhorne Clemens.* New York: William Morrow, 1997.

Howe, Lawrence. *Mark Twain and the Novel.* Cambridge: Cambridge University Press, 1998.

Hunter, Dard. *Papermaking: The History and Technique of an Ancient Craft.* New York: Dover Books, 1974.

Huss, Richard E. *The Development of Printers' Mechanical Typesetting Methods, 1822–1925.* Charlottesville: University Press of Virginia, 1973.

Hyde, Ralph. *Panoramania! The Art and Entertainment of the "All-Embracing" View.* London: Trefoil/Barbican Art Gallery, 1988.

Hyde, William, and Howard L. Conard. *Encyclopedia of the History of Saint Louis.* New York: Southern History Co., 1899.

Hyne, C. J. Cutliffe. *Beneath Your Very Boots.* London: Digby Long, 1889.

Israel, Fred L., ed. *1897 Sears Roebuck Catalogue.* Reprint, New York: Chelsea House, 1968.

Jackson, Mason. *The Pictorial Press: Its Origins and Progress.* London: Hurst and Blackett, 1885. Reprint, Detroit: Gale Research, 1968.

Johannsen, Albert. *The House of Beadle and Adams and Its Dime and Nickel Novels: The Story of a Vanished Literature.* 3 vols. Norman: University of Oklahoma Press, 1962.

Kahan, Basil. *Ottmar Mergenthaler: The Man and His Machine.* New Castle, DE: Oak Knoll Press, 2000.

Kahn, Sholom J. *Mark Twain's Mysterious Stranger: A Study of the Manuscript Texts.* Columbia: University of Missouri Press, 1978.

Kaplan, Fred. *The Singular Mark Twain.* New York: Doubleday, 2003.

Kaplan, Justin. *Mr. Clemens and Mark Twain.* New York: Simon and Schuster, 1966.

Karolevitz, Robert. *Newspapering in the Old West.* New York: Barrage Books, 1965.

Kemble, E. W. "Illustrating *Huckleberry Finn.*" *Colophon: A Book Collector's Quarterly* 1, no. 1 (1930): n.p.

Kielbowicz, Richard. *News in the Mail: The Press, Post Office, and Public Information, 1700–1860s.* New York: Greenwood Press, 1989.

Kittler, Friedrich. *Discourse Networks, 1800/1900.* Translated by Michael Metteer with Chris Cullens. Stanford: Stanford University Press, 1990.

Knight, Charles. *The Old Printer and the Modern Press.* London: John Murray, 1854.

Knoper, Randall. *Acting Naturally: Mark Twain in the Culture of Performance.* Berkeley: University of California Press, 1995.

Korte, Barbara. "Julian Barnes, *England, England:* Tourism as a Critique of Postmodernism." In *The Making of Modern Tourism: The Cultural History of the British Experience, 1600–2000,* edited by Hartmut Berghoff, Barbara Korte, Ralf Schneider, and Christopher Harvie, 285–304. New York: Palgrave, 2002.

Kruse, Horst. *Mark Twain and "Life on the Mississippi."* Amherst: University of Massachusetts Press, 1981.

Kubler, George. *A New History of Stereotyping.* New York: Little and Ives, 1941.

Lee, Judith Yaross. "Anatomy of a Fascinating Failure." *American Heritage of Invention and Technology* 3 (Summer 1987): 55–60.

Legros, Lucien A., and John C. Grant. *Typographical Printing Surfaces.* London: Longmans, Green, 1916.

Lipset, Seymour Martin, Martin A. Trow, and James S. Coleman. *Union Democracy: The Internal Politics of the International Typographical Union.* New York: Free Press, 1956.

Lystra, Karen. *Dangerous Intimacy: The Untold Story of Mark Twain's Final Years.* Berkeley: University of California Press, 2004.

Macnaughton, William R. *Mark Twain's Last Years as a Writer.* Columbia: University of Missouri Press, 1979.

Madison, James A. *Book Publishing in America.* New York: McGraw-Hill, 1966.

Marzio, Peter C. *The Democratic Art: Chromolithography 1840–90, Pictures for a Nineteenth Century America.* Boston: David Godine, 1979.

Mayer, Henry. *All on Fire: William Lloyd Garrison and the Abolition of Slavery.* New York: St. Martin's Press, 1998.

McGarvey, J. W. *Lands of the Bible, a Geographical and Topographical Description of Palestine with Letters of Travel in Egypt, Syria, Asia Minor, and Greece.* New York: Lippincott, 1881.

McGaw, Judith. *Wonderful Machine: Mechanization and Social Change in Berkshire Paper Making, 1801–1865.* Princeton: Princeton University Press, 1987.

McLuhan, Marshall. *The Gutenberg Galaxy.* Toronto: University of Toronto Press, 1962.

———. *Understanding Media: The Extensions of Man.* New York: McGraw-Hill, 1964.

Melton, Jeffrey Alan. *Mark Twain, Travel Books, and Tourism: The Tide of a Great Popular Movement.* Tuscaloosa: University of Alabama Press, 2002.

Messent, Peter. *Mark Twain.* New York: St. Martin's Press, 1997.

Michelson, Bruce. *Mark Twain on the Loose.* Amherst: University of Massachusetts Press, 1995.

"Miss Hutchinson's *Songs and Lyrics.*" *Century: A Popular Quarterly* 23, no. 4 (1882): 626.

Mitchell, W. J. T. *Iconology: Image, Text, Ideology.* Chicago: University of Chicago Press, 1986.

Montague, William M. *The St. Louis Business Directory for 1853–4.* St. Louis: E. A. Louis, 1853.

Moore, Olin Harris. "Mark Twain and Don Quixote." *PMLA* 37 (1922): 324–46.

Moran, James. *Printing Presses: History and Development from the Fifteenth Century to Modern Times.* Berkeley: University of California Press, 1973.

Morel, Edmund Dene. *King Leopold's Rule in Africa.* New York: Funk and Wagnalls, 1905.

Moylan, Michele, and Lane Stiles, eds. *Reading Books: Essays on the Material Text and Literature in America.* Amherst: University of Massachusetts Press, 1996.

Mulvey, Christopher. *Anglo-American Landscapes: A Study of Nineteenth-Century Anglo-American Travel Literature.* New York: Cambridge University Press, 1983.

Nevins, Alan. *The Emergence of Modern America, 1865–1878.* Vol. 8 of *A History of American Life,* edited by Mark C. Carnes and Arthur M. Schlesinger Jr. New York: Macmillan, 1955.

The New York City Directory, 1851–1852. New York: Doggett and Rode, 1852.

Newlin, Lucy. *Reading, Writing, and Romanticism: The Anxiety of Reception.* Oxford: Oxford University Press, 2000.

Official Catalogue of the New-York Exhibition of the Industry of All Nations, 1853. New York: George P. Putnam, 1853.

Okker, Patricia. *Our Sister Editors: Sarah J. Hale and the Tradition of Nineteenth Century American Women Editors.* Athens: University of Georgia Press, 1995.

Ong, Walter J. *Orality and Literacy: The Technologizing of the Word.* New York: Routledge, 1988.

O'Reilly, Bernard. *Life of Pope Leo XIII, from an Authentic Memoir.* New York: Charles Webster, 1886.

Oxford English Dictionary. Edited by James A. H. Murray et al. Compact ed. 2 vols. Oxford: Clarendon Press, 1971.

Paine, Albert Bigelow. *Mark Twain, A Biography.* 3 vols. New York: Harper and Brothers, 1912.

Partridge, C. S. *Electrotyping: A Practical Treatise on the Art of Electrotyping by the Latest Known Methods.* Chicago: Inland Printer, 1908.

Pasko, W. W. *American Dictionary of Printing and Bookmaking.* New York: Lockwood, 1894.

Pearson, Andrea C. "*Frank Leslie's Illustrated Newspaper* and *Harper's Weekly:* Innovation and Imitation in Nineteenth-Century American Pictorial Reporting." *Journal of Popular Culture* 23, no. 4 (1990): 81–111.

Phelps, S. Dryden. *Holy Land with Glimpses of Europe and Egypt.* New York: Sheldon; Boston: Gould and Lincoln, 1863.

Plant, Marjorie. *The English Book Trade.* London: Allen and Unwin, 1965.

Pratt, Mary Louise. *Imperial Eyes: Travel Writing and Transculturation.* New York: Routledge, 1992.

Quirk, Tom. *Coming to Grips with Huckleberry Finn: Essays on a Book, a Boy, and a Man.* Columbia: University of Missouri Press, 1993.

Rader, Howard Allen. "Newspaper History of Callaway Co. Missouri, 1839–60." PhD diss., University of Missouri, 1961.

Randall, D. A. *The Handwriting of God in Egypt, Sinai, and the Holy Land.* Philadelphia: John E. Potter; Chicago: J. W. Godspeed, 1862.

Rasmussen, Kent. *Mark Twain, A to Z.* New York: Oxford University Press, 1995.

Ring, Jim. *How the English Made the Alps.* London: John Murray, 2000.

Ringwalt, J. Luther, ed. *American Encyclopaedia of Printing.* Philadelphia: Menamin and Ringwalt, 1871.

Rose, Jonathan. "Education, Literacy, and the Victorian Reader." In *A Companion to the Victorian Novel,* edited by William Thesing and Patrick Brantlinger, 31–47. Oxford: Basil Blackwell, 2005.

Rugg, Linda Haverty. *Picturing Ourselves: Photography and Autobiography.* Chicago: University of Chicago Press, 1997.

Ruskin, John. *The Works of John Ruskin.* Edited by E. T. Cook and Alexander Wedderburn. 39 vols. London: George Allen, 1903–1912.

Savage, William. *Dictionary of the Art of Printing*. London: Longman, Brown, Green, and Longmans, 1841.

Schlesinger, Carl, ed. *The Biography of Ottmar Mergenthaler, Inventor of the Linotype: A New Edition, with Added Historical Notes Based on Recent Findings*. New Castle, DE: Oak Knoll Press, 1989.

Schudson, Michael. *The Power of News*. Cambridge, MA: Harvard University Press, 1995.

Seelye, John. *Mark Twain in the Movies: A Meditation with Pictures*. New York: Viking Press, 1977.

Sharp, Luke [Robert Barr]. "A Conglomerate Interview with Mark Twain." *Idler Magazine* 1, no. 1 (1892): 79–92.

Shoemaker, Floyd Calvin. *Missouri and Missourians: Land of Contrasts and People of Achievements*. 2 vols. Chicago: Lewis, 1943.

Smith, Artegall. *Sub Sole, or Under the Sun*. London: James Nisbet, 1889.

Smith, Henry Nash, and William Gibson, eds. *Mark Twain–Howells Letters*. Cambridge, MA: Harvard Belknap, 1960.

Sollors, Werner. "Was Roxy Black? Race and Stereotype in Mark Twain, Edward Windsor Kemble, and Paul Laurence Dunbar." In *Mixed Race Literature,* edited by Jonathan Brennan, 70–87. Stanford: Stanford University Press, 2002.

Stafford, Marjorie. "Subscription Book Publishing in the United States, 1865–1930." MA thesis, University of Illinois at Urbana-Champaign, 1943.

Stedman, Laura, and George M. Gould. *Life and Letters of Edmund Clarence Stedman*. 2 vols. New York: Moffat, Yard, 1910.

Steinbrink, Jeffrey. "Mark Twain's Mechanical Marvels." In *Constructing Mark Twain: New Directions in Scholarship,* edited by Laura E. Skandera Trombley and Michael Kiskis. Columbia: University of Missouri Press, 2001.

Stephen, Leslie. *The Playground of Europe*. 1871. Reprint, London: Longmans, Green, 1910.

Stevens, Walter B. *St. Louis: The Fourth City, 1764–1909*. 3 vols. St. Louis: S. J. Clarke, 1909.

Stewart, Guy Harry. "History and Bibliography of Middle Tennessee Newspapers, 1799–1876." PhD diss., University of Illinois at Urbana-Champaign, 1957.

Stoops, J. Walter. *The Art of Canvassing, or, the Experience of a Practical Canvasser*. New York: "Printed for the Author," 1857.

Sutton, Albert A. *The Design and Makeup of the Newspaper*. New York: Prentice-Hall, 1948.

Sylvester, Christopher, ed. *The Norton Book of Interviews*. New York: W. W. Norton, 1996.

Taft, Robert. *Photography and the American Scene: A Social History, 1839–1889*. New York: Macmillan, 1938.

Taylor, Bayard. *The Unpublished Letters of Bayard Taylor*. Edited by John Richie Schultz. San Marino, CA: Huntington Library, 1937.

Tebbel, John. *A History of Book Publishing in the United States.* Vol. 1. *The Creation of an Industry, 1630–1865.* New York: R. R. Bowker, 1972.

———. *A History of Book Publishing in the United States.* Vol. 2. *The Expansion of an Industry, 1865–1919.* New York: R. R. Bowker, 1975.

Thomas, Amy M. "'There Is Nothing So Effective as a Personal Canvass': Revaluing Nineteenth Century American Subscription Books." *Book History* 1, no. 1 (1998): 140–52.

Thoreau, Henry David. *Walden.* Edited by J. Lyndon Shanley. Princeton: Princeton University Press, 1971.

Timperley, C. H. *A Printer's Manual, Containing Instructions to Learners, with Scales of Impositions and Numerous Calculations, Recipes, and Scales of Prices.* London: H. Johnson, 1838.

Toqueville, Alexis de. *Democracy in America.* 2 vols. Translated by Henry Reeve. New York: Vintage Books, 1945.

Tuckey, John S. *Mark Twain and the Little Satan: The Writing of "The Mysterious Stranger."* West Lafayette: Purdue University Press, 1963. Reprint, Westport: Greenwood Press, 1973.

Twain, Mark. *Adventures of Huckleberry Finn.* 1884. Edited by Victor Fischer and Lin Salamo. Berkeley: University of California Press, 2003.

———. *The Adventures of Tom Sawyer.* 1876. Edited by John C. Gerber and Paul Baender. Berkeley: University of California Press, 1982.

———. *Collected Tales, Sketches, Speeches, and Essays, 1852–1890.* Edited by Louis J. Budd. New York: Library of America, 1992.

———. *A Connecticut Yankee in King Arthur's Court.* 1889. Edited by Bernard L. Stein. Berkeley: University of California Press, 1979.

———. *A Connecticut Yankee in King Arthur's Court.* 1889. Edited by Shelley Fisher Fishkin. New York: Oxford University Press, 1996.

———. *The Diaries of Adam and Eve.* Edited by Shelley Fisher Fishkin. New York: Oxford University Press, 1996.

———. *Early Tales and Sketches, 1851–1864.* Edited by Edgar Marquess Branch and Robert H. Hirst. Berkeley: University of California Press, 1979.

———. *Following the Equator and Anti-imperialist Essays.* Edited by Shelley Fisher Fishkin. New York: Oxford University Press, 1996.

———. *Life on the Mississippi.* 1883. Edited by Shelley Fisher Fishkin. New York: Oxford University Press, 1996.

———. *Mark Twain in Eruption: Hitherto Unpublished Pages about Men and Events.* Edited by Bernard DeVoto. New York: Harper and Brothers, 1940.

———. *Mark Twain of the Enterprise.* Edited by Henry Nash Smith. Berkeley: University of California Press, 1957.

———. *Mark Twain Speaking.* Edited by Paul Fatout. Iowa City: University of Iowa Press, 1976.

———. *Mark Twain's Autobiography.* Edited by Albert Bigelow Paine. 2 vols. New York: Harper and Brothers, 1924.

———. *Mark Twain's Correspondence with Henry Huddleston Rogers, 1893–1909*. Edited by Lewis Leary. Berkeley: University of California Press, 1969.

———. *Mark Twain's Letters*. Edited by Albert Bigelow Paine. 2 vols. New York: Harper and Brothers, 1917.

———. *Mark Twain's Letters*. Vol. 1. *1853–1866*. Edited by Edgar Marquess Branch, Michael B. Frank, and Kenneth M. Sanderson. Berkeley: University of California Press, 1988.

———. *Mark Twain's Letters*. Vol. 6. *1874–1875*. Edited by Michael B. Frank and Harriet Elinor Smith. Berkeley: University of California Press, 2002.

———. *Mark Twain's Letters to His Publishers, 1867–1894*. Edited by Hamlin Hill. Berkeley: University of California Press, 1967.

———. *Mark Twain's Notebooks and Journals*. Vol. 2. *1877–1883*. Edited by Frederick Anderson, Lin Salamo, and Bernard L. Stein. Berkeley: University of California Press, 1975.

———. *Mark Twain's Notebooks and Journals*. Vol. 3. *1883–1891*. Edited by Robert Pack Browning, Michael B. Frank, and Lin Salamo. Berkeley: University of California Press, 1979.

———. *Mark Twain's Travels with Mr. Brown*. Edited by Franklin Walker and G. Ezra Dane. New York: Russell and Russell, 1940.

———. *Mark Twain's Which Was the Dream? and Other Symbolic Writings of the Later Years*. Edited by John H. Tuckey. Berkeley: University of California Press, 1967.

———. *The Mysterious Stranger*. Edited by William M. Gibson. Berkeley: University of California Press, 1969.

———. *Roughing It*. Edited by Harriet Elinor Smith, Edgar Marquess Branch, Lin Salamo, and Robert Pack Browning. Berkeley: University of California Press, 1993.

———. *A Tramp Abroad*. 1880. Edited by Shelley Fisher Fishkin. New York: Oxford University Press, 1996.

Urry, John. *The Tourist Gaze: Leisure and Travel in Contemporary Societies*. Thousand Oaks, CA: Sage Publications, 1995.

Vaidhyanathan, Siva. *Copyrights and Copywrongs: The Rise of Intellectual Property and How It Threatens Creativity*. New York: New York University Press, 2001.

Vexler, Robert I. *St. Louis: A Chronological and Documentary History*. Dobbs Ferry, NY: Oceana Publications, 1974.

Wagenknecht, Edward. *Mark Twain, the Man and His Work*. Norman: University of Oklahoma Press, 1961.

Webster, Samuel Charles. *Mark Twain, Business Man*. Boston: Little, Brown, 1946.

Wecter, Dixon. *Sam Clemens of Hannibal*. Boston: Houghton Mifflin, 1952.

Weinstein, Cindy. *The Literature of Labor and the Labors of Literature*. Cambridge: Cambridge University Press, 1995.

Welland, Dennis. *Mark Twain in England*. Atlantic Highlands, NJ: Humanities Press, 1978.

Whybrow, Peter C. *American Mania: When More Is Not Enough.* New York: W. W. Norton, 2005.

Winship, Michael. *American Literary Publishing in the Mid-nineteenth Century: The Business of Ticknor and Fields.* New York: Cambridge University Press, 1995.

Wood, Gillen D'Arcy285. *The Shock of the Real: Romanticism and Visual Culture, 1760–1860.* New York: Palgrave/St. Martin's Press, 2001.

The World's Greatest Books. Selected by William Rainey Harper, Edward Everett Hale, and others. 30 vols. New York: Appleton, 1898–99.

Zboray, Ronald J. "Antebellum Reading and the Ironies of Technological Innovation." In *Reading in America: Literature and Social History,* edited by Cathy N. Davidson. Baltimore: Johns Hopkins University Press, 1989.

———. *A Fictive People: Antebellum Economic Development and the American Reading Public.* New York: Oxford University Press, 1993.

PERMISSIONS

PAGE 211, eight lines, beginning with "Very few persons"; PAGE 212, nine lines, beginning with "prodigious, vine-clad, stately"; PAGE 214, nine lines, beginning with "It turned me sick"; PAGE 216, nine lines, beginning with "A man *originates* nothing"; all from Mark Twain, *The Mysterious Stranger Manuscripts,* ed. William Gibson. © 1969 by The Regents of the University of California.

PAGE 104, eleven lines from a spring 1879 letter to Frank Bliss, beginning with "Now as to illustrations"; PAGE 105, seven lines from a spring 1879 letter to Frank Bliss, beginning with "Brown agrees to submit"; PAGE 106, seven lines, beginning with "If you will send me"; PAGE 106, five lines, beginning with "*In addition* I propose to give"; PAGE 171, eight lines, beginning with "Of course my friend"; all from *Mark Twain's Letters to His Publishers, 1867–1894,* ed. Hamlin Hill. © 1967 by The Regents of the University of California.

PAGE 10, twelve lines from a notebook (ca. 1887), beginning with "To begin, then"; PAGE 13, seven lines from an unpublished manuscript titled "Detailed Instructions," beginning with "We are now ready"; PAGES 13–14, seventeen lines from "Detailed Instructions," beginning with "It is safe"; PAGE 248, nine lines from an undated notebook entry, beginning with "The Thorne, the Burr, & the Macmillan"; PAGE 248, four lines from a manuscript titled "No. Needed," beginning with "There are 60,000"; PAGE 16, fifteen lines from a letter from SLC to Orion Clemens, November 27, 1880; PAGE 261, seven lines from a letter from Webster to SLC, April 17, 1884; PAGE 79, twenty-six lines from a letter from Fred J. Hall to SLC, August 5, 1889; PAGES 105–106, sixteen lines from a letter from Frank Bliss to SLC, June 27, 1879; PAGE 249, fourteen lines from a letter from Fred J. Hall to SLC, October 8, 1889; all courtesy of the Mark Twain Papers, Bancroft Library, University of California, Berkeley.

INDEX

Twain, Mark: bankruptcy, 167, 169, 171, 183, 192, 202, 246n23; celebrity, 184, 199, 234–35, 267n22, 274n7; early publishing experience, 1, 3, 5, 21, 25, 138, 150–51, 209, 213, 243n2; East Coast travels, 25–28; involvement with illustrations, 77, 87, 103–4, 105–6, 127, 165, 182, 184, 187, 195, 200, 273n51; journalistic identity, 29, 53–55, 68–69, 252n72, 257n1; and kaolatype, 16–17, 167, 248n40; mechanization and new printing technologies, 8, 15, 25–28, 188–89; as media tycoon, 165–67, 184; on modern vision, 86, 90, 96, 99, 110–11, 116, 130, 178–79; and Paige compositor, 10, 12–13, 15, 167–68, 184, 210, 246n23; publishing and literary output, 7–8, 164, 245n17; satire of newspapers, 52–55, 68–75; on sensationalism, 64–66, 160–61; views on publishing and identity, 165, 172, 209, 210–11, 216, 222–23, 274n7

Twichell, Joe ("Harris"), 78, 90, 91, 94, 96, 97, 99, 103, 113, 114, 117

typesetting, manual, 5–7, 12

typesetting machines, 247n32; Dow, 247n26; Empire, 247n26; Linotype, 11–12, 14–15, 183, 189, 190, 248n38, 271n31; McMillan, 247n26; Monoline, 14–15; Monotype, 11–12, 183; Munson, 247n26; Paige compositor, 9–12, 14–15, 81, 118, 167, 183, 189, 215, 246nn19–20,24, 247n26, 248n36; Thorne, 247n26

Typographia, or The Printer's Instructor (Johnson), 244n4

Typographical Printing Surfaces (Legros and Grant), 246n20

Ubu Roi (Jarry), 195

Uncle Tom's Cabin (Stowe), 34

Vacation Tourists (Galton), 93

Victorian Poets (Stedman), 168

virtual reality, 110, 233–34, 237, 241

visual arts, 179–80, 192–93, 195, 197–98, 200, 262n16, 264n29, 272n35

Wagner, Richard, 234

Wanderings in the High Alps (Wills), 92

Warner, Charles Dudley, 39, 88. See also *Gilded Age, The*

Warren, R. P., 200

Washoe (NV), 55

Waterhouse, John William, 234

Webster, Charles L., 47, 83, 167, 169, 248n40, 261n13, 270n15

Wecter, Dixon, 252n73

Weinstein, Cindy, 245n17

Wells, H. G., 192

Western Union Company, 43, 79, 80

Whitman, Walt, 107, 169, 269n6

Whymper, Edward, 93, 95, 99, 105, 107

Wide, Wide World, The (Warner), 34

Wilde, Oscar, 197, 198, 237

William F. Gill Company, 257n7

William Heinemann Company, 199

Williams, George Washington, 169–70

William Thompson Walters Collection, 81–82

Wills, Alfred, 92

Wing-and-Wing (Cooper), 34

Winship, Michael, 253nn80–81

Woman in Sacred History (Stowe), 81

Yellow Kid (Outcault), 195

Youth's Companion, 160

Zboray, Ronald J., 253n84

Zenger, Peter, 3

Zermatt, 95, 97, 98, 100

Text:	11/14 Adobe Garamond
Display:	Adobe Garamond and Perpetua
Compositor:	BookMatters, Berkeley
Printer and binder:	Sheridan Books, Inc.

120-150/63